THE HIGH HISTORY OF THE HOLY GRAIL

THE HIGH HISTORY OF
THE HOLY GRAIL

Translated from the
Old French by

SEBASTIAN EVANS

JAMES CLARKE & CO.

Cambridge

Published by
James Clarke & Co. Ltd
7 All Saints Passage
Cambridge
CB2 3LS
England

ISBN 0 227 67891 5

Printed in Great Britain by
Redwood Burn Limited, Trowbridge, Wiltshire
and bound by Pegasus Bookbinding, Melksham, Wiltshire

INTRODUCTION

THIS Book is translated from the first volume of *Perceval le Gallois ou le conte du Graal*; edited by M. Ch. Potvin for 'La Société des Bibliophiles Belges' in 1866,[1] from the MS. numbered 11,145 in the library of the Dukes of Burgundy at Brussels. This MS. I find thus described in M. F. J. Marchal's catalogue of that priceless collection : ' *Le Roman de Saint Graal*, beginning *Ores lestoires*, in the French language ; date, first third of the sixteenth century ; with ornamental capitals.'[2] Written three centuries later than the original romance, and full as it is of faults of the scribe, this manuscript is by far the most complete known copy of the Book of the Graal in existence, being defective only in Branch XXI. Titles 8 and 9, the substance of which is fortunately preserved elsewhere. Large fragments, however, amounting in all to nearly one-seventh of the whole, of a copy in handwriting of the thirteenth century, are preserved in six consecutive leaves and one detached leaf bound up with a number of other works in a MS. numbered 113 in the City Library at Berne. The volume is in folio on vellum closely written in three columns to the page, and the seven leaves follow the last poem contained in it, entitled *Duremart le Gallois*. The manuscript is well known, having been lent to M. de Sainte Palaye for use in the Monuments of French History issued by the Benedictines of the Congregation of St Maur. Selections from the poems it contains are given in Sinner's *Extraits de Poésie du XIII. Siècle*,[3] and it is described, unfortunately without any reference to these particular leaves, by the same learned librarian in the *Catalogus Codicum MSS. Bibl. Bernensis*. J. R. Sinner.[4]

M. Potvin has carefully collated for his edition all that is preserved of the Romance in this manuscript, comprising all the

---

[1] 6 vols. 8vo. Mons, 1866-1871.
[2] Marchal *Cat.*, 2 vols. Brussels, 1842. Vol i. p. 223.
[3] Lausanne, 1759.
[4] 3 vols. 8vo. Berne, 1770, etc. Vol. ii., Introduc. viii. and p. 389 *et seq.*

beginning of the work as far as Branch III. Title 8, about the
middle, and from Branch XVIII. Title 23, near the beginning, to
Branch XIX. Title 5, in the middle. Making allowance for
variations of spelling and sundry minor differences of reading,
by no means always in favour of the earlier scribe, the Berne
fragments are identical with the corresponding portions of the
Brussels manuscript, and it is therefore safe to assume that the
latter is on the whole an accurate transcript of the entire original
Romance.

The only note of time in the book itself is contained in the
declaration at the end. From this it appears that it was written
by order of the Seingnor of Cambrein for Messire Jehan the
Seingnor of Neele. M. Potvin, without giving any reason for
so doing, assumes that this Lord of Cambrein is none other than
the Bishop of Cambrai. If this assumption be correct, the
person referred to was probably either John of Béthune, who
held the see from 1200 till July 27, 1219, or his successor
Godfrey of Fontaines (Condé), who held it till 1237. To me,
however, it seems more likely that the personage intended was
in reality the 'Seingnor' of Cambrin, the chef-lieu of a canton
of the same name, on a small hill overlooking the peat-marshes
of Béthune, albeit I can find no other record of any such landed
proprietor's existence.

Be this as it may, the Messire Jehan, Seingnor of Neele, can
hardly be other than the John de Nesle who was present at the
battle of Bouvines in 1214, and who in 1225 sold the lordship
of Bruges to Joan of Flanders.[1] These dates therefore may be
regarded as defining that of the original Romance within fairly
narrow limits.

This conclusion is confirmed by other evidence. An early
Welsh translation of the story was published with an English
version and a glossary by the Rev. Robert Williams in the first
volume of his *Selections from the Hengwrt MSS.*[2] The first volume
of this work is entitled *Y Seint Greal, being the adventures of King
Arthur's knights of the Round Table, in the quest of the Holy Grail,
and on other occasions. Originally written about the year* 1200. The
volume, following the manuscript now in the library of W. W.
E. Wynne, Esq., at Peniarth, is divided into two parts. The

---

[1] Rigord. *Chron.* 196, p. 288. Wm. le Breton, *Phil.* xi. 547. See also Birch-
Hirschfeld, *Die Gralsage*, p. 143.
[2] 2 vols. 8vo. London, Richards, 1876-1892.

first, fol. 1-109 of the manuscript, represents the thirteenth to the seventeenth book of Sir Thomas Malory's *Morte d'Arthur.* Of the second, which represents the Romance here translated, Mr Williams writes : ' The second portion of the Welsh Greal, folios 110-280, contains the adventures of Gwalchmei Peredur and Lancelot, and of the knights of the Round Table ; but these are not found in the *Morte d'Arthur.* The Peniarth MS. is beautifully written on vellum, and in perfect preservation, and its date is that of Henry VI., the early part of the fifteenth century. The orthography and style of writing agrees literally with that of the Mabinogion of the Llyvr Côch Hergest, which is of that date. This, of course, is a transcript of an earlier copy ; but there is no certainty when it was first translated into Welsh, though Aneurin Owen in his Catalogue of the Hengwrt MSS. assigns it to the sixth year of Henry I. It is mentioned by Davydd ab Gwilym, who died in 1368.'

Whatever may be the date of the Welsh version, the translator had no great mastery of French, and is often at fault as to the meaning both of words and sentences, and when in a difficulty is only too apt to cut the knot by omitting the passage bodily. The book itself, moreover, is not entire. On page 275, all between Branch ix. Title 16 and Branch xi. Title 2, twenty-two chapters in all, is missing. Again, on page 355, Titles 10-16 in Branch xxi. are left out, while the whole of the last Branch, containing 28 Titles, is crumpled up into one little chapter, from which it would seem that the Welshman had read the French, but thought it waste of pains to translate it. In all, not to speak of other defects, there are fifty-six whole chapters in the present book, of which there is not a word in the Welsh.

In one matter, however, Mr Williams' English translation has stood me in good stead. In Branch xxi., as I have said, the French manuscript makes default of two Titles, but almost the whole of their substance is supplied by the Welsh version. By an unlucky accident, before the hiatus in the French is fully filled up, the Welsh version itself becomes defective, though the gap thus left open can hardly extend beyond a very few words. Without this supplement, incomplete as it is, it would have been impossible to give the full drift of one of the Romancer's best stories, which is equally unintelligible in both the French and Welsh texts in their present state.

As the Welsh version gives a number of names both of persons and places widely differing from those in the French, it may be useful here to note the principal changes made. Perceval in the Welsh is called Peredur, which is said to mean *steel suit*. The Welshman, however, adds that the name in French is *Peneffresvo Galief*, which, unless it be a misreading or miswriting for Perceval le Galois, is to me wholly unintelligible. Perceval's father, Alain li Gros, is in the Welsh Earl Evrawg, and his sister Dindrane, Danbrann. King Arthur is Emperor Arthur, his Queen Guenievre, Gwenhwyvar, and their son Lohot, Lohawt or Llacheu. Messire Gawain is Gwalchmei; Chaus, son of Ywain li Aoutres, Gawns, son of Owein Vrych; Messire Kay or Kex is Kei the Long; Ahuret the Bastard, Anores; Ygerne, wife of Uther Pendragon, Eigyr; Queen Jandree, Landyr; and King Fisherman for the most part King Peleur. Of places, Cardoil is Caerlleon on Usk, Pannenoisance, Penvoisins; Tintagel, Tindagoyl; and Avalon, Avallach.

By a double stroke of ill-luck, the complete and wholly independent Romance here translated has thus been printed by its two former editors as if it were only a part of some other story. M. Potvin descrbes it as the 'First Part, the Romance in Prose,' of his *Perceval le Gallois*, and Mr Williams accepts it as the 'Second Portion' of his *Y Seint Greal*. This unhappy collocation has led not a few of M. Potvin's readers to neglect his First Part, under the impression that the story is retold in the other volumes containing the Romance in verse; while not a few of Mr Williams' readers have neglected his Second Portion under the impression that there could be nothing of any special importance in an adjunct referred to by the Editor in so perfunctory a manner. In very truth, however, the Story of the Holy Graal here told is not only the most coherent and poetic of all the many versions of the Legend, but is also the first and most authentic.

This seems to be proved beyond doubt by a passage in the History of Fulke Fitz-Warine, originally written apparently between the years 1256 and 1264. The passage occurs at the end of the History, and is printed in verse of which I give a literal prose translation.

' Merlin saith that in Britain the Great a Wolf shall come from the White Launde. Twelve sharp teeth shall he have, six below and six above. He shall have so fierce a look that he shall chase the Leopard forth of the White Launde, so much force shall he have and great virtue. We now know that Merlin said this for

Fulke the son of Waryn, for each of you ought to understand
of a surety how in the time of the King Arthur that was called
the White Launde which is now named the White Town. For
in this country was the chapel of S. Austin that was fair, where
Kahuz, the son of Ywein, dreamed that he carried off the candlestick and that he met a man who hurt him with a knife and
wounded him in the side. And he, on sleep, cried out so loud
that King Arthur hath heard him and awakened from sleep.
And when Kahuz was awake, he put his hand to his side. There
hath he found the knife that had smitten him through. So
TELLETH US THE GRAAL, THE BOOK OF THE HOLY VESSEL.
There the King Arthur recovered his bounty and his valour
when he had lost all his chivalry and his virtue. From this
country issued forth the Wolf as saith Merlin the Wise, and the
twelve sharp teeth have we known by his shield. He bore a
shield indented as the heralds have devised. In the shield are
twelve teeth of gules and argent. By the Leopard may be
known and well understood King John, for he bore in his shield
the leopards of beaten gold.'[1]

The story of Kahuz or Chaus here indicated by the historian
is told at length in the opening chapters of the present work and,
so far as is known, nowhere else. The inference is therefore
unavoidable that we have here 'The Graal, the Book of the
Holy Vessel' to which the biographer of Fulke refers. The
use, moreover, of the definite article shows that the writer held
this book to be conclusive authority on the subject. By the
time he retold the story of Fulke, a whole library of Romances
about Perceval and the Holy Graal had been written, with some
of which it is hard to believe that any historian of the time was
unacquainted. He nevertheless distinguishes this particular story
as 'The Graal,' a way of speaking he would scarce have adopted
had he known of any other 'Graals' of equal or nearly equal
authority.

Several years later, about 1280, the trouveur Sarrazin also
cites 'The Graal' (*li Graaus*) in the same manner, in superfluous
verification of the then-accepted truism that King Arthur was

---

[1] *L'histoire de Foulkes Fitz-Warin.* Ed. F. Michel, Paris, 1840; p. 110. Ed. T.
Wright (Warton Club), London, 1855; p. 179. Ed. J. Stevenson (*Rolls Pub.
Chron.* of R. Coggeshall), London, 1875; p. 412. The MS. containing the history
(*MS. Reg.* 12. c. xii.) was first privately printed for the late Sir T. Duffus Hardy
from a transcript by A. Berbrugger.

at one time Lord of Great Britain. This appeal to 'The Graal' as the authority for a general belief shows that it was at that time recognised as a well-spring of authentic knowledge; while the fact that the trouveur was not confounding 'The Graal' with the later version of the story is further shown by his going on presently to speak of 'the Romance that Chrestien telleth so fairly of Perceval—the adventures of the Graal.'[1]

Perhaps, however, the most striking testimony to the fact that this work is none other than the original Book of the Graal is to be found in the Chronicle of Helinand, well known at the time the Romance was written not only as a historian but as a troubadour at one time in high favour at the court of Philip Augustus, and in later years as one of the most ardent preachers of the Albigensian Crusade. The passage, a part of which has been often quoted, is inserted in the Chronicle under the year 720, and runs in English thus :

'At this time a certain marvellous vision was revealed by an angel to a certain hermit in Britain concerning S. Joseph, the decurion who deposed from the cross the Body of Our Lord, as well as concerning the paten or dish in the which Our Lord supped with His disciples, whereof the history was written out by the said hermit and is called "Of the Graal" (*de Gradali*). Now, a platter, broad and somewhat deep, is called in French *gradalis* or *gradale*, wherein costly meats with their sauce are wont to be set before rich folk by degrees (*gradatim*) one morsel after another in divers orders, and in the vulgar speech it is called *graalz*, for that it is grateful and acceptable to him that eateth therein, as well for that which containeth the victual, for that haply it is of silver or other precious material, as for the contents thereof, to wit, the manifold courses of costly meats. I have not been able to find this history written in Latin, but it is in the possession of certain noblemen written in French only, nor, as they say, can it easily be found complete. This, however, I have not hitherto been able to obtain from any person so as to read it with attention. As soon as I can do so, I will translate into Latin such passages as are more useful and more likely to be true.'[2]

---

[1] 'Le Roman de Ham,' in the Appendix to F. Michel's *Histoire des Ducs de Normandie*. Soc. de l'Hist. de France, 1840, pp. 225, 230.

[2] Helinandi Op. Ed. Migne. *Patrol.* Vol. ccxii. col. 814. The former part of the passage is quoted with due acknowledgment by Vincent of Beauvais. *Spec. Hist.* B. xxiii. c. 147. Vincent, however, spells the French word '*grail*,' and, by

A comparison of this passage with the Introduction to the present work[1] leaves no doubt that Helinand here refers to this Book of the Graal, which cannot therefore be of a later date than that at which he made this entry in his Chronicle. At the same time, the difficulty he experienced in obtaining even the loan of the volume shows that the work had at that time been only lately written, as in the course of a few years, copies of a book so widely popular must have been comparatively common. The date, therefore, at which Helinand's Chronicle was written determines approximately that of the Book of the Graal.

In its present state, the Chronicle comes to an end with a notice of the capture of Constantinople by the French in 1204, and it has been hastily assumed that Helinand's labours as a chronicler must have closed in that year. As a matter of fact they had not then even begun. At that time Helinand was still a courtly troubadour, and had not yet entered on the monastic career during which his Chronicle was compiled. He was certainly living as late as 1229, and preached a sermon, which assuredly shows no signs of mental decrepitude, in that year at a synod in Toulouse.[2]

Fortunately a passage in the *Speculum Historiale* of Vincent of Beauvais, himself a younger contemporary and probably a personal acquaintance of Helinand, throws considerable light on the real date of Helinand's Chronicle. After recounting certain matters connected with the early years of the thirteenth century, the last date mentioned being 1209, Vincent proceeds :—

'In those times, in the diocese of Beauvais, was Helinand monk of Froid-mont, a man religious and distinguished for his eloquence, who also composed those verses on Death in our vulgar tongue which are publicly read, so elegantly and so usefully that the subject is laid open clearer than the light. He also diligently digested into a certain huge volume a Chronicle

turning Helinand's *nec* into *nunc*, makes him say that the French work can *now* easily be found complete. Vincent finished his *Speculum Historiale* in 1244 B. xxi. c. 105.

[1] Vol. i. p. 1, etc.

[2] Sermon xxvi., printed in Minge, u. s. col. 692. It has been doubted whether this sermon, preached in the church of S. Jacques, was addressed to the Council held at Toulouse in 1219, or to the one held in 1229, but a perusal of the sermon itself decides the question. It is wholly irrelevant to the topics discussed at the former gathering, while it is one continued commentary on the business transacted at the latter. See also Dom Brial, *Hist. Litt. de la France*, xviii. 92.

from the beginning of the world down to his own time. But in truth this work was dissipated and dispersed in such sort that it is nowhere to be found entire. For it is reported that the said Helinand lent certain sheets of the said work to one of his familiars, to wit, Guarin, Lord Bishop of Senlis of good memory, and thus, whether through forgetfulness or negligence or some other cause, lost them altogether. From this work, however, as far as I have been able to find it, I have inserted many passages in this work of mine own also.'

It will thus be seen that about 1209, Helinand became a monk at Froid-mont, and it is exceedingly improbable that any portion of his Chronicle was written before that date. On the other hand, his 'familiar' Guarin only became Bishop of Senlis in 1214, and died in 1227,[1] so that it is certain Helinand wrote the last part of his Chronicle not later than the last-mentioned year. The limits of time, therefore, between which the Chronicle was written are clearly circumscribed; and if it is impossible to define the exact year in which this particular entry was made, it is not, I fancy, beyond the legitimate bounds of critical conjecture.

On the first page of the Romance, Helinand read that an Angel had appeared to a certain hermit in Britain and revealed to him the history of the Holy Graal. In transferring the record of this event to his Chronicle, he was compelled by the exigencies of his system, which required the insertion of every event recorded under some particular year, to assign a date to the occurrence. A vague 'five hundred years ago' would be likely to suggest itself as an appropriate time at which the occurrence might be supposed to have taken place; and if he were writing in 1220, the revelation to the hermit would thus naturally be relegated to the year 720, the year under which the entry actually appears. This, of course, is pure guesswork, but the fact remains that the Chronicle was written in or about 1220, and the Book of the Graal not long before it.

The name of the author is nowhere recorded. He may possibly be referred to in the 'Elucidation' prefixed to the rhymed version of *Percival le Gallois* under the name of 'Master Blihis,' but this vague and tantalising pseudonym affords no hint of his real identity.[2] Whoever he may have been, I hope that

---

[1] *De Mas Latrie. Trés. de Chron.*, col. 1488.
[2] Cf. Potvin, *P. le G.* ii. 1 and 7, with vol. i. p. 131 and vol. ii. p. 112 of the present work. (See also the Proceedings of the "Hon. Soc. of Cymmrodorion," 1908-9. Ed.)

I am not misled by a translator's natural partiality for the author he translates in assigning him a foremost rank among the masters of mediæval prose romance.

With these testimonies to its age and genuineness, I commend the Book of the Graal to all who love to read of King Arthur and his knights of the Table Round. They will find here printed in English for the first time what I take to be in all good faith the original story of Sir Perceval and the Holy Graal, whole and incorrupt as it left the hands of its first author.

SEBASTIAN EVANS.

CONTENTS

CONTENTS

THE HIGH HISTORY OF THE HOLY GRAAL

BRANCH I

INCIPIT

HEAR ye the history of the most holy vessel that is called Graal, wherein the precious blood of the Saviour was received on the day that He was put on rood and crucified in order that He might redeem His people from the pains of hell. Josephus set it in remembrance by annunciation of the voice of an angel, for that the truth might be known by his writing of good knights, and good worshipful men how they were willing to suffer pain and to travail for the setting forward of the Law of Jesus Christ, that He willed to make new by His death and by His crucifixion.

TITLE I

The High Book of the Graal beginneth in the name of the Father and of the Son and of the Holy Ghost. These three Persons are one substance, which is God, and of God moveth the High Story of the Graal. And all they that hear it ought to understand it, and to forget all the wickednesses that they have in their hearts. For right profitable shall it be to all them that shall hear it of the heart. For the sake of the worshipful men and good knights of whose deeds shall remembrance be made, doth Josephus recount this holy history, for the sake of the lineage of the Good Knight that was after the crucifixion of Our Lord. Good Knight was he without fail, for he was chaste and virgin of his body and hardy of heart and puissant, and so were his conditions without wickedness. Not boastful was he of speech, and it seemed not by his cheer that he had so great courage;

A   1

Natheless, of one little word that he delayed to speak came to pass so sore mischances in Greater Britain, that all the islands and all the lands fell thereby into much sorrow, albeit thereafter he put them back into gladness by the authority of his good knighthood. Good knight was he of right, for he was of the lineage of Joseph of Abarimacie. And this Joseph was his mother's uncle, that had been a soldier of Pilate's seven years, nor asked he of him none other guerdon of his service but only to take down the body of Our Saviour from hanging on the cross. The boon him seemed full great when it was granted him, and full little to Pilate seemed the guerdon; for right well had Joseph served him, and had he asked to have gold or land thereof, willingly would he have given it to him. And for this did Pilate make him a gift of the Saviour's body, for he supposed that Joseph should have dragged the same shamefully through the city of Jerusalem when it had been taken down from the cross, and should have left it without the city in some mean place. But the Good Soldier had no mind thereto, but rather honoured the body the most he might, rather laid it along in the Holy Sepulchre and kept safe the lance whereof He was smitten in the side and the most Holy Vessel wherein they that believed on Him received with awe the blood that ran down from His wounds when He was set upon the rood. Of this lineage was the Good Knight for whose sake is this High History treated. Yglais was his mother's name: King Fisherman was his uncle, and the King of the Lower Folk that was named Pelles, and the King that was named of the Castle Mortal, in whom was there as much bad as there was good in the other twain, and much good was there in them; and these three were his uncles on the side of his mother Yglais, that was a right good Lady and a loyal; and the Good Knight had one sister, that hight Dindrane. He that was head of the lineage on his father's side was named Nichodemus. Gais li Gros of the Hermit's Cross was father of Alain li Gros. This Alain had eleven brethren, right good knights, like as he was himself. And none of them all lived in his knighthood but twelve years, and they all died in arms, for their great hardiment in setting forward of the Law that was made new. There were twelve brethren. Alain li Gros was the eldest; Gorgalians was next; Bruns Brandalis was the third; Bertholez li Chauz the fourth; Brandalus of Wales was the fifth; Elinant of Escavalon was the sixth; Calobrutus was the seventh; Meralis of the Palace Meadow was the eighth; Fortunes of the Red Launde was ninth; Melaarmaus of Abanie was the tenth; Galians of the White Tower the eleventh; Alibans of the Waste City was the twelfth. All these died in arms in the service of the Holy Prophet that had renewed the Law by His death, and smote His enemies to the uttermost of their power. Of these two manner of folk, whose names and records you have heard, Josephus the good clerk telleth us was come the Good Knight of whom you shall well hear the name and the manner presently.

II

The authority of the scripture telleth us that after the crucifixion of Our Lord, no earthly King set forward the Law of Jesus Christ so much as did King Arthur of Britain, both by himself and by the good knights that made repair to his court. Good King Arthur after the crucifixion of Our Lord, was such as I tell you, and was a puissant King, and one that well believed in God, and many were the good adventures that befel at his court. And he had in his court the Table Round that was garnished of the best knights in the world. King Arthur after the death of his father led the highest life and most gracious that ever king led, in such sort that all the princes and all the barons took ensample of him in well-doing. For ten years was King Arthur in such estate as I have told you, nor never was earthly king so praised as he, until that a slothful will came upon him and he began to lose the pleasure in doing largesse that he wont to have, nor was he minded to hold court neither at Christmas-tide nor at Easter nor at Pentecost. The knights of the Table Round when they saw his well-doing wax slack departed thence and began to hold aloof from his court, insomuch as that of three hundred and three-score knights and six that he wont to have of his household, there were now not more than a five-and-twenty at most, nor did no adventure befal any more at his court. All the other princes had slackened of their well-doing for that they saw King Arthur maintain so feebly. Queen Guenievre was so sorrowful thereof that she knew not what counsel to take with herself, nor how she might so deal as to amend matters so God amended them not. From this time beginneth the history.

III

It was one Ascension Day that the King was at Cardoil. He was risen from meat and went through the hall from one end to the other, and looked and saw the Queen that was seated at a window. The King went to sit beside her, and looked at her in the face and saw that the tears were falling from her eyes. 'Lady,' saith the King, 'What aileth you, and wherefore do you weep?' 'Sir,' saith she, 'And I weep, good right have I; and you yourself have little right to make joy.' 'Certes, Lady, I do not.' 'Sir,' saith she, 'You are right. I have seen on this high day, or on other days that were not less high than this, when you have had such throng of knights at your court that right uneath might any number them. Now every day are so few therein that much shame have I thereof, nor no more do no adventures befal therein. Wherefore great fear have I lest God hath put you into forgetfulness.' 'Certes, Lady,' saith the King, 'No will have I to do largesse nor aught that turneth to honour. Rather is my desire changed into feebleness of heart. And by this know I well that I lose my knights and the love of my friends.' 'Sir,' saith the Queen, 'And were you to go to the chapel of S. Augustine that is in the White Forest, that may not be found save by adventure only, methinketh that on your back-repair you would again have your desire of well-doing, for never yet did none discounselled ask counsel of God but he would give it for love of him so he asked it of a good heart.' 'Lady,' saith the King, 'And willingly will I go, forasmuch as that you say have I heard well witnessed in many places where I have been.' 'Sir,' saith she, 'The place is right perilous and the chapel right adventurous. But the most worshipful hermit that is in the Kingdom of Wales hath his dwelling beside the chapel, nor liveth he now any longer for nought save only the glory of God.' 'Lady,' saith the King, 'It will behove me go thither all armed and without knights.' 'Sir,' saith she, 'You may well take with you one knight and a squire.' 'Lady,' saith the King, 'That durst not I, for the place is perilous, and the more folk one should take thither, the fewer adventures there should he find.' 'Sir,' saith she, 'One squire shall you take by my good will, nor shall nought betide you thereof save good only, please God!' 'Lady,' saith the King, 'At your pleasure be it, but much dread I that nought shall come of it save evil only.' Thereupon the King riseth up from beside the Queen, and looketh before him and seeth a youth tall and strong and comely and young, that was hight Chaus, and he was the son of Ywain li Aoutres. 'Lady,' saith he to the Queen, 'This one will I take with me and you think well.' 'Sir,' saith she, 'It pleaseth me well, for I have heard much witness to his valour.' The King calleth the squire, and he cometh and kneeleth down before him. The King maketh him rise and saith unto him, 'Chaus,' saith he, 'You shall lie within to-night, in this hall, and take heed that my horse be saddled at break of day and mine arms ready. For I would be moving at the time I tell you, and yourself with me without more company.' 'Sir,' saith the squire, 'At your pleasure.' And the evening drew on, and the King and Queen go to bed. When they had eaten in hall, the knights went to their hostels. The squire remained in the hall, but he would not do off his clothes nor his shoon, for the night seemed him to be too short, and for that he would fain be ready in the morning at the King's commandment. The squire was lying down in such sort as I have told you, and in the first sleep that he slept, seemed him the King had gone without him. The squire was sore scared thereat, and came to his hackney and set the saddle and bridle upon him, and did on his spurs and girt on his sword, as it seemed him in his sleep, and issued forth of the castle a great pace after the King. And when he had ridden a long space he entered into a great forest and looked in the way before him and saw the slot of the King's horse and followed the track a long space, until that he came to a launde of the forest whereat he thought that the King had alighted. The squire thought that the hoof-marks on the way had come to an end, and so thought that the King had alighted there or hard by there. He looketh to the right hand and seeth a chapel in the midst of the launde, and he seeth about it a great graveyard wherein were many coffins, as it seemed him. He thought in his heart that he would go towards the chapel, for he supposed that the King would have entered to pray there. He went thitherward and alighted. When the squire was alighted, he tied up his hackney and entered into the chapel. None did he see there in one part nor another, save a knight that lay dead in the midst of the chapel upon a bier, and he was covered of a rich cloth of silk, and had around him waxen tapers burning that were fixed in four candlesticks of gold. This squire marvelled much how this body was left there so lonely, insomuch that none were about him save only the images, and yet more marvelled he of the King that he found him not, for he knew not in what part to seek him. He taketh out one of the tall tapers, and layeth hand on the golden candlestick, and setteth it betwixt his hose and his thigh and issueth forth of the chapel, and remounteth on his hackney and goeth his way back and passeth beyond the grave-yard and issueth forth of the launde and entereth into the forest and thinketh that he will not cease until he hath found the King.

IV

So, as he entereth into a grassy lane in the wood, he seeth come before him a man black and foul-favoured, and he was somewhat taller afoot than was himself a-horseback. And he held a great sharp knife in his hand with two edges as it seemed him. The squire cometh over against him a great pace and saith unto him, 'You, that come there, have you met King Arthur in this forest?' 'In no wise,' saith the messenger, 'But you have I met, whereof am I right glad at heart, for you have departed from the chapel as a thief and a traitor. For you are carrying off thence the candlestick of gold that was in honour of the knight that lieth in the chapel dead. Wherefore I will that you yield it up to me and so will I carry it back, otherwise, and you do not this, you do I defy!' 'By my faith,' saith the squire, 'Never will I yield it you! rather will I carry it off and make a present thereof to King Arthur.' 'By my faith,' saith the other, 'Right dearly shall you pay for it, and you yield it not up forthwith.' Howbeit, the squire smiteth with his spurs and thinketh to pass him by, but the other hasteth him, and smiteth the squire in the left side with the knife and thrusteth it into his body up to the haft. The squire, that lay in the hall at Cardoil, and had dreamed this, awoke and cried in a loud voice: 'Holy Mary! The priest! Help! Help, for I am a dead man!' The King and the Queen heard the cry, and the chamberlain leapt up and said to the King: 'Sir, you may well be moving, for it is day!' The King made him be clad and shod. And the squire crieth with such strength as he hath: 'Fetch me the priest, for I die!' The King goeth thither as fast as he may, and the Queen and the chamberlain carry great torches and candles. The King asketh him what aileth him, and he telleth him all in such wise as he had dreamed it. 'Ha,' saith the King, 'Is it then a dream?' 'Yea, sir,' saith he, 'But a right foul dream it is for me, for right foully hath it come true!' He lifted his left arm. 'Sir,' saith he, 'Look you there! Lo, here is the knife that was run into my side up to the haft!' After that, he setteth his hand to his hose where the candlestick was. He draweth it forth and showeth it to the King. 'Sir,' saith he, 'For this candlestick that I present to you, am I wounded to the death!' The King taketh the candlestick and looketh thereat in wonderment for none so rich had he never seen tofore. The King showeth it to the Queen. 'Sir,' saith the squire, 'Draw not forth the knife of my body until that I be shriven.' The King sent for one of his own chaplains that made the squire confess and do his houselling right well. The King himself draweth forth the knife of the body, and the soul departed forthwith. The King made do his service right richly and his shrouding and burial. Ywain li Aoutres that was father to the squire was right sorrowful of the death of his son. King Arthur, with the good will of Ywain his father, gave the candlestick to S. Paul in London, for the church was newly founded, and the King wished that this marvellous adventure should everywhere be known, and that prayer should be made in the church for the soul of the squire that was slain on account of the candlestick.

V

King Arthur armed himself in the morning, as I told you and began to tell, to go to the chapel of S. Augustine. Said the Queen to him: 'Whom will you take with you?' 'Lady,' saith he, 'No company will I have thither, save God only, for well may you understand by this adventure that hath befallen, that God will not allow I should have none with me.' 'Sir,' saith she, 'God be guard of your body, and grant you return safely so as that you may have the will to do well, whereby shall your praise be lifted up that is now sore cast down.' 'Lady,' saith he, 'May God remember it.' His destrier was brought to the mounting-stage, and the King mounted thereon all armed. Messire Ywain li Aoutres lent him his shield and spear.   When the King had hung the shield at his neck and held the spear in his hand, sword-girt, on the tall destrier armed, well seemed he in the make of his body and in his bearing to be a knight of great pith and hardiment.   He planteth himself so stiffly in the stirrups that he maketh the saddlebows creak again and the destrier stagger under him that was right stout and swift, and he smiteth him of his spurs, and the horse maketh answer with a great leap.   The Queen was at the windows of the hall, and as many as five-and-twenty knights were all come to the mounting-stage. When the King departed, 'Lords,' saith the Queen, 'How seemeth you of the King?   Seemeth he not a goodly man?' 'Yea, certes, Lady, and sore loss is it to the world that he followeth not out his good beginning, for no king nor prince is known better learned of all courtesy nor of all largesse than he, so he would do like as he was wont.'   With that the knights hold their peace, and King Arthur goeth away a great pace.   And he entereth into a great forest adventurous, and rideth the day long until he cometh about evensong into the thick of the forest.   And he espied a little house beside a little chapel, and it well seemed him to be a hermitage.   King Arthur rode thitherward and alighteth before this little house, and entereth thereinto and draweth his horse after him, that had much pains to enter in at the door, and laid his spear down on the ground and leant his shield against the wall, and hath ungirded his sword and unlaced his ventail.   He looked before him and saw barley and provender, and so led his horse thither and smote off his bridle, and afterwards hath shut the door of the little house and locked it.   And it seemed him that there was a strife in the chapel.   The ones were weeping so tenderly and sweetly as it were angels, and the other spake so harshly as it were fiends.   The King heard such voices in the chapel and marvelled much what it might be.   He findeth a door in the little house that openeth on a little cloister whereby one goeth to the chapel.   The King is gone thither and entereth into the little minster, and looketh everywhere but seeth nought there, save the images and the crucifixes.   And he supposeth not that the strife of these voices cometh of them. The voices ceased as soon as he was within.   He marvelleth how it came that this house and hermitage were solitary, and what had become of the hermit that dwelt therein.   He drew nigh the altar of the chapel and beheld in front thereof a coffin all discovered, and he saw the hermit lying therein all clad in his vestments, and seeth the long beard down to his girdle, and his hands crossed upon his breast. There was a cross above him, whereof the image came as far as his mouth, and he had life in him yet, but he was nigh his end, being at the point of death. The King was before the coffin a long space, and looked right fainly on the hermit, for well it seemed him that he had been of a good life. The night was fully come, but within was a brightness of light as if a score of candles were lighted. He had a mind to abide there until that the good man should have passed away. He would fain have sate him down before the coffin, when a voice warned him right horribly to begone thence, for that it was desired to make a judgment within there, that might not be made so long as he were there. The King departed, that would willingly have remained there, and so returned back into the little house, and sate him down on a seat whereon the hermit wont to sit. And he heareth the strife and the noise begin again within the chapel, and the ones he heareth speaking high and the others low, and he knoweth well by the voices, that the ones are angels and the others devils. And he heareth that the devils are distraining on the hermit's soul, and that judgment will presently be given in their favour, whereof make they great joy. King Arthur is grieved in his heart when he heareth that the angels' voices are stilled. The King is so heavy, that no desire hath he neither to eat nor to drink. And while he sitteth thus, stooping his head toward the ground, full of vexation and discontent, he heareth in the chapel the voice of a Lady that spake so sweet and clear, that no man in this earthly world, were his grief and heaviness never so sore, but and he had heard the sweet voice of her pleading would again have been in joy. She saith to the devils: 'Begone from hence, for no right have ye over the soul of this good man, whatsoever he may have done aforetime, for in my Son's service and mine own is he taken, and his penance hath he done in this hermitage of the sins that he hath done.' 'True, Lady,' say the devils, 'But longer had he served us than he hath served you and your Son. For forty years or more hath he been a murderer and robber in this forest, whereas in this hermitage but five years hath he been. And now you wish to thieve him from us.' 'I do not. No wish have I

to take him from you by theft, for had he been taken in
your service in suchwise as he hath been taken in mine,
yours would he have been, all quit.' The devils go their way
all discomfit and aggrieved; and the sweet Mother of our Lord
God taketh the soul of the hermit, that was departed of his
body, and so commendeth it to the angels and archangels that
they make present thereof to Her dear Son in Paradise. And
the angels take it and begin to sing for joy *Te Deum laudamus.*
And the Holy Lady leadeth them and goeth her way along with
them. Josephus maketh remembrance of this history and
telleth us that this worthy man was named Calixtus.

VI

King Arthur was in the little house beside the chapel, and
had heard the voice of the sweet Mother of God and the angels.
Great joy had he, and was right glad of the good man's soul
that was borne thence into Paradise. The King had slept right
little the night and was all armed. He saw the day break clear
and fair, and goeth his way toward the chapel to cry God
mercy, thinking to find the coffin discovered there where the
hermit lay; but so did he not! Rather, was it covered of the
richest tomb-stone that any might ever see, and had on the top
a red cross, and seemed it that the chapel was all incensed.
When the King had made his orison therein, he cometh back
again and setteth on his bridle and saddle and mounteth, and
taketh his shield and spear and departeth from the little house
and entereth into the forest and rideth a great pace, until he
cometh at right hour of tierce to one of the fairest laundes that
ever a man might see. And he seeth at the entrance a spear set
bar-wise, and looketh to the right or ever he should enter therein,
and seeth a damsel sitting under a great leafy tree, and she
held the reins of her mule in her hand. The damsel was of
great beauty and full seemly clad. The King turneth thitherward and so saluteth her and saith : ' Damsel,' saith he, ' God
give you joy and good adventure.' ' Sir,' saith she, ' So may
He do to you !' ' Damsel,' saith the King, ' Is there no hold in
this launde ?' ' Sir,' saith the damsel, ' No hold is there save
a most holy chapel and a hermit that is beside S. Augustine's
chapel.' ' Is this then S. Augustine's chapel ?' saith the King.
' Yea, Sir, I tell it you for true, but the launde and the forest

about is so perilous that no knight returneth thence but he be
dead or wounded; but the place of the chapel is of so great
worthiness that none goeth thither, be he never so discounselled,
but he cometh back counselled, so he may thence return on live.
And Lord God be guard of your body, for never yet saw I
none aforetime that seemed more like to be good knight, and
sore pity would it be and you were not, and never more shall
I depart me hence and I shall have seen your end.' 'Damsel,'
saith the King, 'Please God, you shall see me repair back
thence.' 'Certes,' saith the damsel, 'Thereof should I be
right fain, for then should I ask you tidings at leisure of him
that I am seeking.' The King goeth to the bar whereby one
entereth into the launde, and looketh to the right into a combe
of the forest and seeth the chapel of S. Augustine and the right
fair hermitage. Thitherward goeth he and alighteth, and it
seemeth him that the hermit is apparelled to sing the mass. He
reineth up his horse to the bough of a tree by the side of the
chapel and thinketh to enter thereinto, but, had it been to conquer all the kingdoms of the world, thereinto might he not
enter, albeit there was none made him denial thereof, for the
door was open and none saw he that might forbid him. Sore
ashamed is the King thereof. Howbeit, he beholdeth an image
of Our Lord that was there within and crieth Him of mercy
right sweetly, and looketh toward the altar. And he looketh
at the holy hermit that was robed to sing mass and said his
Confiteor, and seeth at his right hand the fairest Child that ever
he had seen, and He was clad in an alb and had a golden crown
on his head loaded with precious stones that gave out a full
great brightness of light. On the left hand side, was a Lady
so fair that all the beauties of the world might not compare
them with her beauty. When the holy hermit had said his
Confiteor and went to the altar, the Lady also took her Son and
went to sit on the right hand side towards the altar upon a
right rich chair and set her Son upon her knees and began to
kiss Him full sweetly and saith: 'Sir,' saith she, 'You are my
Father and my Son and my Lord, and guardian of me and of
all the world.' King Arthur heareth the words and seeth the
beauty of the Lady and of the Child, and marvelleth much of
this that She should call Him her Father and her Son. He
looketh at a window behind the altar and seeth a flame come
through at the very instant that mass was begun, clearer than

any ray of sun nor moon nor star, and evermore it threw forth
a brightness of light such that and all the lights in the world
had been together it would not have been the like. And it
is come down upon the altar. King Arthur seeth it who
marvelleth him much thereof. But sore it irketh him of this
that he may not enter therewithin, and he heareth, there where
the holy hermit was singing the mass, right fair responses, and
they seem him to be the responses of angels. And when the
Holy Gospel was read, King Arthur looked toward the altar
and saw that the Lady took her Child and offered Him into
the hands of the holy hermit, but of this King Arthur made
much marvel, that the holy hermit washed not his hands when
he had received the offering. Right sore did King Arthur
marvel him thereof, but little right would he have had to
marvel had he known the reason. And when the Child was
offered him, he set Him upon the altar and thereafter began his
sacrament. And King Arthur set him on his knees before the
chapel and began to pray to God and to beat his breast. And
he looked toward the altar after the preface, and it seemed him
that the holy hermit held between his hands a man bleeding from
His side and in His palms and in His feet, and crowned with
thorns, and he seeth Him in His own figure. And when he
had looked on Him so long and knoweth not what is become
of Him, the King hath pity of Him in his heart of this that he
had seen, and the tears of his heart come into his eyes. And
he looketh toward the altar and thinketh to see the figure of
the man, and seeth that it is changed into the shape of the Child
that he had seen tofore.

VII

When the mass was sung, the voice of a holy angel said *Ite,
missa est.* The Son took the Mother by the hand, and they
evanished forth of the chapel with the greatest company and
the fairest that might ever be seen. The flame that was come
down through the window went away with this company.
When the hermit had done his service and was divested of
the arms of God, he went to King Arthur that was still without the chapel. 'Sir,' saith he to the King, 'Now may you
well enter herein and well might you have been joyous in your
heart had you deserved so much as that you might have come

in at the beginning of the mass.' King Arthur entered into
the chapel without any hindrance. 'Sir,' saith the hermit to
the King, 'I know you well, as did I also King Uther Pendragon your father. On account of your sins and your deserts
might you not enter here while mass was being sung. Nor
will you to-morrow, save you shall first have made amends of
that you have misdone towards God and towards the saint
that is worshipped herewithin. For you are the richest King
of the world and the most adventurous, wherefore ought all
the world to take ensample of you in well-doing and in largesse
and in honour ; whereas you are now an ensample of evil-doing
to all rich worshipful men that be now in the world. Wherefore shall right sore mishap betide you and you set not back
your doing to the point whereat you began. For your court
was the sovran of all courts and the most adventurous, whereas
now is it least of worth. Well may he be sorry that goeth
from honour to shame, but never may he have reproach that
shall do him ill, that cometh from shame to honour, for the
honour wherein he is found rescueth him to God, but blame
may never rescue the man that hath renounced honour for
shame, for the shame and wickedness wherein he is found
declare him guilty.'

VIII

'Sir,' saith King Arthur, 'To amend me have I come hither,
and to be better counselled than I have been. Well do I see
that the place is most holy, and I beseech you that you pray
God that He counsel me and I will do my endeavour herein to
amend me.' 'God grant you may amend your life,' saith the
holy hermit, 'in such sort that you may help to do away the
evil Law and to exalt the Law that is made new by the
crucifixion of the Holy Prophet. But a great sorrow is befallen
in the land of late through a young knight that was harboured
in the hostel of the rich King Fisherman, for that the most
Holy Graal appeared to him and the Lance whereof the point
runneth of blood, yet never asked he to whom was served
thereof nor whence it came, and for that he asked it not are all
the lands commoved to war, nor no knight meeteth other in
the forest but he runneth upon him and slayeth him and he
may, and you yourself shall well perceive thereof or ever you
shall depart of this launde.' 'Sir,' saith King Arthur, 'God

defend me from the anguish of an evil death and from wickedness, for hither have I come for none other thing but to amend my life, and this will I do, so God bring me back in safety.' 'Truly,' saith the hermit, 'He that hath been bad for three years out of forty, he hath not been wholly good.' 'Sir,' saith the King, 'You speak truth.' The hermit departeth and so commendeth him to God. The King cometh to his horse and mounteth the speediest that ever he may, and setteth his shield on his neck, and taketh his spear in his hand and turneth him back a great pace. Howbeit, he had not gone a bowshot's length when he saw a knight coming disorderly against him, and he sate upon a great black horse and he had a shield of the same and a spear. And the spear was somewhat thick near the point and burned with a great flame, foul and hideous, and the flame came down as far as over the knight's fist. He setteth his spear in rest and thinketh to smite the King, but the King swerveth aside and the other passeth beyond. 'Sir knight, wherefor hate you me?' 'Of right ought I not to love you,' saith the knight. 'Wherefore?' saith the King. 'For this, that you have had my brother's candlestick that was foully stolen from him!' 'Know you then who I am?' saith the King. 'Yea,' saith the knight; 'You are the King Arthur that aforetime were good and now are evil. Wherefore I defy you as my mortal enemy.' He draweth him back so that his onset may be the weightier. The King seeth that he may not depart without a stour. He setteth his spear in rest when he seeth the other come towards him with his own spear all burning. The King smiteth his horse with his spurs as hard as he may, and meeteth the knight with his spear and the knight him. And they melled together so stoutly that the spears bent without breaking, and both twain are shifted in their saddles and lose their stirrups. They hurtle so strongly either against other of their bodies and their horses that their eyes sparkle as of stars in their heads and the blood rayeth out of King Arthur by mouth and nose. Either draweth away from other and they take their breath. The King looketh at the Black Knight's spear that burneth, and marvelleth him right sore that it is not snapped in flinders of the great buffet he had received thereof, and him thinketh rather that it is a devil and a fiend. The Black Knight is not minded to let King Arthur go so soon, but rather cometh toward him a great career. The King seeth him come toward him and so covereth him of his shield for fear of the flame. The King receiveth him on the point of his spear and smiteth him with so sore a shock that he maketh him bend backward over his horse croup. The other, that was of great might, leapeth back into the saddle-bows and smiteth the King upon the boss of his shield so that the burning point pierceth the shield and the sleeve of his habergeon and runneth the sharp iron into his arm. The King feeleth the wound and the heat, whereof is he filled with great wrath, and the knight draweth back his spear to him, and hath great joy at heart when he feeleth the King wounded. The King was rejoiced not a whit, and looked at the spear that was quenched thereof and burned no longer. 'Sir,' saith the knight, 'I cry you mercy. Never would my spear have been quenched of its burning, save it were bathed in your blood.' 'Now may never God help me,' saith King Arthur, 'whenever I shall have mercy on you, and I may achieve!' He pricketh towards him a great run, and smiteth him in the broad of the breast and thrusted his spear half an ell into his body, and beareth him to the ground, both him and his horse all in a heap, and draweth his spear back to him and looketh at the knight that lay as dead and leaveth him in the launde, and draweth him towards the issue incontinent. And so as the King went, he heard a great clashing of knights coming right amidst the forest, so as it seemed there were a good score or more of them, and he seeth them enter the launde from the forest, armed and well horsed. And they come with great ado toward the knight that lay dead in the midst of the launde. King Arthur was about to issue forth, when the damsel that he had left under the tree cometh forward to meet him. 'Sir,' saith she, 'For God's sake, return back and fetch me the head of the knight that lieth there dead.' The King looketh back, and seeth the great peril and the multitude of knights that are there all armed. 'Ha, damsel,' saith he, 'You are minded to slay me.' 'Certes, Sir, that I am not, but sore need will there be that I should have it, nor never did knight refuse to do the thing I asked nor deny me any boon I demanded of him. Now God grant you be not the most churlish.' 'Ha, damsel, I am right sore wounded in the arm whereon I hold my shield.' 'Sir,' saith she, 'I know it well, nor never may you be heal thereof save you bring me the head of the knight.' 'Damsel,' he saith, 'I will essay it whatsoever may befal me thereof.'

IX

King Arthur looketh amidst the launde and seeth that they that have come thither have cut the knight to pieces limb by limb, and that each is carrying off a foot or a thigh or an arm or a hand and are dispersing them through the forest. And he seeth that the last knight beareth on the point of his spear the head. The King goeth after him a great gallop and crieth out to him : 'Ha, Sir knight, abide and speak to me!' 'What is your pleasure?' saith the knight. 'Fair Sir,' saith the King, 'I beseech you of all loves that you deign to give me the head of this knight that you are carrying on the point of your lance.' 'I will give it you,' saith the knight, 'on condition.' 'What condition?' saith the King. 'That you tell me who slew the knight whose head I carry that you ask of me.' 'May I not otherwise have it?' saith the King. 'In no wise,' saith he. 'Then will I tell you,' saith the King. 'Know of a very truth that King Arthur slew him.' 'And where is he?' saith the knight. 'Seek him until you shall have found him,' saith King Arthur, 'For I have told you the truth thereof. Give me the head.' 'Willingly,' saith the knight. He lowereth his spear and the King taketh the head. The knight had a horn at his neck. He setteth it to his mouth and soundeth a blast right loud. The knights that were set within the forest hear the horn and return back a great gallop, and King Arthur goeth his way toward the oak-tree at the issue of the launde where the damsel is awaiting him. And the knights come presently to him that had given the head to the King and ask him wherefore he hath sounded the horn. 'For this,' saith he, 'That this knight that is going away yonder hath told me that King Arthur slew the Black Knight, and I was minded you should know it that we may follow him.' 'We will not follow him,' say the knights, 'For it is King Arthur himself that is carrying off the head, and no power have we to do evil to him nor other sith that he hath passed the bar. But you shall aby it that let him go when he was so nigh you!' They rush in upon him and slay him and cut him up, and each one carrieth off his piece the same as they had done with the other. King Arthur is issued forth of the bar, and cometh to the maiden that is waiting for him and presenteth her the head. 'Sir,' saith the damsel, 'Gramercy.' 'Damsel,' saith he, 'With a good will!'

'Sir,' saith the damsel, ' You may well alight, for nought have you to fear on this side the bar.' With that, the King alighteth. 'Sir,' saith she, ' Do off your habergeon heedfully and I will bind up the wound in your arm, for of none may you be made whole save of me only.' The King doeth off his habergeon, and the damsel taketh of the blood of the knight's head that still ran all warm, and therewith washeth King Arthur his wound, and thereafter maketh him do on his habergeon again. 'Sir,' saith she, ' Never would you have been whole save by the blood of this Black Knight. And for this carried they off the body piecemeal and the head, for that they well knew you were wounded ; and of the head shall I have right sore need, for thereby shall a castle be yielded up to me that was reft from me by treason, so I may find the knight that I go seek, through whom it ought to be yielded up to me.' ' Damsel,' saith the King, ' And who is the knight?' ' Sir,' saith she, ' He was the son of Alain li Gros of the Valleys of Camelot, and is named Perlesvax.' ' Wherefore Perlesvax?' saith the King. 'Sir,' saith she, ' When he was born, his father was asked how he should be named in right baptism, and he said that he would he should have the name Perlesvax, for the Lord of the Moors had reft him of the greater part of the Valleys of Camelot, and therefore he would that his son should by this name be re-minded thereof, and God should so multiply him as that he should be knight. The lad was right comely and right gentle and began to go by the forests and launch his javelins, Welsh-fashion, at hart and hind. His father and his mother loved him much, and one day they were come forth of their hold, whereunto the forest was close anigh, to enjoy them. Now, there was between the hold and the forest, an exceeding small chapel that stood upon four columns of marble ; and it was roofed of timber and had a little altar within, and before the altar a right fair coffin, and thereupon was the figure of a man graven. Sir,' saith the damsel to the King, ' The lad asked his father and mother what man lay within the coffin. The father answered : " Fair son," saith he, " Certes, I know not to tell you, for the tomb hath been here or ever that my father's father was born, and never have I heard tell of none that might know who it is therein, save only that the letters that are on the coffin say that when the Best Knight in the world shall come hither the coffin will open and the

B

joinings all fall asunder, and then will it be seen who it
is that lieth therein."'

X

'Damsel,' saith the King, 'Have many knights passed thereby
sithence that the coffin was set there?' 'Yea, sir, so many that
neither I nor none other may tell the number. Yet natheless
hath not the coffin removed itself for none. When the lad
heareth his father and mother talking thus, he asketh what a
knight may be? "Fair son," saith his mother, "Of right
ought you well to know by your lineage." She telleth the
lad that he had eleven uncles on his father's side that had all
been slain in arms, and not one of them lived knight but twelve
years. Sir,' saith she to the King, 'The lad made answer that
this was not that he had asked, but how knights were made?
And the father answered that they were such as had more
valour than any other in the world. After that he said, "Fair
son, they are clad in habergeons of iron to protect their bodies,
and helms laced upon their heads, and shields and spears and
swords girded wherewithal to defend their bodies."'

XI

'Sir,' saith the damsel to the King, 'When that the father
had thus spoken to the lad, they returned together to the castle.
When the morrow morning came, the lad arose and heard the
birds sing and bethought him that he would go for disport into
the forest for the day sith that it was fair. So he mounted on
one of his father's horses of the chase and carried his javelins
Welshman-fashion and went into the forest and found a stag
and followed him a good four leagues Welsh, until that he came
into a launde and found two knights all armed that were there
doing battle, and the one had a red shield and the other a
white. He left of tracking the stag to look on at the melly
and saw that the Red Knight was conquering the White. He
launched one of his javelins at the Red Knight so hard that
he pierced his habergeon and made it pass through the heart.
The knight fell dead. Sir,' saith the damsel, 'The knight of
the white shield made great joy thereof, and the lad asked
him, "were knights so easy to slay? Methought," saith the
lad, "that none might never pierce nor damage a knight's

armour, otherwise would I not have run him through with my javelin," saith the lad. Sir, the lad brought the destrier home to his father and mother, and right grieved were they when they heard the tidings of the knight he had slain. And right were they, for thereof did sore trouble come to them thereafter. Sir, the squire departed from the house of his father and mother and came to the court of King Arthur. Right gladly did the King make him knight when he knew his will, and afterward he departed from the land and went to seek adventure in every kingdom. Now is he the Best Knight that is in the world. So go I to seek him, and full great joy shall I have at heart and I may find him. Sir, and you should meet him by any adventure in any of these forests, he beareth a red shield with a white hart. And so tell him that his father is dead, and that his mother will lose all her land so he come not to succour her; and that the brother of the knight of the Red shield that he slew in the forest with his javelin warreth upon her with the Lord of the Moors.' 'Damsel,' saith the King, 'And God grant me to meet him, right fain shall I be thereof, and right well will I set forth your message.' 'Sir,' saith she, 'Now that I have told you him that I seek, it is your turn to tell me your name.' 'Damsel,' saith the King, 'Willingly. They that know me call me Arthur.' 'Arthur? Have you indeed such name?' 'Yea, damsel,' saith he. 'So help me God,' saith she, 'Now am I sorrier for you than tofore, for you have the name of the worst King in the world, and I would that he were here in such sort as you are now. But never again will he move from Cardoil, do what he may, such dread hath the Queen lest any should take him from her, according as I have heard witness, for never saw I neither the one nor the other. I was moved to go to his court, but I have met full a score knights one after other, of whom I asked concerning him, and one told me the same tale as another, for each told me that the court of King Arthur is the vilest in the world, and that all the knights of the Table Round have renounced it for the badness thereof.' 'Damsel,' saith the King, 'Hereof may he well be sorry, but at the beginning I have heard say he did right well.' 'And who careth,' saith the damsel, 'for his good beginning when the end is bad? And much it misliketh me that so seemly knight and so worshipful man as are you should have the name of so evil a king.'

'Damsel,' saith the King, 'A man is not good by his name, but by his heart.' 'You say true,' saith the damsel, 'But for the King's name have I despite of yours. And whitherward are you going?' 'I shall go to Cardoil, where I shall find King Arthur when I shall come thither.' 'Go to, then, and bestir!' saith she. 'One bad man with another! No better hope have I of you, sith that you go thither!' 'Damsel, you may say your pleasure, for thither I go! God be with you!' 'And may never God guide you,' saith she, 'and you go to the court of King Arthur!'

XII

With that the King mounted again and departed, and left the damsel under the tree and entered into the deep forest and rode with much ado as fast as he might to come to Cardoil. And he had ridden a good ten leagues Welsh when he heard a Voice in the thick of the forest that began to cry aloud: 'King Arthur of Great Britain, right glad at heart mayst thou be of this that God hath sent me hither unto thee. And so He biddeth thee that thou hold court at the earliest thou mayst, for the world, that is now made worse of thee and of thy slackness in well-doing, shall thereof be greatly amended!' With that the Voice is silent, and the King was right joyous in his heart of that he had heard. The story speaketh no more here of other adventure that befel King Arthur in his returning nor on his arriving. Anyway, he hath ridden so long that he is come back to Cardoil. The Queen and the knights made great feast of him and great joy. The King was alighted on the mounting-stage and went up into the hall and made him be disarmed. And he showed the Queen the wound that he had on his arm, that had been right great and painful, but it was healing full fairly. The King goeth into the chamber and the Queen with him, and doeth the King be apparelled in a robe of cloth of silk all furred of ermine, with coat, surcoat and mantle. 'Sir,' saith the Queen, 'Sore pain and travail have you had.' 'Lady, in such wise behoveth worshipful man to suffer in order that he may have honour, for hardly shall none without travail come to honour.' He recounteth to the Queen all the adventures that have befallen him sithence that he was departed, and in what manner he was wounded in the arm, and of the damsel that had so blamed him of his name. 'Sir,' saith the queen, 'Now may you well know how meet it is that a man high and rich and puissant should have great shame of himself when he becometh evil.' 'Lady,' saith the King, 'So much did the damsel do me well to wot, but greatly did a Voice recomfort me that I heard in the forest, for it told me that God bade me hold court presently, and that I shall see there the fairest adventure befal that ever I may see.' 'Sir,' saith she, 'Right joyous ought you to be that your Saviour hath had you in remembrance. Now, therefore, fulfil His commandment.' 'Certes, Lady, so will I do. For never had none better desire of well-doing than have I as at this time, nor of honour nor of largesse.' 'Sir,' saith she, 'God be praised thereof.'

BRANCH II

INCIPIT

Now beginneth here the second branch of the Holy Graal in the name of the Father, and of the Son, and of the Holy Ghost.

TITLE I

King Arthur was at Cardoil with the Queen and right few knights. By God's pleasure, the wish and the will had come back to him to win honour and to do largesse as most he might. He made seal his letters and sent them throughout all his lands and all the islands, and gave notice to the barons and knights that he would hold court at Pannenoisance, that is situate on the sea of Wales, at the feast of S. John after Whitsuntide. And he was minded to put it off until that day, for that Whitsuntide was already too nigh, and they that should be present thereat might not all come by the earlier day. The tidings went through all lands, so that knights come in great plenty thereunto, for well-doing had so waxed feeble in all the kingdoms, that every one had avoided King Arthur as one that should do nought more for ever. Wherefore all began now to marvel whence his new desire had come. The knights of the Table Round that were scattered through the lands and the forests, by God's will learnt the tidings and right great joy had they thereof, and came back to the court with great ado. But neither Messire Gawain nor Lancelot came thither on that day. But all the other came that were then on live. S. John's day came, and the knights were come from all parts, marvelling much that the King had not held the court at Whitsuntide, but they knew not the occasion thereof. The day was fair and clear and the air fresh, and the hall was wide and high and garnished of good knights in great plenty. The cloths were spread on the tables whereof were great plenty in the hall. The King and the Queen had washen and went to sit at the head of one table and the other knights sate them down, whereof were full five score and five as the story telleth. Kay the Seneschal and Messire Ywain the son of King Urien served that day at the tables at meat, and five-and-twenty knights beside. And Lucan the Butler served the golden cup before the King. The sun shone through the windows everywhere amidst the hall that was strown of flowers and rushes and sweet herbs and gave out a smell like as had it been sprinkled of balm. And straightway after the first meat had been served, and while they were yet awaiting the second, behold you three damsels where they enter into the hall! She that came first sate upon a mule white as driven snow and had a golden bridle and a saddle with a bow of ivory banded with precious stones and a saddle-cloth of a red samite dropped of gold. The damsel that was seated on the mule was right seemly of body but scarce so fair of face, and she was robed in a rich cloth of silk and gold and had a right rich hat that covered all her head. And it was all loaded of costly stones that flamed like fire. And great need had she that her head were covered, for she was all bald without hair, and carried on her neck her right arm slung in a stole of cloth of gold. And her arm lay on a pillow, the richest that ever might be seen, and it was all charged of little golden bells, and in this hand held she the head of a King sealed in silver and crowned with gold. The other damsel that came behind rode after the fashion of a squire, and carried a pack trussed behind her with a brachet thereupon, and at her neck she bore a shield banded argent and azure with a red cross, and the boss was of gold all set with precious stones. The third damsel came afoot with her kirtle tucked up like a running footman; and she had in her hand a whip wherewith she drove the two steeds. Each of these twain was fairer than the first, but the one afoot surpassed both the others in beauty. The first cometh before the King, there where he sitteth at meat with the Queen. 'Sir,' saith she, 'The Saviour of the world grant you honour and joy and good adventure and my Lady the Queen and all them of this hall for love of you! Hold it not churlishness and I alight not, for there where knights be may I not alight, nor ought I until such time as the Graal be achieved.' 'Damsel,' saith the King, 'Gladly would I have it so.' 'Sir,' saith she, 'That know I well, and may it not mislike you to hear the errand whereon I am come,' 'It shall not mislike me,' saith the King, 'Say your pleasure!' 'Sir,' saith she, 'The shield that this damsel beareth belonged to Joseph, the good soldier knight that took down Our Lord of hanging on the rood. I make you a present thereof in such wise as I shall tell you, to wit, that you keep the shield for a knight that shall come hither for the same, and you shall make hang it on this column in the midst of your hall, and guard it in such wise as that none may take it and hang at his neck save he only. And of this shield shall he achieve the Graal, and another shield shall he leave here in the hall, red, with a white hart; and the brachet that the damsel carrieth shall here remain, and little joy will the brachet make until the knight shall come.' 'Damsel,' saith the King, 'The shield and the brachet will we keep full safely, and right heartily we thank you that you have deigned to bring them hither.' 'Sir,' saith the damsel, 'I have not yet told you all that I have in charge to deliver. The best King that liveth on earth and the most loyal and the most righteous, sendeth you greeting; of whom is sore sorrow for that he hath fallen into a grievous languishment.' 'Damsel,' saith the King, 'Sore pity is it and it be so as you say; and I pray you tell me who is the King?' 'Sir,' saith she, 'It is rich King Fisherman, of whom is great grief.' 'Damsel' saith the King, 'You say true; and God grant him his heart's desire!' 'Sir,' saith she, 'Know you wherefore he hath fallen into languishment?' 'Nay, I know not at all, but gladly would I learn.' 'And I will tell you,' saith she. 'This languishment is come upon him through one that harboured in his hostel, to whom the most Holy Graal appeared. And, for that he would not ask unto whom one served thereof, were all the lands commoved to war thereby, nor never thereafter might knight meet other but he should fight with him in arms without none other occasion. You yourself may well perceive the same, for your well-doing hath greatly slackened, whereof have you had much blame, and all the other barons that by you have taken ensample, for you are the mirror of the world alike in well-doing and in evil-doing. Sir, I myself have good right to plain me of the knight, and I will show you wherefore.' She lifteth the rich hat from her head and showeth the King and Queen and the knights in the hall her head all bald without hair. 'Sir,' saith she, 'My head was right seemly garnished of hair plaited in rich tresses of gold at such time as the knight came to the hostel of the

rich King Fisherman, but I became bald for that he made
not the demand, nor never again shall I have my hair until
such time as a knight shall go thither that shall ask the
question better than did he, or the knight that shall achieve
the Graal. Sir, even yet have you not seen the sore mischief
that hath befallen thereof. There is without this hall a car
that three white harts have drawn hither, and lightly may you
send to see how rich it is. I tell you that the traces are of
silk and the axletrees of gold, and the timber of the car is
ebony. The car is covered above with a black samite, and
below is a cross of gold the whole length, and under the coverlid of the car are the heads of an hundred and fifty knights
whereof some be sealed in gold, other some in silver and the
third in lead. King Fisherman sendeth you word that this loss
hath befallen of him that demanded not unto whom one serveth
of the Graal. Sir, the damsel that beareth the shield holdeth
in her hand the head of a Queen that is sealed in lead and
crowned with copper, and I tell you that by the Queen whose
head you here behold was the King betrayed whose head I bear,
and the three manner of knights whose heads are within the
car. Sir, send without to see the costliness and fashion of the
car.' The King sent Kay the Seneschal to see. He looked
straitly thereat within and without and thereafter returned to
the King. 'Sir,' saith he, 'Never beheld I car so rich, and
there be three harts withal that draw the car, the tallest and
fattest one might ever see. But and you will be guided by me,
you will take the foremost, for he is scarce so fat, and so might
you bid make right good collops thereof.' 'Avoid there, Kay!'
saith the King. 'Foul churlishness have you spoken! I would
not such a deed were done for another such kingdom as is this
of Logres!' 'Sir,' saith the damsel, 'He that hath been wont
to do churlishness doth right grudgingly withdraw himself
therefrom. Messire Kay may say whatsoever him pleaseth,
but well know I that you will pay no heed to his talk. Sir,'
saith the damsel, 'Command that the shield be hung on this
column and that the brachet be put in the Queen's chamber
with the maidens. We will go on our way, for here have we
been long enough.' Messire Ywain laid hold on the shield and
took it off the damsel's neck by leave of the King, and hung it
on the column in the midst of the hall, and one of the Queen's
maidens taketh the brachet and carrieth him to the Queen's

chamber. And the damsel taketh her leave and turneth again, and the King commendeth her to God. When the King had eaten in hall, the Queen with the King and the knights go to lean at the windows to look at the three damsels and the three white harts that draw the car, and the more part said that the damsel afoot that went after the two that were mounted should have the most misease. The bald damsel went before, and set not her hat on her head until such time as behoved her enter into the forest; and the knights that were at the windows might see them no longer. Then set she her hat again upon her head. The King, the Queen, and the knights when they might see them no more, came down from the windows, and certain of them said that never until this time had they seen bald-headed damsel save this one only.

II

Hereupon the story is silent of King Arthur, and turneth again to speak of the three damsels and the car that was drawn by the three white harts. They are entered into the forest and ride on right busily. When they had left the castle some seven leagues Welsh behind them, they saw a knight coming toward them on the way they had to go. The knight sat on a tall horse, lean and bony. His habergeon was all rusty and his shield pierced in more than a dozen places, and the colour thereon was so fretted away that none might make out the cognizance thereof. And a right thick spear bore he in his hand. When he came anigh the damsel, he saluted her right nobly. 'Fair welcome, damsel, to you and your company.' 'Sir,' saith she, 'God grant you joy and good adventure!' 'Damsel,' saith the knight, 'Whence come you?' 'Sir, from a court high-plenary that King Arthur holdeth at Pannenoisance. Go you thither, sir knight,' saith the damsel, 'to see the King and the Queen and the knights that are there?' 'Nay, not so!' saith he. 'Many a time have I seen them, but right glad am I of King Arthur that he hath again taken up his well-doing, for many a time hath he been accustomed thereof.' 'Whitherward have you now emprised your way?' saith the damsel. 'To the land of King Fisherman, and God allow me.' 'Sir,' saith she, 'Tell me your name and bide awhile beside me.' The knight draweth bridle and the damsels and the car come to a stay. 'Damsel,' saith he, 'Well behoveth me tell you my name. Messire Gawain am I called, King Arthur's nephew.' 'What? are you Messire Gawain? My heart well told me as much.' 'Yea, damsel,' saith he, 'Gawain am I.' 'God be praised thereof, for so good knight as are you may well go see the rich King Fisherman. Now am I fain to pray you of the valour that is in you and the courtesy, that you return with me and convoy me beyond a certain castle that is in this forest whereof is some small peril.' 'Damsel,' saith Messire Gawain, 'Willingly, at your pleasure.' He returneth with the damsel through the midst of the forest that was tall and leafy and little haunted of folk. The damsel relateth to him the adventure of the heads that she carried and that were in the car, like as she did at the court of King Arthur, and of the shield and the brachet she had left there, but much it misliked Messire Gawain of the damsel that was afoot behind them. 'Damsel,' saith Messire Gawain, 'Wherefore doth not this damsel that goeth afoot mount upon the car?' 'Sir,' saith she, 'This shall she not, for behoveth her go not otherwise than afoot. But and you be so good knight as men say, betimes will she have done her penance.' 'How so?' saith Gawain. 'I will tell you,' saith she. 'And it shall so be that God bring you to the hostel of rich King Fisherman, and the most Holy Graal appear before you and you demand unto whom is served thereof, then will she have done her penance, and I, that am bald, shall receive again my hair. And so you also make not demand thereof, then will it behove us suffer sore annoy until such time as the Good Knight shall come and shall have achieved the Graal. For on account of him that first was there and made not the demand, are all the lands in sorrow and warfare, and the good King Fisherman is yet in languishment.' 'Damsel,' saith Messire Gawain, 'God grant me courage and will herein that I may come to do this thing according to your wish, whereof may I win worship both of God and of the world.'

III

Messire Gawain and the damsels go on their way a great pace through the high forest, green and leafy, where the birds are singing, and enter into the most hideous forest and most horrible that any might ever see, and seemed it that no greenery never there had been, so bare and dry were all the branches and all the trees black and burnt as it had been by fire, and the ground all parched and black atop with no green, and full of great cracks. 'Damsel,' saith Messire Gawain, 'Right loathly is this forest and right hideous. Goeth it on far like this?' 'Sir,' saith she, 'For nine leagues Welsh goeth it on the same, but we shall pass not through the whole thereof.' Messire Gawain looketh from time to time on the damsel that cometh afoot, and sore it irketh him that he may not amend her estate. They ride on until that they come to a great valley and Messire Gawain looketh along the bottom and seeth appear a black castle that was enclosed within a girdle of wall, foul and evil-seeming. The nigher he draweth to the castle the more hideous it seemeth him, and he seeth great halls appear that were right foully mis-shapen, and the forest about it he seeth to be like as he had found it behind. He seeth a water come down from the head of a mountain, foul and horrible and black, that went amidst the castle roaring so loud that it seemed to be thunder. Messire Gawain seeth the entrance of the gateway foul and horrible like as it had been hell, and within the castle heard he great outcries and lamentations, and the most part heard he saying: 'Ha, God! What hath become of the Good Knight, and when will he come?' 'Damsel,' saith Messire Gawain, 'What is this castle here that is so foul and hideous, wherein is such dolour suffered and such weary longing for the coming of the Good Knight?' 'Sir, this is the castle of the Black Hermit. Wherefore am I fain to pray you that you meddle not herein for nought that they within may do to me, for otherwise it may well be that your death is at hand, for against them will you have no might nor power.' They come anigh the castle as it were a couple of bow-shots, and behold, through the gateway come knights armed on black horses and their arms all black and their shields and spears, and there were a hundred and fifty and two, right parlous to behold. And they come a great gallop toward the damsel, and toward the car, and take the hundred and fifty-two heads, each one his own, and set them upon their spears and so enter into the castle again with great joy. Messire Gawain seeth the insolence that the knights have wrought, and right great shame hath he of himself that he hath not moved withal. 'Messire Gawain,' saith the damsel, 'Now may you know how little would your

force have availed you herein.' 'Damsel, an evil castle is
this where folk are robbed on such wise.' 'Sir, never may
this mischief be amended, nor this outrage be done away, nor
the evil-doer therein be stricken down, nor they that cry and
lament within the prison there be set free until such time as
the Good Knight shall come for whom are they yearning as
you have heard but now.' 'Damsel, right glad may the knight
be that by his valour and his hardiment shall destroy so many
evil folk!' 'Sir, therefore is he the Best Knight in the world,
and he is yet young enough of age, but right sorrowful am I
at heart that I know not true tidings of him ; for better will
have I to see him than any man on live.' 'Damsel, so also
have I,' saith Messire Gawain, 'For then by your leave would
I turn me again.' 'Not so, sir, but and you shall come beyond
the castle, then will I teach you the way whereby you ought
to go.'

IV

With that they go toward the castle all together. Just as
they were about to pass beyond the castle wall, behold you
where a knight cometh forth of a privy postern of the castle,
and he was sitting upon a tall horse, his spear in his fist, and
at his neck had he a red shield whereon was figured a golden
eagle. 'Sir knight,' saith he to Messire Gawain, 'I pray you
bide.' 'What is your pleasure?' 'You must needs joust with
me,' saith he, 'and conquer this shield, or otherwise I shall
conquer you. And full precious is the shield, insomuch as that
great pains ought you to take to have it and conquer it, for
it belonged to the best knight of his faith that was ever, and
the most puissant and the wisest.' 'Who, then, was he?'
saith Messire Gawain. 'Judas Machabee was he, and he it
was that first wrought how by one bird to take another.' 'You
say true,' saith Messire Gawain ; 'A good knight was he.'
'Therefore right joyful may you be,' saith he, 'and you may
conquer the same, for your own is the poorest and most battered
that ever saw I borne by knight. For hardly may a man know
the colour thereof.' 'Thereby may you well see,' saith the
damsel to the knight, 'that his own shield hath not been idle,
nor hath the horse whereon he sitteth been stabled so well as
yours.' 'Damsel,' saith the knight, 'No need is here of long
pleading. Needs must he joust with me, for him do I defy.'

Saith Messire Gawain, 'I hear well that you say.' He draweth
him back and taketh his career and the knight likewise, and
they come together as fast as their horses may carry them, spear
in rest. The knight smiteth Messire Gawain on the shield
whereof he had no great defence, and passeth beyond, and in
the by-pass the knight to-brake his spear; and Messire
Gawain smiteth him with his spear in the midst of his
breast and beareth him to the ground over the croup of his
horse, all pinned upon his spear, whereof he had a good full
hand's breadth in his breast. He draweth his spear back to
him, and when the knight felt himself unpinned, he leaped to
his feet and came straight to his horse and would fain set his
foot in the stirrup when the damsel of the car crieth out:
'Messire Gawain, hinder the knight! for and he were mounted
again, too sore travail would it be to conquer him!' When
the knight heard name Messire Gawain, he draweth him back:
'How?' saith he; 'Is this then the good Gawain, King
Arthur's nephew?' 'Yea,' saith the damsel, 'He it is without
fail!' 'Sir,' saith the knight to Messire Gawain, 'Are you
he?' 'Yea,' saith he, 'Gawain I am!' 'Sir, so please you,'
saith he, 'I hold me conquered, and right sorry am I that I
knew you not or ever I had ado with you.' He taketh the
shield from his neck and holdeth it to him. 'Sir,' saith he,
'Take the shield that belonged to the best knight that was in
his time of his faith, for none know I of whom it shall be
better employed than of you. And of this shield were vanquished all they that be in prison in this castle.' Messire
Gawain taketh the shield that was right fair and rich. 'Sir,'
saith the knight, 'Now give me yours, for you will not bear
two shields.' 'You say true,' saith Messire Gawain. He
taketh the guige from his neck and would have given him the
shield, when the damsel afoot: 'Hold, sir knight, you that are
named Messire Gawain! What would you do? And he bear
your shield into the castle there, they of the castle will hold
you recreant and conquered, and will come forth thence and
carry you into the castle by force, and there will you be cast
into his grievous prison; for no shield is borne thereinto save
of a vanquished knight only.' 'Sir knight,' saith Messire
Gawain, 'No good you wish me, according to that this damsel
saith.' 'Sir,' saith the knight, 'I cry you mercy, and a second
time I hold me conquered, and right glad should I have been

might I have borne your shield within yonder, and right great worship should I have had thereof, for never yet hath entered there the shield of knight so good. And now ought I to be right well pleased of your coming, sith that you have set me free of the sorest trouble that ever knight had.' 'What is the trouble?' saith Messire Gawain. 'Sir,' saith he, 'I will tell you. Heretofore many a time hath there been a passing by of knights both of hardy and of coward, and it was my business to contend and joust with them and do battle, and I made them present of the shield as did I you. The more part found I hardy and well able to defend themselves, that wounded me in many places, but never was knight so felled me to the ground nor dealt me so sore a buffet as have you. And sith that you are carrying away the shield and I am conquered, never hereafter shall knight that passeth before this castle have no dread of me nor of no knight that is herein.' 'By my head,' saith Messire Gawain, 'Now am I gladder of my conquest than I was before.' 'Sir,' saith the knight, 'By your leave will I go my way, for, and I may hide not my shame in the castle, needs must I show it openly abroad.' 'God grant you do well!' saith Messire Gawain. 'Messire Gawain,' saith the Damsel of the Car, 'give me your shield that the knight would fain have carried off.' 'Willingly, damsel,' saith he. The damsel that went afoot taketh the shield and setteth it in the car. Howbeit, the knight that was conquered mounted again upon his horse, and entered again into the castle, and when he was come thereinto, arose a noise and great outcry so loud that all the forest and all the valley began to resound thereof. 'Messire Gawain,' saith the Damsel of the Car, 'the knight is shamed and there cast in prison another time. Now haste, Messire Gawain! for now may you go!' With that they all set forward again upon their way together, and leave the castle an English league behind. 'Damsel,' saith Messire Gawain, 'When it shall please you, I shall have your leave to go. 'Sir,' saith she, 'God be guard of your body, and right great thanks of your convoy.' 'Lady,' saith he, 'My service is always ready at your command.' 'Sir,' saith the damsel, 'Gramercy, and your own way see you there by yonder great cross at the entrance of yonder forest. And beyond that, will you find the fairest forest and most delightsome when you shall have passed through this that sore is wearisome.' Messire

Gawain turneth him to go, and the damsel afoot crieth out to him : 'Sir, not so heedful are you as I supposed.' Messire Gawain turneth his horse's head as he that was startled : 'Wherefore say you so, damsel?' saith he. 'For this,' saith she, 'That you have never asked of my Damsel wherefore she carrieth her arm slung at her neck in this golden stole, nor what may be the rich pillow whereon the arm lieth. And no greater heed will you take at the court of the rich King Fisherman.' 'Sweet, my friend,' saith the Damsel of the Car, 'blame not Messire Gawain only, but King Arthur before him and all the knights that were in the court. For not one of them all that were there was so heedful as to ask me. Go your ways, Messire Gawain, for in vain would you now demand it, for I will tell you not, nor shall you never know it save only by the most coward knight in the world, that is mine own knight and goeth to seek me and knoweth not where to find me.' 'Damsel,' saith Messire Gawain, 'I durst not press you further.' With that the Damsel departeth, and Messire Gawain setteth him forward again on the way that she had taught him.

BRANCH III

HERE beginneth another branch of the Graal in the name of
the Father, and in the name of the Son, and in the name of the
Holy Ghost.

TITLE I

Here is the story silent of the three damsels and the Car
and saith that Messire Gawain hath passed throughout the
evil forest and is entered into the forest passing fair, the broad,
the high, the plenteous of venison. And he rideth a great
pace, but sore abashed is he of that the damsel had said to him,
and misdoubteth him but he shall have blame thereof in many
places. He rode hard the day long till that it was evensong
and the sun was about to set. And he looketh before him and
seeth the house of a hermit and the chapel in the thick of the
forest; and a spring flowed forth in front of the chapel right
clear and fresh, and above it was a tree full broad and tall that
threw a shadow over the spring. A damsel sate under the tree
and held a mule by the reins and at the saddle-bow had she the
head of a knight hanging. And Messire Gawain cometh
thitherward and alighteth. 'Damsel,' saith he, 'God give
you good adventure!' 'Sir,' saith she, 'And you always.'
When she was risen up over against him, 'Damsel,' saith he,
'For whom are you a-waiting here?' 'Sir,' saith she, 'I am
waiting for the hermit of this holy chapel, that is gone into the
forest, and I would fain ask him tidings of a knight.' 'Think
you he will tell you them and he knoweth any?' 'Yea, sir, I
think so, according to that I have been told.' Therewithal behold you the hermit that was coming, and saluteth the damsel
and Messire Gawain and openeth the door of the house and

33

setteth the two steeds within and striketh off the bridles and giveth them green-meat first and barley after, and fain would he have taken off the saddles when Messire Gawain leapeth before: 'Sir,' saith he, 'Do not so! This business is not for you!' 'Hermit though I be,' saith he, 'yet well know I how to deal withal, for at the court of King Uther Pendragon have I been squire and knight two-score years, and a score or more have I been in this hermitage.' And Messire Gawain looketh at him in wonderment. 'Sir,' saith he, 'Meseemeth you are not of more than forty years.' 'That know I well of a truth,' saith the hermit, and Messire Gawain taketh off the saddles and bethinketh him more of the damsel's mule than of his own horse. And the hermit taketh Messire Gawain by the hand and the damsel and leadeth them into the chapel. And the place was right fair. 'Sir,' saith the hermit to Messire Gawain, 'You will disarm you not,' saith he, 'for this forest is passing adventurous, and no worshipful man behoveth be disgarnished.' He goeth for his spear and for his shield and setteth them within the chapel. He setteth before them such meat as he hath, and when they have eaten giveth them to drink of the spring. 'Sir,' saith the damsel, 'Of a knight that I go seek am I come to ask you tidings.' 'Who is the knight?' saith the hermit. 'Sir, he is the Chaste Knight of most holy lineage. He hath a head of gold, the look of a lion, the navel of a virgin maid, a heart of steel, the body of an elephant, and without wickedness are all his conditions.' 'Damsel,' saith the hermit, 'Nought will I tell you concerning him, for I know not of a certainty where he is, save this, that he hath lain in this chapel twice, not once only, within this twelvemonth.' 'Sir,' saith she, 'Will you tell me no more of him, nor none other witting?' 'In no wise,' saith the hermit. 'And you, Messire Gawain?' saith she. 'Damsel,' saith he, 'As fainly would I see him as you, but none find I that may tell me tidings of him.' 'And the damsel of the Car, Sir, have you seen her?' 'Yea, lady,' saith he, 'It is but just now sithence that I left her.' 'Carried she still her arm slung at her neck?' 'Yea,' saith Messire Gawain, 'in such wise she carried it.' 'Of a long while,' saith the damsel, 'hath she borne it thus.' 'Sir,' saith the hermit, 'how are you named?' 'Sir,' saith he, 'Gawain am I called, King Arthur's nephew.' 'Thereof I love you the better,' saith the hermit. 'Sir,' saith the damsel, 'You are of kindred to the worst King

that is.' 'Of what King speak you?' saith Messire Gawain.
'I speak,' saith she, 'of King Arthur, through whom is all the
world made worser, for he began doing well and now hath
become evil. For hatred of him hate I a knight that found me
nigh S. Augustine's Chapel, and yet was he the comeliest knight
that saw I ever. He slew a knight within the bar right hardily.
I asked him for the head of the knight and he went back for
the same and set himself in sore peril. He brought it me, and
I made him great joy, but when he told me his name was
Arthur I had no fainness of the bounty he had done me, for
that he had the name of that evil King.'

II

'Damsel,' saith Messire Gawain, 'You may say your
pleasure. I tell you that King Arthur hath held the richest
court that he hath held ever, and these evil conditions whereof
you blame him is he minded to put away for evermore, and
more will he do of good and more of largesse than was ever
known aforetime, so long as he shall live; nor know I none
other knight that beareth his name.' 'You are right,' saith
the damsel, 'to come to his rescue, for that he is your uncle,
but your rescue will scarce avail him and he deliver not himself.'
'Sir,' saith the hermit to Messire Gawain, 'The damsel will
say her pleasure. May God defend King Arthur, for his father
made me knight. Now am I priest, and in this hermitage ever
sithence that I came hither have I served King Fisherman by
the will of Our Lord and His commandment, and all they that
serve him do well partake of his reward, for the place of his
most holy service is a refuge so sweet that unto him that hath
been there a year, it seemeth to have been but a month for the
holiness of the place and of himself, and for the sweetness of his
castle wherein have I oftentimes done service in the chapel where
the Holy Graal appeareth. Therefore is it that I and all that
serve him are so youthful of seeming.' 'Sir,' saith Messire
Gawain, 'By what way may a man go to his castle?' 'Sir,'
saith the hermit, 'None may teach you the way, save the will of
God lead you therein. And would you fain go thither?' 'Sir,'
saith Messire Gawain, 'It is the most wish that I have.' 'Sir,'
saith the hermit, 'Now God give you grace and courage to ask

the question that the others to whom the Graal hath appeared would ask not, whereof have many mischances sithence befallen much people.'

III

With that, they left of talking, and the hermit led Messire Gawain into his house to rest, and the damsel abode still in the chapel. On the morrow when dawn appeared, Messire Gawain that had lain all armed, arose and found his saddle ready and the damsel, and the bridles set on, and cometh to the chapel and findeth the hermit that was apparelled to sing mass, and seeth the damsel kneeling before an image of Our Lady, and she prayed God and the sweet Lady that they would counsel her of that whereof she had need, and wept right tenderly so that the tears ran down her face. And when she had prayed of a long space she ariseth, and Messire Gawain biddeth her God give her good day, and she returneth his salute. 'Damsel,' saith he, 'Meseemeth you are not over joyous.' 'Sir,' saith she, 'I have right, for now am I nigh unto my desolation, sith that I may not find the Good Knight. Now must I needs go to the castle of the Black Hermit, and bear thither the head that hangeth at my saddle-bow, for otherwise shall I not be able to pass through the forest but my body should there be cast in prison or shamed, and this shall be the quittance for my passing. Then will I seek the Damsel of the Car and so shall I go in safety through the forest.' With that the hermit had begun the mass and Messire Gawain and the damsel heard it. When mass was sung, Messire Gawain took leave of the hermit and the damsel also. And Messire Gawain goeth one way and the damsel the other, and either biddeth other to God.

IV

Hereupon the story is now silent of the damsel, and saith that Messire Gawain goeth through the high forest and rideth a great pace, and prayeth God right sweetly that He will set him in such way as that thereby he may go to the land of the rich King Fisherman. And he rideth until the hour of noon, and cometh into the fulness of the forest and seeth under a tree a squire alighted of a horse of the chase. Messire Gawain saluteth

him, and the squire saith: 'Sir, right welcome may you be!'
'Fair sweet friend,' saith Messire Gawain, 'Whither go you?'
'Sir, I go to seek the lord of this forest.' 'Whose is the
forest?' saith Messire Gawain. 'Sir, it belongeth to the best
knight in the world.' 'Can you tell me tidings of him?' 'He
ought to bear a shield banded azure and argent with a red cross
thereon and a boss of gold. I say that he is good knight, but
little call have I to praise him, for he slew my father in this
forest with a javelin. The Good Knight was squire what time
he slew him, and fain would I avenge my father upon him and
I may find him, for he reft me of the best knight that was in the
realm of Logres when he slew my father. Well did he bereave
me of him what time he slew him with his javelin without
defiance, nor shall I never be at ease nor at rest until I shall
have avenged him.' 'Fair sweet friend,' saith Messire Gawain,
'Sith that he is knight so good, take heed you increase not your
wrong of your own act, and I would fain that you had found
him, so as that no evil had befallen him thereof.'

V

'So would not I,' saith the squire, 'for never shall I see
him in this place but I shall run upon him as my mortal enemy!'
'Fair sweet friend,' saith Messire Gawain, 'you may say your
pleasure, but tell me, is there no hold in this forest wherein I
may harbour me the night?' 'Sir,' saith the squire, 'No hold
know I within twenty league of your way in any quarter.
Wherefore no leisure have you to tarry, for it is high noon
already.' So Messire Gawain saluteth the squire and goeth a
great pace as he that knoweth neither highway nor byway save
only as adventure may lead him. And the forest pleaseth him
well for that it is so fair and that he seeth the deer pass by
before him in great herds. He rode on until it drew toward
evensong at a corner of the forest. The evening was fair and
calm and the sun was about to set. And a score league Welsh
had he ridden sithence that he parted from the squire, and sore
he misdoubted him that he should find no hold. He found the
fairest meadow-land in the world, and looked before him when
he had ridden a couple of bow-shot lengths and saw a castle
appear nigh the forest on a mountain. And it was enclosed of
high walls with battlements, and within were fair halls whereof

the windows showed in the outer walls, and in the midst was an ancient tower that was compassed round of great waters and broad meadow-lands. Thitherward Messire Gawain draweth him and looketh toward the gateway of the castle and seeth a squire issue forth a great pace upon a hackney, and he came the way that Messire Gawain was coming. And when the squire seeth him and hath drawn somewhat anigh, he saluteth him right nobly.

VI

'Sir, right welcome may you be!' 'Good adventure may you have!' saith Messire Gawain. 'Fair sweet friend, what is this castle here, sir?' 'Sir, it is the castle of the Widow Lady.' 'What is the name thereof?' 'Camelot; and it belonged to Alain li Gros, that was a right loyal knight and worshipful man. He is dead this long time, and my Lady hath remained without succour and without counsel. Wherefore is the castle warred upon of them that would fain reave her thereof by force. The Lord of the Moors and another knight are they that war upon her and would fain reave her of this castle as they have reft her of seven other already. Greatly desireth she the return of her son, for no counsel hath she save only of her one daughter and of five old knights that help her to guard the castle. Sir,' saith he, 'The door is made fast and the bridge drawn up, for they guard the castle closely, but, so please you, you will tell me your name and I will go before and make the bridge be lowered and the gate unfastened, and will say that you will lodge within to-night.' 'Gramercy,' saith Messire Gawain, 'right well shall my name be known or ever I depart from the castle.' The squire goeth his way a great pace, and Messire Gawain rideth softly at a walk for he had yet a long way to go. And he found a chapel that stood between the forest and the castle, and it was builded upon four columns of marble and within was a right fair sepulchre. The chapel had no fence of any kind about it, so that he seeth the coffin within full clearly, and Messire Gawain bideth awhile to look thereon. And the squire is entered into the castle and hath made the bridge be lowered and the door opened. He alighteth and is come into the hall where was the Widow Lady and her daughter. Saith the Lady to the squire: 'Wherefore have you returned from doing my message?' 'Lady, for the comeliest knight that I have seen ever, and fain

would he harbour within to-night, and he is garnished of all
arms and rideth without company.' 'And what name hath he?'
saith the Lady. 'Lady, he told me you should know it well
or ever he depart from this castle.' Therewithal the Lady gan
weep for joy and her daughter also, and, lifting her hands
towards heaven, 'Fair Lord God!' saith the Widow Lady,
'And this be indeed my son, never before have I had joy that
might be likened to this! Now shall I not be disherited of mine
honour, neither shall I lose my castle whereof they would fain
reave me by wrong, for that no Lord nor champion have I!'

VII

Thereupon the Widow Lady ariseth up and her daughter
likewise, and they go over the bridge of the castle and see
Messire Gawain that was yet looking on the coffin within the
chapel. 'Now haste!' saith the Lady; 'At the tomb shall we
be well able to see whether it be he!' They go to the chapel
right speedily, and Messire Gawain seeth them coming and
alighteth. 'Lady,' saith he, 'Welcome may you be, you and
your company.' The Lady answereth never a word until that
they are come to the tomb. When she findeth it not open she
falleth down in a swoon. And Messire Gawain is sore afraid
when he seeth it. The Lady cometh back out of her swoon and
breaketh out into great lamentation. 'Sir,' saith the damsel to
Messire Gawain, 'Welcome may you be! But now sithence
my mother supposed that you had been her son and made great
joy thereof, and now seeth she plainly that you are not he,
whereof is she sore sorrowful, for so soon as he shall return,
this coffin behoveth open, nor until that hour shall none know
who it is that lieth therein.' The Lady riseth up and taketh
Messire Gawain by the hand. 'Sir,' saith she, 'What is your
name?' 'Lady,' saith he, 'I am called Gawain, King Arthur's
nephew.' 'Sir,' saith she, 'You shall be he that is welcome
both for the sake of my son and for your own sake.' The Lady
biddeth a squire lead his horse into the castle and carry his shield
and spear. Then they enter into the castle and lead Messire
Gawain into the hall, and make disarm him. After that, they
fetch him water to wash his hands and his face, for he was dis-
tained of the rust of his habergeon. The Lady maketh apparel
him in a rich robe of silk and gold, and furred of ermine. The

Widow Lady cometh forth of her chamber and maketh Messire
Gawain sit beside her. 'Sir,' saith she, 'Can you tell me any
tidings of my son that I have not seen of this long time past,
and of whom at this present am I sore in need?'

VIII

'Lady,' saith he, 'No tidings of him know I to tell you, and
right heavy am I thereof, for he is the knight of the world that
fainest I would see and he be your son as I am told. What
name hath he?' 'Sir,' saith she, 'His name in right baptism is
Perceval, and a right comely squire was he when he departed
hence. Now as at this time is it said that he is the comeliest
knight on live and the most hardy and the cleanest of all wickedness. And sore need have I of his hardiment, for what time
that he departed hence he left me in the midst of a great warfare
on behalf of the Knight of the Red Shield that he slew. Within
the se'nnight thereafter he went away, nor never once have I
seen him sithence, albeit a full seven year hath passed already.
And now the brother of the knight that he slew and the Lord of
the Moors are warring upon and are fain to reave me of my
castle and God counsel me not. For my brothers are too far
away from me, and King Pelles of the Lower Folk hath renounced his land for God's sake and entered into a hermitage.
But the King of Castle Mortal hath in him as much of wickedness and felony as these twain have in them of good, and enough
thereof have they. But neither succour nor help may they give
me, for the King of Castle Mortal challengeth my Lord King
Fisherman both of the most Holy Graal and of the Lance whereof the point bleedeth every day, albeit God forbid he should
ever have them.'

IX

'Lady,' saith Messire Gawain, 'There was at the hostel of
King Fisherman a knight before whom the Holy Graal appeared
three times, yet never once would he ask whereof it served nor
whom it honoured.' 'Sir,' saith the Widow Lady's daughter,
'You say true, and the Best Knight is he of the world. This
say I for love of my brother, and I love all knights for the love
of him, but by the foolish wit of the knight hath mine uncle
King Fisherman fallen into languishment.' 'Sir,' saith the

Lady, 'Behoveth all good knights go see the rich King Fisherman. Will you not therefore go?' 'Lady,' saith Messire Gawain, 'Yea, that will I, so speedily as I may, for not elsewhither have I emprised my way.' 'Sir,' saith she, 'Then are you going to see my son, wherefore tell my son, and you see him, of mine evil plight and my misease, and King Fisherman my brother. But take heed, Messire Gawain, that you be better mindful than was the knight.' 'Lady,' saith Messire Gawain, 'I shall do as God shall teach me.' In the meanwhile as they were speaking thus together, behold you therewithal the Widow Lady's five knights that were come in from the forest and make bring harts and hinds and wild swine. So they alighted and made great joy of Messire Gawain when they knew who he was.

X

When the meat was ready they sate to eat, and full plenteously were they provided and right well were they served. Thereupon, behold, cometh the squire that had opened the door for Messire Gawain, and kneeleth before the Widow Lady. 'And what tidings?' saith she. 'Lady, there is to be a right great assembly of tourney in the valleys that aforetime were ours. Already have they spread the Welsh booths, and thither are come these two that are warring upon you and great store other knights. And they have ordained that he which shall do best at the assembly shall undertake the garrison of this castle in such sort as that he shall hold it for his own alone against all other.' The Widow Lady beginneth to weep: 'Sir,' saith she to Messire Gawain, 'Now may you understand that the castle is not mine own, sith that these knights say it is theirs as you hear.' 'Certes, Lady,' saith he, 'Herein do they great dishonour and a sin.'

XI

When the table was removed the damsel fell at Messire Gawaine's feet, weeping. He raiseth her forthwith and saith to her, 'Damsel, herein do you ill.' 'For God's sake, Sir, take pity on my Lady mother and me!' 'Certes, damsel, great pity have I of you.' 'Sir, now shall it be seen in this strait whether

you be good knight, for good is the knighthood that doeth well
for God's sake.' The Widow Lady and her daughter go into
the chamber, and Messire Gawain's bed was made in the midst
of the hall. So he went and lay down as did also the five
knights. All the night was Messire Gawain in much thought.
The morrow, when he was risen, he went to hear mass in a
chapel that was within and ate thereafter three sops in wine and
then armed him, and at the same time asked the five knights
that were there in the hall whether they would go see the
assembly. 'Yea, Sir,' say they, 'and you be going thither.'
'In faith, thither verily will I go!' saith Messire Gawain.
The knights are armed forthwith, and their horses brought and
Messire Gawain's, and he goeth to take leave of the Widow
Lady and her daughter. But great joy make they of this that
they have heard say that he will go with their knights to the
assembly.

XII

Messire Gawain and the five knights mounted and issued
forth of the castle and rode a great gallop before a forest.
Messire Gawain looketh before him about the foreclose of the
forest, and seeth the fairest purlieus that he had seen ever, and
so broad they be that he may not see nor know the fourth part
thereof. They are garnished of tall forests on one hand and on
the other, and there are high rocks in the midst with wild deer
among. 'Sir,' say the knights, 'Lo, these be the Valleys of
Camelot whereof my Lady and her daughter have been bereft,
and bereft also hath she been of the richest castles that be in
Wales to the number of seven.' 'A wrong is it and a sin!'
saith Messire Gawain. So far have they ridden that they see
the ensigns and the shields there where the assembly is to be
held, and they see already mounted the more part of the knights
all armed and running their horses down the meadow-land.
And they see the tents stretched on the one hand and on
another. And Messire Gawain bideth, and the five knights
under a tree, and see the knights assembling on one hand
and on another. One of the five knights that were with him
gave him witting of the Lord of the Moors and the brother of
the knight of the Red Shield that had to name Chaos the Red.
So soon as the tournament was assembled, Messire Gawain and

the knights come to the assembly, and Messire Gawain goeth to a Welsh knight and beareth him to the ground, both him and his horse, all in a heap. And the five come after at a great gallop and each overthroweth his own, and greatly pride they themselves of Messire Gawain. Chaos the Red seeth Messire Gawain but knoweth him not. He goeth toward him a full career, and Messire Gawain receiveth him on the point of his spear and hurtleth against him so sore that he all to-brast his collarbone and maketh the spear fly from his fist. And Messire Gawain searcheth the fellowships of one part and the other, and findeth not nor encountereth no knight before him in his way but he putteth him off his horse or woundeth him, either by himself or by one of the five knights, that make right great joy of that they see him do. They show him the Lord of the Moors that was coming with a full great fellowship of folk. He goeth thitherward a great gallop. They mell together either upon other of their spears that they bent and all to-brast in flinders, and hurtle together so stoutly both of their horses and their bodies that the Lord of the Moors loseth his stirrups and hath the hinder saddlebow to-frushed, and falleth down to the ground over his horse croup in such sort that the peak of his helm dinteth a full palm's breadth into the turf. And Messire Gawain taketh the horse that was right rich and good, maugre all of his fellowship, and giveth it to one of the five knights that maketh it be led to Camelot of a squire. Messire Gawain searcheth the ranks on the one hand and on the other, and doeth such feats of arms as never no knight might do the same again. The five knights also showed great hardiment, and did more of arms that day than ever had they done tofore, for not one of them but had overthrown at least a single knight and won his horse. The Lord of the Moors was mounted again on another rich horse and had great shame for that Messire Gawain had overthrown him. He espieth Messire Gawain and goeth toward him a great gallop and thinketh to avenge his shame. They come together either on other with a great shock, and Messire Gawain smiteth him with the truncheon of his spear that he had still left, in the midst of his breast, so that it was all to-splintered. The Lord of the Moors likewise again to-brast his spear upon him. Messire Gawain draweth his sword and flingeth the truncheon to the ground. The Lord of the Moors doth likewise and commandeth his folk not to mell betwixt them twain, for never yet had he found no knight that he had not conquered. They deal them great buffets on the helms, either upon other, in such sort that the sparks fly thereout and their swords are blunted. The buffets of Messire Gawain are heavier than the other's, for he dealeth them so mighty and horrible that the blood rayeth out from the Lord of the Moors by the mouth and the nose so that his habergeon is all bloody thereof and he may no more endure. Thereupon he yieldeth him prisoner to Messire Gawain, that is right glad thereof and his five knights likewise. The Lord of the Moors goeth to his tent to alight, and Messire Gawain with him and alighteth. And Messire Gawain taketh the horse and saith to one of the knights, 'Keep this for me.' And all the knights are repaired to their tents, and with one accord say they all that the knight of the Red Shield with the eagle of gold thereon hath done better than we, and they ask the Lord of the Moors whether he accordeth with them, and he saith 'Aye.' 'Sir,' saith he to Messire Gawain, 'You, then, are the warden of this castle of Camelot.' 'Gramercy, lord!' saith Messire Gawain. He calleth the five knights and saith unto them: 'Lords, my will is that you be there on my behalf and that you shall safeguard the same by consent of the knights that are here present.' 'Sir, right gladly do we agree thereto.' 'Sir,' saith Messire Gawain to the Lord of the Moors, 'I give you more-over as my prisoner to the Widow Lady that harboured me last night.' 'Sir,' saith he, 'This have you no right to do. Assembly of tourney is not war. Hence have you no right to imprison my body in castle, for well am I able to pay my ransom here. But tell me, what is your name?' 'I am called Gawain.' 'Ha, Messire Gawain, many a time have I heard tell of you albeit never tofore have I seen you. But sith that the castle of Camelot is in your keeping, I promise you loyally that before a year and a day neither the castle nor none of the Lady's land need fear nought from me nor from any other so far forth as I may hinder him, and hereto do I pledge me in the presence of all these knights that are here. And, so you would have of me gold or silver, thereof will I give you at your will.' 'Sir,' saith Messire Gawain, 'Gramercy! I consent freely to as much as you have said.' Messire Gawain taketh leave and turneth him again toward the castle of Camelot, and sendeth by a squire the horse of the Lord of the Moors to the daughter of the Widow

Lady, that made great joy thereof. And the five knights drive before them the horses they have taken booty. Whereof great also was the joy. No need to wonder whether Messire Gawain were well harboured that night at the castle. He recounted to the Lady how the castle was in the keeping of these knights. When it came to morning-tide, Messire Gawain took leave and departed from the castle, but not before he had heard mass, for such was his custom. The Widow Lady and her daughter commend him to God, and the castle remaineth in better keeping than he had found it.

BRANCH IV

INCIPIT

HERE beginneth another branch of the Graal in the name of the
Father, and of the Son, and of the Holy Ghost.

TITLE I

And the story is silent here of the mother of the Good
Knight, and saith that Messire Gawain goeth so as God and
adventure lead him toward the land of the rich King Fisherman. And he entereth into a great forest, all armed, his shield
at his neck and his spear in his hand. And he prayeth Our
Lord that He counsel him of this holy errand he hath emprised
so as that he may honourably achieve it. He rode until that he
came at evensong to a hold that was in the midst of the forest.
And it was compassed about of a great water, and had about it
great clumps of trees so as that scarce with much pains might
he espy the hall, that was right large. The river that compassed it about was water royal, for it lost not its right name
nor its body as far as the sea. And Messire Gawain bethought
him that it was the hold of a worshipful man, and draweth him
thitherward to lodge. And as he drew anigh the bridge of the
hold, he looketh and seeth a dwarf sitting on a high bench.
He leapeth up: 'Messire Gawain,' saith he, 'Welcome may
you be!' 'Fair, sweet friend,' saith Messire Gawain, 'God
give you good adventure! You know me, then?' saith he.
'Well do I know you,' saith the dwarf, 'For I saw you at the
tournament. At a better moment could you not have come
hither, for my lord is not here. But you will find my lady, the
fairest and most gentle and most courteous in the realm of
Logres, and as yet is she not of twenty years.' 'Fair friend,'
saith Messire Gawain, 'What name hath the lord of the hold?'

46

'Sir, he is called of Little Gomeret. I will go tell my lady that Messire Gawain is come, the good knight, and bid her make great joy.' Howbeit, Messire Gawain marvelleth much that the dwarf should make him such cheer, for many knaveries hath he found in many places within the bodies of many dwarfs. The dwarf is come into the chamber where the lady was. 'Now, haste, Lady!' saith he, 'Make great joy, for Messire Gawain is come to harbour with you.' 'Certes,' saith she, 'Of this am I right glad and right sorry ; glad, for that the good knight will lie here to-night, sorry, for that he is the knight that my lord most hateth in the world. Wherefore he warneth me against him for love of him, for oftentimes hath he told me that never did Messire Gawain keep faith with dame nor damsel but he would have his will of them.' 'Lady,' saith the dwarf, 'It is not true albeit it is so said.'

II

Thereupon Messire Gawain entereth into the courtyard and alighteth, and the lady cometh to meet him and saith to him : 'May you be come to joy and good adventure.' 'Lady,' saith he, 'May you also have honour and good adventure.' The lady taketh him by the hand and leadeth him into the hall and maketh him be seated on a cushion of straw. And a squire leadeth his horse to stable. And the dwarf summoneth two other squires and doeth Messire Gawain be disarmed, and helpeth them right busily, and maketh fetch water to wash his hands and his face. 'Sir,' saith the dwarf, 'Your fists are still all swollen of the buffets you gave and received at the tournament.' Messire Gawain answered him nought. And the dwarf entereth into the chamber and bringeth a scarlet robe furred of ermine and maketh it be done on Messire Gawain. And meat was made ready and the table set, and the lady sate to eat. Many a time looked he upon the lady by reason of her great beauty, and, had he been minded to trust to his heart and his eyes, he would have all to-changed his purpose ; but so straitly was his heart bound up, and so quenched the desires thereof, that nought would he allow himself to think upon that might turn to wickedness, for the sake of the high pilgrimage he had emprised. Rather 'gan he withdraw his eyes from looking at the lady, that was held to be of passing great beauty. After meat Messire Gawain's bed was made, and he apparelled himself to lie down. The lady bade him God give him good adventure, and he made answer the like. When the lady was in her chamber, the dwarf said to Messire Gawain: 'Sir, I will lie before you, so as to keep you company until you be asleep.' 'Gramercy,' saith he, 'And God allow me at some time to reward you of the service.' The dwarf laid himself down on a mattress before Messire Gawain, and when he saw that he slept, he ariseth as quickly as he may, and cometh to a boat that was on the river that ran behind the hall, and entereth thereinto and roweth up-stream of the river. And he cometh to a fishery, where was a right fair hall on a little eyot enclosed by a marshy arm of the river. The jealous knight was come thither for disport, and lay in the midst of the hall upon a couch. The dwarf cometh forth of his boat thereinto, and lighteth a great candle in his fist and cometh before the couch. 'What ho, there!' saith the dwarf, 'Are you sleeping?' And the other waketh up sore startled, and asketh what is the matter and wherefore is he come? 'In God's name,' saith he, 'You sleep not so much at your ease as doth Messire Gawain!' 'How know you that?' saith he. 'Well know I,' saith the dwarf, 'For I left him but now in your hall, and methinketh he and your lady are abed together arm to arm.' 'How?' saith he, 'I forbade her she should ever harbour Messire Gawain.' 'In faith,' said the dwarf, 'She hath made him greater cheer than ever saw I her make to none other! But haste you and come, for great fear have I lest he carry her away!' 'By my head!' saith the knight; 'I will go not, howsoever it be! But she shall pay for it, even though she go!' 'Then of wrong will it be!' saith the dwarf, 'as methinketh!'

III

Messire Gawain lay in the hall that was ware of nought of this. He seeth that day hath broken fair and clear, and ariseth up. The lady cometh to the door of the hall and seeth not the dwarf, whereby well she understandeth his treachery. She saith to Messire Gawain, 'Sir, for God's sake have pity upon me, for the dwarf hath betrayed me! And you withdraw yourself forth of our forest and help not to rescue me from the smart that my lord will make me suffer, great sin will you have thereof. For well know you that of right ought I not to be held guilty toward my lord nor toward any other, for aught that you have done toward me or I toward you.' 'You say true,' saith Messire Gawain. Thereupon is he armed, and taketh leave of the lady and issueth forth of the fair hold and setteth him in an ambush in the forest nigh thereby. Straightway behold the jealous knight where he cometh, he and his dwarf. He entereth into the hall. The lady cometh to meet him. 'Sir,' saith she, 'Welcome may you be!' 'And you,' saith he, 'Shame and evil adventure may you have, as the most disloyal dame on live, for that this night have you harboured in my hostel and in my bed him that most have I warned you against!' 'Sir,' saith she, 'In your hostel did I harbour him, but never hath your bed been shamed by me, nor never shall be!' 'You lie!' saith he, 'like a false woman!' He armeth himself all incontinent and maketh his horse be armed, then maketh the lady go down and despoil her to her shirt, that crieth him mercy right sweetly and weepeth. He mounteth his horse and taketh his shield and his spear, and maketh the lady be taken of the dwarf by her tresses and maketh her be led before him into the forest. And he bideth above a pool where was a spring, and maketh her enter into the water that flowed forth full cold, and gathereth saplings in the forest for rods and beginneth to smite and beat her across upon her back and her breast in such sort that the stream from the spring was all bloody therewithal. And she began to cry out right loud, until at last Messire Gawain heareth her and draweth forth of the ambush wherein he was, and cometh thitherward a great gallop. 'By my faith,' saith the dwarf, 'Look you here where Messire Gawain cometh!' 'By my faith,' saith the knight, 'Now know I well that nought is there here but treachery, and that the matter is well proven!' By this time, Messire Gawain is come, and saith: 'Avoid, Sir knight! Wherefore slay you the best lady and most loyal that ever have I seen? Never tofore have I found lady that hath done me so much honour, and this ought you to be well pleased to know, for neither in her bearing, nor in her speech, nor in herself found I nought save all goodness only. Wherefore I pray you of franchise and of love that you forbear your wrath and that you set her forth of the water. And so will I swear on all the sacred hallows in this chapel that never did I beseech her of evil nor wantonness nor never had I no desire thereof.' The knight was full of great wrath when he saw that Messire

C

Gawain had not gone his way thence, and an anguish of jealousy burneth him heart and body and overburdeneth him of folly and outrage, and Messire Gawain that is still before him moveth him to yet further transgression. Natheless, for the fear that he hath of him he speaketh to him : ' Messire Gawain,' saith he, ' I will set her forth thence on one condition, that you joust at me and I at you, and, so you conquer me, quit shall she be of misdoing and of blame, but and if I shall conquer you, she shall be held guilty herein. Such shall be the judgment in this matter.' ' I ask no better,' saith Messire Gawain.

IV

Thereupon, the knight biddeth the dwarf make set the lady forth of the pool of the spring and make her sit in a launde whereas they were to joust. The knight draweth him back the better to take his career, and Messire Gawain cometh as fast as his horse may carry him toward Marin the Jealous. And when Marin seeth him coming, he avoideth his buffet and lowereth his spear and cometh to his wife that was right sore distraught, and wept as she that suffered blameless, and smote her throughout the body and slew her, and then turneth him again so fast as his horse might carry him toward his hold. Messire Gawain seeth the damsel dead and the dwarf that fleeth full speed after his lord. He overtaketh him and trampleth him under his horse's feet so that he bursteth his belly in the midst. Then goeth he toward the hold, for he thinketh to enter therein. But he found the bridge shut up and the gate barred. And Marin crieth out upon him. ' This shame and misadventure hath befallen me along of you, but you shall pay for it yet and I may live.' Messire Gawain hath no mind to argue with him, but rather draweth him back and cometh again to where the lady lay dead, and setteth her on the neck of his horse all bleeding, and then beareth her to a chapel that was without the entrance of the hold. Then he alighted and laid her within the chapel as fairly as most he might, as he that was sore grieved and wrathful thereof. After that, he shut the door of the chapel again as he that was afeared of the body for the wild beasts, and bethought him that one should come thither to set her in her shroud and bury her after that he was departed.

V

Thereupon Messire Gawain departeth, sore an-angered, for it seemed him that never had no thing tofore befallen him that weighed so heavy on his heart. And he rideth thoughtful and down-cast through the forest, and seeth a knight coming along the way he came. And in strange fashion came he. He bestrode his horse backwards in right outlandish guise, face to tail, and he had his horse's reins right across his breast and the base of his shield bore he topmost and the chief bottommost, and his spear upside down and his habergeon and chausses of iron trussed about his neck. He seeth Messire Gawain coming beside the forest, that hath great wonderment of him when he seeth him. Natheless, when they draw nigh, he turneth him not to look at Messire Gawain, but crieth to him aloud: 'Gentle knight, you that come there, for God's sake do me no hurt, for I am the Knight Coward.' 'By God,' saith Messire Gawain, 'You look not like a man to whom any ought to do hurt!' And, but for the heaviness of his heart and the sore wrath that he had, he would have laughed at his bearing with a right good will. 'Sir Knight,' saith Messire Gawain, 'nought have you to be afeard of from me!' With that he draweth anigh and looketh on him in the face and the Knight Coward on him. 'Sir,' saith he, 'Welcome may you be!' 'And you likewise!' saith Messire Gawain. 'And whose man are you, Sir knight?' 'The Damsel's man of the Car.' 'Thereof I love you the better,' saith Messire Gawain. 'God be praised thereof,' saith the Knight Coward, 'For now shall I have no fear of you.' 'Nay, truly,' saith Messire Gawain, 'Thereof be well assured!' The Knight Coward seeth Messire Gawain's shield and knoweth it. 'Ha, Sir,' saith he, 'Now know I well who you are. Now will I alight and ride the right way and set my arms to rights. For you are Messire Gawain, nor hath none the right to claim this shield but only you.' The knight alighteth and setteth his armour to rights, and prayeth Messire Gawain abide until he be armed. So he abideth right willingly, and helpeth him withal. Thereupon behold you a knight where he cometh a great gallop athwart the forest like a tempest, and he had a shield party black and white. 'Abide, Messire Gawain!' saith he, 'For on behalf of Marin the Jealous do I defy you, that hath slain his wife on your account.' 'Sir knight,' saith Messire Gawain, 'Thereof am I right heavy of heart, for death had she not deserved.' 'That availeth not,' saith the Party Knight, 'For I hold you to answer for the death. So I conquer you, the wrong is yours; but, and you conquer me, my lord holdeth his blame and shame for known, and will hold you to forfeit and you allow me to escape hence on live.' 'To this will I not agree,' saith Messire Gawain, 'For God well knoweth that no blame have I herein.' 'Ha, Messire Gawain,' saith the Knight Coward, 'Fight him not as having affiance in me, for of me will you have neither succour nor help!' 'Heretofore,' saith Messire Gawain, 'have I achieved adventures without you, and this also, and God help me, will I yet achieve.' They come together a full career and break their lances on their shields, and Messire Gawain hurtleth against the horse and passeth beyond and overthroweth him and his horse together. Then draweth he his sword and runneth upon him. And the knight crieth out: 'Hold, Messire Gawain! Are you minded to slay me? I yield me conquered, for no mind have I to die for another's folly, and so I cry you mercy hereof.' Messire Gawain thinketh that he will do him no further harm, for that of right behoveth him do his lord's bidding. Messire Gawain holdeth his hands, and he doth him homage on behalf of his lord for his hold and all of his land, and becometh his man.

VI

Thereupon the knight departeth and Messire Gawain remaineth there. 'Sir,' saith the Knight Coward to Messire Gawain, 'I have no mind to be so hardy as are you; for, so God help me, had he defied me in such-wise as he defied you, I should have fled away forthwith, or elsewise I should have fallen at his feet and cried him of mercy.' 'You wish for nought but peace,' saith Messire Gawain. 'By S. James,' saith the Coward, 'Therein are you quite right, for of war cometh nought but evil; nor never have I had no hurt nor wound save some branch of a tree or the like gave it me, and I see your face all seamed and scarred in many places. So God help me, of such hardiesse make I but small account, and every day I pray God that He defend me. And so to God I commend you, for I am going after my Damsel of the Car.' 'Not thus shall you go,' saith Messire Gawain, 'save you tell me first wherefore your Damsel of the Car beareth her arm slung to her neck in such-wise.' 'Sir, this may I will tell you. With this hand served she of the most Holy Graal the knight that was in the hostel of King Fisherman that would not ask whereof the Graal served; for that she held therein the precious vessel whereinto the glorious blood fell drop by drop from the point of the lance, so that none other thing is she minded to hold therein until such time as she shall come back to the holy place where it is. Sir,' saith the Knight Coward, 'Now, so please you, may I well go hence, and see, here is my spear that I give you, for nought is there that I have to do therewithal.' Messire Gawain taketh it, for his own was broken short, and departeth from the knight and commendeth him to God. And he goeth his way a great pace, and Messire Gawain also goeth amidst the forest, and full weary is he and forspent with travail. And he rode until the sun was due to set. And he meeteth a knight that was coming athwart the forest and came toward Messire Gawain a great gallop like as he were smitten through the body, and crieth over all the forest: 'What is your name, Sir knight?' 'My name is Gawain.' 'Ha, Messire Gawain,' saith the other, 'In your service am I wounded thus!' 'How in my service?' saith Messire Gawain. 'Sir, I was minded to bury the damsel that you bare into the chapel, and Marin the Jealous ran upon me and wounded me in many places in such manner as you see. And I had already dug a grave with my sword to bury the body when he seized it from me and abandoned it to the wild beasts. Now go I hence yonder to the chapel of a hermit that is in this forest to confess me, for well know I that I have not long to live for that the wound lieth me so nigh my heart. But I shall die the more easily now that I have found you and shown you the hurt that hath been done me for your sake.' 'Certes,' saith Messire Gawain, 'this grieveth me.'

VII

Therewithal the knights depart asunder, and Messire Gawain rode on until he found in the forest a castle right fair and rich, and met an ancient knight that was issued forth of the castle for disport, and held a bird on his fist. He saluteth Messire Gawain and he him again, and he asked him what castle is this that he seeth show so fair? And he telleth him it is the castle

of the Proud Maiden that never deigned ask a knight his name.
'And we, that are her men, durst not do it on her behalf. But
right well will you be lodged in the castle, for right courteous
is she otherwise and the fairest that ever any may know. Nor
never hath she had any lord, nor deigned to love no knight
save she heard tell that he was the best knight in the world.
And I will go to her with you of courtesy.' 'Gramercy,
Sir,' saith Messire Gawain. They enter into the castle both
twain together, and alight at the mounting-stage before the
hall. The knight taketh Messire Gawain by the hand and
leadeth him up, and maketh disarm him, and bringeth him a surcoat of scarlet purfled of vair and maketh him do it on. Then
leadeth he the lady of the castle to Messire Gawain, and he
riseth up to meet her. 'Lady,' saith he, 'Welcome may you
be!' 'And you, Sir, be welcome!' saith she, 'Will you see
my chapel?' 'Damsel,' saith he, 'At your pleasure.' And
she leadeth him and taketh Messire Gawain by the hand, and
he looketh at the chapel and it well seemeth him that never
before had he come into none so fair nor so rich, and he seeth
four tombs within, the fairest that he had seen ever. And on
the right hand side of the chapel were three narrow openings in
the wall that were wrought all about with gold and precious
stones, and beyond the three openings he seeth great circlets of
lighted candles that were before three coffers of hallows that
were there, and the smell thereof was sweeter than balm. 'Sir
knight,' saith the damsel, 'See you these tombs?' 'Yea,
damsel,' saith Messire Gawain. 'These three are made for the
three best knights in the world and the fourth for me. The
one hath for name Messire Gawain and the second Lancelot of
the Lake. Each of them do I love for love's sake, by my faith!
And the third hath for name Perceval. Him love I better than
the other two. And within these three openings are the hallows
set for love of them. And behold what I would do to them and
their three heads were therein; and so I might not do it to the
three together, yet would I do it to two, or even to one only.'
She setteth her hand toward the openings and draweth forth a
pin that was fastened into the wall, and a cutting blade of steel
droppeth down, of steel sharper than any razor, and closeth up
the three openings. 'Even thus will I cut off their heads when
they shall set them into those three openings thinking to adore
the hallows that are beyond. Afterward will I make take the

bodies and set them in the three coffins, and do them be honoured
and enshrouded right richly, for joy of them in their life may I
never have. And when the end of my life shall be come as God
will, even so will I make set me in the fourth coffin, and so shall
I have company of the three good knights.' Messire Gawain
heard the word, whereof he marvelled right sore, and would
right fain that the night were overpassed. They issue forth of
the chapel. The damsel maketh Messire Gawain be greatly
honoured that night, and there was great company of knights
within that served him and helped guard the castle. They show
Messire Gawain much worship, but they knew not that it was
he, nor did none ask him, for such was the custom of the castle.
But well she knew that he oftentimes passed to and fro amidst
the forest, and four of the knights that watched the forest and
the passers-by had she commanded that and if any of these three
knights should pass they should bring him to her without gainsay, and she would increase the land of each for so doing.

VIII

Messire Gawain was in the castle that night until the morrow,
and went to hear mass in the chapel or ever he removed thence.
Afterward, when he had heard mass and was armed, he took
leave of the damsel and issued forth of the castle as he that had
no desire to abide there longer. And he entereth into the forest
and rideth a long league Welsh and findeth two knights sitting
by a narrow path in the forest. And when they see him coming
they leap up on their horses all armed and come against Messire
Gawain, shields on sides and spears in fists. 'Bide, Sir knight!'
say they, 'And tell us your name without leasing!' 'Lords,'
saith he, 'Right willingly! never hath my name been with-
holden when it hath been asked for. I am called Gawain, King
Arthur's nephew.' 'Nay, then, Sir, welcome may you be!
One other demand have we to make of you. Will you come
with us to the lady in the world who most desireth you, and will
make much joy of you at Castle Orguelleux where she is?'
'Lord,' saith Messire Gawain, 'No leisure have I at this time,
for I have emprised my way else-whither.' 'Sir,' say they,
'Needs must you come thither without fail, for in such wise
hath she commanded us that we shall take you thither by force
an you come not of your own good-will.' 'I have told you

plainly that thither will I not go,' saith Messire Gawain. With that, they leap forward and take him by the bridle, thinking to lead him away by force. And Messire Gawain hath shame thereof, and draweth his sword and smiteth one of them in such wrath that he cutteth off his arm. And the other letteth the bridle go and turneth him full speed ; and his fellow with him that was maimed. And away go they toward Castle Orguelleux and the Proud Maiden of the castle and show her the mischief that hath befallen them. 'Who hath mis-handled you thus?' saith she. 'Certes, lady, Messire Gawain.' 'Where found you him?' 'Lady,' say they, 'In the forest, where he came toward us a full gallop, and was minded to pass by the narrows of the way, when we bade him abide and come to you. But come he would not. We offered him force, and he smote my fellow's arm off.' She biddeth a horn be sounded incontinent, and the knights of the castle arm, and she commandeth them follow Messire Gawain, and saith that she will increase the land and the charge of him that shall bring him to her. They were a good fifteen knights armed. Just as they were about to issue out of the castle, behold you forthwith two keepers of the forest where they come, both twain of them smitten through the body. The damsel and the knights ask who hath done this to them, and they say it was Messire Gawain that did it, for that they would have brought him to the castle. 'Is he far away?' saith the damsel. 'Yea,' say they, 'Four great leagues Welsh.' 'Wherefore the greater folly would it be to follow him,' saith one of the sixteen knights, 'For nought should we increase thereby save only our own shame and hurt, and my Lady hath lost him through her own default, for well know we that he it was that lay within, for that he beareth a shield sinople with a golden eagle.' 'Yea,' saith the wounded knight, 'Without fail.' 'Is this then he?' saith the damsel. 'I know him well now that I have lost him by my pride and by my outrage ; nor never more will knight lie in my hostel sith that he will be estranged for that I ask not his name. But it is too late ! Herein have I failed of this one for ever and ever save God bring him back to me, and through this one shall I lose the other two !'

IX

Herewithal cometh to a stay the pursuit of Messire Gawain, that goeth his way and prayeth God that He send him true

counsel of that he hath emprised, and that He allow him to
come into some place where he may hear true witting of the
hostel of King Fisherman. And while he was thus thinking,
he heareth a brachet questing, and he cometh toward him
a great pace. When he is come anigh Messire Gawain he
setteth his nose to the ground and findeth a track of blood
through a grassy way in the forest, and when Messire Gawain
was minded to leave the way where the track of blood was, the
brachet came over against him and quested. Messire Gawain is
minded not to abandon the track, wherefore he followeth the
brachet a great pace until he cometh to a marish in the midst of
the forest, and seeth there in the marish a house, ancient and
decayed. He passeth with the brachet over the bridge, that
was right feeble, and there was a great water under it, and
cometh to the hall, that was wasted and old. And the brachet
leaveth of his questing. Messire Gawain seeth in the midst of
the house a knight that was stricken right through the breast
unto the heart and there lay dead. A damsel was issuing forth
of the chamber and bare the winding-sheet wherein to enshroud
him. 'Damsel,' saith Messire Gawain, 'Good adventure may
you have!' The damsel that was weeping right tenderly, saith
to him: 'Sir, I will answer you not.' She cometh toward the
dead knight, thinking that his wounds should have begun to
bleed afresh, but they did not. 'Sir,' saith she to Messire
Gawain, 'Welcome may you be!' 'Damsel,' saith he, 'God
grant you greater joy than you have!' And the damsel saith
to the brachet: 'It was not this one I sent you back to fetch,
but him that slew this knight.' 'Know you then, damsel, who
hath slain him?' saith Messire Gawain. 'Yea,' saith she,
'well! Lancelot of the Lake slew him in this forest, on whom
God grant me vengeance, and on all them of King Arthur's
court, for sore mischief and great hurt have they wrought us!
But, please God, right well shall this knight yet be avenged,
for a right fair son hath he whose sister am I, and so hath he
many good friends withal.' 'Damsel, to God I commend you!'
saith Messire Gawain. With that, he issueth forth of the
Waste Manor and betaketh him back to the way he had
abandoned, and prayeth God grant he may find Lancelot of the
Lake.

BRANCH V

HERE beginneth again another branch of the Graal in the name
of the Father, and of the Son, and of the Holy Ghost.

TITLE I

Messire Gawain goeth his way and evening draweth on ; and
on his right hand was there a narrow pathway that seemed him
to be haunted of folk.   Thitherward goeth he, for that he seeth
the sun waxeth low, and findeth in the thick of the forest a
great chapel, and without was a right fair manor.   Before the
chapel was an orchard enclosed of a wooden fence that was
scarce so high as a tall man.   A hermit that seemed him a right
worshipful man was leaning against the fence, and looked into
the orchard and made great cheer from time to time.   He seeth
Messire Gawain, and cometh to meet him, and Messire Gawain
alighteth.   'Sir,' saith the hermit, 'Welcome may you be.'
' God grant you the joy of Paradise,' saith Messire Gawain.
The hermit maketh his horse be stabled of a squire, and then
taketh him by the hand and maketh him sit beside him to look
on the orchard.   'Sir,' saith the hermit, 'Now may you see
that whereof I was making cheer.'   Messire Gawain looketh
therewithin and seeth two damsels and a squire and a child that
were guarding a lion.   'Sir,' saith the hermit, 'Here see you
my joy, which is this child.   Saw you ever so fair a child of
his age ?'   'Never,' saith Messire Gawain.   They go into the
orchard to sit, for the evening was fair and calm.   He maketh
disarm him, and thereupon the damsel bringeth him a surcoat of
right rich silk furred of ermine.   And Messire Gawain looketh
at the child that rode upon the lion right fainly.   'Sir,' saith the
hermit, ' None durst guard him or be master over him save this

child only, and yet the lad is not more than six years of age. Sir, he is of right noble lineage, albeit he is the son of the most cruel man and most felon that is. Marin the Jealous is his father, that slew his wife on account of Messire Gawain. Never sithence that his mother was dead would not the lad be with his father, for well knoweth he that he slew her of wrong. And I am his uncle, so I make him be tended here of these damsels and these two squires, but no one thing is there that he so much desireth to see as Messire Gawain. For after his father's death ought he of right to be Messire Gawain's man. Sir, if any tidings you know of him, tell us them.' 'By my faith, Sir,' saith he, ' Tidings true can I give you. Lo, there is his shield and his spear, and himself shall you have this night for guest.' 'Fair sir, are you he?' saith the hermit. 'So men call me,' saith Messire Gawain, 'And the lady saw I slain in the forest, whereof was I sore an-angered.'

II

'Fair nephew,' saith the hermit, 'See here your desire. Come to him and make him cheer.' The lad alighteth of the lion and smiteth him with a whip and leadeth him to the den and maketh the door so that he may not issue forth, and cometh to Messire Gawain, and Messire Gawain receiveth him between his arms. 'Sir,' saith the child, 'Welcome may you be!' 'God give you growth of honour!' saith Messire Gawain. He kisseth him and maketh cheer with him right sweetly. 'Sir,' saith the hermit, 'He will be of right your man, wherefore ought you to counsel him and help him, for through you came his mother by her death, and right sore need will he have of your succour.' The child kneeleth before him and holdeth up his joined hands. 'Look, Sir,' saith the hermit, 'Is he not right pitiful? He offereth you his homage.' And Messire Gawain setteth his hands within his own: 'Certes,' saith Messire Gawain, 'Both your honour and your homage receive I gladly, and my succour and my counsel shall you have so often as you shall have need thereof. But fain would I know your name?' 'Sir, I am called Meliot of Logres.' 'Sir,' saith the hermit, 'He saith true, for his mother was daughter of a rich earl of the kingdom of Logres.'

III

Messire Gawain was well harboured the night and lay in a right fair house and right rich. In the morning, when Messire Gawain had heard mass, the hermit asked him, 'Whitherward go you?' and he said, 'Toward the land of King Fisherman, and God allow me.' 'Messire Gawain,' saith the hermit, 'Now God grant you speed your business better than did the other knight that was there before you, through whom are all the lands fallen into sorrow, and the good King Fisherman languisheth thereof.' 'Sir,' saith Messire Gawain, 'God grant me herein to do His pleasure.' Thereupon he taketh his leave and goeth his way, and the hermit commendeth him to God. And Messire Gawain rideth on his journeys until he hath left far behind the forest of the hermitage, and findeth the fairest land in the world and the fairest meadowlands that ever had he seen, and it lasted a good couple of great leagues Welsh. And he seeth a high forest before him, and meeteth a squire that came from that quarter, and seeth that he is sore downcast and right simple. 'Fair friend,' saith Messire Gawain, 'Whence come you?' 'Sir,' saith he, 'I come from yonder forest down below.' 'Whose man are you?' saith Messire Gawain. 'I belong to the worshipful man that owneth the forest.' 'You seem not over joyful,' saith Messire Gawain. 'Sir, I have right to be otherwise,' saith the squire, 'For he that loseth his good lord ought not to be joyful.' 'And who is your lord?' 'The best in the world.' 'Is he dead?' saith Messire Gawain. 'Nay, of a truth, for that would be right sore grief to the world, but in joy hath he not been this long time past.' 'And what name hath he?' 'They call him Parlui there where he is.' 'And where then, is he, may I know?' 'In no wise, Sir, of me; but so much may I well tell you that he is in this forest, but I ought not to learn you of the place more at large, nor ought I to do any one thing that may be against my master's will.' Messire Gawain seeth that the squire is of passing comeliness and seeth him forthwith bow his head toward the ground and the tears fall from his eyes. Thereupon he asketh what aileth him. 'Sir,' saith he, 'Never may I have joy until such time as I be entered into a hermitage to save my soul. For the greatest sin that any man may do have I wrought; for I have slain my mother that was a Queen, for this only that she

told me I should not be King after my father's death, for that
she would make me monk or clerk, and that my other brother,
who is younger-born than I, should have the kingdom.   When
my father knew that I had slain my mother, he withdrew himself into this forest, and made a hermitage and renounced his
kingdom.   I have no will to hold the land for the great disloyalty that I have wrought, and therefore am I resolved that it
is meeter I should set my body in banishment than my father.'
'And what is your name?' saith Messire Gawain.   'Sir, my
name is Joseus, and I am of the lineage of Joseph of Abarimacie.
King Pelles is my father, that is in this forest, and King Fisherman mine uncle, and the King of Castle Mortal, and the Widow
Lady of Camelot my aunt, and the Good Knight Par-lui-fet is of
this lineage as near akin as I.'

IV

With that, the squire departeth and taketh leave of Messire
Gawain, and he commendeth him to God and hath great pity of
him, and entereth into the forest and goeth great pace, and
findeth the stream of a spring that ran with a great rushing,
and nigh thereunto was a way that was much haunted.   He
abandoneth his high-way, and goeth all along the stream from
the spring that lasteth a long league plenary, until that he
espieth a right fair house and right fair chapel well enclosed
within a hedge of wood.   He looketh from without the entrance
under a little tree and seeth there sitting one of the seemliest
men that he had ever seen of his age.   And he was clad as a
hermit, his head white and no hair on his face, and he held his
hand to his chin, and made a squire hold a destrier right fair
and strong and tall, and a shield with a sun thereon; and he
was looking at a habergeon and chausses of iron that he had
made bring before him.   And when he seeth Messire Gawain
he dresseth him over against him and saith : 'Fair sir,' saith he,
'Ride gently and make no noise, for no need have we of worse
than that we have.'   And Messire Gawain draweth rein, and
the worshipful man saith to him : 'Sir, for God's sake take it not
of discourtesy; for right fainly would I have besought you to
harbour had I not good cause to excuse me, but a knight lieth
within yonder sick, that is held for the best knight in the
world.   Wherefore fain would I he should have no knight

come within this close, for and if he should rise, as sick as he is, none might prevent him nor hold him back, but presently he should arm him and mount on his horse and joust at you or any other; and so he were here, well might we be the worse thereof. And therefore do I keep him so close and quiet within yonder, for that I would not have him see you nor none other, for and he were so soon to die, sore loss would it be to the world.' 'Sir,' saith Messire Gawain, 'What name hath he?' 'Sir,' saith he, 'He hath made him of himself, and therefore do I call him Par-lui-fet, of dearness and love.' 'Sir,' saith Messire Gawain, 'May it not be in any wise that I may see him?' 'Sir,' saith the hermit, 'I have told you plainly that nowise may it not be. No strange man shall not see him within yonder until such time as he be whole and of good cheer.' 'Sir,' saith Messire Gawain, 'Will you in nowise do nought for me whatsoever I may say?' 'Certes, sir, no one thing is there in the world that I would tell him, save he spake first to me.' Hereof is Messire Gawain right sorrowful that he may not speak to the knight. 'Sir,' saith he to the hermit, 'Of what age is the knight, and of what lineage?' 'Of the lineage of Joseph of Abarimacie the Good Soldier.'

V

Thereupon behold you a damsel that cometh to the door of the chapel and calleth very low to the hermit, and the hermit riseth up and taketh leave of Messire Gawain, and shutteth the door of the chapel; and the squire leadeth away the destrier and beareth the arms within door and shutteth the postern door of the house. And Messire abideth without and knoweth not of a truth whether it be the son of the Widow Lady, for many good men there be of one lineage. He departeth all abashed and entereth again into the forest. The history telleth not all the journeys that he made. Rather, I tell you in brief words that he wandered so far by lands and kingdoms that he found a right fair land and a rich, and a castle seated in the midst thereof. Thitherward goeth he and draweth nigh the castle and seeth it compassed about of high walls, and he seeth the entrance of the castle far without. He looketh and seeth a lion chained that lay in the midst of the entrance to the gate, and the chain was fixed in the wall. And on either side of the gate he seeth two serjeants of beaten copper that were fixed to the wall, and by engine shot forth quarrels from their cross-bows with great force and great wrath. Messire Gawain durst not come anigh the gate for that he seeth the lion and these folk. He looketh above on the top of the wall and seeth a sort of folk that seemed him to be of holy life, and saw there priests clad in albs and knights bald and ancient that were clad in ancient seeming garments. And in each crenel of the wall was a cross and a chapel. Above the wall, hard by an issue from a great hall that was in the castle, was another chapel, and above the chapel was a tall cross, and on either side of this cross another that was somewhat lower, and on the top of each cross was a golden eagle. The priests and the knights were upon the walls and knelt toward this chapel, and looked up to heaven and made great joy, and well it seemed him that they beheld God in Heaven with His Mother. Messire Gawain looketh at them from afar, for he durst not come anigh the castle for these that shoot their arrows so strongly that none armour might defend him. Way seeth he none to right nor left save he go back again. He knoweth not what to do. He looketh before him and seeth a priest issue forth of the gateway. 'Fair sir,' saith Messire Gawain, 'Welcome may you be!' 'Good adventure to you also,' saith the good man, 'What is your pleasure?' 'Sir,' saith Messire Gawain, 'So please you, I would fain ask you to tell me what castle is this?' 'It is,' saith he, 'the entrance to the land of the rich King Fisherman, and within yonder are they beginning the service of the Most Holy Graal.' 'Allow me then,' saith Messire Gawain, 'that I may pass on further, for toward the land of King Fisherman have I emprised my way.' 'Sir,' saith the priest, 'I tell you of a truth that you may not enter the castle nor come nigher unto the Holy Graal, save you bring the sword wherewith S. John was beheaded.' 'What?' saith Messire Gawain, 'Shall I be evilly entreated and I bring it not?' 'So much may you well believe me herein,' saith the priest, 'And I tell you moreover that he who hath it is the fellest misbelieving King that lives. But so you bring the sword, this entrance will be free to you, and great joy will be made of you in all places wherein King Fisherman hath power.' 'Then must I needs go back again,' saith Messire Gawain, 'Whereof I have right to be sore sorrowful.' 'So ought you not to be,' saith the priest, 'For, so you bring the sword and conquer it for us, then will it be well known that you are worthy to behold the Holy Graal. But take heed you remember him who would not ask whereof it served.' Thereupon Messire Gawain departeth so sorrowful and full of thought that he remembereth not to ask in what land he may find the sword nor the name of the King that hath it. But he will know tidings thereof when God pleaseth.

VI

The history telleth us and witnesseth that he rode so far that he came to the side of a little hill, and the day was right fair and clear. He looketh in front of him before a chapel and seeth a tall burgess sitting on a great destrier that was right rich and fair. The burgess espieth Messire Gawain and cometh over against him, and saluteth him right courteously and Messire Gawain him. 'Sir,' saith Messire Gawain, 'God give you joy.' 'Sir,' saith the goodman, 'Right sorrowful am I of this that you have a horse so lean and spare of flesh. Better would it become so worshipful man as you seem to be that he were better horsed.' 'Sir,' saith Messire Gawain, 'I may not now amend it, whereof am I sorry; another shall I have when it shall please God.' 'Fair sir,' saith the burgess, 'Whither are you bound to go?' 'I go seek the sword wherewith the head of S. John Baptist was cut off.' 'Ha, sir,' saith the burgess, 'You are running too sore a peril. A King hath it that believeth not in God, and is sore fell and cruel. He is named Gurgalain, and many knights have passed hereby that went thither for the sword, but never thence have they returned. But, and you are willing to pledge me your word that so God grant you to conquer the sword, you will return hither and show it me on your return, I will give you this destrier, which is right rich, for your own.' 'Will you?' saith Messire Gawain, 'Then are you right courteous, for you know me not.' 'Certes, sir,' saith he, 'So worshipful man seem you to be, that you will hold well to this that you have covenanted with me.' 'And to this do I pledge you my word,' saith Messire Gawain, 'that, so God allow me to conquer it, I will show it to you on my return.'

VII

Thereupon the burgess alighteth and mounteth upon Messire Gawain's horse, and Messire Gawain upon his, and taketh leave of the burgess and goeth his way and entereth into a right great forest beyond the city, and rideth until sundown and findeth neither castle nor city. And he findeth a meadow in the midst of the forest, right broad, and it ran on beyond, like as there were the stream of a spring in the midst. He looketh toward the foot of the meadow close by the forest, and seeth a right large tent, whereof the cords were of silk and the pegs of ivory fixed in the ground, and the tops of the poles of gold and upon each was a golden eagle. The tent was white round about, and the hanging above was of the richest silk, the same as red samite. Thitherward goeth Messire Gawain and alighteth before the door of the tent, and smiteth off the bridle of his horse, and letteth him feed on the grass, and leaneth his spear and his shield without the tent, and looketh narrowly within and seeth a right rich couch of silk and gold, and below was a cloth unfolded as it were a feather-bed, and above a coverlid of ermine and vair without any gold, and at the head of the couch two pillows so rich that fairer none ever saw, and such sweet smell gave they forth that it seemed the tent was sprinkled of balm. And round about the couch were rich silken cloths spread on the ground. And at the head of the couch on the one side and the other were two seats of ivory, and upon them were two cushions stuffed with straw, right rich, and at the foot of the couch, above the bed, two candlesticks of gold wherein were two tall waxen tapers. A table was set in the midst of the tent, that was all of ivory banded of gold, with rich precious stones, and upon the table was the napkin spread and the basin of silver and the knife with an ivory handle and the rich set of golden vessels. Messire Gawain seeth the rich couch and setteth him down thereon all armed in the midst, and marvelleth him wherefore the tent is so richly apparelled and yet more that therein he seeth not a soul. Howbeit, he was minded to disarm him.

VIII

Thereupon, behold you, a dwarf that entereth the tent and saluteth Messire Gawain. Then he kneeleth before him and would fain disarm him.   Then Messire Gawain remembereth him of the dwarf through whom the lady was slain.   'Fair sweet friend, withdraw yourself further from me, for as at this time I have no mind to disarm.'   'Sir,' saith the dwarf, 'Without misgiving may you do so, for until to-morrow have you no occasion to be on your guard, and never were you more richly lodged than to-night you shall be, nor more honourably.'   With that Messire Gawain began to disarm him, and the dwarf helpeth him.   And when he was disarmed, he setteth his arms nigh the couch and his spear and sword and shield lying within the tent, and the dwarf taketh a basin of silver and a white napkin, and maketh Messire Gawain wash his hands and his face.   Afterward, he unfasteneth a right fair coffer, and draweth forth a robe of cloth of gold furred of ermine and maketh Messire Gawain be clad therewithal.   'Sir,' saith the dwarf, 'Be not troubled as touching your destrier, for you will have him again when you rise in the morning.   I will lead him close hereby to be better at ease, and then will I return to you.'   And Messire Gawain giveth him leave.   Thereupon, behold you, two squires that bear in the wine and set the meats upon the table and make Messire Gawain sit to eat, and they have great torches lighted on a tall cresset of gold and depart swiftly.   Whilst Messire Gawain was eating, behold you, thereupon, two damsels that come into the tent and salute him right courteously.   And he maketh answer, the fairest he may. 'Sir,' say the damsels, 'God grant you force and power to-morrow to destroy the evil custom of this tent.'   'Is there then any evil custom herein, damsel?' saith he.   'Yea, sir, a right foul custom, whereof much it grieveth me, but well me-seemeth that you are the knight to amend it by the help of God.'

IX

Therewith he riseth from the table, and one of the squires was apparelled to take away the cloths.   And the two damsels take him by the hand and lead him without the tent, and they set them down in the midst of the meadow.   'Sir,' saith the elder damsel, 'What is your name?'   'Damsel,' saith he, 'Gawain is my name.'   'Thereof do we love you the better, for well we know that the evil custom of the tent shall be done away on condition that you choose to-night the one of us two that most shall please you.' 'Damsel, gramercy,' saith he. Thereupon he riseth up, for he was weary, and draweth him toward the couch, and the damsels help him and wait upon his going to bed. And when he was lien down, they seated themselves before him and lighted the taper and leant over the couch and proffered him much service. Messire Gawain answered them naught save 'Gramercy,' for he was minded to sleep and take his rest. 'By God,' saith the one to the other, 'And this were Messire Gawain, King Arthur's nephew, he would speak to us after another sort, and more of disport should we find in him than in this one. But this is a counterfeit Gawain, and the honour we have done him hath been ill bestowed. Who careth? To-morrow shall he pay his reckoning.'

X

Thereupon, lo you, the dwarf where he cometh. 'Fair friend,' say they, 'Keep good watch over this knight that he flee not away, for he goeth a-cadging from hostel to hostel and maketh him be called Messire Gawain, but Messire Gawain meseemeth is he not. For, and it were he, and we had been minded to watch with him two nights, he would have wished it to be three or four.' 'Damsel,' saith the dwarf, 'He may not flee away save he go afoot, for his horse is in my keeping.' And Messire Gawain heareth well enough that which the damsels say, but he answereth them never a word. Thereupon they depart, and say: God give him an ill night, for an evil knight and a vanquished and recreant, and command the dwarf that he move not on any occasion. Messire Gawain slept right little the night, and so soon as he saw the day, arose and found his arms ready and his horse that had been led all ready saddled before the tent. He armed himself as swiftly as he might, and the dwarf helpeth him and saith to him: 'Sir, you have not done service to our damsels as they would fain you should, wherefore they make sore complaint of you.' 'That grieveth me,' saith Messire Gawain, 'if that I have deserved it.' 'It is great pity,' saith the dwarf, 'when knight so comely as be you is so churlish as they say.' 'They may say their pleasure,' saith he, 'for it is their right. I know not to whom to render

thanks for the good lodging that I have had save to God, and
if I shall see the lord of the tent or the lady I shall con them
much thanks thereof.'

XI

Thereupon, lo you, where two knights come in front of the
tent on their horses, all armed, and see Messire Gawain that
was mounted and had his shield on his neck and his spear in his
fist, as he that thinketh to go without doing aught further.
And the knights come before him: 'Sir,' say they, 'Pay for
your lodging! Last night did we put ourselves to misease on
your account and left you the tent and all that is therein at your
pleasure, and now you are fain to go in this fashion.' 'What
pleaseth it you that I should do?' saith Messire Gawain. 'It
is meet I should requite you of my victual and the honour
of the tent.' Thereupon, lo you, where the two damsels
come that were of right great beauty. 'Sir Knight,' say they,
'Now shall we see whether you be King Arthur's nephew!'
'By my faith,' saith the dwarf, 'Methinketh this is not he that
shall do away the evil custom whereby we lose the coming
hither of knights! Albeit if he may do it, I will forego mine ill
will toward him.' Messire Gawain thus heard himself mocked
by day as well as by night and had great shame thereof. He
seeth that he may not depart without a fight. One of the
knights drew to backward and was alighted; the other was
upon his horse all armed, his shield on his neck and grasping
his spear in his fist. And he cometh toward Messire Gawain
full career and Messire Gawain toward him, and smiteth him so
wrathfully that he pierceth his shield and pinneth his shield to
his arm and his arm to his rib and thrusteth his spear into his
body, and hurtleth against him so sore that he beareth him to
the ground, him and his horse together at the first blow. 'By
my head! Look at Messire Gawain the counterfeit! Better
doth he to-day than he did last night!' He draweth back his
spear, and pulleth forth his sword and runneth upon him, when
the knight crieth him mercy and saith that he holdeth himself
vanquished. Messire Gawain bethinketh him what he shall do
and whether the damsels are looking at him. 'Sir knight,'
saith the elder, 'Need you not fear the other knight until such
time as this one be slain, nor will the evil custom be done away

so long as this one is on live. For he is the lord of the other
and because of the shameful custom hath no knight come hither
this right long space.' 'Hearken now,' saith the knight, 'the
great disloyalty of her! Nought in the world is there she loved
so well in seeming as did she me, and now hath she adjudged
me my death!' 'Again I tell you plainly,' saith she, 'that
never will it be done away unless he slay you.' Thereupon
Messire Gawain lifteth the skirt of his habergeon and thrusteth
his sword into his body. Thereupon, lo you, the other knight,
right angry and sorrowful and full of wrath for his fellow that
he seeth dead, and cometh in great rage to Messire Gawain and
Messire Gawain to him, and so stoutly they mell together that
they pierce the shields and pierce the habergeons and break the
flesh of the ribs with the points of their spears, and the bodies
of the knights and their horses hurtle together so stiffly that
saddle-bows are to-frushed and stirrups loosened and girths to-
brast and fewtres splintered and spears snapped short, and the
knights drop to the ground with such a shock that the blood
rayeth forth at mouth and nose. In the fall that the knight
made, Messire Gawain brake his collar-bone in the hurtle.
Thereupon the dwarf crieth out: 'Damsel, your counterfeit
Gawain doth it well!' 'Our Gawain shall he be,' say they,
'so none take him from us!' Messire Gawain draweth from
over the knight and cometh toward his horse, and right
fain would he have let the knight live had it not been
for the damsels. For the knight crieth him mercy
and Messire Gawain had right great pity of him. Howbeit the
damsels cry to him; 'And you slay him not, the evil custom
will not be overthrown.' 'Sir,' saith the younger damsel,
'And you would slay him, smite him in the sole of his foot
with your sword, otherwise will he not die yet.' 'Damsel,'
saith the knight, 'Your love of me is turned to shame! Never
more ought knight to set affiance nor love on damsel. But
God keep the other that they be not such as you!' Messire
Gawain marvelleth at this that the damsel saith to him, and
draweth him back, and hath great pity of the knight, and
cometh to the other side whither the horses were gone, and
taketh the saddle of the knight that was dead and setteth it on
his own horse and draweth him away. And the wounded
knight was remounted, for the dwarf had helped him, and fleeth
toward the forest a great gallop. And the damsels cry out,

'Messire Gawain, your pity will be our death this day! For the Knight without Pity is gone for succour, and if he escape, we shall be dead and you also!'

XII

Thereupon Messire Gawain leapeth on his horse and taketh a spear that was leaning against the tent and followeth the knight in such sort that he smiteth him to the ground. Afterward he saith to him: 'No further may you go!' 'That grieveth me,' saith the knight, 'For before night should I have been avenged of you and of the damsels.' And Messire Gawain draweth his sword and thrusteth it into the sole of his foot a full palm's breadth, and the knight stretcheth himself forth and dieth. And Messire Gawain returneth back, and the damsels make great joy of him and tell him that never otherwise could the evil custom have been done away. For, and he had gone his way, all would have been to begin over again, for he is of such kind seeing that he was of the kindred of Achilles, and that all his ancestors might never otherwise die. And Messire Gawain alighteth, and the damsels would have searched the wound in his side, and he telleth them that he taketh no heed thereof. 'Sir,' say they, 'Again do we proffer you our service, for well we know that you are a good knight. Take for your lady-love which of us you will.' 'Gramercy, damsel,' saith Messire Gawain, 'Your love do I refuse not and to God do I commend you.' 'How?' say the damsels, 'Will you go your way thus? Certes, meeter were it to-day for you to sojourn in this tent and be at ease.' 'It may not be,' saith he, 'for leisure have I none to abide here.' 'Let him go!' saith the younger, 'for the falsest knight is he of the world.' 'By my head,' saith the elder, 'it grieveth me that he goeth, for his stay would have pleased me well.' Therewithal Messire Gawain departeth and is remounted on his horse. Then he entereth into the forest.

BRANCH VI

ANOTHER branch that Josephus telleth us recounteth and witnesseth of the Holy Graal, and here beginneth for us in the name of the Father, and of the Son, and of the Holy Ghost.

TITLE I

Messire Gawain rode until he came to a forest, and seeth a land right fair and rich in a great enclosure of wall, and round the land and country-side within, the wall stretched right far away. Thitherward he cometh and seeth but one entrance thereinto, and he seeth the fairest land that ever he beheld and the best garnished and the fairest orchards. The country was not more than four leagues Welsh in length, and in the midst thereof was a tower on a high rock. And on the top was a crane that kept watch over it and cried when any strange man came into the country. Messire Gawain rode amidst the land and the crane cried out so loud that the King of Wales heard it, that was lord of the land. Thereupon, behold you, two knights that come after Messire Gawain and say to him: 'Hold, Sir Knight, and come speak with the king of this country, for no strange knight passeth through his land but he seeth him.' 'Lords,' saith Messire Gawain, 'I knew not of the custom. Willingly will I go.' They led him thither to the hall where the King was, and Messire Gawain alighteth and setteth his shield and his spear leaning against a mounting stage and goeth up into the hall. The King maketh great joy of him and asketh him whither he would go? 'Sir,' saith Messire Gawain, 'Into a country where I was never.' 'Well I know,' saith the king, 'where it is, for that you are passing through my land. You are going to the country of King Gurgalain to conquer the sword wherewith S. John was beheaded.'

71

II

'Sir,' saith Messire Gawain, 'You say true. God grant me that I may have it!' 'That may not be so hastily,' saith the King, 'For you shall not go forth of my land before a year.' 'Ha, Sir,' saith Messire Gawain, 'For God's sake, mercy!' 'None other mercy is here,' saith the King. Straightway he maketh Messire Gawain be disarmed and afterward maketh bring a robe wherewith to apparel him, and showeth him much honour. But ill is he at ease, wherefore he saith to him: 'Sir, wherefore are you fain to hold me here within so long?' 'For this, that I know well you will have the sword and will not return by me.' 'Sir,' saith Messire Gawain, 'I pledge you my word that, so God give me to conquer it, I will return by you.' 'And I will allow you to depart from me at your will. For nought is there that I so much desire to see.' He lay the night therewithin, and on the morrow departed thence and issued forth of the land right glad and joyful. And he goeth toward the land of King Gurgalain. And he entereth into a noisome forest at the lower part and findeth at the right hour of noon a fountain that was enclosed of marble, and it was overshadowed of the forest like as it were with leaves down below, and it had rich pillars of marble all round about with fillets of gold and set with precious stones. Against the master-pillar hung a vessel of gold by a silver chain, and in the midst of the fountain was an image so deftly wrought as if it had been alive. When Messire appeared at the fountain, the image set itself in the water and was hidden therewith. Messire Gawain goeth down, and would fain have taken hold on the vessel of gold when a voice crieth out to him: 'You are not the Good Knight unto whom is served thereof and who thereby is made whole.' Messire Gawain draweth him back and seeth a clerk come to the fountain that was young of age and clad in white garments, and he had a stole on his arm and held a little square vessel of gold, and cometh to the little vessel that was hanging on the marble pillar and looketh therein, and then rinseth out the other little golden vessel that he held, and then setteth the one that he held in the place of the other.

III

Therewithal, behold, three damsels that come of right great
beauty, and they had white garments and their heads were
covered with white cloths, and they carried, one, bread in a
little golden vessel, and the other wine in a little ivory vessel,
and the third flesh in one of silver. And they come to the
vessel of gold that hung against the pillar and set therein that
which they have brought, and afterward they make the sign of
the cross over the pillar and come back again. But on their
going back, it seemed to Messire Gawain that only one was
there. Messire Gawain much marvelled him of this miracle.
He goeth after the clerk that carried the other vessel of gold,
and saith unto him: 'Fair Sir, speak to me.' 'What is your
pleasure?' saith the clerk. 'Whither carry you this golden
vessel and that which is therein?' 'To the hermits,' saith he,
'that are in this forest, and to the Good Knight that lieth sick
in the house of his uncle King Hermit.' 'Is it far from hence?'
saith Messire Gawain. 'Yea, Sir,' saith the clerk, 'to yourself.
But I shall be there sooner than will you.' 'By God,' saith
Messire Gawain, 'I would fain I were there now, so that I
might see him and speak to him.' 'That believe I well,' saith
the clerk, 'But now is the place not here.' Messire Gawain
taketh leave and goeth his way and rideth until he findeth a
hermitage and seeth the hermit therewithout. He was old and
bald and of good life. 'Sir,' saith he to Messire Gawain,
'Whither go you?' 'To the land of King Gurgalain, Sir; is
this the way?' 'Yea,' saith the hermit, 'But many knights
have passed hereby that hither have never returned.' 'Is it
far?' saith he. 'He and his land are hard by, but far away is
the castle wherein is the sword.' Messire Gawain lay the night
therewithin. On the morrow when he had heard mass, he
departed and rode until he cometh to the land of King
Gurgalain, and heareth the folk of the land making dole right
sore. And he meeteth a knight that cometh a great pace to
a castle.

IV

'Sir,' saith Messire Gawain, 'Wherefore make the folk of
this castle such dole, and they of all this land and all this

country ? For I hear them weep and beat their palms together on every side.' 'Sir,' saith he, 'I will tell you. King Gurgalain had one only son of whom he hath been bereft by a Giant that hath done him many mischiefs and wasted much of his land. Now hath the King let everywhere be cried that to him that shall bring back his son and slay the Giant he will give the fairest sword of the world, the which sword he hath, and of all his treasure so much as he may be fain to take. As at this time, he findeth no knight so hardy that he durst go; and much more blameth he his own law than the law of the Christians, and he saith that if any Christian should come into his land, he would receive him.' Right joyous is Messire Gawain of these tidings, and departeth from the castle and rideth on until he cometh to the castle of King Gurgalain. The tidings come to the King that there is a Christian come into his castle. The King maketh great joy thereof, and maketh him come before him and asketh him of his name and of what land he is. 'Sir,' saith he, 'My name is Gawain and I am of the land of King Arthur.' 'You are,' saith he, 'of the land of the Good Knight. But of mine own land may I find none that durst give counsel in a matter I have on hand. But if you be of such valour that you be willing to undertake to counsel me herein, right well will I reward you. A Giant hath carried off my son whom I loved greatly, and so you be willing to set your body in jeopardy for my son, I will give you the richest sword that was ever forged, whereby the head of S. John was cut off. Every day at right noon is it bloody, for that at that hour the good man had his head cut off.' The King made fetch him the sword, and in the first place showeth him the scabbard that was loaded of precious stones and the mountings were of silk with buttons of gold, and the hilt in likewise, and the pommel of a most holy sacred stone that Enax, a high emperor of Rome, made be set thereon. Then the King draweth it forth of the scabbard, and the sword came forth thereof all bloody, for it was the hour of noon. And he made hold it before Messire Gawain until the hour was past, and thereafter the sword becometh as clear as an emerald and as green. And Messire looketh at it and coveteth it much more than ever he did before, and he seeth that it is as long as another sword, albeit, when it is sheathed in the scabbard, neither scabbard nor sword seemeth of two spans length.

V

'Sir Knight,' saith the King, 'This sword will I give you, and another thing will I do whereof you shall have joy.' 'Sir,' saith Messire Gawain, 'And I will do your need, if God please and His sweet Mother.' Thereupon he teacheth him the way whereby the Giant went, and the place where he had his repair, and Messire Gawain goeth his way thitherward and commendeth himself to God. The country folk pray for him according to their belief that he may back repair with life and health, for that he goeth in great peril. He hath ridden until that he cometh to a great high mountain that lay round about a land that the Giant had all laid waste, and the enclosure of the mountain went round about for a good three leagues Welsh, and therewithin was the Giant, so great and cruel and horrible that he feared no man in the world, and for a long time had he not been sought out by any knight, for none durst won in that quarter. And the pass of the mountain whereby he went to his hold was so strait that no horse might get through; wherefore behoveth Messire Gawain leave his horse and his shield and spear and to pass beyond the mountain by sheer force, for the way was like a cut between sharp rocks. He is come to level ground and looketh before him and seeth a hold that the Giant had on the top of a rock, and espieth the Giant and the lad where they were sitting on the level ground under a tree. Messire Gawain was armed and had his sword girt on, and goeth his way thitherward. And the Giant seeth him coming and leapeth up and taketh in hand a great axe that was at his side, and cometh toward Messire Gawain all girded for the fight and thinketh to smite him a two-handed stroke right amidst the head. But Messire Gawain swerveth aside and bestirreth him with his sword and dealeth him a blow such that he cut off his arm, axe and all. And the Giant returneth backward when he feeleth himself wounded, and taketh the King's son by the neck with his other hand and grippeth him so straitly that he strangleth and slayeth him. Then he cometh back to Messire Gawain and falleth upon him and grippeth him sore strait by the flanks, and lifteth him three foot high off the ground and thinketh to carry him to his hold that was within the rock. And as he goeth thither he falleth, Messire Gawain and all, and he lieth undermost. Howbeit, he thinketh to rise, but cannot, for Messire

Gawain sendeth him his sword right through his heart and beyond. Afterward, he cut off the head and cometh there where the King's child lay dead, whereof is he right sorrowful. And he beareth him on his neck, and taketh the Giant's head in his hand and returneth there where he had left his horse and shield and spear, and mounteth and cometh back and bringeth the King's son before the King and the head of the Giant hanging.

VI

The King and all they of the castle come to meet him with right great joy, but when they see the young man dead, their great joy is turned into right great dole thereby. And Messire Gawain alighteth before the castle and presenteth to the King his son and the head of the Giant. 'Certes,' said he, 'might I have presented him to you on live, much more joyful should I have been thereof.' 'This believe I well,' saith the King, 'Howbeit, of so much as you have done am I well pleased, and your guerdon shall you have.' And he looketh at his son and lamenteth him right sweetly, and all they of the castle after him. Thereafter he maketh light a great show of torches in the midst of the city, and causeth a great fire to be made, and his son be set thereon in a brazen vessel all full of water, and maketh him be cooked and sodden over this fire, and maketh the Giant's head be hanged at the gate.

VII

When his son was well cooked, he maketh him be cut up as small as he may, and biddeth send for all the high men of his land and giveth thereof to each so long as there was any left. After that he maketh bring the sword and giveth it to Messire Gawain, and Messire Gawain thanketh him much thereof. 'More yet will I do for you,' saith the King. He biddeth send for all the men of his land to come to his hall and castle. 'Sir,' saith he, 'I am fain to baptize me.' 'God be praised thereof,' saith Messire Gawain. The King biddeth send for a hermit of the forest, and maketh himself be baptized, and he had the name of Archis in right baptism; and of all them that were not willing to believe in God, he commanded Messire Gawain that he should cut off their heads.

VIII

In such wise was this King baptized that was the lord of Albanie, by the miracle of God and the knighthood of Messire Gawain, that departeth from the castle with right great joy and rideth until he has come into the land of the King of Wales and bethought him he would go fulfil his pledge. He alighted before the hall, and the King made right great cheer when he saw him come. And Messire Gawain hath told him: 'I come to redeem my pledge. Behold, here is the sword.' And the King taketh it in his hand and looketh thereon right fainly, and afterward maketh great joy thereof and setteth it in his treasury and saith: 'Now have I done my desire.' 'Sir,' saith Messire Gawain, 'Then have you betrayed me.' 'By my head,' saith the King, 'That have I not, for I am of the lineage of him that beheaded S. John, wherefore have I better right to it than you.' 'Sir,' say the knights to the King, 'Right loyal and courteous knight is Messire Gawain, wherefore yield him that which he hath conquered, for sore blame will you have of evil-treating him.' 'I will yield it,' saith the King, 'on such condition that the first damsel that maketh request of him, what thing soever she may require and whatsoever it be shall not be denied of him.' And Messire Gawain agreeth thereto, and of this agreement thereafter did he suffer much shame and anguish and was blamed of many knights. And the King yielded him the sword. He lay the night therewithin, and on the morrow so soon as he might, he departed and rode until he came without the city where the burgess gave him the horse in exchange for his own. And he remembered him of his covenant, and abideth a long space and leaneth him on the hilt of his sword until the burgess cometh. Therewithal made they great joy the one of the other, and Messire showeth him the sword, and the burgess taketh it and smiteth his horse with his spurs and goeth a great gallop toward the city. And Messire Gawain goeth after a great pace and crieth out that he doth great treachery. 'Come not after me into the city,' saith the burgess, 'for the folk have a commune.' Howbeit, he followeth after into the city for that he might not overtake him before, and therein he meeteth a great procession of priests and clerks that bore crosses and censers. And Messire Gawain alighteth on account of the procession, and seeth the burgess that hath gone into the church and the procession after. 'Lords,' saith Messire Gawain, 'Make yield me the sword whereof this burgess that hath entered your church hath plundered me.' 'Sir,' say the priests, 'Well know we that it is the sword wherewith S. John was beheaded, wherefore the burgess hath brought it to us to set with our hallows in yonder, and saith that it was given him.' 'Ha, lords!' saith Messire Gawain, 'Not so! I have but shown it to him to fulfil my pledge. And he hath carried it off by treachery.' Afterward he telleth them as it had befallen him, and the priests make the burgess give it up, and with great joy Messire Gawain departeth and remounteth his horse and issueth forth of the city. He hath scarce gone far before he meeteth a knight that came all armed, as fast as his horse could carry him, spear in rest. 'Sir,' saith he to Messire Gawain, 'I have come to help you. We were told that you had been evil-entreated in the city, and I am of the castle that succoureth all strange knights that pass hereby whensoever they have need thereof.' 'Sir,' saith Messire Gawain, 'Blessed be the castle! I plain me not of the trespass for that right hath been done me. And how is the castle named?' 'Sir, they call it the Castle of the Ball. Will you return back thither with me, since you are delivered, and lodge there the night with Messire, that is a right worshipful man, and of good conditions?' Therewith they go together to the castle, that was right fair and well-seeming. They enter in, and when they were within, the Lord, that sate on a mounting-stage of marble, had two right fair daughters, and he made them play before him with a ball of gold, and looked at them right fainly. He seeth Messire Gawain alight and cometh to meet him and maketh him great cheer. Afterward, he biddeth his two daughters lead him into the hall.

IX

When he was disarmed, the one brought him a right rich robe, and after meat the two maidens sit beside him and make him right great cheer. Thereupon behold you, a dwarf that issueth forth of a chamber, and he holdeth a scourge. And he cometh to the damsels and smiteth them over their faces and their heads. 'Rise up,' saith he, 'ye fools, ill-taught! Ye make cheer unto him whom you ought to hate! For this is Messire Gawain, King Arthur's nephew, by whom was your uncle slain!'

Thereupon they rise, all ashamed, and go into the chamber, and
Messire Gawain remaineth there sore abashed.   But their father
comforteth him and saith : ' Sir, be not troubled for aught that
he saith, for the dwarf is our master : he chastiseth and teacheth
my daughters, and he is wroth for that you have slain his
brother, whom you slew the day that Marin slew his wife on
your account, whereof we are right sorrowful in this castle.'
' So also am I,' saith Messire Gawain, ' But no blame of her
death have I nor she, as God knoweth of very truth.'

X

Messire Gawain lay the night at the castle, and departed on
the morrow, and rode on his journeys until he cometh to the
castle at the entrance to the land of the rich King Fisherman,
where he seeth that the lion is not at the entrance nor were the
serjeants of copper shooting.   And he seeth in great procession
the priests and them of the castle coming to meet him, and he
alighteth, and a squire was apparelled ready, that took his
armour and his horse, and he showeth the sword to them that
were come to meet him.   It was the hour of noon.   He draweth
the sword, and seeth it all bloody, and they bow down and
worship it, and sing *Te Deum laudamus*.   With such joy was
Messire Gawain received at the castle, and he set the sword
back in his scabbard, and kept it right anigh him, and made it
not known in all the places where he lodged that it was such.
The priests and knights of the castle make right great joy, and
pray him right instantly that so God should lead him to the
castle of King Fisherman, and the Graal should appear before
him, he would not be so forgetful as the other knights.   And
he made answer that he would do that which God should teach
him.

XI

' Messire Gawain,' saith the master of the priests, that was
right ancient : ' Great need have you to take rest, for meseemeth
you have had much travail.'   ' Sir, many things have I seen
whereof I am sore abashed, nor know I what castle this may
be.'   ' Sir,' saith the priest, ' This Castle is the Castle of
Inquest, for nought you shall ask whereof it shall not tell you
the meaning, by the witness of Joseph, the good clerk and good

hermit through whom we have it, and he knoweth it by annunciation of the Holy Ghost.' 'By my faith,' saith Messire Gawain, ' I am much abashed of the three damsels that were at the court of King Arthur. Two of them carried, the one the head of a king and the other of a queen, and they had in a car an hundred and fifty heads of knights whereof some were sealed in gold, other in silver, and the rest in lead.' 'True,' saith the priest,' For as by the queen was the king betrayed and killed, and the knights whereof the heads were in the car, so saith she truth as Joseph witnesseth to us, for he saith of remembrance that by envy was Adam betrayed, and all the people that were after him and the people that are yet to come shall have dole thereof for ever more. And for that Adam was the first man is he called King, for he was our earthly father, and his wife Queen. And the heads of the knights sealed in gold signify the new law, and the heads sealed in silver the old, and the heads sealed in lead the false law of the Sarrazins. Of these three manner of folk is the world stablished.' 'Sir,' saith Messire Gawain, 'I marvel of the castle of the Black Hermit, there where the heads were all taken from her, and the Damsel told me that the Good Knight should cast them all forth when he should come. And the other folk that are therewithin are longing for him.' 'Well know you,' saith the priest, 'that on account of the apple that Eve gave Adam to eat, all went to hell alike, the good as well as the evil, and to cast His people forth from hell did God become man, and cast these souls forth from hell of His bounty and of His puissance. And to this doth Joseph make us allusion by the castle or the Black Hermit, which signifieth hell, and the Good Knight that shall thence cast forth them that are within. And I tell you that the Black Hermit is Lucifer, that is Lord of hell in like manner as he fain would have been Lord of Paradise.' 'Sir,' saith the priest, 'By this significance is he fain to draw the good hermits on behalf of the new law wherein the most part are not well learned, wherefore he would fain make allusion by ensample.' 'By God,' saith Messire Gawain, 'I marvel much of the Damsel that was all bald, and said that never should she have her hair again until such time as the Good Knight should have achieved the Holy Graal.' 'Sir,' saith the good man, 'Each day full bald behoveth her to be, ever since bald she became when the good King fell into languishment on account of the knight whom he harboured that made not the demand. The bald damsel signifieth Joseu Josephus, that was bald before the crucifixion of Our Lord, nor never had his hair again until such time as He had redeemed His people by His blood and by His death. The car that she leadeth after her signifieth the wheel of fortune, for like as the car goeth on the wheels, doth she lay the burden of the world on the two damsels that follow her; and this you may see well, for the fairest followeth afoot and the other was on a sorry hackney, and they were poorly clad, whereas the third had costlier attire. The shield whereon was the red cross, that she left at the court of King Arthur, signifieth the most holy shield of the rood that never none durst lift save God alone.' Messire Gawain heareth these significances and much pleaseth him thereof, and thinketh him that none durst set his hand to nor lift the shield that hung in the King's hall, as he had heard tell in many places; wherefore day by day were they waiting for the Good Knight that should come for the shield.

XII

'Sir,' saith Messire Gawain, 'By this that you tell me you do me to wit that whereof I was abashed, but I have been right sorrowful of a lady that a knight slew on my account albeit no blame had she therein, nor had I.' 'Sir,' saith the priest, 'Right great significance was there in her death, for Josephus witnesseth us that the old law was destroyed by the stroke of a sword without recover, and to destroy the old law did Our Lord suffer Himself to be smitten in the side of a spear. By this stroke was the old law destroyed, and by His crucifixion. The lady signifieth the old law. Would you ask more of me?' saith the priest. 'Sir,' saith Messire Gawain, 'I met a knight in the forest that rode behind before and carried his arms upside down. And he said that he was the Knight Coward, and his habergeon carried he on his neck, and so soon as he saw me he set his arms to rights and rode like any other knight.' 'The law was turned to the worse,' saith the priest, 'before Our Lord's crucifixion, and so soon as He was crucified, was again restored to right.' 'Even yet have I not asked you of all,' saith Messire Gawain, 'For a knight came and jousted with me party of black and white, and challenged me of the death of the lady on behalf of her husband, and told me and I should van-

D

quish him that he and his men would be my men.   I did vanquish him and he did me homage.'   'It is right,' saith the priest,
'On account of the old law that was destroyed were all they
that remained therein made subject, and shall be for ever more.
Wish you to enquire of aught further?' saith the priest.   'I
marvel me right sore,' saith Messire Gawain, 'of a child that
rode a lion in a hermitage, and none durst come nigh the lion
save the child only, and he was not of more than six years, and
the lion was right fell.   The child was the son of the lady that
was slain on my account.'   'Right well have you spoken,' saith
the priest, 'in reminding me thereof.   The child signifieth the
Saviour of the world that was born under the old law and was
circumcised, and the lion whereon he rode signifieth the world
and the people that are therein, and beasts and birds that none
may govern save by virtue of Him alone.'   'God!' saith Messire
Gawain, 'How great joy have I at heart of that you tell me!
Sir, I found a fountain in a forest, the fairest that was ever
seen, and an image had it within that hid itself when it saw
me, and a clerk brought a golden vessel and took another golden
vessel that hung at the column that was there, and set his own
in place thereof.   Afterward, came three damsels and filled the
vessel with that they had brought thither, and straightway
meseemed that but one was there.'   'Sir,' saith the priest, 'I
will tell you no more thereof than you have heard, and therewithal ought you to hold yourself well apaid, for behoveth not
discover the secrets of the Saviour, and them also to whom they
are committed behoveth keep them covertly.'

XIII

'Sir,' saith Messire Gawain, 'I would fain ask you of a
King.   When I had brought him his son back dead, he made
him be cooked and thereafter made him be eaten of all the folk
of his land.'   'Sir,' saith the priest, 'Already had he leant his
heart upon Jesus Christ, and would fain make sacrifice of his
flesh and blood to Our Lord, and for this did he make all those
of his land eat thereof, and would fain that their thoughts
should be even such as his own.   And therefore was all evil
belief uprooted from his land, so that none remained therein.'
'Blessed be the hour,' saith Messire Gawain, 'that I came
herewithin!'   'Mine be it!' saith the priest.   Messire Gawain

lay therewithin the night, and right well lodged was he. The morrow, when he had heard mass, he departed and went forth of the castle when he had taken leave. And he findeth the fairest land of the world and the fairest meadow-grounds that were ever seen, and the fairest rivers and forests garnished of wild deer and hermitages. And he rideth until he cometh one day as evening was about to draw on, to the house of a hermit, and the house was so low that his horse might not enter therein. And his chapel was scarce taller, and the good man had never issued therefrom of forty years past. The Hermit putteth his head out of the window when he seeth Messire Gawain and saith, 'Sir, welcome may you be,' saith he. 'Sir, God give you joy, Will you give me lodging to-night?' saith Messire Gawain. 'Sir, herewithin none harboureth save the Lord God alone, for earthly man hath never entered herewithin but me this forty year, but see, here in front is the castle wherein the good knights are lodged.' 'What is the castle?' 'Sir, the good King Fisherman's, that is surrounded with great waters and plenteous in all things good, so the lord were in joy. But behoveth them harbour none there save good knights only.' 'God grant,' saith Messire Gawain, 'that I may come therein.'

XIV

When he knoweth that he is nigh the castle, he alighteth and confesseth him to the hermit, and avoweth all his sins and re-penteth him thereof right truly. 'Sir,' saith the hermit, 'Now forget not, so God be willing to allow you, to ask that which the other knight forgat, and be not afeard for ought you may see at the entrance of the castle, but ride on without misgiving and adore the holy chapel you will see appear in the castle, there where the flame of the Holy Spirit descendeth each day for the most Holy Graal and the point of the lance that is served there.' 'Sir,' saith Messire Gawain, 'God teach me to do His will!' He taketh leave, and goeth his way and rideth until the valley appeareth wherein the castle is seated garnished of all things good, and he seeth appear the most holy chapel. He alighteth, and then setteth him on his knees and boweth him down and adoreth right sweetly. Thereafter he re-mounteth and rideth until he findeth a sepulchre right rich, and it had a cover over, and it lay very nigh the castle, and it seemed to be within a little burial-ground that was enclosed all round about, nor were any other tombs therein. A voice crieth to him as he passeth the burial-ground: 'Touch not the sepulchre, for you are not the Good Knight through whom shall it be known who lieth therein.' Messire Gawain passeth beyond when he had heard the voice and draweth nigh the entrance of the castle, and seeth that three bridges are there, right great and right horrible to pass. And three great waters run below, and him seemeth that the first bridge is a bowshot in length and in breadth not more than a foot. Strait seemeth the bridge and the water deep and swift and wide. He knoweth not what he may do, for it seemeth him that none may pass it, neither afoot nor on horse.

XV

Thereupon, lo you, a knight that issueth forth of the castle and cometh as far as the head of the bridge, that was called the Bridge of the Eel, and shouteth aloud: 'Sir Knight, pass quickly before it shall be already night, for they of the castle are awaiting us.' 'Ha,' saith Messire Gawain, 'Fair sir, but teach me how I may pass hereby.' 'Certes, Sir Knight, no passage know I to this entrance other than this, and if you desire to come to the castle, pass on without misgiving.' Messire Gawain hath shame for that he hath stayed so long, and forthinketh him of this that the Hermit told him, that of no mortal thing need he be troubled at the entrance of the castle, and therewithal that he is truly confessed of his sins, wherefore behoveth him be the less adread of death. He crosseth and blesseth himself and commendeth himself to God as he that thinketh to die, and so smiteth his horse with his spurs and findeth the bridge wide and large as soon as he goeth forward, for by this passing were proven most of the knights that were fain to enter therein. Much marvelled he that he found the bridge so wide that had seemed him so narrow. And when he had passed beyond, the bridge, that was a drawbridge, lifted itself by engine behind him, for the water below ran too swiftly for other bridge to be made. The knight draweth himself back beyond the great bridge and Messire Gawain cometh nigh to pass it, and this seemed him as long as the other. And he seeth the water below, that was not less swift nor less deep, and, so far as he could judge, the bridge was of ice, feeble and thin, and of a great height above the water, and he looked at it with much marvelling, yet natheless not for that would he any the more hold back from passing on toward the entrance. He goeth forward and commendeth himself to God, and cometh in the midst thereof and seeth that the bridge was the fairest and richest and strongest he had ever beheld, and the abutments thereof were all full of images. When he was beyond the bridge, it lifted itself up behind him as the other had done, and he looketh before him and seeth not the knight, and is come to the third bridge and nought was he adread for anything he might see. And it was not less rich than the other, and had columns of marble all round about, and upon each a knop so rich that it seemed to be of gold. After that, he beholdeth the gate over against him, and seeth Our Lord there figured even as He was set upon the rood, and His Mother of the one side and S. John of the other, whereof the images were all of gold, with rich precious stones that flashed like fire. And on the right hand he seeth an angel, passing fair, that pointed with his finger to the chapel where was the Holy Graal, and on his breast had he a precious stone, and letters written above his head that told how the lord of the castle was the like pure and clean of all evil-seeming as was this stone.

XVI

Thereafter at the entrance of the gate he seeth a lion right great and horrible, and he was upright upon his feet. So soon as he seeth Messire Gawain, he croucheth to the ground, and Messire Gawain passeth the entrance without gainsay and cometh to the castle, and alighteth afoot, and setteth his shield and his spear against the wall of the hall, and mounteth up a flight of marble steps and cometh into a hall right fair and rich, and here and there in divers places was it painted with golden images. In the midst thereof he findeth a couch right fair and rich and high, and at the foot of this couch was a chess-board right fair and rich, with an orle of gold all full of precious stones, and the pieces were of gold and silver and were not upon the board. Meanwhile, as Messire Gawain was looking at the beauty of the chess-board and the hall, behold you two knights that issue forth of a chamber and come to him. 'Sir,' say the knights, 'Welcome may you be.' 'God give you joy and good adventure,' saith Messire Gawain. They make him sit upon the couch and after that make him be disarmed. They bring him, in two basins of gold, water to wash his face and hands. After that, come two damsels that bring him a rich robe of silk and cloth of gold. Then they make him do on the same. Then say the two damsels to him, 'Take in good part whatsoever may be done to you therewithin, for this is the hostel of good knights and loyal.' 'Damsels,' saith Messire Gawain, 'So will I do. Gramercy of your service.' He seeth well that albeit the night were dark, within was so great brightness of light without candles that it was marvel. And it seemed him the sun shone there. Wherefore marvelled he right sore whence so great light should come.

XVII

When Messire Gawain was clad in the rich robe, right comely was he to behold, and well seemed he to be a knight of great valour. 'Sir,' say the knights, 'May it please you come see the lord of this castle?' 'Right gladly will I see him,' saith he, 'For I would fain present him with a rich sword.' They lead him into the chamber where lay King Fisherman, and it seemed as it were all strown and sprinkled of balm, and it was all strown with green herbs and reeds. And King Fisherman lay on a bed hung on cords whereof the stays were of ivory; and therein was a mattress of straw whereon he lay, and above a coverlid of sables whereof the cloth was right rich. And he had a cap of sables on his head covered with a red samite of silk, and a golden cross, and under his head was a pillow all smelling sweet of balm, and at the four corners of the pillow were four stones that gave out a right great brightness of light; and over against him was a pillar of copper whereon sate an eagle that held a cross of gold wherein was a piece of the true cross whereon God was set, as long as was the cross itself, the which the good man adored. And in four tall candlesticks of gold were four tall wax tapers set as often as was need. Messire Gawain cometh before the King and saluteth him. And the King maketh him right great cheer, and biddeth him be welcome. 'Sir,' saith Messire Gawain, 'I present you with the sword whereof John was

beheaded.' 'Gramercy,' saith the King : 'Certes, I knew well
that you would bring it, for neither you nor other might have
come in hither without the sword, and if you had not been of
great valour you would not have conquered it.' He taketh the
sword and setteth it to his mouth and so kisseth it right sweetly
and maketh right great joy thereof. And a damsel cometh to
sit at the head of the bed, to whom he giveth the sword in
keeping. Two others sit at his feet that look at him right
sweetly. 'What is your name?' saith the King. 'Sir, my
name is Gawain.' 'Ha, Messire Gawain,' saith he, 'This
brightness of light that shineth there within cometh to us of
God for love of you. For every time that a knight cometh
hither to harbour within this castle it appeareth as brightly as
you see it now. And greater cheer would I make you than I
do were I able to help myself, but I am fallen into languishment from the hour that the knight of whom you have heard
tell harboured herewithin. On account of one single word he
delayed to speak, did this languishment come upon me. Wherefore I pray you for God's sake that you remember to speak it,
for right glad should you be and you may restore me my health.
And see here is the daughter of my sister that hath been
plundered of her land and disinherited in such wise that
never can she have it again save through her brother only
whom she goeth to seek; and we have been told that
he is the Best Knight of the world, but we can learn no
true tidings of him.' 'Sir,' saith the damsel to her uncle the
King, 'Thank Messire Gawain of the honour he did to my
lady-mother when he came to her hostel. He stablished our
land again in peace, and conquered the keeping of the castle for
a year, and set my lady-mother's five knights there with us to
keep it. The year hath now passed, wherefore will the war be
now renewed against us and God succour us not, and I find not
my brother whom we have lost so long.' 'Damsel,' saith
Messire Gawain, 'I helped you so far as I might, and so would
I again and I were there. And fainer am I to see your brother
than all the knights of the world. But no true tidings may I
hear of him, save so much, that I was at a hermitage where was
a King hermit, and he bade me make no noise for that the Best
Knight of the world lay sick therewithin, and he told me that
his name was Par-lui-fet. I saw his horse being led by a squire
before the chapel, and his arms and shield whereon was a sun

figured.' 'Sir,' saith the damsel, 'My brother's name is not Par-lui-fet, but Perlesvax in right baptism, and it is said of them that have seen him that never comelier knight was known.' 'Certes,' saith the King, 'Never saw I comelier than he that came in hither nor better like to be good knight, and I know of a truth that such he is, for otherwise never might he have entered hereinto. But good reward of harbouring him had I not, for I may help neither myself nor other. For God's sake, Messire Gawain, hold me in remembrance this night, for great affiance have I in your valour.' 'Certes, Sir, please God, nought will I do within yonder, whereof I may be blamed of right.'

XVIII

Thereupon Messire Gawain was led into the hall and findeth twelve ancient knights, all bald, albeit they seemed not to be so old as they were, for each was of a hundred year of age or more and yet none of them seemed as though he were forty. They have set Messire Gawain to eat at a right rich table of ivory and seat themselves all round about him. 'Sir,' saith the Master of the Knights, 'Remember you of that the good King hath prayed of you and told you this night as you have heard.' 'Sir,' saith Messire Gawain, 'God remember it!' With that bring they larded meats of venison and wild-boar's flesh and other in great plenty, and on the table was rich array of vessels of silver and great cups of gold with their covers, and the rich candlesticks where the great candles were burning, albeit their brightness was hidden of the great light that appeared within.

XIX

Thereon, lo you, two damsels that issue forth of a chapel, whereof the one holdeth in her hands the most Holy Graal, and the other the Lance whereof the point bleedeth thereinto. And the one goeth beside the other in the midst of the hall where the knights and Messire Gawain sat at meat, and so sweet a smell and so holy came to them therefrom that they forgat to eat. Messire Gawain looketh at the Graal, and it seemed him that a chalice was therein, albeit none there was as at this time, and he seeth the point of the lance whence the red blood ran thereinto, and it seemeth him he seeth two angels that bear two candlesticks of gold filled with candles.   And the damsels pass before Messire Gawain, and go into another chapel.   And Messire Gawain is thoughtful, and so great a joy cometh to him that nought remembereth he in his thinking save of God only. The knights are all daunted and sorrowful in their hearts, and look at Messire Gawain.   Thereupon behold you the damsels that issue forth of the chamber and come again before Messire Gawain, and him seemeth that he seeth three there where before he had seen but two, and seemeth him that in the midst of the Graal he seeth the figure of a child.   The Master of the Knights beckoneth to Messire Gawain.   Messire Gawain looketh before him and seeth three drops of blood fall upon the table.   He was all abashed to look at them and spake no word.

XX

Therewith the damsels pass forth and the knights are all adread and look one at the other.   Howbeit Messire Gawain may not withdraw his eyes from the three drops of blood, and when he would fain kiss them they vanish away, whereof he is right sorrowful, for he may not set his hand nor aught that of him is to touch thereof.   Therewithal behold you the two damsels that come again before the table and seemeth to Messire Gawain that there are three, and he looketh up and it seemeth him to be the Graal all in flesh, and he seeth above, as him thinketh, a King crowned, nailed upon a rood, and the spear was still fast in his side.   Messire Gawain seeth it and hath great pity thereof, and of nought doth he remember him save of the pain that this King suffereth.   And the Master of the Knights summoneth him again by word of mouth, and telleth him that if he delayeth longer, never more will he recover it. Messire Gawain is silent, as he that heareth not the knight speak, and looketh upward.   But the damsels go back into the chapel and carry back the most Holy Graal and the Lance, and the knights make the tablecloths be taken away and rise from meat and go into another hall and leave Messire Gawain all alone.   And he looketh all around and seeth the doors all shut and made fast, and looketh to the foot of the hall and seeth two candlesticks with many candles burning round about the chess-board, and he seeth that the pieces are set, whereof the one

sort are silver and the other gold.   Messire Gawain sitteth at
the game, and they of gold played against him and mated him
twice.   At the third time, when he thought to revenge himself
and saw that he had the worse, he swept the pieces off the
board.   And the damsel issued forth of a chamber and made a
squire take the chess-board and the pieces and so carry them
away.   And Messire Gawain, that was way-worn of his wander-
ings to come thither where he now hath come, slept upon the
couch until the morrow when it was day, and he heard a horn
sound right shrill.

XXI

Thereupon he armeth him and would fain go to take leave of
King Fisherman, but he findeth the doors bolted so that he may
not get forth.   And right fair service seeth he done in a chapel,
and right sorrowful is he for that he may not hear the mass.
A damsel cometh into the hall and saith to him : ' Sir, now may
you hear the service and the joy that is made on account of the
sword you presented to the good King, and right glad at heart
ought you to have been if you had been within the chapel.
But you lost entering therein on account of a right little word.
For the place of the chapel is so hallowed of the holy relics
that are therein that man nor priest may never enter therein
from the Saturday at noon until the Monday after mass.'   And
he heard the sweetest voices and the fairest services that were
ever done in chapel.   Messire Gawain answereth her not a word
so is he abashed.   Howbeit the damsel saith to him : ' Sir, God
be guardian of your body, for methinketh that it was not of
your own default that you would not speak the word whereof
this castle would have been in joy.'   With that the damsel
departeth and Messire Gawain heareth the horn sound a second
time and a voice warning him aloud : ' He that is from without,
let him go hence ! for the bridges are lowered and the gate
open, and the lion is in his den.   And thereafter behoveth the
bridge be lifted again on account of the King of the Castle
Mortal, that warreth against this castle, and therefore of this
thing shall he die.'

XXII

Thereupon Messire Gawain issueth forth of the hall and
findeth his horse all made ready at the mounting-stage, together

with his arms. He goeth forth and findeth the bridges broad and long, and goeth his way a great pace beside a great river that runneth in the midst of the valley. And he seeth in a great forest a mighty rain and tempest, and so strong a thunder-storm ariseth in the forest that it seemeth like all the trees should be uprooted. So great is the rain and the tempest that it compelleth him set his shield over his horse's head lest he be drowned of the abundance of rain. In this mis-ease rideth he down beside the river that runneth in the forest until he seeth in a launde across the river a knight and a damsel right gaily appointed riding at pleasure, and the knight carrieth a bird on his fist, and the damsel hath a garland of flowers on her head. Two brachets follow the knight. The sun shineth right fair on the meadow and the air is right clear and fresh. Messire Gawain marvelleth much of this, that it raineth so heavily on his way, whereas, in the meadow where the knight and the damsel are riding, the sun shineth clear and the weather is bright and calm. And he seeth them ride joyously. He can ask them naught for they are too far away. Messire Gawain looketh about and seeth on the other side the river a squire nearer to him than is the knight. 'Fair friend,' saith Messire Gawain, 'How is this that it raineth upon me on this side the river, but on the other raineth it not at all?' 'Sir,' saith the squire, 'This have you deserved, for such is the custom of the forest.' 'Will this tempest that is over me last for ever?' saith Messire Gawain. 'At the first bridge you come to will it be stayed upon you,' saith the squire.

XXIII

Therewith the squire departeth, and the tempest rageth in-continent until he is come to the bridge; and he rideth beyond and cometh to the meadow, and the storm is stayed so that he setteth his shield to rights again upon his neck. And he seeth before him a castle where was a great company of folk that were making great cheer. He rideth until he cometh to the castle and seeth right great throng of folk, knights and dames and damsels. Messire Gawain alighteth, but findeth in the castle none that is willing to take his reins, so busied are they making merry. Messire Gawain presenteth himself on the one side and the other, but all of them avoid him, and he seeth

that he maketh but an ill stay therewithin for himself, wherefore
he departeth from the castle and meeteth a knight at the gate.
'Sir,' saith he, 'What castle is this?' 'And see you not,' saith
the knight, 'that it is a castle of joy?' 'By my faith,' saith
Messire Gawain, 'They of the castle be not over-courteous, for
all this time hath none come to take my reins.' 'Not for this
lose they their courtesy,' saith the knight, 'For this is no more
than you have deserved. They take you to be as slothful of deed
as you are of word, and they saw that you were come through the
Forest Perilous whereby pass all the discomfited, as well
appeareth by your arms and your horse.'   Therewith the knight
departeth, and Messire Gawain hath ridden a great space sorrowful and sore abashed, until he cometh to a land parched and
poor and barren of all comfort, and therein findeth he a poor
castle, whereinto he cometh and seeth it much wasted, but that
within was there a hall that seemed haunted of folk.   And
Messire Gawain cometh thitherward and alighteth, and a knight
cometh down the steps of the hall right poorly clad. 'Sir,' saith
the knight to Messire Gawain, 'Welcome may you be!'   After
that, he taketh him by the hand and leadeth him upward to the
hall, that was all waste.   Therewithal issue two damsels from
a chamber, right poorly clad, that were of passing great beauty,
and make great cheer to Messire Gawain.   So, when he was
fain to disarm, behold you thereupon a knight that entereth into
the hall, and he was smitten with the broken end of a lance
through his body. He seeth Messire Gawain, whom he knoweth.
'Now haste!' saith he, 'and disarm you not! Right joyful am
I that I have found you! I come from this forest wherein have
I left Lancelot fighting with four knights, whereof one is dead,
and they think that it is you, and they are of kindred to the
knight that you slew at the tent where you destroyed the evil
custom.   I was fain to help Lancelot, when one of the knights
smote me as you may see.'   Messire Gawain goeth down from
the hall and mounteth all armed upon his horse.

XXIV

'Sir,' saith the knight of the hall, 'I would go help you to
my power, but I may not issue forth of the castle until such
time as it be replenished of the folk that are wont to come
therein and until my land be again given up to me through the

valour of the Good Knight.' Messire Gawain departeth from the castle as fast as horse may carry him, and entereth the forest and followeth the track of the blood along the way the knight had come, and rideth so far in the forest as that he heareth the noise of swords, and seeth in the midst of the launde Lancelot and the three knights, and the fourth dead on the ground. But one of the knights had drawn him aback, for he might abide the combat no longer, for the knight that brought the tidings to Messire Gawain had sore wounded him. The two knights beset Lancelot full sore, and right weary was he of the buffets that he had given and received. Messire Gawain cometh to one of the knights and smiteth him right through the body and maketh him and his horse roll over all of a heap.

XXV

When Lancelot perceiveth Messire Gawain, much joy maketh he thereof. In the meanwhile as the one held the other, the fourth knight fled full speed through the midst of the forest, and he that the knight had wounded fell dead. They take their horses, and Messire Gawain telleth Lancelot he hath the most poverty-stricken host that ever he hath seen, and the fairest damsels known, but that right poorly are they clad. 'Shall we therefore take them of our booty?' 'I agree,' saith Lancelot, 'But sore grieveth me of the knight that hath thus escaped us.' 'Take no heed,' saith Messire Gawain, 'We shall do well enough herein.' Thereupon they return back toward the poor knight's hostel and alight before the hall, and the Poor Knight cometh to meet them, and the two damsels, and they deliver to them the three horses of the three knights that were dead. The knight hath great joy thereof, and telleth them that now is he a rich man and that betimes will his sisters be better clad than are they now, as well as himself.

XXVI

Thereupon come they into the hall. The knight maketh one of his own squires stable the horses and the two damsels help disarm Lancelot and Messire Gawain. 'Lords,' saith the knight, 'So God help me, nought have I to lend you where-

with to clothe you, for robe have I none save mine own jerkin.'
Lancelot hath great pity thereof and Messire Gawain, and the
two damsels take off their kirtles that were made like surcoats
of cloth that covered their poor shirts, and their jackets that
were all to-torn and ragged and worn, and present them to the
knights to clothe them. They were fain not to refuse, lest the
damsels should think they held them not in honour, and did on
the two kirtles right poor as they were. The damsels had
great joy thereof that so good knights should deign wear garments so poor. 'Lords,' saith the Poor Knight, 'The knight
that brought the tidings hither, and was stricken through of a
lance-shaft, is dead and lieth on a bier in a chapel within the
castle, and he confessed himself right well to a hermit and bade
salute you both, and was right fain you should see him after
that he were dead, and he prayed me instantly that I would ask
you to be to-morrow at his burial, for better knights than be ye
might not be thereat, so he told me.' 'Certes,' saith Lancelot,
'A good knight was he, and much mischief is it of his death;
and sore grieveth me that I know not his name nor of what
country he was.' 'Sir,' saith Messire Gawain, 'He said that
you should yet know it well.' The two good knights lay the
night at the castle, and the Poor Knight lodged them as well as
he might. When it cometh to morning, they go to the chapel
to hear mass and to be at the burial of the body. After that
they take leave of the Poor Knight and the two damsels and
depart from the castle all armed. 'Messire Gawain,' saith
Lancelot, 'They know not at court what hath become of you,
and they hold you for dead as they suppose.' 'By my faith,'
saith Messire Gawain, 'thitherward will I go, for I have had
sore travail, and there will I abide until some will shall come to
me to go seek adventure.' He recounteth to Lancelot how the
Graal hath appeared to him at the court of King Fisherman:
'And even as it was there before me, I forgat to ask how it
served and of what.' 'Ha, Sir,' saith Lancelot, 'Have you
then been there?' 'Yea,' saith he, 'And thereof am I right
sorry and glad: glad for the great holiness I have seen, sorry
for that I asked not that whereof King Fisherman prayed me
right sweetly.' 'Sir,' saith Lancelot, 'Right sorely ill have
you wrought, nor is there not whereof I have so great desire
as I have to go to his castle.' 'By my faith,' saith Messire
Gawain, 'Much shamed was I there, but this doth somewhat

recomfort me, that the Best Knight was there before me that gat blame thereof in like manner as I.' Lancelot departeth from Messire Gawain, and they take leave either of other. They issue forth of a forest, and each taketh his own way without saying a word.

BRANCH VII

TITLE I

HERE the story is silent of Messire Gawain and beginneth to speak of Lancelot, that entereth into a forest and rideth with right great ado and meeteth a knight in the midst of the forest that was coming full speed and was armed of all arms. 'Sir,' saith he to Lancelot, 'Whence come you?' 'Sir,' saith Lancelot, 'I come from the neighbourhood of King Arthur's Court.' 'Ha, Sir, can you tell me tidings of a knight that beareth a green shield such as I bear? If so, he is my brother.' 'What name hath he?' saith Lancelot. 'Sir,' saith he, 'His name is Gladoens, and he is a good knight and a hardy, and he hath a white horse right strong and swift.' 'Be there other knights in your country that bear such arms as your shield and his besides you and he?' 'Certes, Sir, none.' 'And wherefore do you ask?' saith Lancelot. 'For this, that a certain man hath reft him of one of his castles for that he was not there. Howbeit, I know well that he will have it again through his good knighthood.' 'Is he so good knight?' saith Lancelot. 'Certes, Sir, yea! He is the best of the Isles of the Moors.' 'Sir, of your mercy, lower your coif.' He quickly thereon lowereth his coif, and Lancelot looketh at him in the face. 'Certes, Sir Knight,' saith he, 'you very much resemble him.' 'Ha, Sir,' saith the knight, 'Know you then any tidings of him?' 'Certes, Sir,' saith he, 'Yea! and true tidings may I well say, for he rode at my side five leagues Welsh, nor never saw I one man so like another as are you to him.' 'Good right hath he to resemble me,' saith the knight, 'for we are twins, but he was born first and hath more sense and knighthood than I; nor in all the Isles of the Moors is there damsel that hath so much worth and beauty as she of whom he is loved of right true love, and more she desireth to see him than aught else that liveth, for she hath not seen him of more than a year, wherefore hath she gone seek her prize, my brother, by all the forests of the world. Sir,' saith the knight, 'Let me go seek my brother, and tell me where I may find him.' 'Certes,' saith Lancelot, 'I will tell you though it grieve me sore.' 'Wherefore?' saith the knight, 'Hath he done you any mis-deed?' 'In no wise,' saith Lancelot, 'Rather hath he done so much for me that I love you thereof and offer you my service.' 'Sir,' saith the knight, 'I am going my way, but for God's sake tell me where I shall find my brother.' 'Sir,' saith Lancelot, 'I will tell you. This morning did I bid his body farewell and help to bury him.' 'Ha, Sir,' saith the knight, 'Do you tell me true?' 'Certes,' saith Lancelot, 'True it is that I tell you.' 'Is he slain then, my brother?' saith the knight. 'Yea, and of succouring me,' saith Lancelot. 'Ha, sir,' saith the knight, 'For God's sake tell me nought that is not right.' 'By God, Sir,' saith he, 'Sore grieved am I to tell it you, for never loved I knight so much in so brief a time as I loved him. He helped to save me from death, and therefore will I do for you according to that he did for me.' 'Sir,' saith the knight, 'If he be dead, a great grief is it to myself, for I have lost my comfort and my life and my land without recovery.' 'Sir,' saith Lancelot, 'He helped me to save my life, and yours will I help to save henceforth for ever and so be that I shall know of your jeopardy.' The knight heareth that his brother is dead and well believeth Lancelot, and beginneth to make dole thereof the greatest that was ever heard. And Lancelot saith to him, 'Sir Knight, let be this dole, for none recovery is there; but my body do I offer you and my knighthood in any place you please, where I may save your honour.' 'Sir,' saith the knight, 'With good will receive I your help and your love, sith that you deign to offer me the same, and now have I sorer need of them than ever. Sir,' saith the knight, 'Sith that my brother is dead, I will return back and bear with my wrong, though well would he have amended it had he been on live.' 'By my head,' saith Lancelot, 'I will go with you, that so may I reward you of that he hath done for me. He delivered his body to the death for me, and in like manner freely would I fain set mine own in jeopardy for love of you and of him.'

II

'Sir,' saith the knight, 'Right good will do I owe you of this that you say to me, so your deeds be but the same herein.'

' Yea, so help me God,' saith Lancelot, ' The same shall they
be, if God lend me the power.' With that, they go on their
way together, and the knight comforteth him much of that
which Lancelot hath said to him, but of the death of his brother
was he right sorrowful. And they ride until they come to the
land of the Moors; then espy they a castle upon a rock, and
below was a broad meadow-land. ' Sir,' saith the Knight of
the Green Shield to Lancelot, ' This castle was my brother's and
is now mine, and much it misliketh me that it hath fallen to me
on this wise. And the knight that reft it of my brother is of so
great hardihood that he feareth no knight on live, and you will
presently see him issue forth of this castle so soon as he shall
perceive you.' Lancelot and the knight ride until they draw
nigh the castle. And the knight looketh in the way before
him, and seeth a squire coming on a hackney, that was carrying
before him a wild boar dead. The Knight of the Green Shield
asketh him whose man he is, and the squire maketh answer: ' I
am man of the Lord of the Rock Gladoens, that cometh there
behind, and my lord cometh all armed, he and others, for the
brother of Gladoens hath defied him on behalf of his brother,
but right little recketh my lord of his defiance.'

III

Lancelot heareth how he that is coming is the enemy of him
to whom had he been alive, his love most was due. The
Knight of the Green Shield pointed him out so soon as he saw
him. ' Sir,' saith he to Lancelot, ' Behold him by whom I am
disherited, and yet worse would he do to me and he knew that
my brother were dead.' Lancelot, without saying more, so
soon as he had espied the Knight of the Rock, smiteth his horse
with his spurs and cometh toward him. The Lord of the Rock,
that was proud and hardy, seeth Lancelot coming and smiteth
with his spurs the horse whereon he sitteth. They come
with so swift an onset either upon other that they break their
spears upon their shields, and hurtle together so sore that the
Knight of the Rock Gladoens falleth over the croup of his
horse. Lancelot draweth his sword and cometh above him, and
he crieth him mercy and asketh him wherefore he wisheth to slay
him ? Lancelot saith for the sake of Gladoens from whom he
hath reft his land and his castle. ' And what is that to you ?'

saith the knight. 'Behoveth his brother challenge me thereof.'
'As much it behoveth me as his brother,' saith Lancelot.
'Wherefore you?' 'For this,' saith Lancelot, 'That as much
as he did for me will I do to you.' He cutteth off his head and
giveth it incontinent to the Knight of the Green Shield. 'Now
tell me,' saith Lancelot, 'Sith that he is dead, is he purged of that
whereof you appeached him?' 'Sir,' saith the knight, 'I hold
him rightly quit thereof, for, sith that he is dead, all claim on
behalf of his kindred is abated by his death.' 'And I pledge
you my faith loyally,' saith Lancelot, 'as I am a knight, that
never shall you be in peril nor in jeopardy of aught wherein I
may help you, so I be in place and free, but my help shall you
have for evermore, for that your brother staked his life to
help me.'

IV

Lancelot and the knight lay the night at the Rock Gladoens,
and the Knight of the Green Shield had his land at his pleasure,
and all were obedient to him. And the upright and loyal were
right glad, albeit when they heard the tidings of Gladoens'
death they were right sorrowful thereof. Lancelot departed
from the castle on the morrow, and the knight remained therein,
sorrowful for his brother that he had lost, and glad for the
land that he had gotten again. Lancelot goeth back right
amidst the forest and rideth the day long, and meeteth a knight
that was coming, groaning sore. And he was stooping over
the fore saddle-bow for the pain that he had. He meeteth
Lancelot and saith to him: 'Sir, for God's sake, turn back, for
you will find there the most cruel pass in the world there where
I have been wounded through the body. Wherefore I beseech
you not go thither.' 'What pass is it then?' saith Lancelot.
'Sir,' saith he, 'It is the pass of the Castle of Beards, and it
hath the name of this, that every knight that passeth thereby
must either leave his beard there or challenge the same, and in
such sort have I challenged my beard that meseemeth I shall die
thereof.' 'By my head,' saith Lancelot, 'I hold not this of
cowardize, sith that you were hardy to set your life in jeopardy
to challenge your beard, but now would you argue me of
cowardize when you would have me turn back. Rather would
I be smitten through the body with honour, so and I had not
my death thereof, than lose with shame a single hair of my

beard.' 'Sir,' saith the knight, 'May God preserve you, for the castle is far more cruel than you think, and God guide the knight that may destroy the evil custom of the castle, for right shameful is the custom to strange knights that pass thereby.'

V

Lancelot departeth from the knight and cometh toward the castle. Just as he had passed over a great bridge, he looketh about and seeth two knights come all armed to the entrance of the castle, and they made hold their horses before them, and their shields and spears are before them leaning against the wall. Lancelot looketh at the gateway of the castle and seeth the great door all covered with beards fastened thereon, and heads of knights in great plenty hung thereby. So, as he was about to enter the gate, two knights issue therefrom over against him. 'Sir,' saith the one, 'Abide and pay your toll!' 'Do knights, then, pay toll here?' saith Lancelot. 'Yea!' say the knights, 'All they that have beards, and they that have none are quit. Sir, now pay us yours, for a right great beard it is, and thereof have we sore need.' 'For what?' saith Lancelot. 'I will tell you,' saith the knight. 'There be hermits in this forest that make hair-shirts thereof.' 'By my head,' saith Lancelot, 'Never shall they have hair-shirt of mine, so I may help it.' 'That shall they,' say the knights, 'Of yours as of the other, or dearly shall you pay therefor!'

VI

Right wroth waxeth Sir Lancelot, and cometh to the knight, and smiteth him with his spear amidst the breast with such a thrust that it passeth half an ell beyond, and overthroweth him and his horse together. The other knight seeth his fellow wounded to the death, and cometh towards him with a great sweep and breaketh his spear upon his shield. Howbeit, Lancelot beareth him to the ground right over his horse-croup and maketh him fall so heavily that he breaketh one of his legs. The tidings are come to the Lady of the Castle that a knight hath come to the pass that hath slain one of her knights and wounded the other. The Lady is come thither, and bringeth two of her damsels with her. She seeth Lancelot that is fain to slay the knight that lieth wounded on the ground. 'Sir,' saith the Lady to Lancelot, 'Withdraw yourself back and slay him not, but alight and speak to me in safety.' 'Lady,' saith one of the maidens, 'I know him well. This is Lancelot of the Lake, the most courteous knight that is in the court of King Arthur.' He alighteth and cometh before the Lady. 'Lady,' saith he, 'what is your pleasure?' 'I desire,' saith she, 'that you come to my hostel to harbour, and that you make me amends of the shame you have done me.'

VII

'Lady,' saith Lancelot, 'Shame have I never done you nor shall do, but the knights took in hand too shameful a business when they were minded to take the beards of stranger knights by force.' 'Sir,' saith she, 'I will forego mine ill-will on condition that you harbour herewithin to-night.' 'Lady,' saith Lancelot, 'I desire not your ill-will, wherefore will I gladly do your pleasure.' He setteth him within the castle and maketh his horse be led in after him, and the Lady hath the dead knight brought into the chapel and buried. The other she biddeth be disarmed and clothed and commandeth that his wounds be searched. Then maketh she Lancelot be disarmed and clad right richly in a good robe, and telleth him that she knoweth well who he is. 'Lady,' saith Lancelot, 'It is well for me.' Thereupon they sit to eat, and the first course is brought in by knights in chains that had their noses cut off; the second by knights in chains that had their eyes put out; wherefore they were led in by squires. The third course was brought in by knights that had but one hand and were in chains. After that, came other knights that had each but one foot and brought in the fourth course. At the fifth course came knights right fair and tall, and each brought a naked sword in his hand and presented their heads to the Lady.

VIII

Lancelot beheld the martyrdom of these knights, and sore misliking had he of the services of such folk. They are risen from meat and the lady goeth to her chamber and sitteth on a couch. 'Lancelot,' saith the Lady, 'you have seen the justice and the lordship of my castle. All these knights have been conquered at the passing of my door.' 'Lady,' saith Lancelot, 'foul mischance hath befallen them.' 'The like mischance would have befallen you had you not been knight so good. And greatly have I desired to see you this long time past. And I will make you lord of this castle and myself.' 'Lady,' saith he, 'the lordship of this castle hold I of yourself without mesne, and to you have I neither wish nor right to refuse it. Rather am I willing to be at your service.' 'Then,' saith she, 'you will abide with me in this castle, for more do I love you than any other knight that liveth.' 'Lady,' saith Lancelot, 'Gramercy, but in no castle may I abide more than one night until I have been thither whither behoveth me to go.' 'Whither are you bound?' saith she. 'Lady,' saith he, 'to the Castle of Souls.' 'Well know I the castle,' saith she. 'The King hath the name Fisherman, and lieth in languishment on account of two knights that have been at his castle and made not good demand. Would you fain go thither?' saith the Lady. 'Yea,' saith Lancelot. 'Then pledge me your faith that you will return by me to speak to me, so the Graal shall appear to you, and you ask whereof it serveth.' 'Yea, truly,' saith Lancelot, 'were you beyond sea!' 'Sir,' saith one of the damsels, 'So much may you well promise, for the Graal appeareth not to no knight so wanton as be ye. For you love the Queen Guenievre, the wife of your lord, King Arthur, nor so long as this love lieth at your heart may you never behold the Graal.'

IX

Lancelot heard the damsel and blushed of despite. 'Ha, Lancelot,' saith the Lady, 'Love you other than me?' 'Lady,' saith he, 'the damsel may say her pleasure.' Lancelot lay the night at the castle, and right wroth was he of the damsel that calleth the love of him and the Queen disloyal. And the morrow when he had heard mass, he took leave of the Lady of the Castle, and she besought him over and over to keep his covenant, and he said that so would he do without fail. Therewithal he issueth forth of the castle and entereth into a tall and ancient forest, and rideth the day long until he cometh to the outskirt of the forest, and seeth a tall cross at the entrance of a burying-ground enclosed all round about with a hedge of thorns. And the way lay through the burying-ground. Lancelot entered therein and the night was come. He seeth the graveyard full of tombs and sepulchres. He looketh behind and seeth a chapel wherein were candles burning. Thitherward goeth he, and passeth beyond without saying aught more by the side of a dwarf that was digging a grave in the ground. 'Lancelot,' saith the dwarf, 'you are right not to salute me, for you are the man of all the world that most I hate; and God grant me vengeance of your body. So will He what time you are stricken down here within!' Lancelot heard the dwarf, but deigned not to answer him of nought. He is come to the chapel, and alighteth and maketh fast the bridle of his horse to a tree, and leaneth his shield and spear without. After that he entereth into the chapel, and findeth a damsel laying out a knight in his winding-sheet. As soon as Lancelot was entered therewithin the wounds of the knight were swollen up and began to bleed afresh. 'Ha, Sir Knight, now see I plainly that you slew him that I am wrapping in his winding-sheet!'

X

Thereupon, behold you, two knights that are carrying other two knights dead. They alight and then set them in the chapel. And the dwarf crieth out to them: 'Now shall it be seen how you avenge your friends of the enemy that fell upon you!' The knight that had fled from the forest when Messire Gawain came thither where the three lay dead, was come therewithin and knew Lancelot, whereupon saith he: 'Our mortal enemy are you, for by you were these three knights slain.' 'Well had they deserved it,' saith Lancelot, 'and in this chapel am I in no peril of you, wherefore as at this time will I depart not hence, for I know not the ways of the forest.' He was in the chapel until the day broke, when he issued forth thereof, and sore it weighed upon him that his horse was still fasting. He taketh his arms and is mounted. The dwarf crieth out aloud: 'What aileth you?' saith he to the two knights, 'Will you let your mortal enemy go thus?' With that the two knights mount their horses and go to the two issues of the grave-yard, thinking that Lancelot is fain to flee therefrom; but no desire hath he thereof, wherefore he cometh to the knight that was guarding the entrance whereby he had to issue out,

and smiteth him so stiffly that he thrusteth the point of his
spear right through his body.   The other knight that was
guarding the other entrance, that had fled out of the forest
before, had no mind to avenge his fellow, and fled incontinent
so fast as he might.   And Lancelot taketh the horse of the
knight he had slain and driveth him before him, for he thinketh
that some knight may haply have need thereof.   He rideth on
until he cometh to a hermitage in the forest where he alighteth
and hath his horses stabled, and the Hermit giveth them of the
best he hath.   And Lancelot heard mass, and afterward ate a
little and fell on sleep.   Thereafter, behold you, a knight that
cometh to the Hermit and seeth Lancelot that was about to
mount. 'Sir,' saith he, 'Whither go you?' 'Sir Knight,'
saith Lancelot, 'thither shall I go where God may please; but
you, whitherward are you bound to go?' 'Sir, I go to see one
of my brethren and my two sisters, for I have been told that he
hath fallen on such mishap as that he is called the Poor Knight,
whereof am I sore sorrowful.' 'Certes,' saith Lancelot, 'Poor
he is, the more the pity!   Howbeit, will you do him a message
from me?' 'Sir,' saith the knight, 'Right willingly!' 'Will
you present him with this horse on my behalf, and tell him how
Lancelot that harboured with him hath sent it?' 'Sir,' saith
the knight, 'Right great thanks, and blessed may you be, for
he that doth a kindness to a worshipful man loseth it not.'
'Salute the two damsels for me,' saith Lancelot. 'Sir, right
willingly!'   The knight delivereth the horse to his squire, and
taketh leave of Lancelot.

XI

Thereupon, Lancelot departeth from the hermitage and
rideth on until he cometh forth of the forest, and findeth a
waste land, a country broad and long wherein wonned neither
beast nor bird, for the land was so poor and parched that no
victual was to be found therein.   Lancelot looketh before him
and seeth a city appear far away.   Thither rideth he full speed
and seeth that the city is so great that it seemeth him to
encompass a whole country.   He seeth the walls that are
falling all around, and the gates ruined with age.   He entereth
within and findeth the city all void of folk, and seeth the great
palaces fallen down and waste, and the great grave-yards full of

sepulchres, and the tall churches all lying waste, and the markets and exchanges all empty. He rideth amidst the streets and findeth a great palace that seemeth him to be better and more ancient than all the others. He bideth awhile before it and heareth within how knights and ladies are making great dole. And they say to a knight: 'Ha, God, sore grief and pity is this of you, that you must needs die in such manner, and that your death may not be respited! Sore hatred ought we to bear toward him that hath adjudged you such a death.' The knights and ladies swoon over him as he departeth. Lancelot hath heard all this and much marvelleth he thereof, but nought thereof may he see.

XII

Thereupon, lo you, the knight that cometh down into the midst of the hall, clad in a short red jerkin; and he was girt with a rich girdle of gold, and had a rich clasp at his neck wherein were many rich stones, and on his head had he a great cap of gold, and he held a great axe. The knight was of great comeliness and young of age. Lancelot seeth him coming, and looketh upon him right fainly when he seeth him appear. And the knight saith to him, 'Sir, alight!' 'Certes,' saith Lancelot, 'Willingly.' He alighteth and maketh his horse fast to a ring of silver that was on the mounting-stage, and putteth his shield from his neck and his spear from his hand. 'Sir,' saith he to the knight, 'What is your pleasure?' 'Sir, needs must you cut me off my head with this axe, for of this weapon hath my death been adjudged, but and you will not, I will cut off your own therewith.' 'Hold, Sir,' saith Lancelot, 'What is this you tell me?' 'Sir,' saith the knight, 'You must needs do even as I say, sith that you are come into this city.' 'Sir,' saith Lance-lot, 'Right foolish were he that in such a jeopardy should not do the best for himself, but blamed shall I be thereof and I shall slay you when you have done me no wrong.' 'Certes,' saith the Knight, 'In no otherwise may you go hence.' 'Fair Sir,' saith Lancelot, 'So gentle are you and so well nurtured, how cometh it that you take your death so graciously? You know well that I shall kill you before you shall kill me, sith that so it is.' 'This know I well for true,' saith the Knight, 'But you will promise me before I die, that you will return into this city within a year from this, and that you will set your head in the same jeopardy without challenge, as I have set mine.' 'By my head,' saith Lancelot, 'Needeth no argument that I shall choose respite of death to dying here on the spot. But I marvel me of this that you are so fairly apparelled to receive your death.'

XIII

'Sir,' saith the Knight, 'He that would go before the Saviour of the World ought of right to apparel him as fairly as he may. I am by confession purged of all wickedness and of all the misdeeds that ever I have committed, and do repent me truly thereof, wherefore at this moment am I fain to die.' Therewithal he holdeth forth the axe, and Lancelot taketh it and seeth that it is right keen and well whetted. 'Sir,' saith the Knight, 'Hold up your hand toward the minster that you see yonder.' 'Sir,' saith Lancelot, 'Willingly.' 'Thus, then, will you swear to me upon the holy relics that are within this minster, that on this day year at the hour that you shall have slain me, or before, you yourself will come back here and place your head in the very same peril as I shall have placed mine, without default?' 'Thus,' saith Lancelot, 'do I swear and give you thereto my pledge.' With that, the Knight kneeleth and stretcheth his neck as much as he may, and Lancelot taketh the axe in his hands, and then saith to him, 'Sir Knight, for God's sake, have mercy on yourself!' 'Let cut off my head!' saith the Knight, 'For otherwise may I not have mercy upon you!' 'In God's name,' saith Lancelot, 'fain would I deny you.' With that, he swingeth the axe and cutteth off the head with such a sweep that he maketh it fly seven foot high from the body. The Knight fell to the ground when his head was cut off, and Lancelot flung down the axe, and thinketh that he will make but an ill stay there for himself. He cometh to his horse, and taketh his arms and mounteth and looketh behind him, but seeth neither the body of the Knight nor the head, neither knoweth he what hath become of them all, save only that he heard much dole and a great cry far off in the city of knights and ladies, saying that he shall be avenged, please God, at the term set, or before. Lancelot hath heard and understood all that the knights say and the ladies, and issueth forth of the city.

BRANCH VIII

INCIPIT

Of the most Holy Graal here beginneth another branch in such wise as the authority witnesseth and Joseph that made recoverance thereof, in the name of the Father, and of the Son, and of the Holy Ghost.

TITLE I

This high history and profitable witnesseth us that the son of the Widow Lady sojourned still with his uncle King Pelles in the hermitage, and through distress of the evil that he had had since he came forth of the house of King Fisherman, was he confessed to his uncle and told him of what lineage he was, and that his name was Perceval. But the good Hermit the good King had given him the name of Parluifet, for that he was made of himself. King Hermit was one day gone into the forest, and the good knight Parluifet felt himself sounder of health and lustier than he wont to be. He heard the birds sing in the forest, and his heart began to swell of knighthood, and he minded him of the adventures he wont to find in the forest and of the damsels and knights that he wont to meet, and never was he so fain of arms as was he at that time, for that he had been sojourning so long within doors. He felt courage in his heart and lustiness in his limbs and fainness in his thought. Right soon armeth he himself and setteth the saddle on his horse and mounteth forthwith. He prayeth God give him adventure that he may meet good knight, setteth himself forth of his uncle's hermitage and entereth into the forest that was broad and shady. He rideth until he cometh into a launde that was right spacious, and seeth a leafy tree that was at the head of the launde. He alighteth in the shadow, and thinketh to

himself that two knights might joust on this bit of ground fair
and well, for the place was right broad.   And, even as he was
thinking on this wise, he heard a horse neigh full loud in the
forest three times, and right glad was he thereof and said:
'Ha, God, of your sweetness grant that there be a knight with
that horse, so may I prove whether there be any force or valour
or knighthood in me.   For I know not now what strength I
may have, nor even whether my heart be sound and my limbs
whole.   For on a knight that hath neither hardihood nor valour
in himself, may not another knight that hath more force in him
reasonably prove his mettle, for many a time have I heard say
that one is better than other.   And for this pray I to the
Saviour and this be a knight that cometh there, that he may
have strength and hardihood and mettle to defend his body
against mine own, for great desire have I to run upon him.
Grant now that he slay me not, nor I him!'

II

Therewithal, he looketh before him, and seeth the knight
issue from the forest and enter into the launde.   The knight
was armed and had at his neck a white shield with a cross of
gold.   He carried his lance low, and sate upon a great destrier
and rode at a swift pace.   As soon as Perceval seeth him, he
steadieth him in his stirrups and setteth spear in rest and smiteth
his horse with his spurs, right joyous, and goeth toward the
knight a great gallop.   Then he crieth: 'Sir Knight, cover
you of your shield to guard you as I do of mine to defend my
body, for you do I defy on this side slaying, and our Lord God
grant that I find you so good knight as shall try what hardihood
of heart I may have, for I am not such as I have been aforetime, and better may one learn of a good knight than of a bad.'
With that he smiteth the knight upon his shield with such a
sweep that he maketh him lose one of his stirrups and pierceth
his shield above the boss, and passeth beyond full speed.   And
the knight marvelleth much, and maketh demand, saying, 'Fair
Sir, what misdeed have I done you?'   Perceval is silent, and
hath no great joy of this that he hath not overthrown the
knight, but not so easy was he to overthrow, for he was one of
the knights of the world that could most of defence of arms.
He goeth toward Perceval as fast as his horse may carry him

and Perceval toward him. They mell together upon their shields right stiffly, so that they pierce and batter them with the points of their spears. And Perceval thrusteth his spear into the flesh two finger-breadths, and the knight doth not amiss, for he passeth his spear right through his arm so that the shafts of the lances were splintered. They hurtle together either against other at the passing so mightily, that the flinders of iron from the mail of their habergeons stick into their foreheads and faces, and the blood leapeth forth by mouth and nose so that their habergeons were all bloody. They drew their swords with a right great sweep. The knight of the white shield holdeth Perceval's rein and saith : ' Gladly would I know who you are and wherefore you hate me, for you have wounded me right sore, and sturdy knight have I found you and of great strength.' Perceval saith not a word to him and runneth again upon him sword drawn, and the knight upon him, and right great buffets either giveth other on the helm, so that their eyes all sparkle of stars and the forest resoundeth of the clashing of their swords. Right tough was the battle and right horrible, for good knights were both twain. But the blood that ran down from their wounds at last slackened their sinews, albeit the passing great wrath that the one had against the other, and the passing great heat of their will, had so enchafed them they scarce remembered the wounds that they had, and still dealt each other great buffets without sparing.

III

King Hermit cometh from labouring in the forest and findeth not his nephew in the hermitage, whereof is he right sorrowful, and he mounteth on a white mule that he had therewithin. She was starred in the midst of her forehead with a red cross. Josephus the good clerk witnesseth us that this same mule had belonged to Joseph of Abarimacie at the time he was Pilate's soldier, and that he bequeathed her to King Pelles. King Hermit departeth from the hermitage and prayeth God grant him to find his nephew. He goeth through the forest and rideth until he draweth nigh the launde where the two knights were. He heareth the strokes of the swords, and cometh towards them full speed and setteth him between the twain to forbid them. ' Ha, sir,' saith he to the Knight of the White Shield, ' Right great ill do you to combat against this knight that hath lain sick this long time in this forest, and right sorely have you wounded him.' 'Sir,' saith the knight, 'As much hath he done by me, and never would I have run upon him now had he not challenged me, and he is not minded to tell me who he is nor whence ariseth his hatred of me.' 'Fair Sir,' saith the Hermit, 'And you, who are you?' 'Sir,' saith the knight, 'I will tell you. I am the son of King Ban of Benoic.' 'Ha, fair nephew,' saith King Hermit to Perceval, 'See here your cousin, for King Ban of Benoic was your father's cousin-german. Make him right great cheer!' He maketh them take off their helmets and lower their ventails, and then kiss one another, afterward he leadeth them to his hermitage. They alight together. He calleth his own squire that waited upon him, and made them be disarmed right tenderly. There was a damsel within that was cousin-german to King Pelles and had tended Perceval within in his sickness. She washeth their wounds right sweetly and cleanseth them of the blood. And they see that Lancelot is sorer wounded than Perceval. 'Damsel,' saith the Hermit, 'How seemeth you?' 'Sir,' saith she, 'Needs must this knight sojourn here, for his wound is in a right perilous place.' 'Hath he danger of death?' 'Sir,' saith she, 'In no wise of this wound, but behoveth him take good heed thereto.' 'God be praised!' saith he, 'And of my nephew how seemeth you?' 'Sir, the wound that he hath will be soon healed. He will have none ill thereof.'

IV

The damsel, that was right cunning of leech-craft, tended the wounds of the knights, and made them whole as best she might, and King Hermit himself gave counsel therein. But and Perceval had borne his shield that was there within, of sinople with a white hart, Lancelot would have known him well, nor would there have been any quarrel between them, for he had heard tell of this shield at the court of King Arthur. The authority of this story recordeth that the two knights are in hermitage, and that Perceval is well-nigh whole; but Lancelot hath sore pain of his wound and is still far from his healing.

BRANCH IX

TITLE I

Now the story is silent about the two knights for a little time, and speaketh of the squire that Messire Gawain meeteth in the midst of the forest, that told him he went seek the son of the Widow Lady that had slain his father. And the squire saith that he will go to avenge him, wherefore cometh he to the court of King Arthur, for that he had heard tell how all good knights repaired thither. And he seeth the shield hang on the column in the midst of the hall that the Damsel of the Car had brought thither. The squire knoweth it well, and kneeleth before the King and saluteth him, and the King returneth his salute and asketh who he is. 'Sir,' saith he, 'I am the son of the Knight of the Red Shield of the Forest of Shadows, that was slain of the Knight that ought to bear the shield that hangeth on this column, wherefore would I right gladly hear tidings of him.' 'As gladly would I,' saith the King, 'so that no evil came to him thereof, for he is the knight of the world that I most desire.' 'Sir,' saith the Squire, 'Well behoveth me to hate him for that he slew my father. He that ought to bear this shield was squire when he slew him, wherefore am I the more sorrowful for that I thought to be avenged upon him squire. But this I may not do, wherefore I pray you for God's sake that you will make me knight, for the like favour are you accustomed to grant unto others.' 'What is your name, fair friend?' saith the King. 'Sir,' saith he, 'I am called Clamados of the Shadows.' Messire Gawain that had repaired to court, was in the hall, and said to the King: 'If this squire be enemy of the Good Knight that ought to bear this shield, behoveth you not set forward his mortal enemy but rather set him back, for he is the Best Knight of the world and the most chaste that liveth in the world and of the most holy lineage, and therefore have you sojourned right long time in this castle to await his coming. I say not this for the hindering of the squire's advancement, but that you may do nought whereof the Good Knight may have cause of complaint against you.' 'Messire Gawain,' saith Queen Guenievre, 'well know I that you love my Lord's honour, but sore blame will he have if he make not this one knight, for so much hath he never refused to do for any; nor yet will the Good Knight have any misliking thereof, for greater shame should he have, and greater despite of the hatred of a squire than of a knight; for never yet was good knight that was not prudent and well-advised and slow to take offence. Wherefore I tell you that he will assuredly listen to reason, and I commend my Lord the rather that he make him knight, for much blame would he have of gainsaying him.' 'Lady,' saith Messire Gawain, 'So you are content, I am happy.' The King made him knight right richly, and when he was clad in the robes, they of the court declare and witness that never this long time past had they seen at the court knight of greater comeliness. He sojourned therein long time, and was much honoured of the King and all the barons. He was every day on the watch for the Good Knight that should come for the shield, but the hour and the place were not as yet.

II

When he saw that he did not come, he took leave of the King and the Queen and all them of the court, and departed, thinking him that he would go prove his knighthood in some place until he should have heard tidings of his mortal enemy. He rideth amidst the great forests bearing a red shield like as did his father, and he was all armed as for defending of his body. And a long space of time he rideth, until one day he cometh to the head of a forest, and he espied his way that ran between two mountains and saw that he had to pass along the midst of the valley that lay at a great depth. He looketh before him and seeth a tree far away from him, and underneath were three damsels alighted, and one prayed God right heartily aloud that He would send them betimes a knight that durst convoy them through this strait pass.

III

Clamodos heareth the damsel and cometh thitherward. When they espied him, great joy have they thereof and rise up to

meet him. 'Sir,' say they, 'Welcome may you be!'
'Damsels,' saith he, 'Good adventure may you have! And
whom await you here?' saith he. 'We await,' saith the
Mistress of the damsels, 'some knight that shall clear this pass,
for no knight durst pass hereby.' 'What is the pass, then,
damsel?' saith he. 'It is the one of a lion, and a lion, moreover, so fell and horrible that never was none seen more cruel.
And there is a knight with the lion between the two mountains
that is right good knight and hardy and comely. Howbeit none
durst pass without great company of folk. But the knight that
hath repair with the lion is seldom there, for so he were there
we need fear no danger, for much courtesy is there in him and
valour.' And the knight looketh and seeth in the shadow of
the forest three fair stags harnessed to a car. 'Ha,' saith he,
'You are the Damsel of the Car, wherefore may you well tell
me tidings of the knight of whom I am in quest.' 'Who is
he?' saith the Damsel. 'It is he that should bear a shield
banded argent and azure with a red cross.' 'Of him am I likewise in quest,' saith the Damsel; 'please God, we shall hear
tidings of him betimes.' 'Damsel,' saith the knight, 'that
would I. And for that you are in quest of him as am I
likewise, I will convoy you beyond this pass.' The Damsel
maketh her Car go on before, and the damsels go before the
knight; and so enter they into the field of the lion, and right
fair land found they therewithin. Clamados looketh and seeth
the hall within an enclosure and seeth the lion that lay at the
entrance of the gateway. As soon as he espieth Clamados and
the damsels, he cometh toward them full speed, mouth open
and ears pricked up. 'Sir,' saith the Damsel, 'and you defend
not your horse on foot, he is dead at the first onset.'

IV

Clamados is alighted to his feet, by her counsel, and holdeth
his spear in his fist, and the lion rampeth toward him all in a
fury. Clamados receiveth him on the point of his spear, and
smiteth him therewith so stoutly that it passeth a fathom beyond
his neck. He draweth back his spear without breaking it, and
thinketh to smite him again. But the lion cheateth him, and
arising himself on his two hinder feet, setteth his fore feet on
his shoulders, then huggeth him toward him like as one man

E

doth another. But the grip was sore grievous, for he rendeth his habergeon in twain and so teareth away as much flesh as he can claw hold on.

V

When Clamados felt himself wounded, he redoubled his hardihood, and grippeth the lion so straitly to him that he wringeth a huge roar out of him, and then flingeth him to the ground beneath him. Then he draweth his sword and thrusteth it to the heart right through the breast. The lion roareth so loud that all the mountains resound thereof. Clamados cutteth off his head and goeth to hang it at the door of the hall. Then he cometh back to his horse and mounteth the best he may. And the Damsel saith to him, 'Sir, you are sore wounded.' 'Damsel,' said he, 'Please God, I shall take no hurt thereof.' Thereupon, behold you a squire that issueth forth of the hall and cometh after him full speed. 'Hold, Sir Knight,' saith he; 'Foul wrong have you wrought, for you have slain the lion of the most courteous knight that may be known, and the fairest and most valiant of this kingdom, and in his despite have you hung the head at his door! Right passing great outrage have you done hereby!' 'Fair sweet friend,' saith Clamados, 'it may well be that the lord is right courteous, but the lion was rascal and would have slain me and them that were passing by. And your lord loved him so much he should have chained him up, for better liketh me that I slew him than that he should slay me.' 'Sir,' saith the squire, 'There is no road this way, for it is a forbidden land whereof certain would fain reave my lord, and it was against the coming of his enemies that the lion was allowed forth unchained.' 'And what name hath your lord, fair friend?' saith Clamados. 'Sir, he is called Meliot of Logres, and he is gone in quest of Messire Gawain, of whom he holdeth the land, for right dear is he to him.' 'Messire Gawain,' saith Clamados, 'left I at the court of King Arthur, but behoveth him depart thence or ever I return thither.' 'By my head,' saith the squire, 'Fain would I you might meet them both twain, if only my lord knew that you had slain him his lion.' 'Fair friend,' saith Clamados, 'And he be as courteous as you say, no misliking will he have of me thereof, for I slew him in defending mine own body, and God forbid I should meet any that would do me evil therefor.'

VI

Thereupon the knight and the damsels depart and pass the narrow strait in the lion's field, and ride on until they draw nigh a right rich castle seated in a meadowland surrounded of great waters and high forests, and the castle was always void of folk. And they were fain to turn thitherward, but they met a squire that told them that in the castle was not a soul, albeit and they would ride forward they would find great plenty of folk. So far forward have they ridden that they are come to the head of a forest and see great foison of tents stretched right in the midst of a launde, and they were compassed round of a great white sheet that seemed from afar to be a long white wall with crenels, and it was a good league Welsh in length. They came to the entrance of the tents and heard great joy within, and when they had entered they saw dames and damsels, whereof was great plenty, and of right passing great beauty were they. Clamados alighteth, that was right sore wounded. The Damsel of the Car was received with right great joy. Two of the damsels come to Clamados, of whom make they right great joy. Afterward they lead him to a tent and made disarm him. Then they washed his wounds right sweetly and tenderly. Then they brought him a right rich robe and made him be apparelled therein, and led him before the ladies of the tents, that made right great joy of him.

VII

'Lady,' saith the Damsel of the Car, 'This knight hath saved my life, for he hath slain the lion on account of which many folk durst not come to you, wherefore make great joy of him.' 'Greater joy may I not make, than I do, nor the damsels that are herein, for we await the coming of the Good Knight that is healed, from day to day. And now is there nought in the world I more desire to see.' 'Lady,' saith Clamados, 'Who is this Good Knight?' 'The son of the Widow Lady of the Valleys of Camelot,' saith she. 'Tell me, Lady, do you say that he will come hither presently?' 'So methinketh,' saith she. 'Lady, I also shall have great joy thereof, and God grant he come betimes!' 'Sir Knight,' saith she, 'What is your name?' 'Lady,' saith he, 'I am called Clamados, and I am son of the lord of the Forest of Shadows.' She throweth her arms on his neck and kisseth and embraceth him right sweetly, and saith : 'Marvel not that I make you joy thereof, for you are the son of my sister-in-law, nor have I any friend nor blood-kindred so nigh as are you, and fain would I you should be lord of all my land and of me, as is right and reason.' The damsels of the tents make right great joy of him when they know the tidings that he is so nigh of kin to the Lady of the Tents. And he sojourned therewithin until that he was whole and heal, awaiting the coming af the knight of whom he had heard the tidings. And the damsels marvel them much that he cometh not, for the damsel that had tended him was therewithin and telleth them that he was healed of his arm, but that Lancelot is not yet whole, wherefore he is still within the hermitage.

VIII

This high history witnesseth us and recordeth that Joseph, who maketh remembrance thereof, was the first priest that sacrificed the body of Our Lord, and forsomuch ought one to believe the words that come of him. You have heard tell how Perceval was of the lineage of Joseph of Abarimacie, whom God so greatly loved for that he took down His body hanging on the cross, which he would not should lie in the prison there where Pilate had set it. For the highness of the lineage whereof the Good Knight was descended ought one willingly to hear brought to mind and recorded the words that are of him. The story telleth us that he was departed of the hermitage all sound and whole, albeit he hath left Lancelot, for that his wound was not yet healed, but he hath promised him that he will come back to him so soon as he may. He rideth amidst a forest, all armed, and cometh toward evensong to the issue of the forest and seeth a castle before him right fair and well seated, and goeth thitherward for lodging, for the sun was set. He entereth into the castle and alighteth. The lord cometh to meet him that was a tall knight and a red, and had a felon look, and his face scarred in many places ; and knight was there none therewithin· save only himself and his household.

IX

When he seeth Perceval alighted, he runneth to bar the door, and Perceval cometh over against him. For all greeting, the

knight saluteth him thus : 'Now shall you have,' saith he, 'such
guerdon as you have deserved. Never again shall you depart
hence, for my mortal enemy are you, and right hardy are you
thus to throw yourself upon me, for you slew my brother the
Lord of the Shadows, and Chaos the Red am I that war upon
your mother, and this castle have I reft of her. In like manner
will I wring the life out of you or ever you depart hence!'
'Already,' saith Perceval, 'have I thrown myself on this your
hostel to lodge with you, wherefore to blame would you be to
do me evil. But lodge me this night as behoveth one knight do
for another, and on the morrow at departing let each do the best
he may.' 'By my head!' saith Chaos the Red, 'Mortal enemy
of mine will I never harbour here save I harbour him dead.' He
runneth to the hall above, and armeth himself as swiftly as he
may, and taketh his sword all naked in his hand and cometh back
to the place where Perceval was, right full of anguish of heart
for this that he said, that he would war upon his mother and had
reft her of this castle. He flung his spear to the ground, and
goeth toward him on foot and dealeth him a huge buffet above
the helmet upon the coif of his habergeon, such that he cleaveth
the mail and cutteth off two fingers'-breadth of the flesh in such
sort that he made him reel three times round.

X

When Chaos the Red felt himself wounded, he was sore
grieved thereof, and cometh toward Perceval and striketh him a
great buffet above in the midst of his helmet, so that he made
the sparks fly and his neck stoop and his eyes sparkle of stars.
And the blow slippeth down on to the shield, so that it is cleft
right down to the boss. Perceval felt his neck stiff and heavy,
and feeleth that the knight is sturdy and of great might. He
cometh back towards him, and thinketh to strike him above in
the midst of his head, but Chaos swerved aside from him : howbeit Perceval reached him and caught his right arm and cutteth
it sheer from his side, sword and all, and sendeth it flying to the
ground, and Chaos runneth upon him, thinking to grapple him
with his left arm, but his force was waning; nathless right
gladly would he have avenged himself and he might. Howbeit,
Perceval setteth on him again that loved him not in his heart,
and smiteth him again above on the head, and dealeth him such

a buffet as maketh his brains be all to-scattered abroad. His
household and servants were at the windows of the hall. When
they see that their lord is nigh to the death, they cry to Perceval:
'Sir, you have slain the hardiest knight in the kingdom of Logres,
and him that was most redoubted of his enemies; but we can do
no otherwise; we know well that this castle is your mother's
and ought to be yours. We challenge it not; wherefore may
you do your will of whatsoever there is in the castle; but allow
us to go to our lord that there lieth dead, and take away the
body and set it in some seemly place for the sake of his good
knighthood, and for that it behoveth us so to do.' 'Readily do
I grant it you,' saith Perceval. They bear the body to a chapel,
then they disarm him and wind him in his shroud. After that
they lead Perceval into the hall and disarm him and say to him:
'Sir, you may be well assured that there be none but us twain
herewithin and two damsels, and the doors are barred, and
behold, here are the keys which we deliver up to you.' 'And
I command you,' saith Perceval, 'that you go straightway to my
mother, and tell her that she shall see me betimes and I may get
done, and so salute her and tell her I am sound and whole. And
what is the name of this castle?' 'Sir, it hath for name the
Key of Wales, for it is the gateway of the land.'

XI

Perceval lay the night in the castle·he had reconquered for his
mother, and the morrow, when he was armed, he departed.
These promised that they would keep the castle loyally and
would deliver it up to his mother at her will. He rode until he
came to the tents where the damsels were, and drew rein and
listened. But there was not so great joy as when the damsel
that rode like a knight and led the Car came thither with
Clamados. Great dole heard he that was made, and beating of
palms. Wherefore he bethought him what folk they might be.
Natheless he was not minded to draw back without entering.
He alighted in the midst of the tents and set down his shield
and his spear, and seeth the damsels wringing their hands and
tearing their hair, and much marvelleth he wherefore it may be.
A damsel cometh forward that had set forth from the castle
where he had slain the knight: 'Sir, to your shame and ill
adventure may you have come hither!' Perceval looketh at her

and marvelleth much of that she saith, and she crieth out:
'Lady, behold here him that hath slain the best knight of your
lineage! And you, Clamados, that are within there, he hath
slain your father and your uncle! Now shall it be seen what
you will do!' The Damsel of the Car cometh thitherward and
knoweth Perceval by the shield that he bare of sinople with a
white hart. 'Sir,' saith she, 'welcome may you be! Let who
will make dole, I will make joy of your coming!'

XII

Therewith the Damsel leadeth him into a tent and maketh
him sit on a right rich couch; afterward she maketh him
be disarmed of her two damsels and clad in a right rich
robe. Then she leadeth him to the Queen of the Tents
that was still making great dole. 'Lady,' saith the Damsel of
the Car, 'Stint your sorrow, for behold, here is the Good
Knight on whose account were the tents here pitched, and on
whose account no less have you been making this great joy right
up to this very day!' 'Ha,' saith she, 'Is this then the son of
the Widow Lady?' 'Yea, certes,' saith the Damsel. 'Ha,'
saith the Lady, 'He hath slain me the best knight of all my kin,
and the one that protected me from mine enemies.' 'Lady,'
saith the Damsel, 'This one will be better able to protect and
defend us, for the Best Knight is he of the world and the
comeliest.' The Queen taketh him by the hand and maketh him
sit beside her. 'Sir,' saith she, 'Howsoever the adventure may
have befallen, my heart biddeth me make joy of your coming.'
'Lady,' saith he, 'Gramercy! Chaos would fain have slain me
within his castle, and I defended myself to my power.' The
Queen looketh at him amidst his face, and is taken with a love
of him so passing strong and fervent that she goeth nigh to fall
upon him. 'Sir,' saith she, 'And you will grant me your love,
I will pardon you of all the death of Chaos the Red.' 'Lady,'
saith he, 'Your love am I right fain to deserve, and mine you
have.' 'Sir,' saith she, 'How may I perceive that you love
me?' 'Lady,' saith he, 'I will tell you. There is no knight
in the world that shall desire to do you a wrong, but I will help
you against him to my power.' 'Such love,' saith she, 'is the
common love that knight ought to bear to lady. Would you
do as much for another?' 'Lady,' saith he, 'It well may be,

but more readily shall a man give help in one place than in another.' The Queen would fain that Perceval should pledge himself to her further than he did, and the more she looketh at him the better he pleaseth her, and the more is she taken with him and the more desirous of his love. But Perceval never once thought of loving her or another in such wise. He was glad to look upon her, for that she was of passing great beauty, but never spake he nought to her whereby she might perceive that he loved her of inward love. But in no wise might she refrain her heart, nor withdraw her eyes, nor lose her desire. The damsels looked upon her with wonder that so soon had she forgotten her mourning.

XIII

Thereupon, behold you Clamados, that had been told that this was the knight that, as yet only squire, had slain his father and put Chaos his uncle to death. He cometh into the tent and seeth him sitting beside the Queen, that looked at him right sweetly. 'Lady,' saith he, 'Great shame do you to yourself, in that you have seated at your side your own mortal enemy and mine. Never again henceforth ought any to have affiance in your love nor in your help.' 'Clamados,' saith the Queen, 'The knight hath thrown himself upon me suddenly. Wherefore ought I do him no evil, rather behoveth me lodge him and keep his body in safety. Nought, moreover, hath he done whereof he might be adjudged of murder nor of treason.' 'Lady,' saith Clamados, 'He slew my father in the Lonely Forest without defiance, and treacherously cast a javelin at him and smote him through the body, wherefore shall I never be at ease until I have avenged him. Therefore do I appeal and pray you to do me my right, not as being of your kindred, but as stranger. For right willing am I that kinship shall avail me nought herein.' Perceval looketh at the knight and seeth that he is of right goodly complexion of body and right comely of face. 'Fair Sir,' saith he, 'As of treason I would that you hold me quit, for never toward your father nor toward other have had I never a mind to do treason, and God defend me from such shame, and grant me strength to clear myself of any blame thereof.' Clamados cometh forward to proffer his gage. 'By my head,' saith the Queen, 'Not this day shall gage be received herein. But to-morrow will come day, and counsel therewith, and then shall right be done to each.' Clamados is moved of right great wrath, but the Queen of the Tents showeth Perceval the most honour she may, whereof is Clamados right heavy, and saith that never ought any to put his trust in woman. But wrongly he blameth her therein, for she did it of the passing great love she hath for Perceval, inasmuch as well she knoweth that he is the Best Knight of the world and the comeliest. But it only irketh her the more that she may not find in him any sign of special liking toward herself neither in deed nor word, whereof is she beyond measure sorrowful. The knights and damsels lay the night in the tents until the morrow, and went to hear mass in a chapel that was in the midst of the tents.

XIV

When mass was sung, straightway behold you, a knight that cometh all armed, bearing a white shield at his neck. He alighteth in the midst of the tents and cometh before the Queen all armed, and saith : 'Lady, I plain me of a knight that is there within that hath slain my lion, and if you do me not right herein, I will harass you as much or more than I will him, and will harm you in every wise I may. Wherefore I pray and require you, for the love of Messire Gawain, whose man I am, that you do me right herein.' 'What is the knight's name?' saith the Queen. 'Lady,' saith he, 'He is called Clamados of the Shadows, and methinketh I see him yonder, for I knew him when he was squire.' 'And what is your name?' saith the Queen. 'Lady, I am called Meliot of Logres.' 'Clamados,' saith the Queen, 'Hear you what this knight saith?' 'Yea, Lady,' saith he ; 'But again I require that you do me right of the knight that slew my father and my uncle.' 'Lady,' saith Meliot, 'I would fain go. I know not toward whom the knight proffereth his gage, but him do I appeal of felony for my lion that he hath slain.' He taketh in his hand the skirt of his habergeon : 'Lady, behold here the gage I offer you.'

XV

'Clamados,' saith the Queen, 'Hear you then not that which this knight saith?' 'Lady,' saith he, 'I hear him well. Truth it is that I slew his lion, but not until after he had fallen upon me, and made the wounds whereof I have been healed here-within. But well you know that the knight who came hither last night hath done me greater wrong than have I done this other. Wherefore would I pray you that I may take vengeance of him first.' 'You hear,' saith she, 'how this knight that hath come hither all armed is fain to go back forthwith. Quit you, therefore, of him first, and then will we take thought of the other.' 'Lady, gramercy!' saith Meliot, 'and Messire Gawain will take it in right good part, for this knight hath slain my lion that defended me from all my enemies. Nor is it true that the entrance to your tent was deserted on account of my lion; and in despite of me hath he hung the head at my gate.' 'As of the lion,' saith the Queen, 'you have no quarrel against him and he slew him in defending his body, but as of the despite he did you as you say, when in nought had you done him any wrong, it shall not be that right shall be denied you in my court, and if you desire to deliver battle, no blame shall you have thereof.'

XVI

Clamados maketh arm him and mounteth on his horse, and he seemeth right hardy of his arms and valorous. He cometh right in the midst of the tent, where the ground was fair and level, and found Meliot of Logres all armed upon his horse, and a right comely knight was he and a deliver. And the ladies and damsels were round about the tilting-ground. 'Sir,' saith the Queen to Perceval, 'I will that you keep the field for these knights.' 'Lady,' saith he, 'At your pleasure.' Meliot moveth toward Clamados right swiftly and Clamados toward him, and they melled together on their shields in such sort that they pierced them and cleft the mail of their habergeons asunder with the points of their spears, and the twain are both wounded so that the blood rayeth forth of their bodies. The knights draw asunder to take their career, for their spears were broken short, and they come back the one toward the other with a great rush, and smite each other on the breast with their spears so stiffly that there is none but should have been pierced within the flesh, for the habergeons might protect them not. They hurtle against each other so strongly that knights and horses fall together to the ground all in a heap. The Queen and the damsels have great pity of the two knights, for they see that

they are both so passing sore wounded. The two knights rise
to their feet and hold their swords naked and run the one on
the other right wrathfully, with such force as they had left.
'Sir,' saith the Queen to Perceval, 'Go part these two knights
asunder that one slay not the other, for they are sore wounded.'
Perceval goeth to part them and cometh to Meliot of Logres.
'Sir,' saith he, 'Withdraw yourself back; you have done
enough.' Clamados felt that he was sore wounded in two
places, and that the wound he had in his breast was right great.
He draweth himself back. The Queen is come thither. 'Fair
nephew,' saith she, 'Are you badly wounded?' 'Yea, Lady,'
saith Clamados. 'Certes,' saith the Queen, 'This grieveth me,
but never yet saw I knight and he were desirous of fighting,
but came at some time by mischance. A man may not always
stand on all his rights.' She made him be carried on his shield
into a tent, and made search his wounds, and saw that of one
had he no need to fear, but that the other was right sore
perilous.

XVII

'Lady,' saith Clamados, 'Once more do I pray and require
you that you allow not the knight that slew my father to issue
forth from hence, save he deliver good hostage that he will
come back when I shall be healed.' 'So will I do, sith that it
is your pleasure.' The Queen cometh to the other knight that
was wounded, for that he declareth himself Messire Gawain's
man, and maketh search his wounds, and they say that he hath
not been hurt so sore as is Clamados. She commandeth them
to tend him and wait upon him right well-willingly, 'Sir,'
saith she to Perceval, 'Behoveth you abide here until such time
as my nephew be heal, for you know well that whereof he
plaineth against you, nor would I that you should depart hence
without clearing you of the blame.' 'Lady, no wish have I to
depart without your leave, but rather shall I be ready to clear
myself of blame whensoever and wheresoever time and place
may be. But herewithin may I make not so long sojourn.
Natheless to this will I pledge my word, that I will return
thither within a term of fifteen days from the time he shall be
whole.' 'Sir,' saith the Damsel of the Car, 'I will remain here
in hostage for you.' 'But do you pray him,' saith the Queen,
'that he remain herewithin with us.'

XVIII

'Lady,' saith Perceval, 'I may not, for I left Lancelot wounded right sore in my uncle's hermitage.' 'Sir,' saith the Queen, 'I would fain that remaining here might have pleased you as well as it would me.' 'Lady,' saith he, 'None ought it to displease to be with you, but every man behoveth keep his word as well as he may, and none ought to lie to so good a knight as he.' 'You promise me, then,' saith the Queen, 'that you will return hither the soonest you may, or at the least, within the term appointed after you shall have learnt that Clamados is healed, to defend you of the treason that he layeth upon you?' 'Lady,' saith he, 'And if he die shall I be quit?' 'Yea, truly, Sir, and so be that you have no will to come for love of me. For right well should I love your coming.' 'Lady,' saith he, 'Never shall be the day my services shall fail you, so I be in place, and you in need thereof.' He taketh leave and departeth, armed. The Damsel of the Car commendeth him to God, and Perceval departeth full speed and rideth so far on his journeys that he cometh to his uncle's hermitage and entereth in, thinking to find Lancelot. But his uncle telleth him that he hath departed all sound and all heal of his wound, as of all other malady, as him thinketh.

BRANCH X

ANOTHER branch of the Graal again beginneth in the name of the Father, and of the Son, and of the Holy Ghost.

TITLE I

And the story is here silent of Perceval, and saith that Lancelot goeth his way and rideth by a forest until he findeth a castle amidst his way at the head of a launde, and seeth at the gateway of the castle an old knight and two damsels sitting on a bridge. Thitherward goeth he, and the knight and damsels rise up to meet him, and Lancelot alighteth. 'Sir,' saith the Vavasour, 'Welcome may you be.' The damsels make great joy of him and lead him into the castle. 'Sir,' saith the Vavasour, 'Sore need had we of your coming.' He maketh him go up into the hall above and be disarmed of his arms. 'Sir,' saith the Vavasour, 'Now may you see great pity of these two damsels that are my daughters. A certain man would reave them of this castle for that no aid nor succour have they save of me alone. And little enough can I do, for I am old and feeble, and my kin also are of no avail, insomuch that hitherto have I been able to find no knight that durst defend me from the knight that is fain to reave this castle from me. And you seem to be of so great valiance that you will defend me well herein to-morrow, for the truce cometh to an end to-night.' 'How?' saith Lancelot, 'I have but scarce come in hither to lodge, and you desire me so soon already to engage myself in battle?' 'Sir,' saith the Vavasour, 'Herein may it well be proven whether there be within you as much valour as there seemeth from without to be. For, and you make good the claim of these two damsels that are my daughters to the fiefs that are of right their own, you will win thereby the love of God as well as praise of the world.' They fall at his feet weeping, and pray him of mercy that they may not be disherited. And he raiseth them forthwith, as one that hath great pity thereof. 'Damsels,' saith he, 'I will aid you to my power. But I would fain that the term be not long.' 'Sir,' say they, 'To-morrow is the day, and to-morrow, so we have no knight to meet him that challengeth this castle, we shall have lost it. And our father is an old knight, and hath no longer lustihood nor force whereby he might defend it for us, and all of our lineage are fallen and decayed. This hatred hath fallen on us on account of Messire Gawain, whom we har-boured.' Lancelot lay there the night within the castle and was right well lodged and worshipfully entreated. And on the morrow he armed himself when he had heard mass, and leant at the windows of the hall and seeth the gate shut and barred, and heareth a horn sound without the gate three times right loud. 'Sir,' saith the Vavasour, 'The knight is come, and thinketh that within here is no defence.' 'By my head,' saith Lancelot, 'but there is, please God!' The knight bloweth another blast of his horn. 'Hearken, Sir,' saith the Vavasour, 'It is nigh noon, and he thinketh him that none will issue hence to meet him.'

II

Lancelot cometh down below and findeth his horse saddled and is mounted as soon. The damsels are at his stirrup, and pray him for God's sake remember to defend the honour that is theirs of the castle, for, save only he so doth, they must flee like beggars into other lands. Thereupon the Knight soundeth his horn again. Lancelot, when he heareth the blast, hath no mind to abide longer, and forthwith issueth out of the castle all armed, lance in hand and shield at his neck. He seeth the knight at the head of the bridge, all armed under a tree. Thitherward cometh Lancelot full speed. The knight seeth him coming, and crieth to him. 'Sir Knight,' saith he, 'What demand you? Come you hither to do me evil?' 'Yea,' saith Lancelot, 'for that evil are you fain to do to this castle; where-fore on behalf of the Vavasour and his daughters do I defy you.' He moveth against the knight and smiteth him on the shield with his spear and the knight him. But Lancelot pierceth his shield for him with his sword, and smiteth him so stiffly that he pinneth his arm to his side, and hurtleth against him so passing stoutly that he thrusteth him to the ground, him and his horse, and runneth over him, sword drawn. 'Ha,' saith the knight to Lancelot, 'Withdraw a little from over me, and slay me not, and tell me your name, of your mercy.' 'What have you to do with my name?' saith Lancelot. 'Sir,' saith he, 'Gladly would I know it, for a right good knight seem you to be, and so have I well proven in the first encounter.' 'Sir,' saith he, 'I am called Lancelot of the Lake. And what is your name?' 'Sir,' saith he, 'I am called Marin of the castle of Gomeret. So am I father of Meliot of Logres. I pray you, by that you most love in the world, that you slay me not.' 'So will I do,' saith Lancelot, 'and you renounce not your feud against this castle.' 'By my faith,' saith the knight, 'Thus do I renounce it, and I pledge myself that thenceforth for ever shall it have no disturbance of me.' 'Your pledge,' saith Lancelot, 'will I not accept save you come in thither.' 'Sir,' saith the knight, 'You have sore wounded me in such sort that I cannot mount but with right great pain.' Lancelot helpeth him until he was mounted again on his horse, and leadeth him into the castle with him, and maketh him present his sword to the Vavasour and his daughters, and yield up his shield and his arms, and afterward swear upon hallows that never again will he make war upon them. Lancelot thereupon receiveth his pledge to forego all claim to the castle and Marin turneth him back to Gomeret. The Vavasour and his daughters abide in great joy.

III

The story saith that Lancelot went his way by strange lands and by forests to seek adventure, and rode until he found a plain land lying without a city that seemed to be of right great lordship. As he was riding by the plain land, he looketh toward the forest and seeth the plain fair and wide and the land right level. He rideth all the plain, and looketh toward the city and seeth great plenty of folk issuing forth thereof. And with them was there much noise of bag-pipes and flutes and viols and many instruments of music, and they came along the way wherein was Lancelot riding. When the foremost came up to him, they halted and redoubled their joy. 'Sir,' say they, 'Welcome may you be!' 'Lords,' saith Lancelot, 'Whom come ye to meet with such joy?' 'Sir,' say they, 'They that come behind there will tell you clearly that whereof we are in need.'

IV

Thereupon behold you the provosts and the lords of the city, and they come over against Lancelot. 'Sir,' say they, 'All this joy is made along of you, and all these instruments of music are moved to joy and sound of gladness for your coming.' 'But wherefore for me,' saith Lancelot. 'That shall you know well betimes,' say they. 'This city began to burn and to melt in one of the houses from the very same hour that our king was dead, nor might the fire be quenched, nor never will be quenched until such time as we have a king that shall be lord of the city and of the honour thereunto belonging, and on New Year's Day behoveth him to be crowned in the midst of the fire, and then shall the fire be quenched, for otherwise may it never be put out nor extinguished. Wherefore have we come to meet you to give you the royalty, for we have been told that you are a good knight.' 'Lords,' saith Lancelot, 'Of such a kingdom have I no need, and God defend me from it.' 'Sir,' they say, 'You may not be defended thereof, for you come into this land at hazard, and great grief would it be that so good land as you see this is were burnt and melted away by the default of one single man, and the lordship is right great, and this will be right great worship to yourself, that on New Year's Day you should be crowned in the fire and thus save this city and this great people, and thereof shall you have great praise.'

V

Much marvelleth Lancelot of this that they say. They come round about him on all sides and lead him into the city. The ladies and damsels are mounted to the windows of the great houses and make great joy, and say the one to another, 'Look at the new king here that they are leading in. Now will he quench the fire on New Year's Day.' 'Lord!' say the most part, 'What great pity is it of so comely a knight that he shall end on such-wise!' 'Be still!' say the others. 'Rather should there be great joy that so fair city as is this should be saved by his death, for prayer will be made throughout all the kingdom for his soul for ever!' Therewith they lead him to the palace with right great joy and say that they will crown him. Lancelot found the palace all strown with rushes and hung about with curtains of rich cloths of silk, and the lords of the city all apparelled to do him homage. But he refuseth right stoutly, and saith that their king nor their lord will he never be in no such sort. Thereupon behold you a dwarf that entereth into the city, leading one of the fairest dames that be in any kingdom, and asketh whereof this joy and this murmuring may be. They tell him they are fain to make the knight king, but that he is not minded to allow them, and they tell him the whole manner of the fire.

VI

The dwarf and the damsel are alighted, then they mount up to the palace. The dwarf calleth the provosts of the city and the greater lords. 'Lords,' saith he, 'Sith that this knight is not willing to be king, I will be so willingly, and I will govern the city at your pleasure and do whatsoever you have devised to do.' 'In faith, sith that the knight refuseth this honour and you desire to have it, willingly will we grant it you, and he may go his way and his road, for herein do we declare him wholly quit.' Therewithal they set the crown on the dwarf's head, and Lancelot maketh great joy thereof. He taketh his leave, and they commend him to God, and so remounteth he on his horse and goeth his way through the midst of the city all armed. The dames and damsels say that he would not be king for that he had no mind to die so soon. When he came forth of the city right well pleased was he. He entereth a great forest and rideth on till daylight began to fail, and seeth before him a hermitage newly stablished, for the house and the chapel were all builded new. He cometh thitherward and alighteth to lodge. The hermit, that was young without beard or other hair on his face, issued from his chapel. 'Sir,' saith he to Lancelot, 'You are he that is welcome.' 'And you, sir, good adventure to you,' saith Lancelot. 'Never have I seen hermit so young as you.' 'Sir, of this only do I repent me, that I came not hither ere now.'

VII

Therewith he maketh his horse be stabled, and leadeth him into his hermitage, and so maketh disarm him and setteth him at ease as much as he may. 'Sir,' saith the hermit, 'Can you tell me any tidings of a knight that hath lain sick of a long time in the house of a hermit?' 'Sir,' saith Lancelot, 'It is no long time agone sithence I saw him in the house of the good King Hermit, that hath tended me and healed me right sweetly of the wounds that the knight gave me.' 'And is the knight healed, then?' saith the hermit. 'Yea, Sir,' saith Lancelot, 'Whereof is right great joy. And wherefore do you ask me?' 'Well ought I to ask it,' saith the hermit, 'For my father is King Pelles, and his mother is my father's own sister.' 'Ha, Sir, then is the King Hermit your father?' 'Yea, Sir, certes.' 'Thereof do I love you the better,' saith Lancelot, 'For never found I any man that hath done me so much of love as hath he. And what, Sir, is your name?' 'Sir,' saith he, 'My name is Joseus, and yours, what?' 'Sir,' saith he, 'I am called Lancelot of the Lake.' 'Sir,' saith the hermit, 'Right close are we akin, I and you.' 'By my head,' saith Lancelot, 'Hereof am I right glad at heart.' Lancelot looketh and seeth in the hermit's house shield and spear, javelins and habergeon. 'Sir,' saith Lancelot, 'What do you with these arms?' 'Sir,' saith he, 'This forest is right lonely, and this hermitage is far from any folk, and none are there here-within save me and my squire. So, when robbers come hither, we defend ourselves therewith.' 'But hermits, methought, never assaulted nor wounded nor slew?' 'Sir,' saith the hermit, 'God forbid I should wound any man or slay!' 'And how, then, do you defend yourselves?' saith Lancelot. 'Sir, I will tell you thereof. When robbers come to us, we arm our-selves accordingly. If I may catch hold of any in my hands, he cannot escape me. Our squire is so well-grown and hardy that he slayeth him forthwith or handleth him in such sort that he may never help himself after.' 'By my head,' saith Lancelot, 'Were you not hermit, you would be valiant throughout.' 'By my head,' saith the squire. 'You say true, for methinketh there is none so strong nor so hardy as he in all the kingdom of Logres.' The hermit lodged Lancelot the night the best he could.

VIII

When as they were in their first sleep, come four robber-knights of the forest that knew how a knight was lodged there-within, and had coveted his horse and his arms. The hermit that was in his chapel saw them first, and awoke his squire

and made him bring his arms all secretly; then he made his
squire arm. 'Sir,' saith the squire, 'Shall I waken the knight?'
'In nowise,' saith the hermit, 'until such time as we shall know
wherefore.' He maketh open the door of the chapel and taketh
a great coil of rope, and they issue forth, he and his squire, and
they perceived the robbers in the stable where Lancelot's horse
was. The hermit crieth out: the squire cometh forward and
thereupon beareth one to the ground with his spear. The
hermit seizeth him and bindeth him to a tree so strait that he
may not move. The other three think to defend them and to
rescue their fellow. Lancelot leapeth up all startled when he
heareth the noise and armeth himself as quickly as he may, albeit
not so quickly but that or ever he come, the hermit hath taken
the other three and bound them with the fourth. But of them
were some that were wounded right sore. 'Sir,' saith the
hermit to Lancelot, 'It grieveth me that you have been
awakened.' 'Rather,' saith Lancelot, 'have you done me great
wrong for that you ought to have awakened me sooner.' 'Sir,'
saith the hermit, 'We have assaults such as this often enough.'
The four robbers cry mercy of Lancelot that he will pray the
hermit to have pity upon them. And Lancelot saith God help
not him that shall have pity on thieves! As soon as it was
daylight, Lancelot and the squire led them into the forest, their
hands all tied behind their backs, and have hanged them in a
waste place far away from the hermitage. Lancelot cometh
back again and taketh leave of Joseus the young hermit, and
saith it is great loss to the world that he is not knight. 'Sir,'
saith the squire, 'To me is it great joy, for many a man should
suffer thereby.' Lancelot is mounted, and Joseus commendeth
him to God, praying him much that he salute his father and cousin
on his behalf, and Messire Gawain likewise that he met in the
forest what time he came all weeping to the hermitage.

IX

Lancelot hath set him forth again upon his way, and rideth
by the high forests and findeth holds and hermitages enough,
but the story maketh not remembrance of all the hostels wherein
he harboured him. So far hath he ridden that he is come forth
of the forest and findeth a right fair meadow-land all loaded
with flowers, and a river ran in the midst thereof that was right

fair and broad, and there was forest upon the one side and the
other, and the meadow lands were wide and far betwixt the
river and the forest. Lancelot looketh on the river before him
and seeth a man rowing a great boat, and seeth within the boat
two knights, white and bald, and a damsel, as it seemed him,
that held in her lap the head of a knight that lay upon a mattress
of straw and was covered with a coverlid of marten's fur, and
another damsel sate at his feet. There was a knight within in
the midst of the boat that was fishing with an angle, the rod
whereof seemeth of gold, and right great fish he took. A little
cock-boat followed the boat, wherein he set the fish he took.
Lancelot cometh anigh the bank the swiftest he may, and so
saluteth the knights and damsels, and they return his salute
right sweetly. 'Lords,' saith Lancelot, 'is there no castle nigh
at hand nor no harbour?' 'Yea, Sir,' say they, 'Beyond that
mountain, right fair and rich, and this river runneth thither all
round about it.' 'Lords, whose castle is it?' 'Sir,' say they,
'It is King Fisherman's, and the good knights lodge there when
he is in this country; but such knights have been harboured
there as that the lord of the land hath had good right to plain
him thereof.' The knights go rowing along the river, and
Lancelot rideth until he cometh to the foot of the mountain and
findeth a hermitage beside a spring, and bethinketh him, since
it behoveth him to go to so high a hostel and so rich, where the
Holy Graal appeareth, he will confess him to the good man.
He alighteth and confesseth to the good man, and rehearseth
all his sins, and saith that of all thereof doth he repent him save
only one, and the hermit asketh him what it is whereof he is
unwilling to repent. 'Sir,' saith Lancelot, 'It seemeth to me the
fairest sin and the sweetest that ever I committed.' 'Fair Sir,'
saith the hermit, 'Sin is sweet to do, but right bitter be the
wages thereof; neither is there any sin that is fair nor seemly,
albeit there be some sins more dreadfuller than other.' 'Sir,'
saith Lancelot, 'This sin will I reveal to you of my lips, but of
my heart may I never repent me thereof. I love my Lady, which
is the Queen, more than aught else that liveth, and albeit one
of the best kings on live hath her to wife. The affection
seemeth me so good and so high that I cannot let go thereof,
for, so rooted is it in my heart that thence may it nevermore
depart, and the best knighthood that is in me cometh to me
only of her affection.' 'Alas!' saith the hermit, 'Sinner of

mortal sin, what is this that you have spoken? Never may no
knighthood come of such wantonness that shall not cost you
right dear! A traitor are you toward our earthly lord, and a
murderer toward Our Saviour. Of the seven deadly sins, you
are labouring under the one whereof the delights are the falsest
of any, wherefore dearly shall you aby thereof, save you repent
you forthwith.' 'Sir,' saith Lancelot, 'Never the more do I
desire to cast it from me.' 'As much,' saith the hermit, 'is
that as to say that you ought long since to have cast it from you
and renounced it. For so long as you maintain it, so long are
you an enemy of the Saviour!' 'Ha, Sir,' saith Lancelot, 'She
hath in her such beauty and worth and wisdom and courtesy and
nobleness that never ought she to be forgotten of any that hath
loved her!'

X

'The more of beauty and worth she hath in her,' saith the
hermit, 'so much the more blame hath she of that she doeth,
and you likewise. For of that which is of little worth is the loss
not so great as of that which is much worth. And this is a
Queen, blessed and anointed, that was thus, therefore, in her
beginning vowed to God; yet now is she given over to the
Devil of her love for you, and you of your love for her. Fair,
sweet my friend,' saith the hermit, 'Let go this folly, which is
so cruel, that you have taken in hand, and be repentant of these
sins! So every day will I pray to the Saviour for you, that so
truly as He pardoned His death to him that smote Him with a
lance in His side, so may He pardon you of this sin that you
have maintained, and that so you be repentant and truly confessed
thereof, I may take the penance due thereunto upon myself!'
'Sir,' saith Lancelot, 'I thank you much, but I am not
minded to renounce it, nor have I no wish to speak aught wherewith my heart accordeth not. I am willing enough to do penance
as great as is enjoined of this sin, but my lady the Queen will I
serve so long as it may be her pleasure, and I may have her
good will. So dearly do I love her that I wish not even that
any will should come to me to renounce her love, and God is so
sweet and so full of right merciful mildness, as good men bear
witness, that He will have pity upon us, for never no treason
have I done toward her, nor she toward me.' 'Ha, fair sweet

friend,' saith the hermit, 'Nought may you avail you of whatsoever I may say, wherefore God grant her such will and you
also, that you may be able to do the will of Our Saviour.   But
so much am I fain to tell you, that and if you shall lie in the
hostel of King Fisherman, yet never may you behold the Graal
for the mortal sin that lieth at your heart.'   'May our Lord
God,' saith Lancelot, 'counsel me therein at His pleasure and at
His will!'   'So may He do!' saith the hermit, 'For of a truth
you may know thereof am I right fain.'

XI

Lancelot taketh leave of the hermit, and is mounted forthwith
and departeth from the hermitage.   And evening draweth on,
and he seeth that it is time to lodge him.   And he espieth
before him the castle of the rich King Fisherman.   He seeth
the bridges, broad and long, but they seem not to him the same
as they had seemed to Messire Gawain.   He beholdeth the rich
entrance of the gateway there where Our Lord God was figured
as He was set upon the rood, and seeth two lions that guard the
entrance of the gate.   Lancelot thinketh that sith Messire
Gawain had passed through amidst the lions, he would do likewise.   He goeth toward the gateway, and the lions that were
unchained prick up their ears and look at him.   Howbeit
Lancelot goeth his way between them without heeding them,
and neither of them was fain to do him any hurt.   He alighteth
before the master-palace, and mounteth upward all armed. Two
other knights come to meet him and receive him with right great
joy, then they make him be seated on a couch in the midst of
the hall and be disarmed of two servants.   Two damsels bring
him a right rich robe and make him be apparelled therewithal.
Lancelot beholdeth the richness of the hall and seeth nought
figured there save images of saints, men or women, and he seeth
the hall hung about with cloths of silk in many places.   The
knights lead him before King Fisherman in a chamber where he
lay right richly.   He findeth the King, that lieth on a bed so
rich and so fair apparelled as never was seen a better, and one
damsel was at his head and another at his feet. Lancelot
saluteth him right nobly, and the King answereth him full fairly
as one that is a right worshipful man.   And such a brightness
of light was there in the chamber as that it seemed the sun were

beaming on all sides, and albeit the night was dark, no candles, so far as Lancelot might espy, were lighted therewithin. 'Sir,' saith King Fisherman, 'Can you tell me tidings of my sister's son, that was son of Alain li Gros of the Valleys of Camelot, whom they call Perceval?' 'Sir,' saith Lancelot, 'I saw him not long time sithence in the house of King Hermit, his uncle.' 'Sir,' saith the King, 'They tell me he is a right good knight?' 'Sir,' saith Lancelot, ' He is the best knight of the world. I myself have felt the goodness of his knighthood and his valour, for right sorely did he wound me or ever I knew him or he me.' 'And what is your name?' saith the King. 'Sir, I am called Lancelot of the Lake, King Ban's son of Benoic.' 'Ha,' saith the King, 'You are nigh of our lineage, you ought to be good knight of right, and so are you as I have heard witness, Lancelot,' saith the King. 'Behold there the chapel where the most Holy Graal taketh his rest, that appeared to two knights that have been herewithin. I know not what was the name of the first, but never saw I any so gentle and quiet, nor had better likelihood to be good knight. It was through him that I have fallen into languishment. The second was Messire Gawain.' 'Sir,' saith Lancelot, 'The first was Perceval your nephew.' 'Ha!' saith King Fisherman, 'Take heed that you speak true!' 'Sir,' saith Lancelot, 'I ought to know him well!' 'Ha, God!' saith the King, 'Wherefore then did I know him not? Through him have I fallen into this languishment, and had I only known then that it was he, should I now be all whole of my limbs and of my body, and right instantly do I pray you, when you shall see him, that he come to see me or ever I die, and that he be fain to succour and help his mother, whose men have been slain, and whose land hath been reaved in such sort that never may she have it again save by him alone. And his sister hath gone in quest of him throughout all kingdoms.' 'Sir,' saith Lancelot, 'This will I tell him gladly, if ever I may find him in any place, but it is great adventure of finding him, for oft-times will he change his cognizance in divers fashion and conceal his name in many places.'

XII

King Fisherman is right joyous of the tidings he hath heard of his nephew, wherefore he maketh Lancelot be honoured greatly. The knights seat them in the hall at a table of ivory at meat, and the King remaineth in his chamber. When they had washen, the table was dight of rich sets of vessels of gold and silver, and they were served of rich meats of venison of hart and wild boar. But the story witnesseth that the Graal appeared not at this feast. It held not aloof for that Lancelot was not one of the three knights of the world of the most renown and mightiest valour, but for his great sin as touching the Queen, whom he loved without repenting him thereof, for of nought did he think so much as of her, nor never might he remove his heart therefrom. When they had eaten they rose from the tables. Two damsels waited on Lancelot at his going to bed, and he lay on a right rich couch, nor were they willing to depart until such time as he was asleep. He rose on the morrow as soon as he saw the day, and went to hear mass. Then he took leave of King Fisherman and the knights and damsels, and issued forth of the castle between the two lions, and prayeth God that He allow him to see the Queen again betimes, for this is his most desire. He rideth until he hath left the castle far behind and entereth the forest, and is in right great desire to see Perceval, but the tidings of him were right far away. He looketh before him in the forest and seeth come right amidst the launde a knight, and a damsel clad in the richest robe of gold and silk that ever he had seen tofore.

XIII

The damsel came weeping by the side of the knight and prayed him oftentimes that he would have mercy upon her. The knight is still and holdeth his peace, and saith never a word. 'Ha, Sir,' saith the damsel to Lancelot, 'Be pleased to beseech this knight on my behalf.' 'In what manner?' saith Lancelot. 'Sir,' saith she, 'I will tell you. He hath shown me semblance of love for more than a year, and had me in covenant that he would take me to wife, and I apparelled myself in the richest garments that I had to come to him. But my father is of greater power and riches than is he, and therefore was not willing to allow the marriage. Wherefore come I with him in this manner, for I love him better than ever another knight beside. Now will he do nought of that he had me in covenant to do, for he loveth another, better, methinketh, than me. And this hath he done, as I surmise, to do shame to my

friends and to me.' Lancelot seeth the damsel of right great
beauty and weeping tenderly, whereof hath he passing great
pity. 'Hold, Sir!' saith Lancelot to the knight, 'This shall
you not do! You shall not do such shame to so fair a damsel
as that you shall fail to keep covenant with her. For not a
knight is there in the kingdom of Logres nor in that of Wales
but ought to be right well pleased to have so fair a damsel to
wife, and I pray and require that you do to the damsel that
whereof you held her in covenant. This will be a right worshipful deed, and I pray and beseech that you do it, and thereof
shall I be much beholden unto you.' 'Sir,' saith the knight,
'I have no will thereunto, nor for no man will I do it, for ill
would it beseem me.' 'By my head, then,' saith Lancelot, 'the
basest knight are you that ever have I seen, nor ought dame nor
damsel ever hereafter put trust in you, sith that you are minded
to put such disgrace upon this lady.' 'Sir,' saith the knight,
'A worthier lover have I than this, and one that I more value;
wherefore as touching this damsel will I do nought more than I
have said.' 'And whither, then, mean you to take her?' saith
Lancelot. 'I mean to take her to a hold of mine own that is in
this forest, and to give her in charge to a dwarf of mine that
looketh after my house, and I will marry her to some knight or
some other man.' 'Now never God help me,' saith Lancelot,
'but this is foul churlishness you tell me, and, so you do not
her will, it shall betide you ill of me myself, and, had you been
armed as I am, you should have felt my first onset already.'
'Ha,' saith the damsel to Lancelot, 'Be not so ready to do him
any hurt, for nought love I so well as I love his body, whatsoever he do unto me. But for God's sake pray him that he do
me the honour he hath promised me.' 'Willingly,' saith
Lancelot. 'Sir Knight, will you do this whereof you had the
damsel in covenant?' 'Sir,' saith the knight, 'I have told you
plainly that I will not.' 'By my head,' saith Lancelot, 'you
shall do it, or otherwise sentence of death hath passed upon
you, and this not so much for the sake of the damsel only, but
for the churlishness that hath taken possession of you, that it
be not a reproach to other knights. For promise that knight
maketh to dame or damsel behoveth him to keep. And you, as
you tell me, are knight, and no knight ought to do churlishly
to his knowledge, and this churlishness is so far greater than
another, that for no prayer that the damsel may make will I

suffer that it shall be done, but that if you do not that whereof
you held her in covenant, I shall slay you, for that I will not
have this churlishness made a reproach unto other knights.'
He draweth his sword and would have come toward him, when
the knight cometh over against him and saith to him : 'Slay me
not.   Tell me rather what you would have me do?'   'I
would,' saith he, 'that you take the damsel to wife without
denial.'   'Sir,' saith he, 'It pleaseth me better to take her than
to die.   Sir, I will do your will.'   'I thank you much therefor,'
saith Lancelot.   'Damsel, is this your pleasure also?'   'Yea,
Sir, but, so please you, take not your departure from us until
such time as he shall have done that which you tell him.'   'I will
well that so it be,' saith Lancelot, 'for love of you.'   They ride
together right through the forest, until they came to a chapel at
a hermitage, and the hermit wedded them and made much joy
thereof.   When it cometh to after-mass, Lancelot would fain
depart, but the damsel prayeth him right sweetly that he should
come right to her father's house to witness that the knight had
wedded her.

XIV

'Sir,' saith she, 'My father's hold is not far away.'   'Lady,'
saith Lancelot, 'Willingly will I go sith that you beseech me
thereof.'   They ride so long right amidst the forest, that
presently they come to the castle of the Vavasour, that was
sitting on the bridge of his castle, right sorrowful and troubled
because of his daughter.   Lancelot is gone on before and
alighteth.   The Vavasour riseth up to meet him, and Lancelot
recounteth unto him how his daughter hath been wedded, and
that he hath been at the wedding.   Thereof the Vavasour
maketh right great joy.   Therewithal, behold you, the knight
and the Vavasour's daughter that are straightway alighted, and
the Vavasour thanketh Lancelot much of the honour he hath
done his daughter.   Therewith he departeth from the castle and
rideth amidst the forest the day long, and meeteth a damsel and
a dwarf that came a great gallop.   'Sir,' saith the damsel to
Lancelot, 'From whence come you?'   'Damsel,' saith he, 'I
come from the Vavasour's castle that is in this forest.'   'Did
you meet,' saith she, 'a knight and a damsel on your way?'
'Yea,' saith Lancelot, 'He hath wedded her.'   'Say you true?'
saith she.   'I tell you true,' saith Lancelot, 'But had I not been

there, he would not have wedded her.' 'Shame and ill adventure may you have thereof, for you have reft me of the thing in the world that most I loved. And know you well of a truth that joy of him shall she never have, and if the knight had been armed as are you, never would he have done your will, but his own. And this is not the first harm you have done me; you and Messire Gawain between you have slain my uncle and my two cousins-german in the forest, whom behoved me bury in the chapel where you were, there where my dwarf that you see here was making the graves in the burial-ground.' 'Damsel,' saith Lancelot, 'True it is that I was there, but I departed from the grave-yard, honour safe.' 'True,' saith the dwarf, 'For the knights that were there were craven, and failed.' 'Fair friend,' saith Lancelot, 'Rather would I they should be coward toward me than hardy.' 'Lancelot,' saith the damsel, 'Much outrage have you done, for you slew the Knight of the Waste House, there whither the brachet led Messire Gawain, but had he there been known, he would not have departed so soon, for he was scarce better loved than you, and God grant you may find a knight that may abate the outrages that are in your heart and in his; for great rejoicing would there be thereof, for many a good knight have you slain, and I myself will bring about trouble for you, so quickly as I may.'

XV

Thereupon the dwarf smiteth the mule with his whip, and she departeth. Lancelot would answer none of her reviling, wherefore he departed forthwith, and rideth so long on his journeys that he is come back to the house of the good King Hermit, that maketh right great joy of him. And he telleth him that he hath been unto the house of King Fisherman, his brother that lieth in languishment, and telleth him also how he hath been honoured in his hostel, and of the salutations that he sent him. King Hermit is right joyous thereof, and asketh him of his nephew, and he telleth him he hath seen him not since he departed thence. King Hermit asketh him whether he hath seen the Graal, and he telleth him he hath seen it not at all. 'I know well,' saith the King, 'wherefore this was so. And you had had the like desire to see the Graal that you have to see the Queen, the Graal would you have seen.' 'Sir,' saith Lancelot,

'The Queen do I desire to see for the sake of her good intent, her wisdom, courtesy and worth, and so ought every knight to do. For in herself hath she all honourable conditions that a lady may have.' 'God grant you good issue therein,' saith King Hermit, 'and that you do nought whereof He may visit you with His wrath at the Day of Judgment.' Lancelot lay the night in the hermitage, and on the morrow departed thence and took leave when he had heard mass, and cometh back as straight as he may to Pannenoisance on the sea of Wales, where were the King and Queen with great plenty of knights and barons.

BRANCH XI

TITLE I

THIS High History witnesseth whereof this account cometh, and saith that Perceval is in the kingdom of Logres, and came great pace toward the land of the Queen of the Tents to release the Damsel of the Car, that he had left in hostage on account of Clamados, that had put upon him the treason whereof behoved him to defend himself. But, or ever he entered into the land of the Queen of the Tents, he met the Damsel of the Car that was coming thence. She made right great joy of him, and told him that Clamados was dead of the wound that Meliot of Logres had dealt him, and that Meliot of Logres was heal. 'Sir,' saith she, 'The tents and the awnings are taken down, and the Queen hath withdrawn herself to the castle with her maidens, and by my coming back from thence may you well know that you are altogether quit. Wherefore I tell you that your sister goeth in quest of you, and that never had your mother so sore need of help as now she hath, nor never again shall your sister have joy at heart until such time as she shall have found you. She goeth seeking for you by all the kingdoms and strange countries in sore mis-ease, nor may she find any to tell her tidings of you.' Therewith Perceval departeth from the Damsel, without saying more, and rideth until he cometh into the kingdom of Wales to a castle that is seated above the sea upon a high rock, and it was called the Castle of Tallages. He seeth a knight issue from the castle and asketh whose hold it is, and he telleth him that it belonged to the Queen of the Maidens. He entereth into the first baily of the castle, and alighteth at the mounting-stage and setteth down his shield and his spear, and looketh toward the steps whereby one goeth up to the higher hall, and seeth upon them row upon row of knights and damsels. He cometh thitherward, but never a knight nor dame was there that gave him greeting of any kind. So he saluted them at large. He went his way right amidst them toward the door of the great hall, which he findeth shut, and rattled the ring so loud that it made the whole hall resound thereof. A knight cometh to open it and he entereth in. 'Sir Knight, welcome may you be!' 'Good adventure may you have!' saith Perceval. He lowereth his ventail and taketh off his helm. The knight leadeth him to the Queen's chamber, and she riseth to meet him, and maketh great joy of him, and maketh him sit beside her all armed.

II

With that, cometh a damsel and kneeleth before the Queen and saith : 'Lady, behold here the knight that was first at the Graal. I saw him in the court of the Queen of the Tents, there where he was appeached of treason and murder.' 'Now haste,' saith the Queen to the knight, 'Let sound the ivory horn upon the castle.' The knights and damsels that were sitting on the steps leapt up, and make right great joy, and the other knights likewise. They say that now they know well that they have done their penance. Thereupon they enter into the hall, and the Lady issueth from her chamber and taketh Perceval by the hand and goeth to meet them. 'Behold here,' saith she, 'the knight through whom you have had the pain and travail, and by whom you are now released therefrom!' 'Ha!' say the knights and dames, 'Welcome may he be!' 'By my head,' saith the Queen, 'so is he, for he is the knight of the world that I had most desire to see.' She maketh disarm him, and bring the rich robe of cloth of silk to apparel him. 'Sir,' saith the Queen, 'Four knights and three damsels have been under the steps at the entrance of the hall ever since such time as you were at the hostel of King Fisherman, there where you forgot to ask whereof the Graal might serve, nor never since have they had none other house nor hold wherein to eat nor to drink nor to lie, nor never since have they had no heart to make joy, nor would not now and you had not come hither. Wherefore ought you not to marvel that they make joy of your coming. Howbeit, on the other hand, sore need have we in this castle of your coming, for a knight warreth upon me that is brother of King Fisherman, and his name is the King of Castle Mortal.' 'Lady,' saith he,

'He is my uncle, albeit I knew it not of a long time, nor of the good King Fisherman either, and the good King Hermit is my uncle also. But I tell you of a very truth, the King of Castle Mortal is the most fell and cruel that liveth, wherefore ought none to love him for the felony that is in him, for he hath begun to war upon King Fisherman my uncle, and challengeth him his castle, and would fain have the Lance and the Graal.' 'Sir,' saith the Queen, 'In like sort challengeth he my castle of me for that I am in aid of King Fisherman, and every week cometh he to an island that is in this sea, and oft-times cometh plundering before this castle and hath slain many of my knights and damsels, whereof God grant us vengeance upon him.' She taketh Perceval by the hand and leadeth him to the windows of the hall that were nighest the sea. 'Sir,' saith she, 'Now may you see the island, there, whereunto your uncle cometh in a galley, and in this island sojourneth he until he hath seen where to aim his blow and laid his plans. And here below, see, are my gallies that defend us thereof.'

III

Perceval, as the history telleth, was much honoured at the castle of the Queen of the Maidens, that was right passing fair. The Queen loved him of a passing great love, but well she knew that she should never have her desire, nor any dame nor damsel that might set her intent thereon, for chaste was he and in chastity was fain to die. So long was he at the castle as that he heard tell his uncle was arrived at the island whither he wont to come. Perceval maketh arm him forthwith and entereth into a galley below the hall, and maketh him be rowed toward his uncle, that much marvelleth when he seeth him coming, for never aforetime durst no knight issue out alone from this castle to meet him, nor to come there where he was, body to body. But had he known that it was Perceval, he would not have marvelled. Thereupon the galley taketh the ground and Perceval is issued forth. The Queen and the knights and her maidens are come to the windows of the castle to behold the bearing of the nephew and the uncle. The Queen would have sent over some of her knights with him, but Perceval would not. The King of Castle Mortal was tall and strong and hardy. He seeth his nephew come all armed, but knoweth him not. But Perceval knew him well, and kept his sword drawn and his shield on his arm, and sought out his uncle with right passing wrathfulness, and dealeth him a heavy buffet above upon his helm that he maketh him stoop withal.   Howbeit, the King spareth him not, but smiteth him so passing stoutly that he had his helm all dinted in thereby.   But Perceval attacketh him again, thinking to strike him above on the head, but the King swerveth aside and the blow falleth on the shield and cleaveth it right down as far as the boss.   The King of Castle Mortal draweth him backward and hath great shame within himself for that Perceval should thus fettle him, for he searcheth him with his sword in every part, and dealeth him great buffets in such sort that, and his habergeon had not been so strong and tough, he would have wounded him in many places.

IV

The King himself giveth him blows so heavy that the Queen and all they that were at the windows marvelled how Perceval might abide such buffets.   The King took witting of the shield that Perceval bare, and looketh on it of a long space.   'Knight,' saith he, 'Who gave you this shield, and on behalf of whom do you bear such an one?'   'I bear it on behalf of my father,' saith he.   'Did your father, then, bear a red shield with a white hart?'   'Yea,' saith Perceval, 'Many a day.'   'Was your father, then, King Alain of the Valleys of Camelot?'   'My father was he without fail.   No blame ought I to have of him, for a good knight was he and a loyal.'   'Are you the son of Yglais my sister, that was his wife?'   'Yea!' saith Perceval. 'Then are you my nephew,' saith the King of Castle Mortal, 'For she was my sister.'   'That misliketh me,' saith Perceval, 'For thereof have I neither worship nor honour, for the most disloyal are you of all my kindred, and I knew well when I came hither that it was you, and, for the great disloyalty that is in you, you war upon the best King that liveth and the most worshipful man, and upon the Lady of this castle for that she aideth him in all that she may.   But, please God, henceforward she shall have no need to guard her to the best of her power against so evil a man as are you, nor shall her castle never be obedient to you, nor the sacred hallows that the good King hath in his keeping.   For God loveth not you so much as He doth him, and so long as you war upon him, you do I defy and hold you as mine enemy.'   The King wotteth well that his nephew holdeth him not over dear, and that he is eager to do him a hurt, and that he holdeth his sword in his fist and that he is well roofed-in of his helmet, and that he is raging like a lion. He misdoubteth him sore of his strength and his great hardiment. He hath well proven and essayed that he is the Best Knight of the world. He durst no longer abide his blows, but rather he turneth him full speed toward his galley, and leapeth thereinto forthwith. He pusheth out from the shore incontinent, and Perceval followeth him right to the beach, full heavy that he hath gotten him away. Then he crieth after him : 'Evil King, tell me not that I am of your kindred ! Never yet did knight of my mother's lineage flee from other knight, save you alone ! Now have I conquered this island, and never on no day hereafter be you so over-hardy as be seen therein again ! ' The King goeth his way as he that hath no mind to return, and Perceval cometh back again in his galley to the Queen's castle, and all they of the palace come forth to meet him with great joy. The Queen asketh him how it is with him and whether he is wounded ? 'Lady,' saith he, 'Not at all, thank God.' She maketh disarm him, and honoureth him at her pleasure, and commandeth that all be obedient to him, and do his command-ment so long as he shall please to be there. Now feel they safer in the castle for that the king hath so meanly departed thence, and it well seemeth them that never will he dare come back for dread of his nephew more than of any other, whereof make they much joy in common.

F

BRANCH XII

Title I

Now is the story silent about Perceval, and saith that King Arthur is at Pannenoisance in Wales with great plenty of knights. Lancelot and Messire Gawain are repaired thither, whereof all the folk make great joy. The King asketh of Messire Gawain and Lancelot whether they have seen Lohot his son in none of these islands nor in none of these forests, and they answer him that they have seen him nowhere. 'I marvel much,' saith the King, 'what hath become of him, for no tidings have I heard of him beyond these, that Kay the Seneschal slew Logrin the giant, whose head he brought me, whereof I made great joy, and right willingly did I make Kay's lands the broader thereof, and well ought I to do him such favour, for he avenged me of him that did my land more hurt than any other, wherefore I love him greatly.' But, and the King had only known how Kay had wrought against him, he would not have so highly honoured his chivalry and his hardiment. The King sate one day at meat and Queen Guenievre at his side. Thereupon behold you, a damsel that alighteth before the palace, then mounteth the steps of the hall and is come before the King and the Queen. 'Sir, I salute you as the sorest dismayed and most discounselled damsel that ever you have seen! Wherefore am I come to demand a boon of you for the nobleness and valour of your heart.' 'Damsel,' saith the King, 'God counsel you of His will and pleasure, and I myself am full fain to partake therein.' The damsel looketh at the shield that hangeth in the midst of the hall. 'Sir,' saith she, 'I beseech you that you deign grant me the aid of the knight that shall bear this shield from hence. For sorer need have I thereof than ever another of them that are discounselled.' 'Damsel,' saith the King, 'Full well shall I be pleased, so the knight be also fain to do as you say.' 'Sir,' saith she, 'And he be so good knight as he is

146

reported, never will he refuse your prayer, nor would he mine, if only I were here at such time as he shall come. For, had I been able to find my brother that I have been seeking this long time, then well should I have been succoured long agone! But I have sought him in many lands, nor never could I learn where he is. Therefore to my sorrow, behoveth me to ride all lonely by the strange islands and put my body in jeopardy of death, whereof ought these knights to have great pity.'

II

'Damsel,' saith the King, 'For this reason do I refuse you nought of that you wish, and right willingly will I put myself to trouble herein.' 'Sir,' saith she, 'Much thanks to God thereof!' He maketh her be set at meat, and much honour be done her. When the cloths were drawn, the Queen leadeth her into her chamber with the maidens, and maketh much joy of her. The brachet that was brought thither with the shield was lying on a couch of straw. He would not know the Queen nor her damsels nor the knights that were in the court, but so soon as ever he heard the damsel he cometh to her and maketh greater joy of her than ever was brachet seen to make before. The Queen and her damsels marvelled much thereof, as did the damsel herself to whom the brachet made such joy, for never since that he was brought into the hall had they seen him rejoice of any. The Queen asked her whether she knew him. 'Certes, Lady, no, for never, so far as I know, have I seen him before.' The brachet will not leave her, but will be always on her lap, nor can she move anywhither but he followeth her. The damsel is long time in the court in this manner, albeit as she that had sore need of succour she remained in the chapel every day after that the Queen was come forth, and wept right tenderly before the image of the Saviour, and prayed right sweetly that His Mother would counsel her, for that she had been left in sore peril of losing her castle. The Queen asked her one day who her brother was. 'Lady,' saith she, 'one of the best knights of the world, whereof have I heard witness. But he departed from my father's and mother's hostel a right young squire. My father is since dead, and my Lady mother is left without help and without counsel, wherefore hath a certain man reaved her of her land and her castles and slain her men. The very castle wherein she hath her hold would he have seized long agone had it not been for Messire Gawain that made it be safe-guarded against her enemies for a year. The term is now ended and my Lady mother is in dread lest she shall lose her castle, for none other hold hath she. Wherefore is it that she hath sent me to seek for my brother, for she hath been told that he is a good knight, and for that I may not find him am I come to this court to beseech of King Arthur succour of the knight that shall bear away the shield, for I have heard tell that he is the Best Knight of the world; and, for the bounty that is in him will he therefore have pity on me.' 'Damsel,' saith the Queen, 'Would that you had found him, for great joy would it be unto me that your mother were succoured, and God grant that he that ought to bear the shield come quickly, and grant him courage that he be fain to succour your mother.' 'So shall he be, please God, for never was good knight that was without pity.'

III

The Queen hath much pity of the damsel, for she was of right great beauty, and well might it be seen by her cheer and her semblant that no joy had she. She had told the Queen her name and the name of her father and mother, and the Queen told her that many a time had she heard tell of Alain li Gros, and that he was said to be a worshipful man and good knight. The King lay one night beside the Queen, and was awoke from his first sleep so that he might not go to sleep again. He rose and did on a great grey cape and issueth forth of the chamber and cometh to the windows of the hall that opened toward the sea, calm and untroubled, so that much pleasure had he of looking thereat and leaning at the windows. When he had been there of a long space, he looked out to sea and saw coming afar off as it were the shining of a candle in the midst of the sea. Much he marvelled what it might be. He looked at it until he espied what seemed him to be a ship wherein was the light, and he was minded not to move until such time as he should know whether a ship it were or something other. The longer he looketh at it, the better perceiveth he that it is a ship, and that it was coming with great rushing toward the castle as fast as it might. The King espieth it nigh at hand, but none seeth he within nor without save one old man, ancient and bald, of right passing seemliness that held the rudder of the ship.

The ship was covered of a right rich cloth in the midst and the sail was lowered, for the sea was calm and quiet. The ship was arrived under the palace and was quite still. When the ship had taken ground, the King looketh thereat with much marvelling, and knoweth not who is there within, for not a soul heareth he speak. Him thinketh that he will go see what is within the ship, and he issueth forth of the hall, and cometh thither where the ship was arrived, but he might not come anigh for the flowing of the sea. 'Sir,' saith he that held the rudder, 'Allow me a little!' He launcheth forth of the ship a little boat, and the King entereth thereinto, and so cometh into the great ship, and findeth a knight that lay all armed upon a table of ivory, and had set his shield at his head. At the head of his bed had he two tall twisted links of wax in two candlesticks of gold, and the like at his feet, and his hands were crossed upon his breast. The King draweth nigh toward him and so looketh at him, and seemed him that never had he seen so comely a knight.

IV

'Sir,' saith the master of the ship, 'For God's sake draw you back and let the knight rest, for thereof hath he sore need.' 'Sir,' saith the King, 'Who is the knight?' 'Sir, this would he well tell you were he willing, but of me may you know it not.' 'Will he depart forthwith from hence?' saith the King. 'Sir,' saith the master, 'Not before he hath been in this hall, but he hath had sore travail and therefore he taketh rest.' When the King heard say that he would come into his palace, thereof had he great joy. He cometh to the Queen's chamber and telleth her how the ship is arrived. The Queen riseth and two of her damsels with her, and apparelleth her of a kirtle of cloth of silk, furred of ermine, and cometh into the midst of the hall. Thereupon behold you, the knight that cometh all armed and the master of the ship before him bearing the twisted link of wax in the candlestick of gold in front of him, and the knight held his sword all naked. 'Sir,' saith the Queen, 'Well may you be welcome!' 'Lady,' saith he, 'God grant you joy and good adventure.' 'Sir,' saith she, 'Please God we have nought to fear of you?' 'Lady,' saith he, 'No fear ought you to have!' The King seeth that he beareth the red shield with the white hart whereof he had heard tell. The brachet that was in the hall heareth the knight. He cometh racing toward him and leapeth about his legs and maketh great joy of him. And the knight playeth with him, then taketh the shield that hung at the column, and hangeth the other there, and cometh back thereafter toward the door of the hall. 'Lady,' saith the King, 'Pray the knight that he go not so hastily.' 'Sir,' saith the knight, 'No leisure have I to abide, but at some time shall you see me again.' The knights also say as much, and the King and Queen are right heavy of his departure, but they durst not press him beyond his will. He is entered into the ship, and the brachet with him. The master draweth the boat within, and so they depart and leave the castle behind. King Arthur abideth at Pannenoisance, and is right sorrowful of the knight, that he hath gone his way so soon. The knights arose throughout the castle when the day waxed light, and learnt the tidings of the knight that had borne the shield thence, and were right grieved for that they had not seen him. The damsel that had asked the boon cometh to the King. 'Sir,' saith she, 'Did you speak of my business to the knight?' 'Damsel,' saith the King, 'Never a whit! to my sorrow, for he hath departed sooner than I would!' 'Sir,' saith she, 'You have done a wrong and a sin, but, please God, so good a King as are you shall not fail of his covenants to damsel so forlorn as am I.' The King was right sorrowful for that he had remembered not the damsel. She departeth from the court, and taketh leave of the King and Queen, and saith that she herself will go seek the knight, and that, so she may find him, she will hold the King quit of his covenant. Messire Gawain and Lancelot are returned to the court, and have heard the tidings of the knight that hath carried away the shield, and are right grieved that they have not seen him, and Messire Gawain more than enough, for that he had lien in his mother's house. Lancelot seeth the shield that he had left on the column, and knoweth it well, and saith, 'Now know I well that Perceval hath been here, for this shield was he wont to bear, and the like also his father bore.' 'Ha,' saith Messire Gawain, 'What ill-chance have I that I may not see the Good Knight!' 'Messire Gawain,' saith Lancelot, 'So nigh did I see him that methought he would have killed me, for never before did I essay onset so stout nor so cruel of force of arms, and I myself wounded him, and when he knew me he made right great joy of me. And I was with him at the house of King Hermit a long space until that I was healed. 'Lancelot,' saith Messire Gawain, 'I would that he had wounded me, so I were not too sore harmed thereof, so that I might have been with him so long time as were you.' 'Lords,' saith the King, 'Behoveth you go on quest of him or I will go, for I am bound to beseech his aid on behalf of a damsel that asked me thereof, but she told me that, so she might find him first, I should be quit of her request.' 'Sir,' saith the Queen, 'You will do a right great service and you may counsel her herein, for sore discounselled is she. She hath told me that she was daughter of Alain li Gros of the Valleys of Camelot, and that her mother's name is Yglais, and her own Dindrane.' 'Ha, Lady,' saith Messire Gawain, 'She is sister to the knight that hath borne away the shield, for I lay at her mother's house wherein I was right well lodged.' 'By my head,' saith the Queen, 'it may well be, for so soon as she came in hither, the brachet that would have acquaintance with none, made her great joy, and when the knight came to seek the shield, the brachet, that had remained in the hall, played gladly with him and went away with him.' 'By my faith,' saith Messire Gawain, 'I will go in quest of the knight, for right great desire have I to see him.' 'And I,' saith Lancelot, 'Never so glad have I been to see him aforetime as I should be now.' 'Howsoever it be,' saith the King, 'I pray you so speed my business that the damsel shall not be able to plain her of me.'

V

'Sir,' saith Lancelot, 'We will tell him and we may find him, that his sister is gone in quest of him, and that she hath been at your court.' The two knights depart from the court to enter on the quest of the Good Knight, and leave the castle far behind them and ride in the midst of a high forest until they find a cross in the midst of a launde, there where all the roads of the forest join together. 'Lancelot,' saith Messire Gawain, 'Choose which road soever you will, and so let each go by himself, so that we may the sooner hear tidings of the Good Knight, and let us meet together again at this cross at the end of a year and let either tell other how he hath sped, for please God in one place or another we shall hear tidings of him.' Lancelot taketh the way to the right, and Messire Gawain to the left. Therewithal they depart and commend them one another to God.

BRANCH XIII

Title I

HERE the story is silent of Lancelot, and saith that Messire Gawain goeth a great pace riding, and prayeth God that He will so counsel him that he may find the knight. He rideth until the day cometh to decline, and he lay in the house of a hermit in the forest, that lodged him well. 'Sir,' saith the hermit to Messire Gawain, 'Whom do you go seek?' 'Sir,' saith he, 'I am in quest of a knight that I would see right gladly.' 'Sir,' saith the hermit, 'In this neighbourhood will you find no knight.' 'Wherefore not?' saith Messire Gawain, 'Be there no knights in this country?' 'There was wont to be plenty,' saith the hermit, 'But now no longer are there any, save one all alone in a castle and one all alone on the sea that have chased away and slain all the others.' 'And who is the one of the sea?' saith Messire Gawain. 'Sir,' saith the hermit, 'I know not who he is, save only that the sea is hard by here, where the ship runneth oftentimes wherein the knight is, and he repaireth to an island that is under the castle of the Queen of the Maidens, from whence he chased an uncle of his that warred upon the castle, and the other knights that he had chased thence and slain were helping his uncle, so that now the castle is made sure. And the knights that might flee from this forest and this kingdom durst not repair thither for the knight, for they dread his hardiment and his great might, sith that they know well they might not long endure against him.' 'Sir,' saith Messire Gawain, 'Is it so long a space sithence that he hath haunted the sea?' 'Sir,' saith the hermit, 'It is scarce more than a twelvemonth.' 'And how nigh is this to the sea?' saith Messire Gawain. 'Sir,' saith the hermit, 'It is not more than two leagues Welsh. When I have gone forth to my toil, many a time have I seen the ship run close by me, and the knight, all armed, within, and meseemed he was of right great comeliness, and had as passing proud a look as any lion. But I

152

can well tell you never was knight so dreaded in this kingdom
as is he.   The Queen of the Maidens would have lost her
castle ere now but for him.   Nor never sithence that he hath
chased his uncle from the island, hath he entered the Queen's
castle even once, but from that time forth hath rather rowed
about the sea and searched all the islands and stricken down all
the proud in such sort that he is dreaded and warily avoided
throughout all the kingdoms.   The Queen of the Maidens is
right sorrowful for that he cometh not to her castle, for so dear
she holdeth him of very love, that and he should come and she
might keep him so that he should never issue forth again, she
would sooner lock him up with her there safe within.'   'Know
you,' saith Messire Gawain, 'what shield the knight beareth?'
'Sir,' saith the hermit, 'I know not how to blazon it, for
nought know I of arms.   Three score years and more have I
been in this hermitage, yet never saw I this kingdom before so
dismayed as is it now.'   Messire Gawain lay the night therewithin, and departed when he had heard mass.   He draweth
him as nigh the sea as he may, and rideth along beside the
shore and many a time draweth rein to look forth if he might
see the knight's ship.   But nowhere might he espy it.   He
hath ridden until he cometh to the castle of the Queen of the
Maidens.   When she knew that it was Messire Gawain, she
made thereof great joy, and pointed him out the island whither
Perceval had repaired, and from whence he had driven his uncle.
'Sir,' saith she to Messire Gawain, 'I plain me much of him,
for never hath he been fain to enter herewithin, save the one
time that he did battle with his uncle, but ever sithence hath he
made repair to this island and rowed about this sea.'   'Lady,'
saith Messire Gawain, 'and whereabout may he be now?'
'Sir, God help me,' saith she, 'I know not, for I have not seen
him now of a long space, and no earthly man may know his
intent nor his desire, nor whitherward he may turn.'   Messire
Gawain is right sorrowful for that he knoweth not where to
seek him albeit he hath so late tidings of him.   He lay at the
castle and was greatly honoured, and on the morrow he heard
mass and took leave of the Queen, and rideth all armed beside
the seashore, for that the hermit had told him, and the Queen
herself, that he goeth oftener by sea than by land.   He entereth
into a forest that was nigh the sea, and seeth a knight coming a
great gallop as if one were chasing him to slay him,   'Sir

knight,' saith Messire Gawain, 'Whither away so fast?' 'Sir, I am fleeing from the knight that hath slain all the others.' 'And who is the knight?' saith Messire Gawain. 'I know not who he is,' saith the knight, 'But and you go forward you are sure to find him.' 'Meseemeth,' saith Messire Gawain, 'that I have seen you aforetime.' 'Sir,' saith he, 'So have you! I am the Knight Coward that you met in the forest there where you conquered the knight of the shield party black and white, and I am man of the Damsel of the Car. Wherefore I pray you for God's sake that you do me no hurt, for the knight that I found down yonder hath a look so fierce that I thought I was dead when I saw it.' 'Need you fear nought of me,' saith Messire Gawain, 'For I love your damsel well.' 'Sir,' saith the knight, 'I would that all the other knights would say as much in respect of me, for no fear have I save for myself alone.'

II

Messire Gawain departeth from the knight, and goeth his way amidst the forest that overshadowed the land as far as the seashore, and looketh forth from the top of a sand-hill, and seeth a knight armed on a tall destrier, and he had a shield of gold with a green cross. 'Ha, God,' saith Messire Gawain, 'Grant that this knight may be able to tell me tidings of him I seek!' Thitherward goeth he a great gallop, and saluteth him worshipfully and he him again. 'Sir,' saith Messire Gawain, 'Can you tell me tidings of a knight that beareth a shield banded of argent and azure with a red cross?' 'Yea, Sir,' saith the knight, 'That can I well. At the assembly of the knights may you find him within forty days.' 'Sir,' saith Messire Gawain, 'Where will the assembly be?' 'In the Red Launde, where will be many a good knight. There shall you find him without fail.' Thereof hath Messire Gawain right great joy, and so departeth from the knight and the knight from him, and goeth back toward the sea a great gallop. But Messire Gawain saw not the ship whereinto he entered, for that it was anchored underneath the cliff. The knight entered thereinto and put out to sea as he had wont to do. Howbeit Messire Gawain goeth his way toward the Red Launde where the assembly was to be, and desireth much the day that it shall be. He rideth until he cometh one eventide nigh to a castle that was of right fair seeming. He met a damsel that was following after a dead knight that two other knights bare upon a horse-bier, and she rode a great pace right amidst the forest. And Messire Gawain cometh to meet her and saluteth her, and she returned the salute as fairly as she might. 'Damsel,' saith Messire Gawain, 'Who lieth in this bier?' 'Sir, a knight that a certain man hath slain by great outrage.' 'And whither shall you ride this day?' 'Sir, I would fain be in the Red Launde, and thither will I take this knight, that was a right worshipful man for his age.' 'And wherefore will you take him there?' saith Messire Gawain. 'For that he that shall do best at the assembly of knights shall avenge this knight's death.'

III

The damsel goeth her way thereupon. And Messire Gawain goeth to the castle that he had seen, and found none within save only one solitary knight, old and feeble, and a squire that waited upon him. Howbeit, Messire Gawain alighteth at the castle. The Vavasour lodged him well and willingly, and made his door be well shut fast and Messire Gawain be disarmed, and that night he showed him honour as well as he might. And when it came to the morrow and Messire Gawain was minded to depart thence, the Vavasour saith to him, 'Sir you may not depart thus, for this door hath not been opened this long while save only yesterday, when I made it be opened before you, to the intent that you should meet on my behalf a certain knight that is fain to slay me, for that the King of Castle Mortal hath had his hold herewithin, he that warreth on the Queen of the Maidens. Wherefore I pray you that you help me to defend it against the knight.' 'What shield beareth he?' saith Messire Gawain. 'He beareth a golden shield with a green cross.' 'And what sort of knight is he?' saith Messire Gawain. 'Sir,' saith the Vavasour, 'A good knight and a hardy and a sure.' 'By my faith,' saith Messire Gawain, 'And you can tell me tidings of another knight whereof I am in quest, I will protect you against this one to the best I may, and if he will do nought for my prayer, I will safeguard you of my force.' 'What knight, then, do you seek?' saith the Vavasour. 'Sir, a knight that is called Perceval, and he hath carried away from the court of King Arthur a shield banded argent and azure with a red cross on a band of gold. He will be at the assembly in the Red Launde. These tidings had I of the knight you dread so much.'

IV

Thereupon, whilst Messire Gawain was thus speaking to the Vavasour, behold you the Knight of the Golden Shield, that draweth rein in the midst of a launde that was betwixt the castle and the forest. The Vavasour seeth him from the windows of the hall, and pointeth him out to Messire Gawain. Messire Gawain goeth and mounteth on his destrier, his shield at his neck and his spear in his fist, all armed, and issueth forth of the door when it had been unfastened, and cometh toward the knight, that awaited him on his horse. He seeth Messire Gawain coming, but moveth not, and Messire Gawain marvelleth much that the knight cometh not toward him, for him thinketh well that the Vavasour had told him true. But he had not, for never had the knight come thither to do the Vavasour any hurt, but on account of the knights that passed by that way that went to seek adventure, for right glad was he to see them albeit he was not minded to make himself known unto any. Messire Gawain looketh before him and behind him and seeth that the door was made fast and the bridge drawn up so soon as he was departed thence, whereof he marvelled much and saith to the knight, 'Sir, is your intent nought but good only?' 'By my head,' saith he, 'Nought at all, and readily will I tell it you.' Thereupon, behold you a damsel that cometh a great pace, and held a whip wherewith she hurrieth her mule onward, and she draweth rein there where the two knights were. 'Ha, God!' saith she, 'Shall I ever find one to wreak me vengeance of the traitor Vavasour that dwelleth in this castle?' 'Is he then traitor?' saith Messire Gawain. 'Yea, Sir, the most traitor you saw ever! He lodged my brother the day before yesterday, and bore him on hand at night that a certain knight was warring upon him for that the way whereby the knights pass is here in front of this place, and lied to him so much as that my brother held him in covenant that he would assault a certain knight that he should point out to him, for love of him. This knight came passing hereby, that had no thought to do hurt neither to the Vavasour nor to my brother. The knight was right strong and hardy, and was born at the castle of Escavalon.

My brother issued forth of the castle filled with fool-hardiness for the leasing of the Vavasour, and ran upon the knight without a word. The knight could do no less than avenge himself. They hurtled together so sore that their horses fell under them and their spears passed either through other's heart. Thus were both twain killed on this very piece of ground.

V

'The Vavasour took the arms and the horses and put them in safe keeping in his castle, and the bodies of the knights he left to the wild beasts, that would have devoured them had I not chanced to come thither with two knights that helped me bury them by yonder cross at the entrance of the forest.' 'By my head,' saith Messire Gawain, 'In like manner would he have wrought me mischief had I been minded to trust him; for he bore me in hand that this knight was warring upon him, and besought me that I should safeguard him against him. But our Lord God so helped me that I intermeddled not therein, for lightly might I have wrought folly.' 'By the name of God,' saith the other, 'Meseemeth it clear that the Vavasour would fain that knights should kill each other. 'Sir,' saith the damsel, 'You say true; it is of his covetise of harness and horses that he entreateth the knights on this-wise.' 'Damsel,' saith Messire Gawain, 'Whither go you?' 'Sir,' saith she, 'After a knight that I have made be carried in a litter for the dead.' 'I saw him,' saith he, 'pass by here last night, full late last night.' The knight taketh leave of Messire Gawain, and Messire Gawain saith that he holdeth himself a churl in that he hath not asked him of his name. But the knight said, 'Fair Sir, I pray you of love that you ask not my name until such time as I shall ask you of yours.'

VI

Messire Gawain would ask nought further of the knight, and the knight entered into the Lonely Forest and Messire Gawain goeth on his way. He meeteth neither knight nor damsel to whom he telleth not whom he goeth to seek, and they all say that he will be in the Red Launde. He lodged the night with a hermit. At night, the hermit asked Messire Gawain whence he came? 'Sir, from the land of the Queen of the Maidens.'

' Have you seen Perceval, the Good Knight that took the shield
in King Arthur's court and left another there?' 'No, certes,'
saith Messire Gawain, 'whereof am I right sorrowful.   But a
knight with a shield of gold and a green cross thereon told me
that he would be at the Red Launde.' 'Sir,' saith the hermit,
'You say true, for it was he himself to whom you spake.   To-
night is the third night since he lay within yonder, and see here
the brachet he brought from King Arthur's court, which he
hath commanded me to convey to his uncle, King Hermit.'
' Alas!' saith Messire Gawain, 'What ill chance is mine if this
be true!' 'Sir,' saith the hermit, 'I ought not to lie, neither to
you nor other.   By the brachet may you well know that this is
true.' 'Sir,' saith Messire Gawain, 'Of custom beareth he no
such shield.' 'I know well,' saith the hermit, 'what shield he
ought to bear, and what shield he will bear hereafter.   But this
doth he that he may not be known, and this shield took he in
the hermitage of Joseus, the son of King Hermit, there where
Lancelot was lodged, where he hanged the four thieves that
would have broken into the hermitage by night.   And within
there hath remained the shield he brought from King Arthur's
court, with Joseus the son of my sister, and they are as brother
and sister between the twain, and you may know of very truth
that albeit Joseus be hermit, no knight is there in Great Britain
of his heart and hardiment.'

VII

' Certes,' saith Messire Gawain, ' It was sore mischance for me
that I should see him yesterday before the castle where the
knights pass by, and speak to him and ask him his name, but he
besought me that I should not ask him his name until such time
as he should ask me mine ; and with that he departed from me
and entered into the forest, and I came hitherward.   Now am I
so sorrowful that I know not what I may do for the best, for
King Arthur sendeth me in quest of him, and Lancelot hath also
gone to seek him in another part of the kingdom of Logres.
But now hath too great mischance befallen me of this quest, for
twice have I seen him and found him and spoken to him, and
now have I lost him again.' 'Sir,' saith the hermit, 'He is so
close and wary a knight, that he is fain never to waste a word,
neither will he make false semblant to any nor speak word that

he would not should be heard, nor do shame of his body to his knowledge, nor carnal sin, for virgin and chaste is he and doth never outrage to any.' 'I know well,' saith Messire Gawain, 'that all the valours and all the cleannesses that ought to be in a knight are in him, and therefore am I the more sorrowful that I am not of them that he knoweth, for a man is worth the more that hath acquaintance with a good knight.'

VIII

Messire Gawain lay the night in the hermit's house, right sorrowful, and in the morning departed when he had heard mass. Josephus the good clerk witnesseth us in this high history that this hermit had to name Josuias, and was a knight of great worship and valour, but he renounced all for the love of God, and was fain to set his body in banishment for Him. And all these adventures that you hear in this high record came to pass, Josephus telleth us, for the setting forward the law of the Saviour. All of them could he not record, but only these whereof he best remembered him, and whereof he knew for certain all the adventures by virtue of the Holy Spirit. This high record saith that Messire Gawain hath wandered so far that he is come into the Red Launde whereas the assembly of knights should be held. He looketh and seeth the tents pitched and the knights coming from all quarters. The most part were already armed within and before their tents. Messire Gawain looketh everywhere, thinking to see the knight he seeketh, but seemeth him he seeth him not, for no such shield seeth he as he beareth. All abashed is he thereof, for he hath seen all the tents and looked at all the arms. But the knight is not easy to recognise, for he hath changed his arms, and nigh enough is he to Messire Gawain, albeit you may well understand that he knoweth it not. And the tournament assembleth from all parts, and the divers fellowships come the one against other, and the melly of either upon other as they come together waxeth sore and marvellous. And Messire Gawain searcheth the ranks to find the knight, albeit when he meeteth knight in his way he cannot choose but do whatsoever a knight may do of arms, and yet more would he have done but for his fainness to seek out the knight. The damsel is at the head of the tournament, for that she would fain know the one that shall have the mastery and the prize therein.

The knight that Messire Gawain seeketh is not at the head of
the fellowships, but in the thickest of the press, and such feats
of arms doth he that more may no knight do, and smiteth down
the knights about him, that flee from him even as the deer-
hound fleeth from the lion. 'By my faith,' saith Messire Gawain,
'sith that they have lied to me about the knight, I will seek him
no more this day, but forget my discontent as best I may until
evening.' He seeth the knight, but knoweth him not, for he
had a white shield and cognisances of the same. And Messire
Gawain cometh to him as fast as his horse may carry him, and
the knight toward Messire Gawain. So passing stoutly they
come together that they pierce their shields below the boss.
Their spears were so tough that they break not, and they draw
them forth and come together again so strongly that the spears
wherewith they smote each other amidst the breast were bended
so that they unriveted the holdfasts of their shields, and they
lost their stirrups, and the reins fly from their fists, and they
stagger against the back saddlebows, and the horses stumbled
so as that they all but fell. They straighten them in saddle and
stirrup, and catch hold upon their reins, and then come together
again, burning with wrath and fury like lions, and either smiteth
on other with their spears that may endure no longer, for the
shafts are all to-frushed as far as the fists in such sort that they
that look on marvel them much how it came to pass that the
points had not pierced their bodies. But God would not that
the good knights should slay each other, rather would He that
the one should know the true worth of the other. The
habergeons safeguarded not their bodies, but the might of God
in whom they believed, for in them had they all the valour that
knight should have; and never did Messire Gawain depart from
hostel wherein he had lien, but he first heard mass before he
went if so he might, nor never found he dame nor damsel discounselled whereof he had not pity, nor did he ever churlishness
to other knight, nor said nor thought it, and he came, as you
have heard, of the most holy lineage of Josephus and the good
King Fisherman.

IX

The good knights were in the midst of the assembly, and
right wrathful was the one against the other, and they held their
swords naked and their shields on their arms and dealt each

other huge buffets right in the midst of the helms. The most part of the knights come to them and tell them that the assembly waiteth for them to come thereunto. They have much pains to part them asunder, and then the melly beginneth again on all sides, and the evening cometh on that parteth them at last. And on this wise the assembly lasted for two days. The damsel that brought the knight on a bier in a coffin, dead, prayed the assembly of all the knights to declare which one of all the knights had done the best, for the knight that she made be carried might not be buried until such time as he were avenged. And they say that the knight of the white shield and the other with the shield sinople and the golden eagle had done better than all the other, but, for that the knight of the white shield had joined in the melly before the other, they therefore would give him the prize ; but they judged that for the time that Messire Gawain had joined therein he had not done worse than the other knight. The damsel seeketh the knight of the white shield among the knights and throughout all the tents, but cannot find him, for already hath he departed. She cometh to Messire Gawain and saith: 'Sir, sith that I find not the knight of the white shield, you are he that behoveth avenge the knight that lieth dead in the litter.' 'Damsel,' saith Messire Gawain, 'Do me not this shame, for it hath been declared that the other knight hath better done herein than I.'

X

'Damsel, well you know that no honour should I have thereof, were I to emprise to do that whereof you beseech me, for you have said that behoveth none to avenge him, save only he that hath borne him best at this assembly, and that is he of the white shield, and, so God help me, this have I well felt and proven.'

XI

The damsel well understandeth that Messire Gawain speaketh reason. 'Ha, Sir,' saith she, 'He hath already departed hence and gone into the forest, and the most divers-seeming knight is he and the best that liveth, and great pains shall I have or ever I find him again.' 'The best?' saith Messire Gawain; 'How know you that?' 'I know it well,' saith she, 'For that in the house of King Fisherman did the Graal appear unto him for the goodness of his knighthood and the goodness of his heart and for the chastity of his body. But he forgat to ask that one should serve thereof, whence hath sore harm befallen the land. He came to the court of King Arthur, where he took a shield that none ought to bear save he alone. Up to this time have I well known his coming and going, but nought shall I know thereof hereafter for that he hath changed the cognisance of his shield and arms. And now am I entered into sore pain and travail to seek him, for I shall not have found him of a long space, and I came not to this assembly save for him alone.' 'Damsel,' saith Messire Gawain, 'You have told me tidings such as no gladness have I thereof, for I also am seeking him, but I know not how I may ever recognise him, for he willeth not to tell me his name, and too often changeth he his shield, and well I know that so I shall ever come in place where he hath changed his cognisance, and he shall come against me and I against him, I shall only know him by the buffets that he knoweth how to deal, for never in arms have I made acquaintance with so cruel a knight. But again would I suffer sorer blows than I have suffered yet, so only I might be where he is.' 'Sir,' saith the damsel, 'What is your name?' 'Damsel,' saith he, 'I am called Gawain.' With that he commendeth the damsel to God, and goeth his way in one direction and the damsel in another, and saith to herself that Perceval is the most marvellous knight of the world, that so often he discogniseth himself. For when one seeth him one may recognise him not. Messire Gawain rideth amidst the forest, and prayeth the Saviour lead him into such place as that he may find Perceval openly, in such sort that he may have his acquaintance and his love that so greatly he desireth.

BRANCH XIV

TITLE I

HEREWITHAL the story is silent of Messire Gawain, and saith
that Lancelot seeketh Perceval in like manner as did Messire
Gawain, and rideth until that he cometh to the hermitage where
he hanged the thieves. Joseus made right great joy of him.
He asked him whether he knew any tidings of the son of the
Widow Lady. 'I have seen him sithence that he came from
King Arthur's court but once only, and whither he is gone I know
not.' 'Sir,' saith Lancelot, 'I would see him right fain. King
Arthur sendeth for him by me.' 'Sir,' saith the hermit, 'I
know not when I may see him again, for when once he departeth
hence he is not easy to find.' Lancelot entereth the chapel with
the hermit, and seeth the shield that Perceval brought from
King Arthur's court beside the altar. 'Sir,' saith Lancelot, 'I
see his shield yonder. Hide him not from me.' 'I will not do
so,' saith the hermit. 'This shield, truly, is his, but he took
with him another from hence, of gold with a green cross.'
'And know you no tidings of Messire Gawain?' 'I have not
seen Messire Gawain sithence tofore I entered into this hermitage. But you have fallen into sore hatred on account of the
four robbers that were knights whom you hanged. For their
kinsmen are searching for you in this forest and in other, and
are thieves like as were the others, and they have their hold in
this forest, wherein they bestow their robberies and plunder.
Wherefore I pray you greatly be on your guard against them.'
'So will I,' saith Lancelot, 'please God.' He lay the night in
the hermitage, and departeth on the morrow after that he hath
heard mass, and prayeth God grant he may find Perceval or Messire
Gawain. He goeth his way amidst the strange forests until
that he cometh to a strong castle that was builded right seemly.

He looketh before him and seeth a knight that was issued there-out, and was riding a great pace on a strong destrier, and carried a bird on his fist toward the forest.

II

When he saw Lancelot coming he drew up. 'Sir,' saith he, 'Be welcome.' 'Good adventure to you,' saith Lancelot. 'What castle is this?' 'Sir, it is the Castle of the Golden Circlet. And I go to meet the knights and dames that come to the castle, for this day is the day ordained for the adoration of the Golden Circlet.' 'What is the Golden Circlet?' saith Lancelot. 'Sir, it is the Crown of Thorns,' saith the knight, 'that the Saviour of the world had on His head when He was set upon the Rood. Wherefore the Queen of this castle hath set it in gold and precious stones in such sort that the knights and dames of this kingdom come to behold it once in the year. But it is said that the knight that was first at the Graal shall conquer it, and there-fore is no strange knight allowed to enter. But, so please you, I will lead you to mine own hold that is in this forest.' 'Right great thanks,' saith Lancelot, 'But as yet it is not time to take lodging.' He taketh leave of the knight, and so departeth and looketh at the castle, and saith that in right great worship should the knight be held that by the valour of his chivalry shall conquer so noble a hallow as is the Golden Circlet when it is kept safe in a place so strong. He goeth his way right amidst the forest, and looketh forth before him and seeth coming the damsel that hath the knight carried in the litter for the dead. 'Damsel,' saith Lancelot, 'Be welcome.' 'Sir, God give you good adventure! Sir,' saith the damsel, 'Greatly ought I to hate the knight that slew this knight, for that he hath forced me thus to lead him in this wise by fell and forest. So also ought I to mislike me much of the knight that it standeth upon to avenge him, whom I may not find.' 'Damsel,' saith Lancelot, 'Who slew this knight?' 'Sir,' saith she, 'The Lord of the Burning Dragon.' 'And who ought of right to avenge him?' 'Sir,' saith she, 'The knight that was in the Red Launde at the assembly, that jousted with Messire Gawain, and had the prize of the tournament.' 'Did he better than Messire Gawain?' saith Lancelot. 'Sir, so did they adjudge him; for that he was a longer time in the assembly.' 'A good knight was he, then,' saith Lancelot, 'sith that he did better than Messire Gawain!'

'By my head,' saith the damsel, 'You say true, for he is the Best
Knight of the World.' 'And what shield beareth he?' saith
Lancelot. 'Sir,' saith the damsel, 'At the assembly he bore
white arms, but before that, he had arms of another semblance,
and one shield that he had was green, and one gold with a green
cross.' 'Damsel,' saith he, 'Did Messire Gawain know him!'
'Sir, not at all, whereof is he right sorrowful.' 'Is he, then,'
saith he, 'Perceval, the son of the Widow Lady?' 'By my
head, you say true!' 'Ha, God!' saith Lancelot, 'The more
am I mazed how Messire Gawain knew him not. Damsel,' saith
he, 'And know you whitherward they are gone?' 'Sir,' saith
she, 'I know not whither, nor have I any tidings, neither of the
one nor the other.' He departeth from the damsel and rideth
until the sun was set. He found the rocks darkling and the
forest right deep and perilous of seeming. He rode on, troubled
in thought, and weary and full of vexation. Many a time looketh
he to right and to left, and he may see any place where he may
lodge. A dwarf espied him, but Lancelot saw him not. The dwarf
goeth right along a by-way that is in the forest, and goeth to a
little hold of robber-knights that lay out of the way, where was
a damsel that kept watch over the hold. The robbers had
another hold where was the damsel where the passing knights
are deceived and entrapped. The dwarf cometh forthright to
the damsel, and saith: 'Now shall we see what you will do, for
see, here cometh the knight that hanged your uncle and your
three cousins german.' 'Now shall I have the best of him,'
saith she, 'as for mine own share in this matter, but take heed
that you be garnished ready to boot.' 'By my head,' saith the
dwarf, 'That will I, for, please God, he shall not escape us
again, save he be dead.' The damsel was of passing great beauty
and was clad right seemingly, but right treacherous was she of
heart, nor no marvel was it thereof, for she came of the lineage
of robbers and was nurtured on theft and robbery, and she
herself had helped to murder many a knight. She is come upon
the way, so that Lancelot hath to pass her, without her kerchief.
She meeteth Lancelot and saluteth him and maketh him right great
joy, of semblant. 'Sir,' saith she, 'Follow this path that goeth
into the forest, and you will find a hold that my forefathers
stablished for harbouring of such knights as might be passing
through the forest. The night is dark already, and if you pass
on further no hold will you find nearer than a score leagues
Welsh.' 'Damsel,' saith Lancelot, 'Gramercy heartily of this

that it pleaseth you to say, for right gladly will I harbour me here, for it is more than time to take lodging, and with you more willingly than another.'

III

On this wise they go their way talking, as far as the hold. There was none therewithin save only the dwarf, for the five robber knights were in their hold at the lower end of the forest. The dwarf took Lancelot's horse, and stabled him, then went up into the hall above, and gave himself up wholly to serving him. 'Sir,' saith the damsel, 'Allow yourself to be disarmed, and have full assurance of safety.' 'Damsel,' saith he, 'Small trouble is it for me to wear mine arms, and lightly may I abide it.' 'Sir,' saith she, 'Please God, you shall not lie armed within yonder. Never yet did knight so that harboured therein.' But the more the damsel presseth him to disarm, the more it misliketh him, for the place seemeth him right dark and foul-seeming, wherefore will he not disarm nor disgarnish himself. 'Sir,' saith she, 'Meseemeth you are suspicious of something, but no call have you to misdoubt of aught here within, for the place is quite safe. I know not whether you have enemies?' 'Damsel,' saith Lancelot, 'Never yet knew I knight that was loved of everybody, yet sometimes might none tell the reason thereof.'

IV

Lancelot, so saith the story, would not disarm him, wherefore he made the table be set, and sate thereat beside the damsel at meat. He made his shield and his helmet and spear be brought into the hall. He leant back upon a rich couch that was therewithin, with his sword by his side, all armed. He was weary and the bed was soft, so he went to sleep. Howbeit, the dwarf mounteth on his horse that he had left still saddled, and goeth his way to the other hold where the robbers were, all five, that were Lancelot's mortal enemies. The damsel remained all alone with him that she hated of a right deadly hate. She thought to herself that gladly would she slay him, and that, so she might compass it, she would be thereof held in greater worship of all the world, for well she knew that he was a good knight, and that one so good she had never slain. She filched away the sword that was at his side, then drew it from the scabbard, then looketh to see where she may lightliest smite him to slay him. She seeth that his head is so covered of armour that nought appeareth thereof save only the face, and she bethinketh her that one stroke nor two on the helmet would scarce hurt him greatly, but that and she might lift the skirt of his habergeon without awakening him she might well slay him, for so might she thrust the sword right through his heart. Meanwhile, as she was searching thus, Lancelot, that was sleeping and took no heed thereof, saw, so it seemed him, a little cur-dog come there-within, and brought with him sundry great mongrel ban-dogs that ran upon him on all sides, and the little cur bit at him like-wise among the others. The ban-dogs held him so fast that he might not get away from them. He seeth that a greyhound bitch had hold of his sword, and she had hands like a woman, and was fain to slay him. And it seemed him that he snatched the sword from her and slew the greyhound bitch and the biggest and most masterful of the ban-dogs and the little cur. He was scared of the dream and started up and awoke, and felt the scabbard of his sword by his side, that the damsel had left there all empty, the which he perceived not, and soon thereafter he fell on sleep again. The dwarf that had stolen his horse cometh to the robber knights, and crieth to them, 'Up, Sirs, and haste you to come and avenge you of your mortal enemy that sent the best of your kindred out of the world with such shame! See, here is his horse that I bring you for a token!' He alighteth of the horse, and giveth him up to them. Right joyous are the robbers of the tidings he telleth them. The dwarf bringeth them all armed to the hold.

V

Lancelot was awake, all scared of the dream he had dreamed. He seeth them enter within all armed, and the damsel crieth to them: 'Now will it appear,' saith she, 'what you will do!' Lancelot hath leapt up, thinking to take his sword, but findeth the scabbard all empty. The damsel that held the sword was the first of all to run upon him, and the five knights and the dwarf set upon him from every side. He perceived that it was his own sword the damsel held, the one he prized above all other. He taketh his lance that was at his bed's head and cometh toward the master of the knights at a great sweep, and smiteth him so fiercely that he thrusteth him right through the body so that the lance passeth a fathom beyond, and beareth him to the ground dead.　His spear broke as he drew it back.　He runneth to the damsel that held the sword, and wresteth it forth of her hands and holdeth it fast with his arm right against his flank and grippeth it to him right strait; albeit she would fain snatch it again from him by force, whereat Lancelot much marvelled.　He swingeth it above him, and the four knights come back upon him.　He thinketh to smite one with the sword, when the damsel leapeth in between them, thinking to hold Lancelot fast, and thereby the blow that should have fallen on one of the knights caught the damsel right through the head and slew her, whereof he was right sorrowful, howsoever she might have wrought against him.

VI

When the four knights saw the damsel dead, right grieved were they thereof.　And the dwarf crieth out to them: ' Lords, now shall it be seen how you will avenge the sore mischief done you.　So help me God, great shame may you have and you cannot conquer a single knight.'　They run upon him again on all sides, but maugre all their heads he goeth thither where he thinketh to find his horse; but him findeth he not.　Thereby well knoweth he that the dwarf hath made away with him, wherefore he redoubled his hardiment and his wrath waxed more and more. And the knights were not to be lightly apaid when they saw their lord dead and the damsel that was their cousin.　Sore buffets they dealt him of their swords the while he defended himself as best he might.　He caught the dwarf that was edging them on to do him hurt, and clave him as far as the shoulders, and wounded two of the knights right badly, and he himself was hurt in two places; but he might not depart from the house, nor was his horse there within, nor was there but a single entrance into the hall.　The knights set themselves without the door and guard the issue, and Lancelot was within with them that were dead.　He sate himself down at the top of the hall to rest him, for he was sore spent with the blows he had given and received.　When he had rested himself awhile, he riseth to his feet and seeth that they have sate them down in the entrance to the hall.　He mounteth up to the windows and flingeth them down them that were dead within through the windows.　Just then the day appeared, fair and clear, and the birds began to sing amidst the forest, whereof the hall was overshadowed. He maketh fast the door of the hall and barreth it and shutteth the knights without; and they say one to the other and swear it, that they will not depart thence until they have taken him or famished him to death. Little had Lancelot recked of their threats and he might have had his horse at will, but he was not so sure of his stroke afoot as a-horseback, as no knight never is. Him thinketh he may well abide the siege as long as God shall please, for the hall was well garnished of meat in right great joints. He is there within all alone, and the four knights without that keep watch that he goeth not, but neither wish nor will hath he to go forth afoot; but, and he had had his horse, the great hardiment that he hath in him would have made that he should go forth honourably, howsoever they without might have taken it and what grievance soever they might have had thereof.

BRANCH XV

TITLE I

HERE the story is silent of Lancelot, and talketh of Messire Gawain that goeth to seek Perceval, and is right heavy for that twice hath he found him when he knew him not. He cometh back again to the cross whereas he told Lancelot he would await him so he should come thither before him. He went and came to and fro by the forest more than eight days to wait for him, but could hear no tidings. He would not return to King Arthur's court, for had he gone thither in such case, he would have had blame thereof. He goeth back upon the quest and saith that he will never stint therein until he shall have found both Lancelot and Perceval. He cometh to the hermitage of Joseus, and alighted of his horse and found the young hermit Joseus, that received him well and made full great joy of him. He harboured the night therewithin. Messire Gawain asked him tidings of Perceval, and the hermit telleth him he hath not seen him since before the assembly of the Red Launde. 'And can you tell me where I may find him?' saith Messire Gawain. 'Not I,' saith the hermit, 'I cannot tell you whereabout he is.' While they were talking on this wise, straightway behold you a knight coming that hath arms of azure, and alighteth at the hermitage to lodge there. The hermit receiveth him right gladly. Messire Gawain asketh him if he saw a knight with white arms ride amidst the forest. 'By my faith,' saith the knight, 'I have seen him this day and spoken with him, and he asked me and I could tell him tidings of a knight that beareth a shield of sinople with a golden eagle, and I told him, no. Afterward, I enquired wherefore he asked it, and he made answer that he had jousted at him in the Red Launde, nor never before had he found so sturdy assault of any knight, wherefore he was right sorrowful for that he was not acquainted with him, for the sake of his good knighthood.' 'By my faith,' saith

Gawain, ' The knight is more sorrowful than he, for nought is there in the world he would gladlier see than him.' The knight espieth Messire Gawain's shield and saith, ' Ha, Sir, methinketh you are he.' ' Certes,' saith Messire Gawain, ' you say true. I am he against whom he jousted, and right glad am I that so good a knight smote upon my shield, and right sorrow- ful for that I knew him not ; but tell me where I may find him ? '

II

' Sir,' saith Joseus the Hermit, ' He will not have gone forth from this forest, for this is the place wherein he wonneth most willingly, and the shield that he brought from King Arthur's court is in this chapel.' So he showeth the shield to Messire Gawain that maketh great joy thereof. ' Ha, Sir,' saith the knight of the white arms, ' Is your name Messire Gawain ? ' ' Fair Sir,' saith he, ' Gawain am I called.' ' Sir,' saith the knight, ' I have not ceased to seek you for a long while past. Meliot of Logres, that is your man, the son of the lady that was slain on your account, sendeth you word that Nabigant of the Rock hath slain his father on your account ; wherefore he challengeth the land that hath fallen to him ; and hereof he prayeth you that you will come to succour him as behoveth lord to do to his liege man.' ' By my faith,' saith Messire Gawain, ' Behoveth me not fail him therein, wherefore tell him I will succour him so soon as I may ; but tell him I have emprised a business that I cannot leave but with loss of honour until such time as it be achieved.' They lay the night at the hermitage until after mass was sung on the morrow.

III

The knight departed and Messire Gawain remained. So when he was apparelled to mount, he looketh before him at the issue of the forest toward the hermitage, and seeth coming a knight on a tall horse, full speed and all armed, and he bore a shield like the one he saw Perceval bearing the first time. ' Sir,' saith he, · Know you this knight that cometh there ! ' ' Truly, Sir, well do I know him. This is Perceval whom you seek, whom you so much desire to see ! ' ' God be praised thereof ! ' saith Messire Gawain, ' Inasmuch as he cometh hither.' He goeth afoot to meet him, and Perceval alighteth ro

soon as he seeth him. 'Sir,' saith Messire Gawain, 'Right
welcome may you be!' 'Good joy may you have,' saith
Perceval. 'Sir,' saith the hermit, 'Make great joy of him! this
is Messire Gawain, King Arthur's nephew.' 'Thereof do I
love him the better!' saith he. 'Honour and joy ought all they
to do him that know him!' He throweth his arms on his neck,
and so maketh him great joy. 'Sir,' saith he, 'Can you tell me
tidings of a knight that was in the Red Launde at the assembly
of knights?' 'What shield beareth he?' saith Messire Gawain.
'A red shield with a golden eagle,' saith Perceval. 'And more
by token, never made I acquaintance with any so sturdy in
battle as are he and Lancelot.' 'Fair sir, it pleaseth you to say
so,' saith Messire Gawain. 'In the Red Launde was I at the
assembly, and such arms bore I as these you blazon, and I
jousted against a knight in white arms, of whom I know this,
that all of knighthood that may be lodged in the body of a man
is in him.' 'Sir,' saith Perceval to Messire Gawain, 'You
know not how to blame any man.' So they hold one another by
the hands, and go into the hermitage. 'Sir,' saith Messire
Gawain, 'When you were in the court of King Arthur for the
shield that is within yonder, your sister was also there, and
prayed and besought the help of the knight that should bear
away the shield, as being the most discounselled damsel in the
world. The King granted it her, and you bore away the
shield. She asked your aid of the King as she that deemed not
you were her brother, and said that if the King failed of his
covenant, he would do great sin, whereof would he have much
blame. The King was fain to do all he might to seek you, to
make good that he had said, and sent us forth in quest of you,
so that the quest lieth between me and Lancelot. He himself
would have come had we been unwilling to go. Sir, I have
found you three times without knowing you, albeit great desire
had I to see you. This is the fourth time and I know you now,
whereof I make myself right joyous; and much am I beholden
to you of the fair lodging your mother gave me at Camelot;
but right sore pity have I of her, for a right worshipful woman
is she, and a widow lady and ancient, and fallen into much war
without aid nor comfort, through the evil folk that harass her
and reave her of her castles. She prayed me, weeping the while
right sweetly, that and if I should find you that are her son, I
should tell you of her plight, that your father is dead, and that

she hath no succour nor aid to look for save from you alone, and if you succour her not shortly, she will lose her own one castle that she holdeth, and must needs become a beggar, for of the fifteen castles she wont to have in your father's time, she hath now only that of Camelot, nor of all her knights hath she but five to guard the castle.   Wherefore I pray you on her behalf and for your own honour, that you will grant her herein of your counsel and your valour and your might, for of no chivalry that you may do may you rise to greater worship.   And so sore need hath she herein as you hear me tell, nor would I that she should lose aught by default of message, for thereof should I have sin and she harm, and you yourself also, that have the power to amend it and ought of right so to do!'   'Well have you delivered yourself herein,' saith Perceval, 'And betimes will I succour her and our Lord God will.'   'You will do honour to yourself,' saith Messire Gawain.   'Thereof will you have praise with God and worship with the world.'   'Well know I,' saith Perceval, 'that in me ought she to have aid and counsel as of right, and that so I do not accordingly, I ought to have reproach and be blamed as recreant before the world.'

IV

'In God's name,' saith the hermit, 'You speak according to the scripture, for he that honoureth not his father and mother neither believeth in God nor loveth Him.'   'All this know I well,' saith Perceval, 'And well pleased am I to be reminded thereof, and well know I also mine intent herein, albeit I tell it to none.   But if any can tell me tidings of Lancelot, right willingly shall I hear them, and take it kindly of the teller thereof.'   'Sir,' saith Joseus, 'It is but just now since he lay here within, and asked me tidings of Messire Gawain, and I told him such as I knew.   Another time before that, he lay here when the robbers assailed us that he hanged in the forest, and so hated is he thereof of their kinsfolk that and they may meet him, so they have the might, he is like to pay for it right dear, and in this forest won they rather than in any other.   I told him as much, but he made light thereof in semblant, even as he will in deed also if their force be not too great.'   'By my head,' saith Perceval, 'I will not depart forth of this forest until I know tidings of him, if Messire Gawain will pledge himself thereto.'

And Messire saith he desireth nothing better, sith that he hath found Perceval, for he may not be at ease until such time as he shall know tidings of Lancelot, for he hath great misgiving sith that he hath enemies in the forest.

V

Perceval and Messire Gawain sojourned that day in the forest in the hermitage, and the morrow Perceval took his shield that he brought from King Arthur's court, and left that which he brought with him, and Messire Gawain along with him that made himself right joyous of his company. They ride amidst the forest both twain, all armed, and at the right hour of noon they meet a knight that was coming a great gallop as though he were all scared. Perceval asketh him whence he cometh, that he seemeth so a-dread. 'Sir, I come from the forest of the robbers that won in this forest wherethrough you have to pass. They have chased me a full league Welsh to slay me, but they would not follow me further for a knight that they have beset in one of their holds, that hath done them right sore mischief, for he hath hanged four of their knights and slain one, as well as the fairest damsel that was in the kingdom. But right well had she deserved the death for that she harboured knights with fair semblant and showed them much honour, and afterward brought about their death and destruction, between herself and a dwarf that she hath, that slew the knights.' 'And know you who is the knight?' saith Perceval. 'Sir,' saith the knight, 'Not I, for no leisure had I to ask him, for sorer need had I to flee than to stay. But I tell you that on account of the meat that failed him in the hold wherein they beset him, he issued forth raging like a lion, nor would he have suffered himself be shut up so long but for two wounds that he had upon his body; for he cared not to issue forth of the house until such time as they were healed, and also for that he had no horse. And so soon as he felt himself whole, he ventured himself against the four knights, that were so a-dread of him that they durst not come a-nigh. And moreover he deigneth not to go a-foot, wherefore if they now come a-nigh, it may not be but he shall have one at least out of their four horses, but they hold them heedfully aloof.' 'Sir,' saith Perceval, 'Gramercy of these tidings.' They were fain to depart from the knight, but said he : 'Ha, Lords, allow me so much as to see the destruction of

this evil folk that have wrought such mischief in this forest!
Sir,' saith he to Messire Gawain, 'I am cousin to the Poor
Knight of the Waste Forest that hath the two poor damsels to
sister, there where you and Lancelot jousted between you, and
when the knight that brought you tidings thereof died in the
night.' 'By my faith,' saith Messire Gawain, 'These tidings
know I well, for you say true, and your company hold I right
dear for the love of the Poor Knight, for never yet saw I more
courteous knight, nor more courteous damsels, nor better
nurtured, and our Lord God grant them as much good as I
would they should have.' Messire Gawain made the knight go
before, for well knew he the robbers' hold, but loath enough
had he been to go thither, had the knights not followed him
behind. Lancelot was issued forth of the hold sword in hand,
all armed, angry as a lion. The four knights were upon their
horses all armed, but no mind had they come a-nigh him, for
sore dreaded they the huge buffets he dealt, and his hardiment.
One of them came forward before the others, and it seemed him
shame that they might not vanquish one single knight. He
goeth to smite Lancelot a great stroke of his sword above in the
midst of his head, nor did Lancelot's sword fail of its stroke, for
before he could draw back, Lancelot dealt him such a blow as
smote off all of his leg at the thigh, so that he made him leave
the saddlebows empty. Lancelot leapt up on the destrier, and
now seemed him he was safer than before. The three robber-
knights that yet remained whole ran upon him on all sides and
began to press him of their swords in right sore wrath. Thereupon behold you, the knight cometh to the way that goeth to
the hold and saith to Messire Gawain and Perceval, 'Now may
you hear the clashing of swords and the melly.' Therewithal
the two good knights smite horse with spur and come thither
where the three robber-knights were assailing Lancelot. Each
of the twain smiteth his own so wrathfully that they thrust their
spears right through their bodies and bear them to the ground
dead. Howbeit the third knight was fain to flee, but the knight
that had come to show Messire Gawain the way took heart and
hardiment from the confidence of the good knights, and smote
him as he fled so sore that he pierced him with his spear to the
heart and toppled him to the ground dead. And the one whose
leg Lancelot had lopped off was so trampled underfoot of the
knights that he had no life in him.

VI

When Lancelot knew Perceval and Messire Gawain he made great joy of them and they of him. 'Lancelot,' saith Messire Gawain, 'This knight that led us hither to save your life is cousin to the Poor Knight of the Waste Castle, the brother of the two poor damsels that lodged us so well. We will send him these horses, one for the knight that shall be the messenger, and the two to the lord of the Waste Castle, and this hold that we have taken shall be for the two damsels, and so shall we make them safe all the days of their life. This, methinketh, will be well.' 'Certes,' saith Perceval, 'You speak of great courtesy.' 'Sir,' saith Lancelot, 'Messire Gawain hath said, and right willingly will I grant him all his wish.' 'Lords,' saith the knight, 'They have in this forest a hold wherein the knights did bestow their plunder, for the sake whereof they murdered the passers by. If the goods remain there they will be lost, for therein is so great store as might be of much worth to many folk that are poverty-stricken for want thereof.' They go to the hold and find right great treasure in a cave underground, and rich sets of vessels and rich ornaments of cloth and armours for horses, that they had thrown the one over another into a pit that was right broad. 'Certes,' saith he, 'Right well hath it been done to this evil folk that is destroyed!' 'Sir,' saith Lancelot, 'In like manner would they have dealt with me and killed me if they might; whereof no sorrow have I save of the damsel that I slew, that was one of the fairest dames of the world. But I slew her not knowingly, for I meant rather to strike the knight, but she leapt between us, like the hardiest dame that saw I ever.' 'Sirs,' saith the knight, 'Perceval and Lancelot, by the counsel of Messire Gawain, granted the treasure to the two damsels, sisters to the Poor Knight of the Waste Castle, whereupon let them send for Joseus the Hermit and bid him guard the treasure until they shall come hither.' And Joseus said that he would do so, and is right glad that the robbers of the forest are made away withal, that had so often made assault upon him. He guarded the treasure and the hold right safely in the forest; but the dread and the renown of the good knights that had freed the forest went far and wide. The knight that led the three destriers was right joyfully received at the Waste Castle; and when he told the

message wherewith he was charged by Messire Gawain, the
Poor Knight and two damsels made great joy thereof. Perceval
taketh leave of Messire Gawain and Lancelot, and saith that
never will he rest again until he shall have found his sister and
his widow mother. They durst not gainsay him, for they know
well that he is right, and he prayeth them right sweetly that
they salute the King and Queen and all the good knights of the
court, for, please God, he will go see them at an early day.
But first he was fain to fulfil the promise King Arthur made to
his sister, for he would not that the King should be blamed in
any place as concerning him, nor by his default; and he himself
would have the greater blame therein and he succoured her not,
for the matter touched him nearer than it did King Arthur.

VII

With that the Good Knight departeth, and they commend
him to God, and he them in like sort. Messire Gawain and
Lancelot go their way back toward the court of King Arthur,
and Perceval goeth amidst strange forests until he cometh to a
forest far away, wherein, so it seemed him, he had never been
before. And he passed through a land that seemed him to have
been laid waste, for it was all void of folk. Wild beast only
seeth he there, that ran through the open country. He entered
into a forest in this waste country, and found a hermitage in the
combe of a mountain. He alighted without and heard that the
hermit was singing the service of the dead, and had begun the
mass with a requiem betwixt him and his clerk. He looketh
and seeth a pall spread upon the ground before the altar as
though it were over a corpse. He would not enter the chapel
armed, wherefore he hearkened to the mass from without right
reverently, and showed great devotion as he that loved God
much and was a-dread. When the mass was sung, and the
hermit was disarmed of the armour of Our Lord, he cometh to
Perceval and saluteth him and Perceval him again. 'Sir,' saith
Perceval, 'For whom have you done such service? meseemed
that the corpse lay therewithin for whom the service was
ordained.' 'You say truth,' saith the hermit. 'I have done it
for Lohot, King Arthur's son, that lieth buried under this pall.'
'Who, then, hath slain him?' saith Perceval. 'That will I tell
you plainly,' saith the hermit.

G

VIII

'This wasted land about this forest wherethrough you have
come is the beginning of the kingdom of Logres.   There wont
to be therein a Giant so big and horrible and cruel that none
durst won within half a league round about, and he destroyed
the land and wasted it in such sort as you see.   Lohot was
departed from the land and the court of King Arthur his father
in quest of adventure, and by the will of God arrived at this
forest, and fought against Logrin, right cruel as he was, and
Logrin against him.   As it pleased God, Lohot vanquished him;
but Lohot had a marvellous custom: when he had slain a man,
he slept upon him.   A knight of King Arthur's court, that is
called Kay the Seneschal, was come peradventure into this forest
of Logres.   He heard the Giant roar when Lohot dealt him the
mortal blow.   Thither came he as fast as he might, and found
the King's son sleeping upon Logrin.   He drew his sword and
therewith cut off Lohot's head, and took the head and the body
and set them in a coffin of stone.   After that he hacked his
shield to pieces with his sword, that he should not be recognised; then came he to the Giant that lay dead, and so cut off
his head, that was right huge and hideous, and hung it at his
fore saddle-bow.   Then went he to the court of King Arthur
and presented it to him.   The King made great joy thereof and
all they of the court, and the King made broad his lands right
freely for that he believed Kay had spoken true.   I went,' saith
the hermit, 'on the morrow to the piece of land where the Giant
lay dead, as a damsel came within here to tell me with right great
joy.   I found the corpse of the Giant so big that I durst not come
a-nigh it.   The damsel led me to the coffin where the King's
son was lying.   She asked the head of me as her guerdon, and
I granted it to her willingly.   She set it forthwith in a coffer
laden with precious stones that was all garnished within of
balsams.   After that, she helped me carry the body into this
chapel and enshroud and bury it.

IX

'Afterwards the damsel departed, nor have I never heard talk
of her since, nor do I make remembrance hereof for that I would
King Arthur should know it, nor for aught that I say thereof

that he should do evil to the knight; for right sore sin should I have thereof, but deadly treason and disloyalty hath he wrought.' 'Sir,' saith Perceval, 'This is sore pity of the King's son, that he is dead in such manner, for I have heard witness that he ever waxed more and more in great chivalry, and, so the King knew thereof, Kay the Seneschal, that is not well-loved of all folk, would lose the court for ever more, or his life, so he might be taken, and this would be only right and just.' Perceval lay the night in the hermitage, and departed on the morrow when he had heard mass. He rideth through the forest as he that right gladly would hear tidings of his mother, nor never before hath he been so desirous thereof as is he now. He heard, at right hour of noon, a damsel under a tree that made greater dole than ever heard he damsel make before. She held her mule by the reins and was alighted a-foot and set herself on her knees toward the East. She stretched her hands up toward heaven and prayed right sweetly the Saviour of the World and His sweet Mother that they would send her succour betimes, for that the most discounselled damsel of the world was she, and never was alms given to damsel to counsel her so well bestowed as it would be upon her, for that needs must she go to the most perilous place that is in the world, and that, save she might bring some one with her, never would that she had to do be done.

X

Perceval drew himself up when he heard the damsel bemoaning thus. He was in the shadow of the forest so that she saw him not. The damsel cried out all weeping, 'Ha, King Arthur, great sin did you in forgetting to speak of my business to the knight that bare away the shield from your court, by whom would my mother have been succoured, that now must lose her castle presently save God grant counsel herein; and so unhappy am I, that I have gone through all the lands of Great Britain, yet may I hear no tidings of my brother, albeit they say that he is the Best Knight of the world. But what availeth us his knighthood, when we have neither aid nor succour thereof? So much the greater shame ought he to have of himself, if he love his mother, as she, that is the most gentle lady that liveth and the most loyal, hath hope that, and he knew, he would come thither. Either he is dead or he is in lands so far away that

none may hear tidings of him.   Ha, sweet Lady, Mother of Our
Saviour, aid us when we may have no aid of any other! for if
my lady mother loseth her castle, needs must we be forlorn
wanderers in strange lands, for so have her brothers been long
time; he that had the most power and valour lieth in languishment, the good King Fisherman that the King of Castle Mortal
warreth on, albeit he also is my uncle, my mother's brother,
and would fain reave my uncle, that is his brother, of his castle
by his felony.   Of a man so evil my lady mother looketh for
neither aid nor succour.   And the good King Pelles hath renounced his kingdom for the love of his Saviour, and hath
entered into a hermitage.   He likewise is brother of my mother,
and behoveth him make war upon none, for the most worshipful
hermit is he of the world.   And all they on my father's side
have died in arms.   Eleven were there of them, and my father
was the twelfth.   Had they remained on live, well able would
they have been to succour us, but the knight that was first at
the Graal hath undone us, for through him our uncle fell in
languishment, in whom should have been our surest succour.'

XI

At this word Perceval rode forward, and the damsel heareth
him.   She riseth up, and looketh backward and seeth the knight
come, the shield at his neck banded argent and azure, with a
red cross.   She clasped her two hands toward heaven, and
saith, 'Ha, sweet Lady that didst bear the Saviour of the
World, you have not forgotten me, nor never may be discounselled he nor she that calleth upon you with the heart.   Here
see I the knight come of whom we shall have aid and succour,
and our Lord God grant him will to do His pleasure, and lend
him courage and strength to protect us!'   She goeth to meet
him, and holdeth his stirrup and would have kissed his foot, but
he avoideth it and crieth to her: 'Ill do you herein, damsel!'
And therewith she melteth in tears of weeping and prayeth him
right sweetly.   'Sir,' saith she, 'Of such pity as God had of
His most sweet Mother on that day He took His death, when
He beheld Her at the foot of the cross, have pity and mercy of
my lady mother and of me.   For, and your aid fail us, we know
not to whom to fly for rescue, for I have been told that you are
the Best Knight of the world.   And for obtaining of your help

went I to King Arthur's court. Wherefore succour us for pity's sake and God's and for nought beside, for, so please you, it is your duty so to do, albeit, had you been my brother that is also such a knight as you, whom I cannot find, I might have called upon you of a greater right. Sir,' saith she, ' Do you remember you of the brachet you had at the court waiting for you until such time as you should come for the shield, and that went away with you, how he would never make joy nor know any save me alone? By this know I well that if you knew the soreness of our need you would succour us. But King Arthur, that should have prayed you thereof, forgat it.' 'Damsel,' saith he, ' So much hath he done that he hath not failed of his covenant with you, for he sent for me by the two best knights of his court, and, so I may speed, so much will I do herein as that God and he shall be well pleased thereof.'

XII

The damsel had right great joy of the knight that he should grant her his aid, but she knew not he was her brother, or otherwise she would have doubled her joy. Perceval knoweth well that she is his sister, but he would not yet discover himself and manifest his pity outwardly. He helpeth the damsel to mount again and they rode on together. 'Sir,' saith the damsel, ' Needs must I go to-night by myself to the Grave-yard Peril-ous.' ' Wherefore go you thither?' saith Perceval. 'Sir,' saith she, 'I have made vow thereof, and moreover a holy hermit hath told me that the knight that warreth upon us may not be overcome of no knight, save I bring him not some of the cloth wherewith the altar in the chapel of the Grave-yard Perilous is covered. The cloth is of the most holiest, for our Lord God was covered therewith in the Holy Sepulchre, on the third day when He came back from death to life. Nor none may enter the holy grave-yard that bringeth another with him, wherefore behoveth me go by myself, and may God save my life this night, for the place is sore perilous, and so ought I greatly to hate him that hath procured me this dolour and travail. Sir,' saith she, ' You will go your way toward the castle of Camelot: there is the Widow Lady my mother, that awaiteth the return and the succour of the Good Knight, and may you remember to succour and aid us when you shall see how sore is our need of succour.'

XIII

'Damsel,' saith Perceval, 'So God allow me I will aid you to the utmost of my power.' 'Sir,' saith she, 'See, this is my way, that is but little frequented, for I tell you that no knight durst tread therein without great peril and great dread. And our Lord God have your body in keeping, for mine own this night shall be in sore jeopardy and hazard.' Perceval departeth from the damsel, his sister, and hath right great pity for that she goeth in so perilous place all alone. Natheless would he not forbid her, for he knew well that she might not go thither with him nor with other, sith that such was the custom of the grave-yard that twain might not pass the entrance, wherefore needs must one remain without. Perceval was not willing that his sister should break her vow, for never none of his lineage did at any time disloyalty nor base deed knowingly, nor failed of nought that they had in covenant, save only the King of Castle Mortal, from whom he had as much evil as he had good of the others.

XIV

The damsel goeth her way all alone and all forlorn toward the grave-yard and the deep of the forest, all dark and shadowy. She hath ridden until the sun was set and the night draweth nigh. She looketh before her and seeth a cross, high and wide and thick. And on this cross was the figure of Our Lord graven, whereof is she greatly comforted. She draweth nigh the cross, and so kisseth and adoreth it, and prayeth the Saviour of the world that was nailed on Holy Rood that He would bring her forth of the burial-ground with honour. The cross was at the entrance of the grave-yard, that was right spacious, for, from such time as the land was first peopled of folk, and that knights began to seek adventure by the forest, not a knight had died in the forest, that was full great of breadth and length, but his body was borne thither, nor might never knight there be buried that had not received baptism and had repented him not of his sins at his death.

XV

Thereinto entered the damsel all alone, and found great multitude of tombs and coffins. Nor none need wonder whether she had shuddering and fear, for such place must needs be dreadful to a lonely damsel, there where lay so many knights that had been slain in arms. Josephus the good clerk witnesseth us that within the grave-yard might no evil spirit meddle, for that Saint Andrew the apostle had blessed it with his hand. But never might no hermit remain within for the evil things that appeared each night all round about, that took the shapes of the knights that were dead in the forest, wherof the bodies lay not in the blessed burial-ground.

XVI

The damsel beholdeth their sepulchres all round about the grave-yard whereinto she was come. She seeth them surrounded of knights, all black, and spears had they withal, and came one against another, and made such uproar and alarm as it seemed all the forest resounded thereof. The most part held swords all red as of fire, and ran either upon other, and gashed one another's hands and feet and nose and face. And great was the clashing they made, but they could not come a-nigh the grave-yard. The damsel seeth them, and hath such affright thereof that she nigh fell to the ground in a swoon. The mule whereon she sate draweth wide his nostrils and goeth in much fear. The damsel signeth her of the cross and commendeth her to the Saviour and to His sweet Mother. She looketh before her to the head of the grave-yard, and seeth the chapel, small and ancient. She smiteth her mule with her whip, and cometh thitherward and alighteth. She entered therewithin and found a great brightness of light. Within was an image of Our Lady, to whom she prayeth right sweetly that She will preserve her senses and her life and enable her to depart in safety from this perilous place. She seeth above the altar the most holy cloth for the which she was come thither, that was right ancient, and a smell came thereof so sweet and glorious that no sweetness of the world might equal it. The damsel cometh toward the altar thinking to take the cloth, but it goeth up into the air as if the wind had lifted it, and was so high that she might not reach it above an ancient crucifix that was there within. 'Ha, God!' saith the damsel, 'It is for my sin and my disloyalty that this most holy cloth thus draweth itself away from me!'

XVII

'Fair Father God, never did I evil to none, nor never did I shame nor sinned deadly in myself, nor never wrought against your will, so far as in me lay, but rather do I serve you and love and fear you and your sweet Mother; and all the tribulation I receive, accept I in patience for your love, for well I know that such is your pleasure, nor have I no will to set myself against nought that pleaseth you.

XVIII

'When it shall please you, you will release me and my mother of the grief and tribulation wherein we are. For well you know that they have reaved her of her castles by wrong, and of her land, for that she is a Widow Lady without help. Lord, you who have all the world at your mercy and do your commandment in all things, grant me betimes to hear tidings of my brother and he be on live, for sore need have we of him. And so lend force to the knight and power against all our enemies, that for your love and for pity is fain to succour and aid my mother that is sore discounselled. Lord, well might it beseem you to remember of your pity and the sweetness that is in you, and of compassion that she hath been unrighteously disherited, and that no succour nor aid nor counsel hath she, save of you alone. You are her affiance and her succour, and therefore ought you to remember that the good knight Joseph of Abarimacie, that took down your Body when it hung upon the rood, was her own uncle. Better loved he to take down your Body than all the gold and all the fee that Pilate might give him. Lord, good right of very truth had he so to do, for he took you in his arms beside the rood, and laid your Body in the holy sepulchre, wherein were you covered of the sovran cloth for the which have I come in hither. Lord, grant it be your pleasure that I may have it, for love of the knight by whom it was set in this chapel; sith that I am of his lineage it ought well to manifest itself in this sore need, so it come according to your pleasure.' Forthwith the cloth came down above the altar, and she straightway found taken away therefrom as much as it pleased Our Lord she should have. Josephus telleth us of a truth, that never did none enter into the chapel that might touch the cloth save only this one damsel. She set her face to it and her mouth or ever the cloth removed.

XIX

Thereafter, she took the piece that God would and set it near herself full worshipfully, but still the stour went on of the evil spirits round about the church-yard, and they dealt one another blows so sore that all the forest resounded thereof, and it seemed that it was all set on fire of the flame that issued from them. Great fear would the damsel have had of them, had she not comforted herself in God and in His dear, sweet Mother, and the most holy cloth that was within there. A Voice appeared upon the stroke of midnight from above the chapel, and speaketh to the souls whereof the bodies lie within the grave-yard : ' How sore loss hath befallen you of late, and all other whose bodies lie in other hallowed church-yards by the forests of this kingdom ! For the good King Fisherman is dead that made every day our service be done in the most holy chapel there where the most Holy Graal every day appeared, and where the Mother of God abode from the Saturday until the Monday that the service was finished. And now hath the King of Castle Mortal seized the castle in such sort that never sithence hath the Holy Graal appeared, and all the other hallows are hidden, so that none knoweth what hath become of the priests that served in the chapel, nor the twelve ancient knights, nor the damsels that were therein. And you, damsel, that are within, have no affiance in the aid of strange knight in this need, for succoured may you never be save of your brother only ! '

XX

With that the Voice is still, and a wailing and a lamentation goeth up from the bodies that lay in the church-yard, so dolorous that no man is there in the world but should have pity thereof, and all the evil spirits that were without departed groaning and making so mighty uproar at their going away that it seemed all the earth trembled. The damsel heard the tidings of her uncle that was dead, and fell on the ground in a swoon, and when she raised herself, took on to lament and cried : ' Ha, God ! Now have we lost the most comfort and the best friend that we had, and hereof am I again discomforted that I may not be succoured in this my next need by the Good Knight of whom I thought to have succour and aid, and that was so fain to render it. Now shall I know not what to ask of him, for he would grant it right willingly, and may God be as pleased with him thereof as if he had done it.' The damsel was in sore misdoubting and dismay, for she knew not who the knight was, and great misgiving had she of her uncle's death and right sore sorrow. She was in the chapel until it was day, and then commended herself to God and departed and mounted on her mule and issued forth of the church-yard full speed, all alone.

XXI

The story saith that the damsel went her way toward her mother's castle as straight as she might, but sore dismayed was she of the Voice that had told her she might not be succoured save of her brother alone. She hath ridden so far of her journeys that she is come to the Valley of Camelot, and seeth her mother's castle that was surrounded of great rivers, and seeth Perceval, that was alighted under the shadow of a tree at the top of the forest in order that he might behold his mother's castle, whence he went forth squire what time he slew the Knight of the Red Shield. When he had looked well at the castle and the country round about, much pleasure had he thereof, and mounted again forthwith. Thereupon, behold you, the damsel cometh. 'Sir,' saith she, 'In sore travail and jeopardy have I been sithence that last I saw you, and tidings have I heard as bad as may be, and right grievous for my mother and myself. For King Fisherman mine uncle is dead, and another of my uncles, the King of Castle Mortal, hath seized his castle, albeit my lady mother ought rather to have it, or I, or my brother.' 'Is it true,' saith Perceval, 'that he is dead?' 'Yea, certes, Sir, I know it of a truth.' 'So help me God!' saith he, 'This misliketh me right sore. I thought not that he would die so soon, for I have not been to see him of a long time.'

XXII

'Sir,' saith she, 'I am much discomforted as concerning you, for I have likewise been told that no force nor aid of any knight may avail to succour nor aid me from this day forward save my brother's help alone. Wherefore, and it be so, we have lost all, for my lady mother hath respite to be in her castle only until the fifteenth day from to-day, and I know not where to seek my brother, and the day is so nigh as you hear. Now behoveth us do the best we may and abandon this castle betimes, nor know I any refuge that we now may have save only King Pelles in the hermitage. I would fain that my lady mother were there, for he would not fail us.' Perceval is silent, and hath great pity in his heart of this that the damsel saith. She followeth him weeping, and pointeth out to him the Valleys of Camelot and the castles that were shut in by combes and mountains, and the broad meadow-lands and the forest that girded them about. 'Sir,' saith she, 'All this hath the Lord of the Moors reaved of my lady mother, and nought coveteth he so much as to have this castle, and have it he will, betimes.'

XXIII

When they had ridden until that they drew nigh the castle, the Lady was at the windows of the hall and knew her daughter. 'Ha, God!' saith the Lady, 'I see there my daughter coming, and a knight with her. Fair Father God, grant of your pleasure that it be my son, for and it be not he, I have lost my castle and mine heirs are disherited.' Perceval cometh nigh the castle in company with his sister, and knoweth again the chapel that stood upon four columns of marble between the forest and the castle, there where his father told him how much ought he to love good knights, and that none earthly thing might be of greater worth, and how none might know yet who lay in the coffin until such time as the Best Knight of the world should come thither, but that then should it be known. Perceval would fain have passed by the chapel, but the damsel saith to him: 'Sir, no knight passeth hereby save he go first to see the coffin within the chapel.' He alighteth and setteth the damsel to the ground, and layeth down his spear and shield and cometh toward the tomb, that was right fair and rich. He set his hand above it. So soon as he came nigh, the sepulchre openeth on one side, so that one saw him that was within the coffin. The damsel falleth at his feet for joy. The Lady had a custom such that every time a knight stopped at the coffin she made the five ancient knights that she had with her in the castle accompany her, wherein they would never fail her, and bring her as far as the chapel. So soon as she saw the coffin open and the joy her daughter made, she knew that it was her son, and ran to him and embraced him and kissed him and began to make the greatest joy that ever lady made.

XXIV

'Now know I well,' saith she, 'that our Lord God hath not forgotten me. Sith that I have my son again, the tribulations and the wrongs that have been done me grieve me not any more. Sir,' saith she to her son, 'Now is it well known and proven that you are the Best Knight of the world! For otherwise never would the coffin have opened, nor would any have known who he is that you now see openly.' She maketh her chaplain take certain letters that were sealed with gold in the coffin. He looketh thereat and readeth, and then saith that these letters witness of him that lieth in the coffin that he was one of them that helped to un-nail Our Lord from the cross. They looked beside him and found the pincers all bloody wherewith the nails were drawn, but they might not take them away, nor the body, nor the coffin, according as Josephus telleth us, for as soon as Perceval was forth of the chapel, the coffin closed again and joined together even as it was before. The Widow Lady led her son with right great joy into her castle, and recounted to him all the shame that had been done her, and also how Messire Gawain had made safe the castle for a year by his good knighthood.

XXV

'Fair son,' saith she, 'now is the term drawn nigh when I should have lost my castle and you had not come. But now know I well that it shall be safe-guarded of you. He that coveteth this castle is one of the most outrageous knights on live. And he hath reaved me of my land and the Valleys of Camelot without reasonable occasion. But, please God, you shall well repair the harm he hath done you, for nought claim I any longer of the land since you are come. But so avenge your shame as to increase your honour, for none ought to allow his right to be minished of an evil man, and the mischiefs that have

been done me for that I had no aid, let them not wax cold in
you, for a shame done to one valiant and strong ought not to
wax cold in him, but rankle and prick in him, so ought he to
have his enemies in remembrance without making semblant, but
so much as he shall show in his cheer and making semblant and
his menaces, so much ought he to make good in deed when he
shall come in place. For one cannot do too much hurt to an
enemy, save only one is willing to let him be for God's sake.
But truth it is that the scripture saith, that one ought not to do
evil to one's enemies, but pray God that He amend them. I
would fain that our enemies were such that they might amend
toward us, and that they would do as much good to us without
harming themselves as they have done evil, on condition that
mine anger and yours were foregone against them. Mine own
anger I freely forbear against them so far forth as concerneth
myself, for no need have I to wish evil to none, and Solomon
telleth how the sinner that curseth other sinner curseth himself
likewise.

XXVI

'Fair son, this castle is yours, and this land round about
whereof I have been reft ought to be yours of right, for it
falleth to you on behalf of your father and me. Wherefore
send to the Lord of the Moors that hath reft it from me, that he
render it to you. I make no further claim, for I pass it on to
you ; for nought have I now to do with any land save only so
much as will be enough wherein to bury my body when I die,
nor shall I now live much longer since King Fisherman my
brother is dead, whereof right sorrowful am I at heart, and still
more sorrowful should I be were it not for your coming. And,
son, I tell you plainly that you have great blame of his death,
for you are the knight through whom he fell first into languishment, for now at last I know well that and if you had afterwards gone back and so made the demand that you made not at
the first, he would have come back to health. But our Lord
God willed it so to be, wherefore well beseemeth us to yield to
His will and pleasure.'

XXVII

Perceval hath heard his mother, but right little hath he
answered her, albeit greatly is he pleased with whatsoever she

hath said. His face is to-flushed of hardiment, and courage hath
taken hold on him. His mother looketh at him right fainly, and
hath him disarmed and apparelled in a right rich robe. So
comely a knight was he that in all the world might not be found
one of better seeming nor better shapen of body. The Lord of
the Moors, that made full certain of having his mother's castle,
knew of Perceval's coming. He was not at all dismayed in
semblant, nor would he stint to ride by fell nor forest, and
every day he weened in his pride that the castle should be his
own at the hour and the term he had set thereof. One of the
five knights of the Widow Lady was one day gone into the
Lonely Forest after hart and hind, and had taken thereof at his
will. He was returning back to the castle and the huntsmen
with him, when the Lord of the Moors met him and told him he
had done great hardiment in shooting with the bow in the
forest, and the knight made answer that the forest was not his
of right, but the Lady's of Camelot and her son's that had
repaired thither.

XXVIII

The Lord of the Moors waxed wroth. He held a sword in
his hand and thrust him therewith through the body and slew
him. The knight was borne dead to the castle of Camelot
before the Widow Lady and her son. 'Fair son,' saith the
Widow Lady, 'More presents of such-like kind the Lord of the
Moors sendeth me than I would. Never may he be satisfied of
harming my land and shedding the blood of the bodies of my
knights. Now may you well know how many a hurt he hath
done me sithence that your father hath been dead and you were
no longer at the castle, sith that this hath he done me even
now that you are here. You have the name of Perceval on this
account, that tofore you were born, he had begun to reave your
father of the Valleys of Camelot, for your father was an old
knight and all his brethren were dead, and therefore he gave
you this name in baptism, for that he would remind you of the
mischief done to him and to you, and that you might help to
retrieve it and you should have the power.' The Dame maketh
shroud the knight, for whom she is full sorrowful, and on the
morrow hath mass sung and burieth him. Perceval made arm
two of the old knights with him, then issued forth of the castle
and entered the great dark forest. He rode until he came before

a castle, and met five knights that issued forth all armed. He asked whose men they were. They answer, the Lord's of the Moors, and that he goeth seek the son of the Widow Lady that is in the forest. 'If we may deliver him up to our lord, good guerdon shall we have thereof.' 'By my faith,' saith Perceval, 'You have not far to seek. I am here!'

XXIX

Percival smiteth his horse of his spurs and cometh to the first in such sort that he passeth his spear right through his body and beareth him to the ground dead. The other two knights each smote his man so that they wounded them in the body right sore. The other two would fain have fled, but Perceval preventeth them, and they gave themselves up prisoners for fear of death. He bringeth all four to the castle of Camelot and presenteth them to his lady mother. 'Lady,' saith he, 'see here the quittance for your knight that was slain, and the fifth also remaineth lying on the piece of ground shent in like manner as was your own.' 'Fair son,' saith she, 'I should have better loved peace after another sort, and so it might be.' 'Lady,' saith he, 'Thus is it now. One ought to make war against the warrior, and be at peace with the peaceable.' The knights are put in prison. The tidings are come to the Lord of the Moors that the son of the Widow Lady hath slain one of his knights and carried off four to prison. Thereof hath he right great wrath at heart, and sweareth and standeth to it that never will he be at rest until he shall have either taken or slain him, and that, so there were any knight in his land that would deliver him up, he would give him one of the best castles in his country. The more part are keen to take Perceval. Eight came for that intent· before him all armed in the forest of Camelot, and hunted and drove wild deer in the purlieus of the forest so that they of the castle saw them.

XXX

Perceval was in his mother's chapel, where he heard mass; and when the mass was sung, his sister said: 'Fair brother, see here the most holy cloth that I brought from the chapel of the Grave-yard Perilous. Kiss it and touch it with your face, for a holy hermit told me that never should our land be conquered back until such time as you should have hereof.' Perceval kisseth it, then toucheth his eyes and face therewith.   Afterward he goeth to arm him, and the four knights with him ; then he issueth forth of the chamber and mounteth on his horse, then goeth out of the gateway like a lion unchained.   He sitteth on a tall horse all covered.   He cometh nigh the eight knights that were all armed, man and horse, and asketh them what folk they be and what they seek, and they say that they are enemies of the Widow Lady and her son.   'Then you do I defy!' saith Perceval.   He cometh to them a great run, and the four knights with him, and each one overthroweth his own man so roughly that either he is wounded in his body or maimed of arm or leg. The rest held the melly to the utmost they might endure. Perceval made take them and bring to the castle, and the other five that they had overthrown.   The Lord of the Moors was come to shoot with a bow, and he heard the noise of the knights, and cometh thitherward a great gallop all armed.   'Sir,' saith one of the old knights to Perceval, 'Look! here is the Lord of the Moors coming, that hath reft your mother of her land and slain her men.   Of him will it be good to take vengeance.   See, how boldly he cometh.'   Perceval looketh on him as he that loveth him not, and cometh toward him as hard as his horse may carry him, and smiteth him right through the breast so strongly that he beareth to the ground him and his horse together all in a heap.   He alighteth to the ground and draweth his sword. 'How?' saith the Lord of the Moors, 'Would you then slay me and put me in worse plight than I am?'   'By my head,' saith Perceval, 'No, not so swiftly, but I will slay you enough, betimes!'   'So it seemeth you,' saith the Lord of the Moors, 'But it shall not be yet!'   He leapeth up on his feet and runneth on Perceval, sword drawn, as one that fain would harm him if he might.   But Perceval defendeth himself as good knight should, and giveth such a buffet at the outset as smiteth off his arm together with his sword.   The knights that came after fled back all discomfited when they saw their lord wounded.   And Perceval made lift him on a horse and carry him to the castle and presenteth him to his mother.   'Lady,' saith he, 'See here the Lord of the Moors!   Well might you expect him eftsoons, sith that you were to have yielded him up your castle the day after to-morrow!'

XXXI

'Lady,' saith the Lord of the Moors, 'Your son hath wounded me and taken my knights and myself likewise. I will yield you up your castle albeit I hold it mine as of right, on condition you cry me quit.' 'And who shall repay her,' saith Perceval, 'for the shame that you have done her, for her knights that you have slain, whereof never had you pity? Now, so help me God, if she have mercy or pity upon you, never hereafter will I trouble to come to her aid how sore soever may be her need. Such pity and none other as you have had for her and my sister will I have for you. Our Lord God commanded in both the Old Law and the New, that justice should be done upon man-slayers and traitors, and justice will I do upon you that His commandment be not transgressed.' He hath a great vat made ready in the midst of the court, and maketh the eleven knights be brought. He maketh their heads be stricken off into the vat and bleed therein as much blood as might come from them, and then made the heads and the bodies be drawn forth so that nought was there but blood in the vat. After that, he made disarm the Lord of the Moors and be brought before the vat wherein was great abundance of blood. He made bind his feet and his hands right strait, and after that saith: 'Never might you be satisfied of the blood of the knights of my lady mother, now will I satisfy you of the blood of your own knights!' He maketh hang him by the feet in the vat, so that his head were in the blood as far as the shoulders, and so maketh him be held there until that he was drowned and quenched. After that, he made carry his body and the bodies of the other knights and their heads, and made them be cast into an ancient charnel that was beside an old chapel in the forest, and the vat together with the blood made he be cast into the river, so that the water thereof was all bloody. The tidings came to the castles that the son of the Widow Lady had slain the Lord of the Moors and the best of his knights. Thereof were they in sore misgiving, and the most part said that the like also would he do to them save they held themselves at his commandment. They brought him the keys of all the castles that had been reft of his mother, and all the knights that had before renounced their allegiance returned thereunto and pledged themselves to be at his will for dread of death. All the land was assured in safety, nor was there nought to trouble the Lady's joy save only that King Fisherman her brother was dead, whereof she was right sorrowful and sore afflicted.

XXXII

One day the Widow Lady sate at meat, and there was great plenty of knights in the hall. Perceval sate him beside his sister. Thereupon, behold you the Damsel of the Car that came with the other two damsels before the Widow Lady and her son, and saluted them right nobly. 'Damsel,' saith Perceval, 'Good adventure may you have!' 'Sir,' saith she, 'You have speeded right well of your business here, now go speed it elsewhere, for thereof is the need right sore. King Hermit, that is your mother's brother, sendeth you word that, and you come not with haste into the land that was King Fisherman's your uncle, the New Law that God hath stablished will be sore brought low. For the King of Castle Mortal, that hath seized the land and castle, hath made be cried throughout all the country how all they that would fain maintain the Old Law and abandon the New shall have protection of him and counsel and aid, and they that will not shall be destroyed and outlawed.' 'Ha, fair son,' saith the Widow Lady, 'Now have you heard the great disloyalty of the evil man that is my brother, whereof am I right sorrowful, for that he is of my kindred.' 'Lady,' saith Perceval, 'Your brother nor my uncle is he no longer, sith that he denieth God! Rather is he our mortal enemy that we ought of right to hate more than any stranger!'

XXXIII

'Fair son,' saith the Widow Lady, 'I pray and beseech you that the Law of the Saviour be not set aside in forgetfulness and neglect there where you may exalt it, for better Lord in no wise may you serve, nor one that better knoweth how to bestow fair guerdon. Fair son, none may be good knight that serveth Him not and loveth Him. Take heed that you be swift in His service nor delay not for no intent, but be ever at His commandment alike at eventide as in the morning, so shall you not bely your lineage. And the Lord God grant you good intent therein and good will to go on even as you have begun.'

The Widow Lady, that much loved her son, riseth up from the tables, and all the other knights, and seemeth it that she is Lady of her land in such sort as that never was she better. But full often doth she give thanks to the Saviour of the World with her whole heart, and prayeth Him of His pleasure grant her son length of life for the amendment both of soul and body. Perceval was with his mother of a long space, and with his sister, and was much feared and honoured of all the knights of the land, alike for his great wisdom and great pains taking, as well as for the valour of his knighthood.

BRANCH XVI

TITLE I

THIS High History saith that Messire Gawain and Lancelot were repaired to the court of King Arthur from the quest they had achieved. The King made great joy thereof and the Queen. King Arthur sate one day at meat by the side of the Queen, and they had been served of the first meats. Thereupon come two knights all armed, and each bore a dead knight before him, and the knights were still armed as they had been when their bodies were alive. 'Sir,' say the knights, 'This shame and this mischief is yours. In like manner will you lose all your knights betimes and God love you not well enough to give counsel herein forthwith of his mercy.' 'Lords,' saith the King, 'How came these knights to be in so evil case?' 'Sir,' say they, 'It is of good right you ought to know. The Knight of the Fiery Dragon is entered into the head of your land, and is destroying knights and castles and whatsoever he may lay hands on, in such sort that none durst contend against him, for he is taller by a foot than any knight ever you had, and of grisly cheer, and so is his sword three times bigger than the sword of ever another knight, and his spear is well as heavy as a man may carry. Two knights might lightly cover them of his shield, and it hath on the outer side the head of a dragon that casteth forth fire and flame whensoever he will, so eager and biting that none may long endure his encounter.

II

'None other, how strong soever he be, may stand against him, and, even as you see, hath he burnt and evil-entreated all other knights that have withstood him.' 'From what land hath come such manner of man?' 'Sir,' say the knights, 'He is come from the Giant's castle, and he warreth upon you for the love of Logrin the Giant, whose head Messire Kay brought you into your court, nor never, saith he, will he have joy until such time as he shall have avenged him on your body or upon the knight that you love best.' 'Our Lord God,' saith the King, 'will defend us from so evil a man.' He is risen from the table, all scared, and maketh carry the two dead knights to be buried, and the others turn back again when they have told their message. The King calleth Messire Gawain and Lancelot and asketh them what he shall do of this knight that is entered into his land? 'By my head, I know not what to say, save you give counsel herein.' 'Sir,' saith Lancelot, 'We will go against him, so please you, I and Messire Gawain between us.' 'By my head,' saith the King, 'I would not let you go for a kingdom, for such man as is this is no knight but a devil and a fiend that hath issued from the borders of Hell. I say not but that it were great worship and prize to slay and conquer him, but he that should go against him should set his own life in right sore jeopardy and run great hazard of being in as bad plight as these two knights I have seen.' The King was in such dismay that he knew not neither what to say nor to do, and so was all the court likewise in such sort as no knight neither one nor another was minded to go to battle with him, and so remained the court in great dismay.

BRANCH XVII

INCIPIT

HERE beginneth one of the master branches of the Graal in the name of the Father, and of the Son, and of the Holy Ghost.

TITLE I

Perceval had been with his mother as long as it pleased him. He hath departed with her good will and the good will of his sister, and telleth them he will return into the land as speedily as he may. He entereth into the great Lonely Forest, and rideth so far on his journeys that he cometh one day at the right hour of noon into a passing fair launde, and seeth a forest. He looketh amidst the launde and seeth a red cross. He looketh to the head of the launde and seeth a right comely knight sitting in the shadow of the forest, and he was clad in white garments and held a vessel of gold in his hand. At the other end of the launde he seeth a damsel likewise sitting, young and gentle and of passing great beauty, and she was clad in a white samite dropped of gold. Josephus telleth us by the divine scripture that out of the forest issued a beast, white as driven snow, and it was bigger than a fox and less than a hare. The beast came into the launde all scared, for she had twelve hounds in her belly, that quested within like as it were hounds in a wood, and she fled adown the launde for fear of the hounds, the questing whereof she had within her. Perceval rested on the shaft of his spear to look at the marvel of this beast, whereof he had right great pity, so gentle was she of semblance, and of so passing beauty, and by her eyes it might seem that they were two emeralds. She runneth to the knight, all affrighted, and when she hath been there awhile and the hounds rend her again, she runneth to the damsel, but neither there may she stay long time, for the hounds that are within her cease not of their questing, whereof is she sore adread.

II

She durst not venture herself in the forest. She seeth Perceval and so cometh toward him for protection. She maketh as though she would lie down on his horse's neck, and he holdeth forth his hands to receive her there so as that she might not hurt herself, and evermore the hounds quested. Howbeit the knight crieth out to him, 'Sir Knight, let the beast go and hold her not, for this belongeth neither to you nor to other, but let her dree her weird.' The beast seeth that no protection hath she. She goeth to the cross, and forthwith might the hounds no longer be in her, but issued forth all as it were live hounds, but nought had they of her gentleness nor her beauty. She humbled herself much among them and crouched on the ground and made semblant as though she would have cried them mercy, and gat herself as nigh the cross as she might. The hounds had compassed her round about and ran in upon her upon all sides and tore her all to pieces with their teeth, but no power had they to devour her flesh, nor to remove it away from the cross.

III

When the hounds had all to-mangled the beast, they fled away into the wood as had they been raging mad. The knight and the damsel came there where the beast lay in pieces at the cross, and so taketh each his part and setteth the same on their golden vessels, and took the blood that lay upon the earth in like manner as the flesh, and kiss the place, and adore the cross, and then betake them into the forest. Perceval alighteth and setteth him on his knees before the cross and so kisseth and adoreth it, and the place where the beast was slain, in like manner as he had seen the knight and damsel do; and there came to him a smell so sweet of the cross and of the place, such as no sweetness may be compared therewith. He looketh and seeth coming from the forest two priests all afoot; and the first shouteth to him: 'Sir Knight, withdraw yourself away from the cross, for no right have you to come nigh it': Perceval draweth

him back, and the priest kneeleth before the cross and adoreth
it and boweth down and kisseth it more than a score times, and
manifesteth the most joy in the world.   And the other priest
cometh after, and bringeth a great rod, and setteth the first
priest aside by force, and beateth the cross with the rod in
every part, and weepeth right passing sore.

IV

Perceval beholdeth him with right great wonderment, and
saith unto him, 'Sir, herein seem you to be no priest! wherefore
do you so great shame?'   'Sir,' saith the priest, 'It nought
concerneth you of whatsoever we may do, nor nought shall you
know thereof for us!'   Had he not been a priest, Perceval
would have been right wroth with him, but he had no will to
do him any hurt.   Therewithal he departeth and mounteth his
horse and entereth the forest again, all armed, but scarce had
he ridden away in such sort or ever he met the Knight Coward,
that cried out to him as far as he could see him, 'Sir, for God's
sake, take heed to yourself!'   'What manner man are you?'
saith Perceval.   'Sir,' saith he, 'My name is the Knight
Coward, and I am man of the Damsel of the Car.   Wherefore
I pray you for God's sake and for your own valour that you
touch me not.'   Perceval looketh on him and seeth him tall and
comely and well-shapen and adroit and all armed upon his horse,
so he saith to him, 'Sith that you are so coward, wherefore are
you armed thus?'   'Sir,' saith he, 'Against the evil intent of
any knight of whom I am adread, for such an one might haply
meet me as would slay me forthwith.'

V

'Are you so coward as you say?' saith Perceval.   'Yea,'
saith he, 'And much more.'   'By my head,' saith he, 'I will
make you hardy.   Come now along with me, for sore pity is
it that cowardize should harbour in so comely a knight.   I am
fain that your name be changed speedily, for such name beseemeth no knight.'   'Ha, Sir, for God's sake, mercy!   Now
know I well that you desire to slay me!   No will have I to
change neither my courage nor my name!   'By my head,'
saith Perceval, 'Then will you die therefor, betimes!'   He

maketh him go before him, will he or nill he ; and the knight
goeth accordingly with right sore grudging. They had scarce
ridden away, when he heard in the forest off the way, two
damsels that bewailed them right sore, and prayed our Lord
God send them succour betimes.

VI

Perceval cometh towards them, he and the knight he driveth
before him perforce, and seeth a tall knight all armed that
leadeth the damsels all dishevelled, and smiteth them from time
to time with a great rod, so that the blood ran down their faces.
' Ha, Sir Knight,' saith Perceval, ' What ask you of these two
damsels that you entreat so churlishly ? ' ' Sir,' saith he, ' They
have disherited me of mine own hold in this forest that Messire
Gawain gave them.' ' Sir,' say they to Perceval, ' This knight
is a robber, and none other but he now wonneth in this forest,
for the other robber-knights were slain by Messire Gawain and
Lancelot and another knight that came with them, and, for the
sore suffering and poverty that Messire Gawain and Lancelot
saw in us aforetime, and in the house of my brother in whose
castle they lay, were they fain to give us this hold and the
treasure they conquered from the robber-knights, and for this
doth he now lead us away to slay and destroy us, and as much
would he do for you and all other knights, so only he had the
power.' ' Sir Knight,' saith Perceval, ' Let be these damsels,
for well I know that they say true, for that I was there when
the hold was given them.' ' Then you helped to slay my
kindred,' saith the knight, ' And therefore you do I defy ! '
' Ha,' saith the Knight Coward to Perceval, ' Take no heed of
that he saith, and wax not wroth, but go your way ! ' ' Certes,'
saith Perceval, ' This will I not do : Rather will I help to
challenge the honour of the damsels.'

VII

' Ha, Sir,' saith the Knight Coward, ' Never shall it be
challenged of me ! ' Perceval draweth him back. ' Sir,' saith
he, ' See here my champion that I set in my place.' The robber
knight moveth toward him, and smiteth him so sore on the
shield that he breaketh his spear, but he might not unseat the

Coward Knight, that sate still upright as aforehand in the saddle-bows. He looketh at the other knight that hath drawn his sword. The Knight Coward looketh on the one side and the other, and would fain have fled and he durst. But Perceval crieth to him : 'Knight, do your endeavour to save my honour and your own life and the honour of these two damsels !' And the robber-knight dealeth him a great buffet of his sword so as that it went nigh to stun him altogether. Howbeit the Coward Knight moveth not. Perceval looketh at him in wonderment and thinketh him that he hath set too craven a knight in his place, and now at last knoweth well that he spake truth. The robber-knight smiteth him all over his body and giveth him so many buffets that the knight seeth his own blood. 'By my head,' saith he, 'You have wounded me, but you shall pay therefor, for I supposed not that you were minded to slay me !' He draweth his sword, that was sharp and strong, and smiteth his horse right sore hard of his spurs, and catcheth the knight with his sword right in the midst of his breast with a sweep so strong that he beareth him to the ground beside his horse. He alighteth over him, unlaceth his ventail and smiteth down his coif, then striketh off his head and presenteth it to Perceval. 'Sir,' saith he, 'Here give I you of my first joust.' 'By my head,' said Perceval, 'Right dearly love I this present ! Now take heed that you never again fall back into the cowardize wherein you have been. For it is too sore shame to a knight !' 'Sir,' saith he, 'I will not, but never should I have believed that one could become hardy so speedily, or otherwise long ago would I have become so, and so should I have had worship and honour thereof, for many a knight hath held me in contempt herein, that elsewise would have honoured me.' Perceval answereth that right and reason it is that worshipful men should be more honoured than the other. 'I commend these two damsels to your protection, and lead them to their hold in safety, and be at their pleasure and their will, and so say everywhere that you have for name the Knight Hardy, for more of courtesy hath this name than the other.' 'Sir,' saith he, 'You say true, and you have I to thank for the name.' The damsels give great thanks to Perceval, and take leave of him, and so go their way with right good will toward the knight that goeth with them on account of the knight he had slain, so that thereof called they him the Knight Hardy.

VIII

Perceval departeth from the place where the knight lieth dead, and rideth until that he draweth nigh to Cardoil where King Arthur was, and findeth the country round in sore terror and dismay. Much he marvelleth wherefore it may be, and demandeth of some of the meaner sort wherefore they are in so sore affright. 'Doth the King, then, live no longer?' 'Sir,' say the most part, 'Yea, he is there within in this castle, but never was he so destroyed nor so scared as he is at this present. For a knight warreth upon him against whom no knight in the world may endure.' Perceval rideth on until he cometh before the master hall, and is alighted on the mounting-stage. Lancelot and Messire Gawain come to meet him and make much joy of him, as do the King and Queen and all they of the court; and they made disarm him and do upon him a right rich robe. They that had never seen him before looked upon him right fainly for the worship and valour of his knighthood. The court also was rejoiced because of him, for sore troubled had it been. So as the King sate one day at meat, there came four knights into the hall, and each one of them bore before him a dead knight. And their feet and arms had been stricken off, but their bodies were still all armed, and the habergeons thereon were all black as though they had been blasted of lightning. They laid the knights in the midst of the hall. 'Sir,' say they to the King, 'Once more is made manifest this shame that is done you that is not yet amended. The Knight of the Dragon destroyeth you your land and slayeth your men and cometh as nigh us as he may, and saith that in your court shall never be found knight so hardy as that he durst abide him or assault him.' Right sore shame hath the King of these tidings, and Messire Gawain and Lancelot likewise. Right sorrowful are they of heart for that the King would not allow them to go thither. The four knights turn back again and leave the dead knights in the hall, but the King maketh them be buried with the others.

IX

A great murmuring ariseth amongst the knights in the hall, and the most part say plainly that they never heard tell of none that slew knights in such cruel sort, nor so many as did he;

and that neither Messire Gawain nor Lancelot ought to be
blamed for that they went not thither, for no knight in the
world might conquer such a man and our Lord God did not, for
he casteth forth fire and flame from his shield whensoever him
listeth. And while this murmur was going on between the
knights all round about the hall, behold you therewithal the
Damsel that made bear the knight in the horse-bier and cometh
before the King. 'Sir,' saith she, 'I pray and beseech you that
you do me right in your court. See, here is Messire Gawain
that was at the assembly in the Red Launde where were many
knights, and among them was the son of the Widow Lady, that
I see sitting beside you. He and Messire Gawain were they
that won the most prize of the assembly. This knight had
white arms, and they of the assembly said that he had better
done than Messire Gawain, for that he had been first in the
assembly. It had been granted me, before the assembly began,
that he that should do best thereat, should avenge the knight.
Sir, I have sought for him until I have now found him at your
court. Wherefore I pray and beseech you that you bid him do
so much herein as that he be not blamed, for Messire Gawain
well knoweth that I have spoken true. But the knight departed
so soon from the assembly, that I knew not what had become of
him, and Messire Gawain was right heavy for that he had
departed, for he was in quest of him, but knew him not.'

X

'Damsel,' saith Messire Gawain, 'Truth it is that he it was
that did best at the assembly in the Red Launde, and moreover,
please God, well will he fulfil his covenant towards you.'
'Messire Gawain,' saith Perceval, 'Meseemeth you did best
above all other.' 'By my faith,' saith Messire Gawain, 'You
speak of your courtesy, but howsoever I or other may have
done, you had the prize therein by the judgment of the knights.
Of so much may I well call upon the damsel to bear witness.'
'Sir,' saith she, 'Gramercy! He ought not to deny me that I
require of him. For the knight that I have so long followed
about and borne on a bier was son of his uncle Elinant of
Escavalon.'

XI

'Damsel,' saith Perceval, 'Take heed that you speak truth. I know well that Elinant of Escavalon was mine uncle on my father's side, but of his son know I nought.' 'Sir,' saith she, 'Of his deeds well deserved he to be known, for by his great valour and hardiment came he by his death, and he had to name Alein of Escavalon. The Damsel of the Circlet of Gold loved him of passing great love with all her might. The comeliest knight that was ever seen of his age was he, and had he lived longer would have been one of the best knights known, and of the great love she had in him made she his body be embalmed when the Knight of the Dragon had slain him, he that is so cruel and maketh desolate all the lands and all the islands. The Damsel of the Circlet of Gold hath he defied in such sort that already hath he slain great part of her knights, and she is held fast in her castle, so that she durst not issue forth, insomuch that all the knights that are there say, and the Lady of the castle also, that he that shall avenge this knight shall have the Circlet of Gold, that never before was she willing to part withal, and the fairest guerdon will that be that any knight may have.

XII

'Sir,' saith she, 'Well behoveth you, therefore, to do your best endeavour to avenge your uncle's son, and to win the Circlet of Gold, for, and you slay the knight, you will have saved the land of King Arthur that he threateneth to make desolate, and all the lands that march with his own, for no King hateth he so much as King Arthur on account of the head of the Giant whereof he made such joy at his court.' 'Damsel,' saith Perceval, 'Where is the Knight of the Dragon?' 'Sir,' saith she, 'He is in the isles of the Elephants that wont to be the fairest land and the richest in the world. Now hath he made it all desolate, they say, in such sort that none durst inhabit there, and the island wherein he abideth is over against the castle of the Damsel of the Golden Circlet, so that every day she seeth him carry knights off bodily from the forest that he slayeth and smiteth limb from limb, whereof hath she right sore grief at heart.'

XIII

'Perceval heareth this that the damsel telleth him, and marvelleth much thereat, and taketh thought within himself, sith
that the adventure is thus thrown upon him, that great blame
will he have thereof and he achieveth it not.   He taketh leave
of the King and Queen, and so goeth his way and departeth
from the Court.   Messire Gawain departeth and Lancelot with
him, and say they will bear him company to the piece of
ground, and they may go thither.   Perceval holdeth their
fellowship right dear.   The King and Queen have great pity
of Perceval, and say all that never until now no knight went
into jeopardy so sore, and that sore loss to the world will it be
if there he should die.   They send to all the hermits and worshipful men in the forest of Cardoil and bid them pray for
Perceval that God defend him from this enemy with whom he
goeth forth to do battle.   Lancelot and Messire Gawain go
with him by the strange forests and by the islands, and found
the forests all void and desolate and wasted in place after place.
The Damsel followeth them together with the dead knight.
And so far have they wandered that they come into the plain
country before the forest.   So they looked before them and
saw a castle that was seated in the plain without the forest, and
they saw that it was set in a right fair meadow-land, and was
surrounded of great running waters and girdled of high walls,
and had within great halls with windows.   They draw nigh
the castle and see that it turneth all about faster than the wind
may run, and it had at the top the archers of crossbows of
copper that draw their shafts so strong that no armour in the
world might avail against the stroke thereof.   Together with
them were men of copper that turned and sounded their horns
so passing loud that the ground all seemed to quake.   And
under the gateway were lions and bears chained, that roared
with so passing great might and fury that all the ground and
the valley resounded thereof.   The knights draw rein and look
at this marvel.   'Lords,' saith the damsel, 'Now may you see
the Castle of Great Endeavour.   Messire Gawain and Lancelot,
draw you back, and come not nigher the archers, for otherwise
ye be but dead men.   And you, sir,' saith she to Perceval,
'And you would enter into this castle, lend me your spear and
shield, and so will I bear them before for warranty, and you

come after me and make such countenance as good knight should, and so shall you pass through into the castle. But your fellows may well draw back, for now is not the hour for them to pass. None may pass thither save only he that goeth to vanquish the knight and win the Golden Circlet and the Graal, and do away the false law with its horns of copper.'

XIV

Perceval is right sorrowful when he heareth the damsel say that Messire Gawain and Lancelot may not pass in thither with him albeit they be the best knights in the world. He taketh leave of them full sorrowfully, and they also depart sore grudgingly; but they pray him right sweetly, so Lord God allow him escape alive from the place whither he goeth, that he will meet them again at some time and place, and at ease, in such sort as that they may see him without discognisance. They wait awhile to watch the Good Knight, that hath yielded his shield and spear to the damsel. She hath set his shield on the bier in front, then pointeth out to them of the castle all openly the shield that belonged to the Good Soldier; after that she maketh sign that it belongeth to the knight that is there waiting behind her. Perceval was without shield in the saddle-bows, and holdeth his sword drawn and planteth him stiffly in the stirrups after such sort as maketh them creak again and his horse's chine swerve awry. After that, he looketh at Lancelot and Messire Gawain. 'Lords,' saith he, 'To the Saviour of the World commend I you.' And they answer, 'May He that endured pain of His body on the Holy True Cross protect him in his body and his soul and his life.' With that he smiteth with his spurs and goeth his way to the castle as fast as his horse may carry him, —toward the Turning Castle. He smiteth with his sword at the gate so passing strongly that he cut a good three fingers into a shaft of marble. The lions and the beast that were chained to guard the gate slink away into their dens, and the castle stoppeth at once. The archers cease to shoot. There were three bridges before the castle that uplifted themselves so soon as he was beyond.

XV

Lancelot and Messire Gawain departed thence when they had beholden the marvel, but they were fain to go toward the castle when they saw it stop turning. But a knight cried out to them from the battlements, 'Lords, and you come forward, the archers will shoot and the castle will turn, and the bridges be lowered again, wherefore you would be deceived herein.' They draw back, and hear made within the greatest joy that ever was heard, and they hear how the most part therewithin say that now is he come of whom they shall be saved in twofold wise,—saved as of life, and saved as of soul, so God grant him to vanquish the knight that beareth the spirit of the devil. Lancelot and Messire Gawain turn them back thoughtful and all heavy for that they may not pass into the castle, for none other passage might they see than this. So they ride on, until that they draw nigh the Waste City where Lancelot slew the knight. 'Ha,' saith he to Messire Gawain, 'Now is the time at hand that behoveth me to die in this Waste City, and God grant not counsel herein.' He told Messire Gawain all the truth of that which had befallen him therein. So, even as he would have taken leave of him, behold you, the Poor Knight of the Waste Castle!

XVI

'Sir,' saith he to Lancelot, 'I have taken respite of you in the city within there, of the knight that you slew, until forty days after that the Graal shall be achieved, nor have I issued forth of the castle wherein you harboured you until now, nor should I now have come forth had I not seen you come for fulfilling of your pledge, nor never shall I come forth again until such time as you shall return hither on the day I have named to you. And so, gramercy to you and Messire Gawain for the horses you sent me, that were a right great help to us, and for the treasure and the hold you have given to my sisters that were sore poverty-stricken. But I may not do otherwise than abide in my present poverty until such time as you shall be returned, on the day whereunto I have taken respite for you, sore against the will of your enemies, for the benefits you have done me. Wherefore I pray yon forget me not, for the saving of your loyalty.' 'By my head,' saith Lancelot, 'That will I not, and gramercy for having put off the day for love of me.' They depart from the knight and come back again toward Cardoil where King Arthur was.

BRANCH XVIII

TITLE I

HERE the story is silent of Lancelot and Messire Gawain, and saith that Perceval is in the Turning Castle, whereof Joseus recounteth the truth, to wit, that Virgil founded it in the air by his wisdom in such fashion, when the philosophers went on the Quest of the Earthly Paradise, and it was prophesied that the castle should not cease turning until such time as the Knight should come thither that should have a head of gold, the look of a lion, a heart of steel, the navel of a virgin maiden, conditions without wickedness, the valour of a man and faith and belief of God ; and that this knight should bear the shield of the Good Soldier that took down the Saviour of the World from hanging on the rood.   It was prophesied, moreover, that all they of the castle and all other castles whereof this one was the guardian should hold the old law until such time as the Good Knight should come, by whom their souls should be saved and their death respited.   For, so soon as he should be come, they should run to be baptized, and should firmly believe the new law.   Wherefore was the joy great in the castle for that their death should now be respited, and that they should be released of all terror of the knight that was their foe, whom they dreaded even to the death, and of the sin of the false law whereof they had heretofore been attaint.

II

Right glad is Perceval when he seeth the people of the castle turn them to the holy faith of the Saviour, and the damsel saith to him, 'Sir, right well have you speeded thus far on your way ; nought is there now to be done save to finish that which

209

H

remaineth.   For never may they that are within issue forth so
long as the Knight of the Dragon is on live.   Here may you
not tarry, for the longer you tarry, the more lands will be
desolate and the more folk will he slay.   Perceval taketh leave
of them of the castle, that make much joy of him, but sore
misgiving have they of him on account of the knight with
whom he goeth to do battle, and they say that if he shall
conquer him, never yet befell knight so fair adventure.   They
have heard mass before that he departeth, and made rich
offerings for him in honour of the Saviour and His sweet
Mother.   The damsel goeth before, for that she knew the
place where the evil knight had his repair.   They ride until
they come into the Island of Elephants.   The Knight was
alighted under an olive tree, and had but now since slain four
knights that were of the castle of the Queen of the Golden
Circlet.   She was at the windows of her castle and saw her
Knights dead, whereof made she great dole.   'Ha, God,' saith
she, 'Shall I never see none that may avenge me of this evil-
doer that slayeth my men and destroyeth my land on this wise?
She looketh up and seeth Perceval come and the damsel.   'Sir
Knight, and you have not force and help and valour in you
more than is in four knights, come not nigh this devil!   Howbeit, and you feel that you may so do battle as to overcome and
vanquish him, I will give you the Golden Circlet that is within,
and will hold with the New Law that hath been of late
established.   For I see well by your shield that you are a
Christian, and, so you may conquer him, then ought I at last to
be assured that your law availeth more than doth ours, and
that God was born of the Virgin.'

III

Right joyous is Perceval of this that he heareth her say.   He
crosseth and blesseth him, and commendeth him to God and
His sweet Mother; and is pricked of wrath and hardiment like
a lion.   He seeth the Knight of the Dragon mounted, and
looketh at him in wonderment, for that he was so big that
never had he seen any man so big of his body.   He seeth the
shield at his neck, that was right black and huge and hideous.
He seeth the Dragon's head in the midst thereof, that casteth
out fire and flame in great plenty, so foul and hideous and

horrible that all the field stank thereof. The damsel draweth her toward the castle and leaveth the knight on the horsebier nigh the plain.

IV

'Sir,' saith she to Perceval, 'On this level plot was slain your uncle's son whom here I leave, for I have brought him far enough. Now avenge him as best you may, I render and give him over to you, for so much have I done herein as that none have right to blame me.' With that she departeth. The Knight of the Dragon removeth and seeth Perceval coming all alone, wherefore hath he great scorn of him and deigneth not to take his spear, but rather cometh at him with his drawn sword, that was right long and red as a burning brand. Perceval seeth him coming and goeth against him, spear in rest, as hard as his horse may carry him, thinking to smite him through the breast. But the Knight setteth his shield between, and the flame that issued from the Dragon burnt the shaft thereof even to his hand. And the Knight smiteth him on the top of his helmet, but Perceval covereth him of his shield, whereof had he great affiance that the sword of the foeman knight might not harm it. Josephus witnesseth us that Joseph of Abarimacie had made be sealed in the boss of the shield some of the blood of Our Lord and a piece of His garment.

V

When the Knight seeth that he hath not hurt Perceval's shield, great marvel hath he thereof, for never aforetime had he smitten knight but he had dealt him his death-blow. He turneth the head of the Dragon towards Perceval's shield, but the flame that issued from the Dragon's head turned back again as it had been blown of the wind, so that it might not come nigh him. The Knight is right wroth thereof, and passeth beyond and cometh to the bier of the dead knight and turneth his shield with the dragon's head against him. He scorcheth and burneth all to ashes the bodies of the knight and the horses. Saith he to Perceval, 'Are you quit as for this knight's burial?' 'Certes,' saith Perceval, 'You say true, and much misliketh me thereof, but please God I shall amend it.'

VI

The damsel that had brought the knight was at the windows of the palace beside the Queen. She crieth out. 'Perceval, fair sir,' saith the damsel, 'Now is the shame the greater and the harm the greater, and you amend them not.' Right sorrowful is Perceval of his cousin that is all burnt to a cinder, and he seeth the Knight that beareth the devil with him, but knoweth not how he may do vengeance upon him. He cometh to him sword-drawn, and dealeth him a great blow on the shield in such sort that he cleaveth it right to the midst thereof where the dragon's head was, and the flame leapeth forth so burning hot on his sword that it waxed red-hot like as was the Knight's sword. And the damsel crieth to him: "Now is your sword of the like power as his; now shall it be seen what you will do! I have been told of a truth that the Knight may not be vanquished save by one only and at one blow, but how this is I may not tell, whereof irketh me.' Perceval looketh and seeth that his sword is all in a flame of fire, whereof much he marvelleth. He smiteth the Knight so passing sore that he maketh his head stoop down over the fore saddle-bow. The Knight righteth him again, sore wrath that he may not put him to the worse. He smiteth him with his sword a blow so heavy that he cleaveth the habergeon and his right shoulder so that he cutteth and burneth the flesh to the bone. As he draweth back his blow, Perceval catcheth him and striketh him with such passing strength that he smiteth off his hand, sword and all. The Knight gave a great roar, and the Queen was right joyous thereof. The Knight natheless made no semblant that he was yet conquered, but turneth back toward Perceval at a right great gallop and launched his flame against his shield, but it availeth him nought, for he might not harm it. Perceval seeth the dragon's head, that was broad and long and horrible, and aimeth with his sword and thrusteth it up to the hilt into his gullet as straight as ever he may, and the head of the dragon hurleth forth a cry so huge that forest and fell resound thereof as far as two leagues Welsh.

VII

The dragon's head turneth it toward his lord in great wrath, and scorcheth him and burneth him to dust, and thereafter departed up into the sky like lightning. The Queen cometh to Perceval, and all the knights, and see that he is sore hurt in his right shoulder. And the damsel telleth him that never will he be healed thereof save he setteth thereon of the dust of the knight that is dead. And they lead him up to the castle with right great joy. Then they make him be disarmed, and have his wound washed and tended and some of the knight's dust that was dead set thereon that it might have healing. She maketh send to all the knights of her land : 'Lords,' saith she, 'See here the knight that hath saved my land for me and protected your lives. You know well how it hath been prophesied that the knight with head of gold should come, and through him should you be saved. And now, behold, hath he come hither. The prophecy may not be belied. I will that you do his commandment.' And they said that so would they do right willingly. She bringeth him there where the Circlet of Gold is, and she herself setteth it on his head. After that, she bringeth his sword and delivereth it unto him, wherewith he had slain the giant devil, both the knight that bare the devil, and the devil that the knight bare in his shield.

VIII

'Sir,' saith she, 'May all they that will not go to be baptized, nor accept your New Law, be slain of this your sword, and hereof I make you the gift.' She herself made her be held up and baptized first, and all the other after. Josephus maketh record that in right baptism she had for name Elysa, and a good life she led and right holy, and she died a virgin. Her body still lieth in the kingdom of Ireland, where she is highly honoured. Perceval was within the castle until that he was heal. The tidings spread throughout the lands that the Knight of the Golden Circlet had slain the Knight of the Dragon, and great everywhere was the joy thereof. It was known at the court of King Arthur, but much marvelled they that it was said the Knight of the Golden Circlet had slain him, for they knew not who was the Knight of the Golden Circlet.

IX

When Perceval was whole, he departed from the castle of the Queen of the Golden Circlet, all of whose land was at his

commandment.   The Queen told him that she would keep the
Golden Circlet until he should will otherwise, and in such sort
he left it there, for he would not carry it with him, sith that he
knew not whitherward he might turn.   The history telleth us
that he rode on until one day he came to the Castle of Copper.
Within the castle were a number of folk that worshipped the
bull of copper and believed not in any other God.   The bull of
copper was in the midst of the castle upon four columns of
copper, and bellowed so loud at all hours of the day that it was
heard for a league all round about, and there was an evil spirit
within that gave answers concerning whatsoever any should ask
of it.

X

At the entrance to the gateway of the castle were two men
made of copper by art of nigromancy, and they held two
great mallets of iron, and they busied themselves striking the
one after the other, and so strongly they struck that nought
mortal is there in the world that might pass through amongst
their blows but should be all to-crushed thereby.   And on the
other side was the castle so fast enclosed about that nought
might enter thereinto.

XI

Perceval beholdeth the fortress of the castle, and the entrance
that was so perilous, whereof he marvelleth much.   He passeth
a bridge that was within the entry, and cometh nigh them that
guard the gate.   A Voice began to cry aloud above the gate
that he might go forward safely, and that he need have no care
for the men of copper that guarded the gate nor be affrighted
of their blows, for no power had they to harm such a knight
as was he.   He comforteth himself much of that the Voice
saith to him.   He cometh anigh the serjeants of copper, and
they cease to strike at once, and hold their iron mallets quite
still.   And he entereth into the castle, where he findeth within
great plenty of folk that all were misbelievers and of feeble
belief.   He seeth the bull of copper in the midst of the castle
right big and horrible, that was surrounded on all sides by folk
that all did worship thereunto together round about.

XII

The bull bellowed so passing loud that right uneath was it to hear aught else within the castle besides. Perceval was therewithin, but none was there that spake unto him, for so intent were they upon adoring the bull that, and any had been minded to slay them what time they were yet worshipping the same, they would have allowed him so to do, and would have thought that they were saved thereby; and save this had they none other believe in the world. It was not of custom within there to be armed, for the entrance of the fortress was so strong that none might enter but by their will and command-ment, save it were the pleasure of our Lord God. And the devil that had deceived them, and in whom they believed, gave them such great abundance therewithin of everything they could desire, that nought in the world was there whereof they lacked. When he perceived that they held no discourse with him, he draweth himself on one side by a great hall, and so called them around him. The more part came thither, but some of them came not. The Voice warneth him that he make them all pass through the entrance of the gateway there where the men with the iron mallets are, for there may he well prove which of them are willing to believe in God and which not. The Good Knight draweth his sword and surroundeth them all and maketh them all go in common before him, would they or nould they. And they that would not go willingly and kindly might be sure that they should receive their death. He made them pass through the entrance there where the serjeants of copper were striking great blows with their iron mallets. Of one thousand five hundred that there were, scarce but thirteen were not all slain and brained of the iron mallets. But the thirteen had firmly bound their belief in Our Lord, wherefore the serjeants took no heed of them.

XIII

The evil spirit that was in the bull of copper issued forth thereof as it had been lightning from heaven, and the bull of copper melted all in a heap so as that nought remained in that place thereof. Then the thirteen that remained sent for a hermit of the forest and so made themselves be held up and baptized. After that, they took the bodies of the misbelievers and made cast them into a water that is called the River of Hell. This water runneth into the sea, so say many that have seen it, and there where it spendeth itself in the sea is it most foul and most horrible, so that scarce may ship pass that is not wrecked.

XIV

Josephus maketh record that the hermit that baptized the thirteen had the name of Denis, and that the castle was named the Castle of the Trial. They lived within there until the New Law was assured and believed in throughout all the kingdoms, and a right good life led they and a holy. Nor never might none enter with them thereinto but was slain and crushed save he firmly believed in God. When the thirteen that were baptized in the castle issued forth thereof they scattered themselves on every side among strange forests, and made hermitages and buildings, and put their bodies to penance for the false law they had maintained and to win the love of the Saviour of the World.

XV

Perceval, as you may hear, was soldier of Our Lord, and well did God show him how He loved his knighthood, for the Good Knight had much pain and sore travail and pleased Him greatly. He was come one day to the house of King Hermit that much desired to see him, and made much joy of him when he saw him, and rejoiced greatly of his courage. Perceval relateth to him all the greater adventures that have befallen him at many times and in many places sithence that he departed from him, and King Hermit much marvelleth him of many. 'Uncle,' saith Perceval, 'I marvel me much of an adventure that befell me at the outlet of a forest; for I saw a little white beast that I found in the launde of the forest, and twelve hounds had she in her belly, that bayed aloud and quested within her. At last they issued forth of her and slew her beside the cross that was at the outlet of the forest, but they might not eat of her flesh. A knight and a damsel, whereof one was at one end of the launde and the other at the other, came thither and took the flesh and the blood, and set them in two vessels of gold. And the hounds that were born of her fled away into the forest.' 'Fair nephew,' saith the Hermit, 'I know well that God loveth you sith that such things appear to you, for His valour and yours and for the chastity that is in your body. The beast, that was kindly and gentle and sweet, signifieth Our Lord Jesus Christ, and the twelve dogs that yelped within her signify the people of the Old Law that God created and made in His own likeness, and after that He had made and created them He desired to prove how much they loved Him. He sent them forty years into the wilderness, where their garments never wasted, and sent them manna from heaven that served them whatsoever they would to eat and to drink, and they were without evil and without trouble and without sickness, and such joy and pleasance had they as they would. And they held one day their council, and the master of them said that and God should wax wroth with them and withhold this manna, they would have nought to eat, and that it might not last always albeit that God sent it in so passing great plenty. Wherefore they purposed to set aside great part thereof in store, so that if the Lord God should wax wroth they might take of that which was stored and so save themselves for a long space. They agreed among themselves and did thereafter as they had purposed and determined amongst them.

XVI

'God, that seeth and knoweth all things, knew well their thought. He withdrew from them the manna from heaven that had come to them in such abundance, and which they had bestowed in caverns underground, thinking to find there the manna they had set aside, but it was changed by the will of God into efts and adders and worms and vermin, and when they saw that they had done evil, they scattered themselves over strange lands. Fair, sweet nephew,' saith the Hermit, 'These twelve hounds that bayed in the beast are the Jews that God had fed, and that were born in the Law that He established, nor never would they believe on Him, nor love Him, but rather crucified Him and tore His Body after the shamefullest sort they might, but in no wise might they destroy His flesh. The knight and damsel that set the pieces of flesh in vessels of gold signify the divinity of the Father, which would not that His flesh should be minished. The hounds fled to the forest and became savage what time they had torn the beast to pieces, so in like manner are the Jews that were and ever shall be savage, subject to them of the New Law henceforth for ever.'

XVII

'Fair uncle,' saith Perceval, 'Good right and reason is it that they should have shame and tribulation and evil reward sith that they slew and crucified Him that had created and made them and deigned to be born as a man in their Law. But two priests came after, whereof the one kissed the cross and worshipped it right heartily and made great joy thereof, and the other did violence thereunto and beat it with a great rod, and wept right sore and made the greatest dole in the world. With this last was I right sore wrath, and willingly would I have run upon him had he not been a priest.' 'Fair nephew,' saith the Hermit, 'He that beat it believed in God equally as well as he that adored, for that the holy flesh of the Saviour of the World was set thereon, that abhorred not the pains of death. One smiled and made great joy for that He redeemed His souls from the pains of hell that would otherwise have been therein for evermore; and for this made he yet greater joy, that he knew He was God and Man everlastingly in His nature, for he that hath not this in remembrance shall never believe aright Fair nephew, the other priest beat the cross and wept for the passing great anguish and torment and dolour that our Lord God suffered thereon, for so sore was the anguish as might have melted the rock, nor no tongue of man may tell the sorrow He felt upon the cross. And therefore did he beat it and revile it for that He was crucified thereon, even as I might hate a spear or sword wherewith you had been slain. For nought else did he thus, and ever, so often as he remembereth the pain that God suffered thereon, cometh he to the cross in such manner as you saw. Both twain are hermits and dwell in the forest, and he is named Jonas that kissed and adored the cross, and he that beat and reviled it is named Alexis.'

XVIII

Willingly heareth Perceval this that his uncle telleth and recordeth him. He relateth how he did battle with the devil-

knight that bare in his shield the head of a dragon that cast
forth fire and flame, and how the dragon burnt up his lord at
the last.   ' Fair nephew,' saith the hermit, ' Right glad am I of
these tidings that you tell me, for I have been borne on hand
that the Knight of the Golden Circlet had slain him.'   ' Sir,'
saith Perceval, ' It may well be, but never at any time saw I
knight so big and horrible.'   ' Fair nephew,' saith the Hermit,
' None might overcome him save the Good Knight only, for all
true worshipful men behoveth do battle with the Devil, nor
never may he be worshipful man that fighteth not against him.
And even as the devil withal that was figured on his shield
slew and burnt up his master, even so doth one devil torment
and molest other in the world to come ; and greater evil might
not the Knight of the Devil do you than burn the body of your
uncle's son that he had killed, as I have heard tell.   Power had
he over his body, but, please God, not over his soul to burn it.'
' Fair uncle,' saith Perceval, ' I went thither by a Turning
Castle, where were archers of copper that shot bolts, and
bears and lions chained at the entrance of the gateway.   So
soon as I drew nigh and smote thereon with my sword the
castle stopped still.'   ' Fair nephew,' said King Hermit,
' Nought had the Devil outwardly besides this castle.   It was
the entrance to his fortress, nor would they within ever have
been converted save you had been there.'   ' Sir,' saith he,
' Right sorrowful am I of Messire Gawain and Lancelot, for
well I loved their fellowship, and great aid would they have
been in my need.'   ' Fair nephew, had they been chaste as are
you, well might they have entered on account of their good
knighthood.   For were they not wanton, the two best knights
in the world are they.

XIX

' Fair nephew, in the time of your knighthood have you
much advanced the Law of the Saviour, for you have destroyed
the falsest believe in the world, and this was of them that
believed on the bull of copper and the devil that was therein.
If this folk had remained, and had failed of you, never would
it have been destroyed until the end of the world.   Wherefore
marvel not that you have travail in serving God, but endure it
willingly, for never had worshipful man honour without pains.
But now behoveth you achieve another matter.   All they of the

land of King Fisherman your uncle have abandoned the New
Law, and returned to that which God hath forbidden.   But the
most part do so rather perforce and for fear of the King that
hath seized the land, who is my brother and your uncle, than
on account of aught else.   Wherefore behoveth you set
counsel therein, for this thing may not be achieved by any
earthly man save by you only.   For the castle and land should
be yours of right, and sore mischief is it when one that cometh
of lineage so high and so holy is traitor to God, and disloyal to
the world.

XX

'Fair nephew,' saith the good man, 'The castle hath been
much strengthened, for there are now nine bridges newly made,
and at each bridge are there three knights tall and strong and
hardy, whereof hath he much defence, and your uncle is there
within that keepeth the castle.   But never sithence, none of the
knights of King Fisherman nor of his priests have there
appeared, nor knoweth any what hath befallen them.   The
chapel wherein the most Holy Graal appeared is all emptied of
its sacred hallows; the hermits that are by the forest are fain
of your coming, for never see they there a knight pass by that
believeth in God.   And, so you shall have achieved this
enterprise, it is a thing whereof shall God be well pleased.'

XXI

'Fair uncle,' saith Perceval, 'Thither will I go, sith that you
commend it to me, for no reason is it that he should have the
castle that hath entered thereinto.   Of better right ought my
mother to have it, that was the next-born to King Fisherman,
of whose death am I right sorrowful.'   'Fair nephew, you are
right! for on your account fell he into languishment, and, had
you then gone again, so say many, then would he have been
whole, but how this might have been I know not of a certainty.
But methinketh our Lord God willed his languishment and
death, for had it been His will, you would have made the
demand, but He willed otherwise, wherefore ought we to give
thanks and praise Him whatsoever He doth, for He hath
foreseen of every man that which shall come to him.   I have
within here a white mule that is very old.   Fair nephew, you

will take her with you.   She will follow you right willingly,
and a banner shall you bear, for the power of God and His
virtue shall avail more than your own.   Seven-and-twenty
knights guard the nine bridges, all chosen and of approved
great valour, and none ought now to believe that a single
knight may vanquish so many, save the miracle of Our Lord
and His virtue shall open a way for him.   So I pray and
beseech you that you have God always in remembrance and His
sweet Mother, and, so at any time you be put to the worse of
your knighthood, mount upon the mule and take the banner,
and your enemies shall forthwith lose their force, for nought
confoundeth any enemy so swiftly as doth the virtue and
puissance of God.   It is a thing well known that you are the
Best Knight of the World, but set not affiance in your strength
nor in your knighthood as against so many knights, for against
them may you not endure.'

XXII

Perceval hearkeneth unto his uncle's discourse and his chasten-
ing, and layeth fast hold on all that he saith, wherewith is he
pleased full well, for great affiance hath he in his words. 'Fair
nephew,' saith the Hermit, ' Two lions are there at the entry
of the gateway, whereof the one is red and the other white.
Put your trust in the white, for he is on God's side, and look
at him whensoever your force shall fail you, and he will look
at you likewise in such sort as that straightway you shall know
his intent, by the will and pleasure of Our Saviour.   Wherefore
do according as you shall see that he would, for no intent will
he have save good only, and to help you; nor may you not
otherwise succeed in winning past the nine bridges that are
warded of the twenty-seven knights.   And God grant you may
win past in such wise that you may save your body and set
forward withal the Law of Our Lord that your uncle hath
hindered all that he might.'

XXIII

Perceval departeth from the hermitage, and carrieth away the
banner, according to his uncle's counsel, and the white mule
followeth after. He goeth his way toward the land that was

the land of King Fisherman, and findeth a hermit that was issued forth of his hermitage and was going at a great pace through the forest. He abideth so soon as he beholdeth the cross on Perceval's shield. 'Sir,' saith he, 'I well perceive that you are a Christian, of whom not a single one have I seen this long time past. For the King of Castle Mortal is driving us forth of this forest, for he hath renounced God and His sweet Mother, so that we durst not remain in His defence.' 'By my faith,' saith Perceval, 'But you shall! for God shall lead you forward, and I after. Are there more hermits in this forest?' saith Perceval. 'Yea, Sir, there be twelve here that are waiting for me at a cross yonder before us, and we are minded to go to the kingdom of Logres and put our bodies to penance for God's sake, and to abandon our cells and chapels in this forest for dread of this felon King that hath seized the land, for he willeth that none who believeth in God should here abide.'

XXIV

Perceval is come with the hermit to the cross where the good men had assembled them together, and findeth Joseus, the young man that was King Pelles' son, of whom he maketh right great joy, and he maketh the hermits turn back again with him, saying that he will defend them and make them safe, by God's help, in the kingdom, and prayeth them right sweetly that they make prayer for him to our Lord that He grant him to win back that which of right is his own. He is come forth of the forest and the hermits with him. He draweth nigh to the castle of King Fisherman, and strong was the defence at the entrance thereof. Some of the knights well knew that Perceval would conquer him, for long since had it been prophesied that he who bare such shield should win the Graal of him that sold God for money.

XXV

The knights saw Perceval coming and the company of hermits with him right seemly to behold, and much marvel had they thereof. About a couple of bowshots above the bridge was a chapel fashioned like the one at Camelot, wherein was a sepulchre, and none knew who lay therein. Perceval abideth thereby and his company. He leaneth his shield and spear against the chapel, and maketh fast his horse and mule by the reins. He beholdeth the sepulchre, that was right fair, and forthwith the sepulchre openeth and the joinings fall apart and the stone lifteth up in such wise that a man might see the knight that lay within, of whom came forth a smell of so sweet savour that it seemed to the good men that were looking on that it had been all embalmed. They found a letter which testified that this knight was named Josephus. So soon as the hermits beheld the sepulchre open, they said to Perceval: 'Sir, now at last know we well that you are the Good Knight, the chaste, the holy.' The knights that warded the bridge heard the tidings that the sepulchre had opened at the coming of the knight, whereof were they in the greater dismay, and well understood that it was he that was first at the Graal. The tidings came to the King that held the castle, and he bade his knights not be dismayed for dread of a single knight, for that he would have no force nor power against them, nor might it never befall but that one only of his own knights should be enough to conquer him.

XXVI

Perceval was armed upon his horse. The hermits make the sign of the cross over him, and bless him and commend him to God. And he holdeth his spear in rest and cometh toward the three knights that guard the first bridge. They all set upon him at once and break their spears upon his shield. One of them he smiteth with such force that he maketh him topple over into the river that runneth under the bridge, both him and his horse. Of him was he quit, for the river was wide and deep and swift. The others held out against him a much longer bout with sharp sword-play, but he vanquished them and smote them to pieces, and flung their bodies into the water. They of the second bridge came forward, that were right good knights, and many a tough bout had he of them and many a felon onslaught. Joseus that was his uncle's son was there, and said to the other hermits that right fainly would he go help him, but that he deemed it might be sin, and they bade him take no heed of that, for that great work of mercy would it be to destroy the enemies of Our Lord. He doeth off his grey cape and fettleth him in his frock, and taketh one of them that were doing battle

with Perceval and trusseth him on his neck and so flingeth him
into the river all armed, and Perceval slayeth the other twain
and hurleth them into the river in like manner as the other.

XXVII

By the time he had won the two bridges he was full spent
and weary, wherefore he bethinketh him of the lion, the manner
whereof his uncle had told him. Then looketh he toward the
entrance of the gateway and seeth the white lion, that stood
upright on his two hinder feet, for that he was fain to see him.
Perceval looketh him full between the two eyes, and understandeth that the lion is minded by the will of God to do him
to wit that the knights of the third bridge are so hardy and of
such strength that they may not be overcome of a single knight
and our Lord God of his holy bounty open not the way, but
that he must fain take the mule and carry the banner if he would
conquer them. Perceval understandeth the white lion's intent,
and giveth God thanks thereof and draweth him back, and
Joseus the young man likewise. As soon as they look back,
they see that the first bridge is already lifted up behind them.

XXVIII

Perceval cometh to where the white mule was, and she was
starred on the forehead with a red cross. He mounteth thereupon, and taketh the banner and holdeth his sword drawn. So
soon as the white lion seeth him coming, he unchaineth himself
and runneth incontinent to the bridge that was lifted, right
amidst the knights, and lowereth it forthwith. The King of
Castle Mortal was on the battlements of the greater fortress
of the castle, and crieth to the knights that warded the bridge,
'Lords,' saith he, 'You are the most chosen knights of my land
and the hardiest, but no hardiment is it to lift the bridges on
account of a single knight whom you durst not abide body to
body, whereof meseemeth it great cowardize and not hardiment.
But the lion is hardier than you all, that of his hardiment hath
lowered the bridge. Wherefore now know I well that had I
set him to ward the first bridge, he would have warded it better
than these that have allowed themselves to be slain.'

XXIX

Thereupon, behold you Perceval come upon his white mule, sword drawn all naked in his fist, and cometh toward them of the third bridge, whereof he smiteth the first so sore that he overthroweth him into the water. Joseus the hermit cometh forward and would fain have seized the other twain, but they cry mercy of Perceval, and say that they will be at his will in all things, and so will believe on God and His sweet Mother and abandon their evil lord. And they of the fourth bridge say likewise. On such condition he alloweth them to live by the counsel of Joseus, and they cast away their arms and yield up the bridges at his will. Perceval thinketh within himself that God's virtue hath right great power, but that knight who hath force and power ought well to approve his prowess for God's sake. For of all that he shall do or suffer for Him, shall God be well pleased. For, were all the world against our Lord God, and He should grant to any single one that should be His champion all His power and might, he would conquer them all in one hour of the day. But He willeth that a man should travail for Him, even as He Himself suffered travail for His people.

XXX

Perceval cometh again back and alighteth of the white mule and delivereth the banner to Joseus, and then mounteth again on his destrier and cometh back to them of the fifth bridge, and these defend themselves right stoutly, for that hardy knights are they, and do battle against Perceval full sturdily. Joseus the hermit cometh thither and assaulteth them with passing great lustihood, that had the Lord God not saved him they would have overthrown and slain him. Howbeit, he holdeth the banner and grappleth them when he may lay hold, and grippeth them so straight that they may not help themselves. Perceval slayeth them and crusheth them and maketh them topple over into the water that ran swiftly beneath the bridge. When they of the sixth bridge saw that these were conquered, they cried mercy of Perceval and yielded themselves to him and delivered up their swords to him, and they of the seventh bridge likewise. When the red lion saw that the seventh bridge was won, and that the knights of the two bridges had yielded themselves up to Perceval, he leapt up with such fury that he burst his chain as had he been wood mad. He came to one of the knights and bit him and slew him, whereof the white lion was full wroth, and runneth upon the other lion and teareth him to pieces with his claws and teeth.

XXXI

Straightway thereafter he raiseth himself up on his two hinder feet and looketh at Perceval, and Perceval at him. Perceval understandeth well the lion's intent, to wit, that they of the last bridge are worse to conquer than the others, and that they may not be conquered at all save by the will of God and by him that is the lion. And the lion warned him that he go not against them with the banner, holy though it were, nor receive them into mercy what surety soever they might make, for that they are traitors, but that he must fain mount upon the white mule, for that she is a beast on God's side, and that Joseus should bring the banner and all the hermits go before, that are worshipful men and of good life, so as to dismay the traitor King, and so shall the end and the conquest of the castle be brought nigh. Of all this the lion made signs to Perceval, for speak he could not. Great affiance hath Perceval in the lion's warning. He alighteth of his destrier and remounteth on the mule, and Joseus holdeth the banner. The company of twelve hermits was there, right seemly and holy. They draw nigh the castle. The knights on the last bridge see Perceval coming towards them and Joseus the hermit holding the banner, by whom they had seen their other fellows wrestled withal and put to the worse.

XXXII

The virtue of Our Lord and the dignity of the banner and the goodness of the white mule and the holiness of the good hermits that made their orisons to Our Lord so struck the knights that they lost all power over themselves, but treason might not go forth of their hearts, wherefore right heavy were they of their kinsmen that they had seen slain before them. They bethought them that and if by mercy they might escape thence, they would never end until they had slain Perceval. They come to meet him and so cry him mercy passing sweetly in semblance, and say that they will do his will for ever and ever, so only he will let them depart safe and sound. Perceval looketh at the lion to know what he shall do; he seeth that the lion thinketh them traitors and disloyal, and that so they were destroyed and dead the King that was in the castle would have lost his force; and that, so Perceval will run upon them, the lion will help him slay them. Perceval telleth the knights that never will he have mercy upon them, and forthwith runneth upon them, sword drawn, and sorely it misliked him that they defended not themselves, insomuch that he all but left to slay them for that no defence found he in them. But the lion is so far from holding them in the like disdain, that he runneth upon them and biteth and slayeth them, and then casteth forth their limbs and bodies into the water. Perceval alloweth that this is well and seemly, and pleaseth him much of that he seeth the lion do, nor never before had he seen any beast that he might love and prize so highly as this one.

XXXIII

The King of Castle Mortal was on the battlements of the wall, and seeth how his knights are dead, and how the lion helpeth to slay the last. He setteth himself on the highest place of the walls, then lifteth the skirt of his habergeon and holdeth his sword all naked, that was right keen and well-tempered, and so smiteth himself right through the body, and falleth all adown the walls into the water, that was swift and deep, in such sort that Perceval saw him, and all the good hermits likewise, that marvelled much of a King that should slay himself in such manner; but they say according to the judgment of the scripture, that by right of evil man should the end be evil. On such wise was the end of this King of whom I tell you. Josephus relateth us how none ought to marvel that of three brothers, even though they be sons of the same father and mother, one brother should be evil; and the real marvel, saith he, is when one evil corrupteth not the two that are good, for that wickedness is so hard and keen and beguiling, and goodness so kindly and simple and humble. Cain and Abel were brothers-german, yet Cain slew his brother Abel, the one flesh betrayed the other. But great sorrow is it, saith Josephus, when the flesh that ought to be one becometh twain, and the one flesh goeth about by wickedness to deceive and destroy the other.   Josephus recordeth us by this evil king that was so traitorous and false and yet was of the lineage of the Good Soldier Joseph of Abarimacie.   This Joseph, as the scripture witnesseth, was his uncle, and this evil king was brother-german of King Fisherman, and brother of the good King Pelles that had abandoned his land, in order that he might serve God, and brother of the Widow Lady that was Perceval's mother, the most loyal that was ever in Great Britain.   All these lineages were in the service of Our Lord from the beginning of their lives unto the end, save only this evil King that perished so evilly as you have heard.

XXXIV

You have heard how the King that had seized the castle that had been King Fisherman's slew himself in such wise, and how his knights were discomfited.   Perceval entered into the castle and the worshipful hermits together with him.   It seemed them when they were come within into the master hall, that they heard chant in an inner chapel *Gloria in excelsis Deo*, and right sweet praising of Our Lord.   They found the halls right rich and seemly and fairly adorned within.   They found the chapel open where the sacred hallows were wont to be.   The holy hermits entered therein and made their orisons, and prayed the Saviour of the World that He would swiftly restore to them the most Holy Graal and the sacred hallows that wont to be therewithin whereby they might be comforted.

XXXV

The good men were there within with Perceval, that much loved their company.   Josephus witnesseth us that the ancient knights that were of the household of King Fisherman, and the priests and damsels, departed so soon as the King that slew himself had seized the castle, for that they would not be at his court, and the Lord God preserved them from him and made them go into such a place as that they should be in safety.   The Saviour of the World well knew that the Good Knight had won the castle by his valour that should have been his own of right, and sent back thither all them that had served King Fisherman.   Perceval made right great joy of them when he saw

them, and they of him. They seemed well to be a folk that
had come from some place where God and His commandments
were honoured, and so indeed had they.

XXXVI

The High History witnesseth us that when the conquest of
the castle was over, the Saviour of the World was right joyous
and well pleased thereof. The Graal presented itself again in
the chapel, and the lance whereof the point bleedeth, and the
sword wherewith St John was beheaded that Messire Gawain
won, and the other holy relics whereof was right great plenty.
For our Lord God loved the place much. The hermits went
back to their hermitages in the forest and served Our Lord as
they had been wont. Joseus remained with Perceval at the
castle as long as it pleased him, but the Good Knight searched
out the land there where the New Law had been abandoned
and its maintenance neglected. He reft the lives of them that
would not maintain it and believe. The country was supported
by him and made safe, and the Law of Our Lord exalted by his
strength and valour. The priests and knights that repaired to
the castle loved Perceval much, for, so far from his goodness
minishing in ought, they saw from day to day how his valour
and his faith in God increased and multiplied. And he showed
them the sepulchre of his uncle King Fisherman in the chapel
before the altar. The coffin was rich and the tabernacle costly
and loaded of precious stones. And the priests and knights
bear witness that as soon as the body was placed in the coffin
and they were departed thence, they found on their return that
it was covered by the tabernacle all dight as richly as it is now
to be seen, nor might they know who had set it there save only
the commandment of Our Lord. And they say that every night
was there a great brightness of light as of candles there, and
they knew not whence it should come save of God. Perceval
had won the castle by the command of God. The Graal was
restored in the holy chapel, and the other hallows as you have
heard. The evil believe was done away from the kingdom,
and all were assured again in the New Law by the valour of the
Good Knight.

BRANCH XIX

Title I

Now is the story silent of Perceval and cometh back to King
Arthur, the very matter thereof, like as testifieth the history,
that in no place is corrupted and the Latin lie not.   King Arthur
was at Cardoil on one day of Whitsuntide that was right fair
and clear, and many knights were in the hall.   The King sate
at meat and all the knights about him.   The King looketh at
the windows of the hall to right and left, and seeth that two
sunbeams are shining within that fill the whole hall with light.
Thereof he marvelleth much and sendeth without the hall to see
what it might be.   The messenger cometh back again and saith
thereof that two suns appear to be shining, the one in the East
and the other in the West.   He marvelleth much thereat, and
prayeth Our Lord that he may be permitted to know wherefore
two suns should appear in such wise.   A Voice appeared at one
of the windows that said to him : ' King, marvel not hereof that
two suns should appear in the sky, for our Lord God hath well
the power, and know well that this is for joy of the conquest
that the Good Knight hath made that took away the shield from
herewithin.   He hath won the land that belonged to good
King Fisherman from the evil King of Castle Mortal, that did
away thence the good believe, and therefore was it that the
Graal was hidden.   Now God so willeth that you go thither,
and that you choose out the best knights of your court, for
better pilgrimage may you never make, and what time you shall
return hither, your faith shall be doubled and the people of
Great Britain shall be better disposed and better taught to
maintain the service of the Saviour.'

II

Thereupon the Voice departed, and well pleased was the
King of that it had said.   He sitteth at meat beside the Queen.

Straightway behold you, a damsel that cometh of such beauty as never was greater, and clad right richly, and she beareth a coffer richer than ever you saw, for it was all of fine gold and set with precious stones that sparkled like fire. The coffer is not large. The damsel holdeth it between her hands. When she was alighted she cometh before the King and saluteth him the fairest she may and the Queen likewise. The King returneth her salute. 'Sir,' saith she, 'I am come to your court for that it is the sovran of all other, and so bring I you here this rich vessel that you see as a gift; and it hath within the head of a knight, but none may open the coffer save he alone that slew the knight. Wherefore I pray and beseech you, as you are the best king that liveth, that you first set your hand thereon, and in like manner afterwards make proof of your knights, and so the crime and the blood-wite thereof be brought home to you or to any knight that may be within yonder. I pray you that the knight who shall be able to open the coffer wherein the head of the knight lieth, and who therefore is he that slew him, shall have grace of forty days after that you shall be returned from the Graal.' 'Damsel,' saith the King, 'How shall it be known who the knight was?' 'Sir,' saith she, 'Right eath, for the letters are sealed within that tell his name and the name of him that slew him.' The King granteth the damsel her will in such wise as she had asked of him. He hath received the coffer, then maketh her be set at meat and right richly honoured.

III

When the King had eaten, the damsel cometh before him. 'Sir,' saith she, 'Make your knights be summoned and ready for that which you have granted me, and you yourself first of all. 'Damsel,' saith the King, 'Right willingly.' He setteth his hand to the coffer, thinking to open it, but it was not right that it should open for him. As he set his hand thereon the coffer sweated through just as had it been sprinkled all over and was wet with water. The King marvelled greatly, and so made Messire Gawain set his hand to it and Lancelot and all those of the court, but he that might open it was not among them. Messire Kay the Seneschal had served at meat. He heard say that the King and all the others had essayed and proved the coffer but might not open it. He is come thither, all uncalled for. 'Now, then, Kay,' saith the King, 'I had forgotten you.' 'By my head,' saith Kay, 'You ought not to forget me, for as good knight am I and of as much worth as they that you have called before me, and you ought not to have delayed to send for me. You have summoned all the others, and me not a whit, and yet am I as well able, or ought to be, to open the coffer as are they; for against as many knights have I defended me as they, and as many have I slain in defending my body as have they.' 'Kay,' saith the King, 'shall you be so merry and you may open the coffer, and if you have slain the knight whose head lieth therein? By my head, I that am King would fain that the coffer should not open for me, for never was no knight so poor as that he should have neither kinsman nor friend, for he is not loved of all the world that is hated by one man.' 'By my head,' saith Kay, 'I would that all the heads of all the knights I have slain, save one only, were in the midst of this hall, and that there were letters sealed with them to say that they were slain by me. Then would you believe what you are not willing to believe for the envious ones that think they are better worth than I, and yet have not served you so well.'

IV

'Kay,' saith the King, 'Come forward, there is no need of this.' Messire Kay the Seneschal cometh to the dais before the King, whereon was the coffer, and taketh it right boldly and setteth one of his hands below it and the other above. The coffer opened as soon as he clapped hand thereon, and the head within could be seen all openly. A passing delicate-savoured smell and right sweet issued therefrom, so that not a knight in the hall but smelt it. 'Sir,' saith Kay to the King, 'Now may you know that some prowess and some hardiment have I done in your service, nor might none of your knights that you prize so highly open the coffer this day, nor would you have known this day who is therein for them! But now you know it by me, and therefore of so much ought you to be well pleased with me!'

V

'Sir,' saith the damsel that had brought the coffer, 'Let the
letters be read that are within, so shall you know who the
knight was and of what lineage, and what was the occasion of
his death.' The King sitteth beside the Queen, and biddeth
call one of his own chaplains. Then maketh he all the knights
in the hall be seated and keep silence, and commandeth the
chaplain that he should spell out the letters of gold all openly
according as he should find them written. The chaplain
looketh at them, and when he had scanned them down, began
to sigh. 'Sir,' saith he to the King and Queen, 'hearken unto
me, and all the other, your knights.

VI

'These letters say that the knight whose head lieth in this
vessel was named Lohot, and he was son of King Arthur and
Queen Guenievre. He had slain on a day that is past, Logrin
the Giant, by his hardiment. Messire Kay the Seneschal was
passing by there, and so found Lohot sleeping upon Logrin,
for such was his custom that he went to sleep upon the man
after that he had slain him. Messire Kay smote off Lohot's
head, and so left the head and the body on the piece of
ground. He took the head of the Giant and so bore it to
the court of King Arthur. He gave the King and Queen
and all the barons of the court to understand that he had
slain him, but this did he not; rather, that he did was to
slay Lohot, according to the writing and the witness of these
letters.' When the Queen heareth these letters and this witting
of her son that came thus by his death, she falleth in a swoon
on the coffer. After that she taketh the head between her two
hands, and knew well that it was he by a scar that he had on
his face when he was a child. The King himself maketh
dole thereof so sore that none may comfort him, for before
these tidings he had thought that his son was still on live and
that he was the Best Knight in the world, and when the news
came to his court that the Knight of the Golden Circlet had
slain the Knight of the Dragon, he supposed that it had been
Lohot his son, for that none had named Perceval nor Gawain

nor Lancelot.   And all they of the court are right sorrowful
for the death of Lohot, and Messire Kay hath departed, and if
the damsel had not respited the day until the fortieth after the
King's return, vengeance would have been taken of Kay or
ever he might have turned him thence.   For never did no
man see greater dole made in the King's court than they of the
Table Round made for the youth.   King Arthur and the
Queen were so stricken of sorrow that none durst call upon
them to make cheer.   The damsel that brought thither the
coffer was well avenged of the shame that Messire Kay the
Seneschal had done her on a day that was past, for this thing
would not have been known so soon save it had been by her.

VII

When the mourning for the King's son was abated, Lancelot
and many others said unto him, 'Sir, you know well that God
willeth you should go to the castle that was King Fisherman's
on pilgrimage to the most Holy Graal, for it is not right to
delay a thing that one hath in covenant with God.'   'Lords,'
saith the King, 'right willingly will I go, and thereto am I
right well disposed.'   The King apparelleth himself for the
pilgrimage, and saith that Messire Gawain and Lancelot shall
go with him, without more knights, and taketh a squire to wait
upon his body, and the Queen herself would he have taken
thither but for the mourning she made for her son, whereof
none might give her any comfort.   But or ever the King
departed he made the head be brought into the Isle of Avalon,
to a chapel of Our Lady that was there, where was a worshipful
holy hermit that was well loved of Our Lord.   The King
departed from Cardoil and took leave of the Queen and all the
knights.   Lancelot and Messire Gawain go along with him and
a squire that carrieth their arms.   Kay the Seneschal was
departed from the court for dread of the King and his knights.
He durst not abide in the Greater Britain, and so betook himself
into the Lesser.   Briant of the Isles was of great power in
those times, a knight of great strength and hardiment, for all
Great Britain had had many disputes between him and King
Arthur.   His land was full strong of castles and forests and
right fruitful, and many good knights had he in his land.   When
he knew that Kay the Seneschal had departed in such sort from

the court, and that he had crossed the sea, he sent for him and held him of his household, and said that he would hold him harmless against the King and against all men. When he knew that the King had departed he began to war upon the land and to slay his men and to challenge his castles.

BRANCH XX

Title I

THE story saith that King Arthur goeth his way and Lancelot and Messire Gawain with him, and they had ridden so far one day that night came on in a forest and they might find no hold. Messire Gawain marvelled him much that they had ridden the day long without finding neither hold nor hermitage. Night was come and the sky was dark and the forest full of gloom. They knew not whitherward to turn to pass the night. 'Lords,' saith the King, 'Where may we be able to alight to-night?' 'Sir, we know not, for this forest is right wearisome.' They make the squire climb up a tall tree and tell him to look as far as he may to try whether he may espy any hold or house where they may lodge. The squire looketh on all sides, and then telleth them he seeth a fire a long way off as if it were in a waste house, but that he seeth nought there save the fire and the house. 'Take good heed,' saith Lancelot, 'in which quarter it is, so that you may know well how to lead us thither.' He saith that right eath may he lead them.

II

With that he cometh down and mounteth again on his hackney, and they go forward a great pace and ride until they espy the fire and the hold. They pass on over a bridge of wattles, and find the courtyard all deserted and the house from within great and high and hideous. But there was a great fire within whereof the heat might be felt from afar. They alight of their horses, and the squire draweth them on one side amidst the hall, and the knights set them beside the fire all armed. The squire seeth a chamber in the house and entereth thereinto

236

to see if he may find any meat for the horses, but he cometh forth again the swiftest he may and crieth right sweetly on the Mother of the Saviour. They ask him what aileth him, and he saith that he hath found the most treacherous chamber ever he found yet, for he felt there, what with heads and what with hands, more than two hundred men dead, and saith that never yet felt he so sore afeared. Lancelot went into the chamber to see whether he spake true, and felt the men that lay dead, and groped among them from head to head and felt that there was a great heap of them there, and came back and sate at the fire all laughing. The King asketh whether the squire had told truth. Lancelot answereth him yea, and that never yet had he found so many dead men together. 'Methinketh,' saith Messire Gawain, 'Sith that they are dead we have nought to fear of them, but God protect us from the living.'

III

While they were talking thus, behold you a damsel that cometh into the dwelling on foot and all alone, and she cometh lamenting right grievously. 'Ha, God!' saith she, 'How long a penance is this for me, and when will it come to an end?' She seeth the knights sitting in the midst of the house. 'Fair Lord God,' saith she, 'Is he there within through whom I am to escape from this great dolour?' The knights hearken to her with great wonderment. They look and see her enter within the door, and her kirtle was all torn with thorns and briars in the forest. Her feet were all bleeding for that she was unshod. She had a face of exceeding great beauty. She carried the half of a dead man, and cast it into the chamber with the others. She knew Lancelot again so soon as she saw him. 'Ha, God!' saith she, 'I am quit of my penance! Sir,' saith she, 'Welcome may you be, you and your company!' Lancelot looketh at her in wonderment. 'Damsel,' saith he, 'Are you a thing on God's behalf?' 'Certes, Sir,' saith she, 'Yea! nor be you adread of nought! I am the Damsel of the Castle of Beards, that was wont to deal with knights so passing foully as you have seen. You did away the toll that was levied on the knights that passed by, and you lay in the castle that demanded it of them that passed through the demesne thereof. But you had me in covenant that so the Holy Graal should appear unto you, you would come back to me, for otherwise never should I have been willing to let you go. You returned not, for that you saw not the Graal. For the shame that I did to knights was this penance laid upon me in this forest and this manor, to last until such time as you should come. For the cruelty I did them was sore grievous, for never was knight brought to me but I made his nose be cut off or his eyes thrust out, and some were there as you saw that had their feet or their hands stricken off. Now have I paid full dear thereof since, for needs must I carry into this chamber all the knights that are slain in this forest, and within this manor must I cast them according to the custom thereof, alone, without company; and this knight that I carried in but now hath lain so long in the forest that wild beasts have eaten half of his body. Now am I quit of this foul penance, thanks to God and to you, save only that I must go back when it shall be daylight in like manner as I came here.'

IV

'Damsel,' saith Lancelot, 'Right glad am I that we should have come to lodge the night here within, for love of you, for never saw I damsel that might do so cruel penance.' 'Sir,' saith she, 'You know not yet what it is, but you will know it ere long this night, both you and your fellows, and the Lord God shield you from death and from mischief! Every night cometh a rout of knights that are black and foul and hideous, albeit none knoweth whence they come, and they do battle right sore the one against other, and the stour endureth of a right long while; but one knight that came within yonder by chance, the first night I came hither, in like manner as you have come, made a circle round me with his sword, and I sate within it as soon as I saw them coming, and so had I no dread of them, for I had in remembrance the Saviour of the World and His passing sweet Mother. And you will do the same, and you believe me herein, for these are knights fiends.' Lancelot draweth his sword and maketh a great circle round the house-place, and they were within.

V

Thereupon, behold you the knights that come through the forest with such a rushing as it seemed they would rend it all up by the roots. Afterward, they enter into the manor and snatch great blazing firebrands and fling them one at another. They enter into the house battling together, and are keen to fall upon the knights, but they may not. They hurl the firebrands at them from afar, but they are holding their shields and their swords naked. Lancelot maketh semblant as though he would leap towards them, and sore great cowardize it seemeth him not to go against them. 'Sir,' saith the damsel, 'Take heed that you go not forth of the circle, for you will be in sore jeopardy of death, for well you see what evil folk be these.' Lancelot was not minded to hold himself back, but that he would go toward them sword drawn, and they run upon him on all sides, but he defendeth him stoutly and smiteth the burning firebrands so that he maketh red-hot charcoal fly, and thrusteth his sword amidst their faces. King Arthur and Messire Gawain leap up to help Lancelot and smite upon these evil folk and cut them limb from limb, and they bellow like fiends so that the whole forest resoundeth thereof. And when they fell to the ground, they may no longer endure, but become fiends and ashes, and their bodies and their horses become devils all black in the shape of ravens that come forth of their bodies. They marvel right sore what this may be, and say that such hostel is right grievous.

VI

When they had put them all to the worse, they sate them down again and rested; but scarce were they seated or ever another rout of yet blacker folk came about them, and they bare spears burning and flaming, and many of them carried dead knights that they had slain in the forest, and dropped them in the midst of the house, and then bid the damsel carry and set them with the others. Howbeit, she answereth that she is quit of their commandment and service, nor no longer is forced to do nought for them sith that she hath done her penance. They thrust forward their spears toward the King and the two knights, as though they were come to avenge their companions; but they all three leapt up together and attacked them right stoutly. But this rout was greater and of knights more hideous. They began to press the King and his knights hard, and they might not put them to the worse as they did the

others.   And while they were thus in the thickest of the
conflict, they heard the stroke of a bell sounding, and forthwith
the knight fiends departed and hurried away a great pace.
'Lords,' saith the damsel, 'Had this sound not been heard,
scarce might you have endured, for yet another huge rout of
this folk was coming in such sort as that none might have
withstood them, and this sound have I heard every night,
whereby my life hath been saved.'

VII

Josephus telleth us that as at this time was there no bell
neither in Greater Britain nor in Lesser; but folk were called
together by a horn, and in many places there were sheets of
steel, and in other places clappers of wood.   King Arthur
marvelled him much of this sound, so clear and sweet was it,
and it well seemed him that it came on God's behalf, and right
fain was he to see a bell and so he might.   They were the
night until the morrow in the house, as I tell you.   The damsel
took leave of them and so departed.   As they came forth of the
hold, they met three hermits that told them they were going to
search for the bodies that were in this manor so that they might
bury them in a waste chapel that was hard by, for such knights
had lain there as that henceforward the haunting of the evil
folk would be stayed in such sort as that they would have no
more power to do hurt to any, wherefore they would set
therewithin a worshipful hermit that should build up the place
in holiness for the service of God.   The King was right joyful
thereof, and told them that it had been too perilous.   They
parted from the hermits and entered into a forest, nor was there
never a day so long as King Arthur was on pilgrimage, so saith
the history, but he heard the sound of one single bell every
hour, whereof he was right glad.   He bade Messire Gawain
and Lancelot that they should everywhere conceal his name, and
that they should call him not Lord but Comrade.   They
yielded him his will, and prayed to Our Lord that He would
guide and lead them to such a castle and such a hostel as that
they might be lodged honourably therein.   They rode on until
evening drew nigh, and they found a right fair hold in the
forest, whereinto they entered and alighted.   The damsel of
the hold came to meet them and made them right great cheer,

then made them be disarmed, afterward bringeth them right rich robes to wear. She looketh at Lancelot and knoweth him again.

VIII

'Sir,' saith she, 'You had once, on a day that is past, right great pity of me, and saved me my honour, whereof am I in great unhappiness. But better love I to suffer misease in honour, than to have plenty and abundance in shame or reproach, for shame endureth, but sorrow is soon overpassed.' Thereupon behold you the knight of the hold, whither he cometh from shooting in the forest and maketh carry in full great plenty venison of deer and wild boar. He alighted to greet the knights, and began to laugh when he saw Lancelot. 'By my head,' saith he, 'I know you well. For you disappointed me of the thing I best loved in the world, and made me marry this damsel that never yet had joy of me, nor never shall have.' 'Faith, Sir,' saith Lancelot, 'You will do your pleasure therein, for she is yours. Truth it is that I made you marry her, for you were fain to do her a disgrace and a shame in such sort that her kinsfolk would have had shame of her.' 'By my head,' saith the knight, 'the damsel that I loved before loveth you no better hereof, nay, rather, fain would she procure your vexation and your hurt and your shame if she may, and great power hath she in this forest.' 'Sir,' saith Lancelot, 'I have sithence spoken to her and she to me, and so hath she told me her will and her wish.' Thereupon the knight bade the knights take water, and the lady taketh the basins and presenteth water to the knights. 'Avoid, damsel,' saith the King, 'Take it away! Never, please God, shall it befall that we should accept such service from you.' 'By my head,' saith the knight, 'But so must you needs do, for other than she shall not serve you to-night in this matter, or otherwise shall you not eat with me this night there within.'

IX

Lancelot understandeth that the knight is not overburdened of courtesy, and he seeth the table garnished of good meat, and bethinketh him he will not do well to lose such ease, for misease enough had they the night before. He maketh the King take

1

water of the lady, and the same service did she for all of them.
The knight biddeth them be seated. The King would have
made the lady sit beside him at the table, but the knight said that
there she should not sit. She goeth to sit among the squires as
she was wont to do. The knights are sorry enough thereof,
but they durst not gainsay the will of her lord. When they
had eaten, the knight said to Lancelot, 'Now may you see what
she hath gained of me by your making me take her perforce,
nor never, so help me God, so long as I live shall she be
honoured otherwise by me, for so have I promised her that I
love far more.' 'Sir,' saith Lancelot, 'To my thinking, you do
ill herein and a sin, and meseemeth you should have great
blame thereof of them that know it, and may your churlishness
be your own, for nought thereof take I to myself.'

X

Lancelot telleth the King and Messire Gawain that were he
not lodged in his hostel, and had him outside of the hold, he
would willingly have set the blood of his body on it but he
would have handled him in such sort as that the lady should be
maintained in greater honour, either by force or by prayer, in like
manner as he did when he made him marry her. They were
right well lodged the night and lay in the hold until the
morrow, when they departed thence, and rode right busily on
their journeys until they came into a very different land, scarce
inhabited of any folk, and found a little castle in a combe.
They came thitherward and saw that the enclosure of the castle
was fallen down into an abysm, so that none might approach it
on that side, but it had a right fair gateway and a door tall and
wide whereby one entered. They beheld a chapel that was
right fair and rich, and below was a great ancient hall. They
saw a priest appear in the midst of the castle, bald and old,
that had come forth of the chapel. They are come thither and
alighted, and asked the priest what the castle was, and he told
them that it was the great Tintagel. 'And how is this ground
all caved in about the castle?' 'Sir,' saith the priest, 'I will
tell you. Sir,' saith he, 'King Uther Pendragon, that was father
of King Arthur, held a great court and summoned all his
barons. The King of this castle that then was here was named
Gorlois. He went to the court and took his wife with him,

that was named Ygerne, and she was the fairest dame in any
kingdom. King Uther sought acquaintance of her for her
great beauty, and regarded her and honoured her more than all
the others of his court. King Gorlois departed thence and
made the Queen come back to this castle for the dread that he
had of King Uther Pendragon. King Uther was very wroth
with him, and commanded him to send back the Queen his
wife. King Gorlois said that he would not. Thereupon King
Uther Pendragon defied him, and then laid siege about this
castle where the Queen was. King Gorlois was gone to seek
for succour. King Uther Pendragon had Merlin with him of
whom you have heard tell, that was so crafty. He made him
be changed into the semblance of King Gorlois, so that he
entered there within by Merlin's art and lay that night with the
Queen, and so begat King Arthur in a great hall that was next to
the enclosure there where this abysm is. And for this sin hath
the ground sunken in on this wise.' He cometh with them
toward the chapel that was right fair, and had a right rich
sepulchre therein. 'Lords, in this sepulchre was placed the
body of Merlin, but never mought it be set inside the chapel,
wherefore perforce it remained outside. And know of a very
truth that the body lieth not within the sepulchre, for, so soon
as it was set therein, it was taken out and snatched away, either
on God's behalf or the Enemy's, but which we know not.'

XI

'Sir,' saith King Arthur, 'And what became of King
Gorlois?' 'Sir,' saith he, 'The King slew him on the morrow
of the night he lay with his wife, and so forthwith espoused
Queen Ygerne, and in such manner as I tell you was King
Arthur conceived in sin that is now the best King in the world.'
King Arthur hath heard this as concerning his birth that he knew
not, and is a little shamed thereof and confounded on account
of Messire Gawain and Lancelot. He himself marvelleth much
thereof, and much it misliketh him that the priest hath said so
much. They lay the night in the hold, and so departed thence
on the morrow when they had heard mass. Lancelot and
Messire Gawain, that thought they knew the forest, found the
land so changed and different that they knew not whither they
were become, and such an one as should come into the land

that had been King Fisherman's, and he should come again another time within forty days, should not find the castle within a year.

XII

Josephus telleth us that the semblances of the islands changed themselves by reason of the divers adventures that by the pleasure of God befell therein, and that the quest of adventures would not have pleased the knights so well and they had not found them so different. For, when they had entered into a forest or an island where they had found any adventure, and they came there another time, they found holds and castles and adventures of another kind, so that their toils and travails might not weary them, and also for that God would that the land should be conformed to the New Law. And they were the knights that had more toil and travail in seeking adventures than all the knights of the world before them, and in holding to that whereof they had made covenant; nor of no court of no king in the world went forth so many good knights as went forth from the court of King Arthur, and but that God loved them so much, never might they have endured such toil and travail as they did from day to day; for without fail, good knights were they, and good knights not only to deal hard buffets, but rather in that they were loyal and true, and had faith in the Saviour of the World and His sweet Mother, and therefore dreaded shame and loved honour. King Arthur goeth on his way and Messire Gawain and Lancelot with him, and they pass through many strange countries, and so enter into a great forest. Lancelot called to remembrance the knight that he had slain in the Waste City whither behoved him to go, and knew well that the day whereon he should come was drawing nigh. He told King Arthur as much, and then said, that and he should go not, he would belie his covenant. They rode until they came to a cross where the ways forked. 'Sir,' saith Lancelot, 'Behoveth me go to acquit me of my pledge, and I go in great adventure and peril of death, nor know I whether I may live at all thereafter, for I slew the knight, albeit I was right sorry thereof, but or ever I slew him, I had to swear that I would go set my head in the like jeopardy as he had set his. Now the day draweth nigh that I must go thither, for I am unwilling to fail of my covenant, whereof I should be blamed,

and, so God grant me to escape therefrom, I will follow you
speedily.' The King embraceth him and kisseth him at parting
and Messire Gawain also, and they pray God preserve his body
and his life, and that they may see him again ere it be long.
Lancelot would willingly have sent salute to the Queen had he
durst, for she lay nearer his heart than aught beside, but he
would not that the King nor Messire Gawain should misdeem
of the love they might carry to their kinswoman. The love is
so rooted in his heart that he may not leave it, into what peril
soever he may go; rather, he prayeth God every day as sweetly
as he may, that He save the Queen, and that he may deliver his
body from this jeopardy. He hath ridden until that he cometh
at the hour of noon into the Waste City, and findeth the city
empty as it was the first time he was there.

XIII

In the city wherein Lancelot had arrived were many waste
houses and rich palaces fallen down. He had scarce entered
within the city when he heard a great cry and lamentation of
dames and damsels, but he knew not on which side it was, and
they say: 'Ha, God, how hath the knight betrayed us that
slew the knight, inasmuch as he returneth not! This day is
the day come that he ought to redeem his pledge! Never
again ought any to put trust in knight, for that he cometh not!
The others that came hither before him have failed us, and so
will he also for dread of death; for he smote off the head of
the comeliest knight that was in this kingdom and the best,
wherefore ought he also to have his own smitten off, but good
heed taketh he to save it if he may!' Thus spake the damsels.
Lancelot much marvelled where they might be, for nought
could he espy of them, albeit he cometh before the palace,
there where he slew the knight. He alighteth, then maketh
fast his horse's reins to a ring that was fixed in the mounting-
stage of marble. Scarce hath he done so, when a knight
alighteth, tall and comely and strong and deliver, and he was
clad in a short close-fitted jerkin of silk, and held the axe in his
hand wherewith Lancelot had smitten off the head of the other
knight, and he came sharpening it on a whetstone to cut the
better. Lancelot asketh him, 'What will you do with this
axe?' 'By my head,' saith the knight, 'That shall you know

in such sort as my brother knew when you cut off his head, so
I may speed of my business.' 'How?' saith Lancelot, 'Will
you slay me then?' 'That shall you know,' saith he, 'or ever
you depart hence. Have you not loyally promised hereof that
you would set your head in the same jeopardy as the knight set
his, whom you slew without defence? And no otherwise may
you depart therefrom. Wherefore now come forward without
delay and kneel down and stretch your neck even as my brother
did, and so will I smite off your head, and, if you do not this
of your own good will, you shall soon find one that shall make
you do it perforce, were you twenty knights as good as you are
one. But well I know that you have not come hither for this,
but only to fulfil your pledge, and that you will raise no contention herein.' Lancelot thinketh to die, and is minded to
abide by that he hath in covenant without fail, wherefore he
lieth down on the ground as it were on a cross, and crieth
mercy of God. He mindeth him of the Queen, and crieth God
of mercy and saith, 'Ha, Lady,' saith he, 'Never shall I see
you more! but, might I have seen you yet once again before I
die, exceeding great comfort had it been to me, and my soul
would have departed from me more at ease. But this, that
never shall I see you more, as now it seemeth me, troubleth
me more than the death whereby behoveth me to die, for die
one must when one hath lived long enough. But faithfully do
I promise you that my love shall fail you not yet, and never
shall it be but that my soul shall love you in the other world
like as my body hath loved you in this, if thus the soul may
love!' With that the tears fell from his eyes, nor, never
sithence that he was knight, saith the story, had he wept for
nought that had befallen him nor for heaviness of heart, but
this time and one other. He taketh three blades of grass and
so eateth thereof in token of the holy communion, then signeth
him of the cross and blesseth him, riseth up, setteth himself on
his knees and stretcheth forth his neck. The knight lifteth up
the axe. Lancelot heareth the blow coming, boweth his head
and the axe misseth him. He saith to him, 'Sir Knight, so did
not my brother that you slew; rather, he held his head and
neck quite still, and so behoveth you to do!' Two damsels
appeared at the palace-windows of passing great beauty, and
they knew Lancelot well. So, as the knight was aiming a
second blow, one of the damsels crieth to him, 'And you would

have my love for evermore, throw down the axe and cry the knight quit! Otherwise have you lost me for ever!' The knight forthwith flingeth down the axe and falleth at Lancelot's feet and crieth mercy of him as of the most loyal knight in the world. 'But you? Have mercy on me, you! and slay me not!' saith Lancelot, 'For it is of you that I ought to pray mercy!' 'Sir,' saith the knight, 'Of a surety will I not do this! Rather will I help you to my power to save your life against all men, for all you have slain my brother.' The damsels come down from the palace and are come to Lancelot.

XIV

'Sir,' say they to Lancelot, 'Greatly ought we to love you, yea, better than all knights in the world beside. For we are the two damsels, sisters, that you saw so poor at the Waste Castle where you lay in our brother's house. You and Messire Gawain and another knight gave us the treasure and the hold of the robber-knights that you slew; for this city which is waste and the Waste Castle of my brother would never again be peopled of folk, nor should we never have had the land again, save a knight had come hither as loyal as are you. Full a score knights have arrived here by chance in the same manner as you came, and not one of them but hath slain a brother or a kinsman and cut off his head as you did to the knight, and each one promised to return at the day appointed; but all failed of their covenant, for not one of them durst come to the day; and so you had failed us in like manner as the others, we should have lost this city without recovery and the castles that are its appanages.'

XV

So the knight and the damsels lead Lancelot into the palace and then make him be disarmed. They hear presently how the greatest joy in the world is being made in many parts of the forest, that was nigh the city. 'Sir,' say the damsels, 'Now may you hear the joy that is made of your coming. These are the burgesses and dwellers in the city that already know the tidings.' Lancelot leaneth at the windows of the hall, and seeth the city peopled of the fairest folk in the world, and great thronging in the broad streets and the great palace, and clerks and priests coming in long procession praising God and blessing Him for that they may now return to their church, and giving benison to the knight through whom they are free to repair thither. Lancelot was much honoured throughout the city. The two damsels are at great pains to wait upon him, and right great worship had he of all them that were there-within and them that came thither, both clerks and priests.

BRANCH XXI

TITLE I

THEREWITHAL the history is silent of Lancelot, and speaketh word of the King and Messire Gawain, that are in sore misgiving as concerning him, for right gladly would they have heard tidings of him. They met a knight that was coming all armed, and Messire Gawain asketh him whence he came, and he said that he came from the land of the Queen of the Golden Circlet, to whom a sore loss hath befallen; for the Son of the Widow Lady had won the Circlet of Gold for that he had slain the Knight of the Dragon, and she was to keep it safe for him and deliver it up to him at his will. 'But now hath Nabigant of the Rock reft her thereof, and a right outrageous knight is he and puissant; wherefore hath he commanded a damsel that she bring it to an assembly of knights that is to be held in the Meadow of the Tent of the two damsels, there where Messire Gawain did away the evil custom. The damsel that will bring the Golden Circlet will give it to the knight that shall do best at the assembly. Nabigant is keenly set upon having it, and maketh the more sure for that once aforetime he hath had it by force of arms. And I am going to the knights that know not these tidings, in order that when they shall hear them, they shall go to the assembly.' Therewithal the knight departeth. The King and Messire Gawain have ridden so far that they come to the tent where Messire Gawain destroyed the evil custom by slaying the two knights. He found the tent garnished within and without in like manner as it was when he was there, and Messire Gawain made the King be seated on a quilted mattress of straw, right costly, and thereafter be disarmed of a squire, and he himself disarmed him, and they washed their hands and faces for the rust wherewith both of them were besmuttered. And Messire Gawain found the chests unlocked that were at the head of the couch, and made the King be apparelled of white rich stuffs that he found, and a robe of cloth of silk and gold, and he clad himself in the like manner, neither was the chest not a whit disfurnished thereby, for the tent was all garnished of rich adornments. When they were thus dight, a man might have sought far or ever he should find so comely knights.

II

Thereupon, behold you the two Damsels of the Tent coming. 'Damsels,' saith Messire Gawain, 'Welcome may you be.' 'Sir,' say they, 'Good adventure may you have both twain. It seemeth us that you take right boldly that which is ours, yet never for neither of us would you do a thing whereof you were beseeched.' 'Messire Gawain,' saith the elder, 'No knight is there in this kingdom but would be right joyous and he supposed that I loved him, and I prayed you of your love on a day that is past, for the valour of your knighthood, yet never did you grant it me. How durst you have affiance in me of aught, and take the things that are mine own so boldly, when I may not have affiance in you?' 'Damsel, for your courtesy and the good custom of the land; for you told me when the evil customs were overthrown, that all the honours and all the courtesies that are due to knights should ever be ready within for all them that should come hither for harbour.' 'Messire Gawain, you say true, but of right might one let the courtesy tarry and pay back churlishness by churlishness.

III

'The assembly of knights will begin to-morrow in this launde that is so fair. There will be knights in plenty, and the prize will be the Circlet of Gold. Now shall we see who will do best. The assembly will last three whole days, and of one thing at least you may well make boast between you and your comrade, that you have the fairest hostel and the most pleasant and the most quiet of any knights at the assembly.' The younger damsel looketh at King Arthur. 'And you,' saith she, 'What will you do? Will you be as strange toward us as Messire Gawain is friendly with others?'

IV

'Damsel,' saith the king, 'Messire Gawain will do his pleasure and I mine. Strange shall I not be in respect of you, nor toward other damsels; rather shall they be honoured on my part so long as I live, and I myself will be at your commandment.' 'Sir,' saith she, 'Gramercy greatly. I pray you, therefore, that you be my knight at the tournament.' 'Damsel, this ought I not to refuse you, and right glad at heart shall I be and I may do aught that shall please you; for all knights ought to be at pains for the sake of dame or damsel.' 'Sir,' saith she, 'what is your name?'

V

'Damsel,' saith he, 'My name is Arthur, and I am of Tincardoil.' 'Have you nought to do with King Arthur?' 'Damsel, already have I been many times at his court, and, if he loved me not nor I him, I should not be in Messire Gawain's company. In truth, he is the King in the world that I love best.' The damsel looketh at King Arthur, but wotteth not a whit that it is he, and full well is she pleased with the seeming and countenance of him. As for the King, lightly might he have trusted that he should have her as his lady-love so long as he remained with her; but there is much to say betwixt his semblant and his thought, for he showeth good semblant toward the damsel, that hath over much affiance therein, but his thought is on Queen Guenievre in what place soever he may be. For nought loveth he so well as her.

VI

The damsels made stable the horses and purvey for the bodies of the knights right richly at night, and they lay in two right rich beds in the midst of the hall, and their arms were all set ready before. The damsels would not depart until such time as they were asleep. The harness of the knights that came to the assembly came on the morrow from all parts. They set up their booths and stretched their tents all round about the launde of the forest. King Arthur and Messire Gawain were risen in the morning and saw the knights come from all parts. The elder damsel cometh to Messire Gawain and saith unto him, 'Sir,' saith she, 'I will that you bear to-day red arms that I will lend you, for the love of me, and take heed that they be well employed, and I desire that you should not be known by your arms; rather let it be said that you are the Red Knight, and you shall allow it accordingly.' 'Damsel, Gramercy greatly!' saith Messire Gawain, 'I will do my endeavour in arms the best I may for love of you.' The younger damsel cometh to King Arthur; 'Sir,' saith she, 'My sister hath made her gift and I will make mine. I have a suit of arms of gold, the richest that knight may wear, that I will lend you, for methinketh they will be better employed on you than on ever another knight; so I pray you that you remember me at the assembly in like manner as I shall ofttimes remember you.'

VII

'Damsel,' saith the King, 'Gramercy! No knight is there that should see you but ought to have you in remembrance in his heart for your courtesy and your worth.' The knights were come about the tents. The King and Messire Gawain were armed and had made caparison their horses right richly. The damsel that should give the Golden Circlet was come. Nabigant of the Rock had brought great fellowships of knights together with him, and ordinance was made for the assembly.

VIII

The younger damsel saith to King Arthur: 'Well may you know that no knight that is here this day hath better arms than are yours, wherefore take heed that you show you to be good knight for love of me.' 'Damsel,' saith King Arthur, 'God grant that I be so.' So they laid hold on their reins and mounted their horses, that made great leaping and went away a great gallop. Saith the younger damsel to her sister: 'What think you of my knight, doth he not please you?' 'Yea,' saith the elder, 'But sore misliketh me of Messire Gawain for that he is not minded to do as I would have him. But he shall yet aby it dear.' King Arthur and Messire Gawain strike into the midst of the assembly like as it were two lions unchained, and at their first coming they smite down two knights to the ground under the feet of their horses. Messire Gawain taketh the two horses

and sendeth them by a squire to the Damsels of the Tent, that
made much joy thereof.   After that were they not minded to
take more booty as of horses or arms, but searched the fellowships on one side and the other; nor was there no knight that
came against them but they pierced his shield or bore him to the
ground, insomuch as none was there that might endure their
buffets.   Nabigant espieth Messire Gawain and cometh toward
him, and Messire Gawain toward him again, and they hurtle
together either on other so strongly that Messire Gawain
beareth Nabigant to the ground, him and his horse together all
in a heap.   And King Arthur was not idle, for no knight durst
come against him but he overthrew him, so as that all withdrew
them back and avoided his buffets.   And many knights did well
that day at the assembly, but none might be the match of either
of them twain in deeds of arms, for, save it were Lancelot or
Perceval, were no knights on live that had in them so much
hardiment and valour.   After that it was evensong the knights
drew them back to their tents, and they say all that the Knight
of the Golden Arms and the Knight of the Red Arms had done
better than they all at the assembly.   King Arthur and Messire
Gawain come back to the tent of the damsels, that make disarm
them and do upon them the rich robes and make great joy of
them.   Thereupon, behold you, a dwarf that cometh : ' Damsels,
make great joy ! for all they of the assembly say with one
accord that your knights have done best this day.'   King Arthur
and Messire Gawain sate to eat, and right well were they served of
every kind of meats and of great cups of wine and sops in wine.
King Arthur made the younger damsel sit beside him, and
Messire Gawain the elder in like manner, and when they had
eaten they went to lie down and fell on sleep, for right sore
weary were they and forespent of the many buffets they had
given and received, and they slept until the morrow.

IX

When the day appeared they rose up.   Thereupon, behold
you the younger damsel where she cometh and saluteth King
Arthur.   ' And you, damsel ! ' saith King Arthur, ' God give
you joy and good adventure ! '   ' Sir,' saith she, ' I will that you
bear to-day these white arms that you see here, and that you do
no worse to-day than yesterday you did, sith that better you

may not do.' 'Messire Gawain,' saith the elder damsel, 'Remember you of the King there where his land was compassed about of a wall of stone, and you harboured one night in his castle, what time you went to seek for the sword wherewith John Baptist was beheaded, when he was fain to take away the sword from you, whereof you had so sore misliking? Natheless, he yielded you up the sword upon covenant that you should do that which a damsel should first ask you to do thereafter, and you promised him loyally that so would you do?' 'Certes, damsel,' saith Messire Gawain, 'Well do I remember the same.' 'Now, therefore,' saith the damsel, 'would I fain prove whether you be indeed so loyal as men say, and whether you will hold your covenant that you made. Wherefore I pray and beseech you that this day you shall be he that doth worst of all the knights at the assembly, and that you bear none other arms save your own only, so as that you shall be known again of all them that are there present. And, so you will not do this, then will you have failed of your covenant, and I myself will go tell the King that you have broken the promise that you made to him right loyally.' 'Damsel,' saith Messire Gawain, 'Never yet brake I covenant with none, so it were such as I might fulfil or another on my behalf.' King Arthur made arm him of the white arms that the younger damsel had given him, and Messire Gawain of his own, but sore it irked him of this that the damsel hath laid upon him to do, sith that needs must he lose worship and he hold to his covenant, albeit not for nought that is in the world will he fail of the promise he hath made. So they come into the assembly.

X

King Arthur smiteth with his spurs like a good knight and overthroweth two knights in his onset, and Messire Gawain rideth a bandon betwixt two fellowships to be the better known. The most part say, 'See! There is Messire Gawain, the good knight that is King Arthur's nephew.' Nabigant of the Rock cometh toward him as fast as his horse may carry him, lance in rest. Messire Gawain seeth him coming toward him right furiously. He casteth his shield down on the ground and betaketh him to flight as swiftly as he may. They that beheld him, some two score or more, marvel thereof, and say, 'Did ever one see the like overpassing cowardize!' Nabigant saith that he never yet followed a knight that was vanquished, nor never will follow one of such conditions, for no great prize would it be to take him and win his horse. Other knights come to joust with him, but Messire Gawain fleeth and avoideth them the best he may, and maketh semblance that none is there he durst abide. He draweth toward King Arthur for safety. The King hath great shame of this that he seeth him do, and right sore pains hath he of defending Messire Gawain, for he holdeth as close to him as the pie doth to the bramble when the falcon would take her. In such shame and dishonour was Messire Gawain as long as the assembly lasted, and the knights said that he had gotten him off with much less than he deserved, for that never had they seen so craven knight at assembly of tournament as was he, nor never henceforth would they have dread of him as they had heretofore. From this day forward may many lightly avenge themselves upon him of their kinsfolk and friends that he hath slain by the forest. The assembly brake up in the evening, whereof the King and Messire Gawain were right well pleased. The knights disarm them at their hostels and the King and Messire Gawain at the damsels' tent.

XI

With that, behold you! the dwarf that cometh. 'By my head, damsels, your knights go from bad to worse! Of him in the white arms one may even let pass, but Messire Gawain is the most coward ever saw I yet, and so he were to run upon me to-morrow and I were armed like as is he, I should think me right well able to defend me against him. 'Tis the devil took him to a place where is such plenty of knights, for the more folk that are there the better may one judge of his ill conditions. And you, Sir,' saith he to the King, 'Wherefore do you keep him company? You would have done best to-day had he not been there. He skulked as close by you, to be out of the buffets, as a hare doth to the wood for the hounds. No business hath good knight to hold company with a coward. I say not this for that I would make him out worse than he is, for I remember the two knights he slew before this tent.' The damsel heareth the dwarf talking and smileth thereat, for she understandeth that blame enough hath Messire Gawain had at the assembly. The knights said at their hostels that they knew not to whom to give the Circlet of Gold, sith that the Knight of the Golden Armour and he of the Red Armour were not there ; for they did the best the first day of the assembly, and much they marvelled that they should not come when it was continued on the morrow. 'Gawain,' saith the King, 'Sore blame have you had this day, and I myself have been all shamed for your sake. Never thought I that so good a knight as you might ever have known how to counterfeit a bad knight as you did. You have done much for the love of the damsel, and right well had she avenged herself of you and you had done her great annoy. Howbeit, and to-morrow your cowardize be such as it hath been to-day, never will the day be when you shall not have blame thereof.'

XII

'By my faith,' saith Messire Gawain, 'Behoveth me do the damsel's pleasure sith that we have fallen by ill-chance into her power.' They went to bed at night and took their rest as soon as they had eaten, and on the morrow the damsel came to Messire Gawain. 'I will,' saith she, 'that you be clad in the same arms as was your comrade on the first day, right rich, that I will lend you, and I will, moreover, that you be knight so good as that never on any day were you better. But I command you, by the faith you pledged me the other day, to obey this caution, that you make yourself known to none, and, so any man in the world shall ask your name, you shall say that you are the knight of the Golden Arms.' 'Damsel,' saith Gawain, 'Gramercy, I will do your pleasure.' The younger damsel cometh back to the King : 'Sir,' saith she, 'I will that you wear new arms : You shall bear them red, the same as Messire Gawain bore the first day, and I pray you be such as you were the first day, or better.'

XIII

'Damsel, I will do my best to amend myself and my doings, and right well pleased am I of that it pleaseth you to say.' Their horses were caparisoned and the knights mounted, all armed. They come together to the tournament with such an onset as that they pass through the thickest of the press and

overthrew knights and horses as many as they encountered.
King Arthur espieth Nabigant that came right gaily caparisoned,
and smiteth him so passing strong a buffet in the midst of his
breast that he beareth him down from his horse, in such sort
that he breaketh his collar-bone, and presenteth the destrier, by
his squire, to the younger damsel, that maketh great joy
thereof. And Messire Gawain searcheth the fellowships on all
sides, and so well did he search that scarce was one might
endure his blows. King Arthur is not idle, but pierceth
shields and beateth in helms, the while all look on in wonderment at him and Messire Gawain. The story saith that the
King would have done still better, but that he put not forth
his full strength in deeds of arms, for that Messire Gawain had
done so ill the day before, and now he would fain that he should
have the prize.

XIV

The damsel that held the Golden Circlet was in the midst of
the assembly of knights, and had set it in a right rich casket
of ivory with precious stones, right worshipfully. When the
damsel saw that the assembly was at an end, she made all the
knights stay, and prayed them they should speak judgment
true, concealing nought, who had best deserved of arms, and
ought therefore of right to have the Golden Circle. They
said all, that of right judgment the Knight of the Golden Arms
and he of the Red Arms ought to have the prize above all
the others, but that of these two, he of the Golden Arms
ought to have the prize, for so well did he the first day
as that no knight might do better, and on the last day likewise, and that if he of the Red Arms had put forth his
full strength on the last day, he would have done full as
well or better. The Circlet of Gold was brought to Messire
Gawain, but it was not known that it was he; and Messire
Gawain would fain that it had been given to my Lord King
Arthur. The knights departed from the assembly. The King
and Messire Gawain came back to the tent and brought the
Golden Circlet, whereof the damsels made great joy. Thereupon, behold you! the dwarf that cometh back. 'Damsels,
better is it to lodge knights such as these than Messire Gawain
the coward, the craven that had so much shame at the assembly!

You yourselves would have been sore blamed had you lodged him. This knight hath won the Golden Circlet by force of arms, and Messire Gawain nought but shame and reproach.' The damsel laugheth at this that the dwarf saith, and biddeth him on his eyes and head, begone !

XV

The King and Messire Gawain were disarmed. 'Sir,' saith the damsel, 'What will you do with the Golden Circlet?' 'Damsel,' saith Messire Gawain, 'I will bear it to him that first won it in sore peril of death, and delivered it to the Queen that ought to have kept it safe, of whom it hath been reft by force.' The King and Messire Gawain lay the night in the tent. The younger damsel cometh to the King. 'Sir, many feats of arms have you done at the assembly, as I have been told, for love of me, and I am ready to reward you.' 'Damsel, right great thanks. Your reward and your service love I much, and your honour yet more, wherefore I would that you should have all the honour that any damsel may have, for in damsel without honour ought none to put his affiance. Our Lord God grant you to preserve yours.' 'Damsel,' saith she to the other that sitteth before Messire Gawain, 'This Knight and Messire Gawain have taken counsel together. There is neither solace nor comfort in them. Let us leave them to go to sleep, and ill rest may they have, and Lord God defend us ever hereafter from such guests.' 'By my head,' saith the elder damsel, ' were it not for the Golden Circlet that he is bound of right to deliver again to the Queen that had it in charge, who is my Lady, they should not depart from this land in such sort as they will. But, and Messire Gawain still be nice as concerneth damsels, at least I now know well that he is loyal in another-wise, so as that he will not fail of his word.'

XVI

With that the damsels departed, as did likewise the King and Messire Gawain as soon as they saw the day. Nabigant, that was wounded at the tournament, was borne away on a litter. Meliot of Logres was in quest of Messire Gawain. He met the knights and the harness that came from the assembly, and asked of many if they could tell him tidings of King Arthur's nephew, Messire Gawain, and the most part answer, ' Yea, and right bad tidings enough.' Then they ask him wherefore he demandeth. ' Lords,' saith he, ' His liege man am I, and he ought of right to defend my land against all men, that Nabigant hath taken from me without right nor reason, whom they are carrying from thence in a litter, wherefore I am fain to beseech Messire Gawain that he help me to recover my land.' ' In faith, Sir Knight,' say they, ' We know not of what avail he may be to others that may not help himself. Messire Gawain was at the assembly, but we tell you for true, it was he that did worst thereat.' ' Alas,' saith Meliot of Logres, ' Then have I lost my land, and he hath become even such an one as you tell me.' ' You would readily believe us,' say they, ' had you seen him at the assembly ! ' Meliot turneth him back, right sorrowful.

XVII

King Arthur and Messire Gawain depart from the tent, and come a great pace as though they fain would escape thence to come nigher the land where they would be, and great desire had they of the coming of Lancelot. They rode until that they came one night to the Waste Manor whither the brachet led Messire Gawain when he found the dead knight that Lancelot had slain. They lodged there the night, and found there knights and damsels of whom they were known. The Lady of the Waste Manor sent for succour to her knights, saying that she held there King Arthur that slew other knights, and that his nephew Messire Gawain was also there within, but dearly would she have loved that Lancelot had been with them that slew her brother. Knights in plenty came to her to do hurt to King Arthur and Messire Gawain, but she had at least so much courtesy in her that she would not suffer any of them to do them ill within her hold, albeit she kept seven of their number, full of great hardiment, to guard the entrance of the bridge, so that King Arthur and Messire Gawain might not depart thence save only amidst the points of their spears.

XVIII

This high history witnesseth us that Lancelot was departed from the Waste City wherein he was much honoured, and rode until that he came to a forest where he met Meliot of Logres, that was sore dismayed of the tidings he had heard of Messire Gawain. Lancelot asketh him whence he cometh, and he saith from seeking Messire Gawain, of whom he had tidings whereof he was right sorrowful. 'How,' saith Lancelot, 'Is he then otherwise than well?' 'Yea,' saith he, 'As I have heard tell: for he wont to be good knight and hath now become evil. He was at the assembly of knights whereof I met the harness and the fellowships, and they told me that never yet was such cowardize in any knight, but that a knight who was with him did right well. But howsoever he may have borne himself, right fain am I to find him, for, maugre what any may say, I may scarce believe that he is so bad after all.' 'Sir,' saith Lancelot, 'I will seek him for you, and you can come along with me and it seemeth you good.' Meliot of Logres betaketh him back with Lancelot. They ride until they happen by chance upon the Waste Manor where the King and Messire Gawain were lodged; and they were armed, and were minded to go forth from thence. But the seven knights guarded the issue, all armed. The King and Messire Gawain saw that no good would it do them to remain there within, wherefore they passed over the bridge and came perforce to the place where the seven knights were watching for them. Thereupon, they went toward them all armed and struck among them, and the knights received them on the points of their lances.

XIX

Thereupon, behold you! Lancelot and the knight with him, whom they had not been looking for. Lancelot espied the King and Messire Gawain; then the knights cried out and struck among them as a hawk striketh amongst larks, and made them scatter on one side and the other. Lancelot hath caught one at his coming, and smiteth him with his spear through the body, and Meliot of Logres slayeth another. King Arthur knew Lancelot, and right glad was he to see him safe and sound, as was Messire Gawain likewise. Lancelot and Meliot of Logres made clear the passage for them. The knights departed, for longer durst they not abide. The damsel of the castle held a squire by the hand, that was right passing comely. She knew Lancelot, and when she saw him she called him.

XX

'Lancelot, you slew this squire's brother, and, please God, either he or another shall take vengeance thereof.' Lancelot holdeth his peace when he heareth the dame speak, and departeth from the Waste Hold. Meliot of Logres knew Messire Gawain and Messire Gawain him again, and great joy made they the one of the other. 'Sir,' saith Meliot, 'I am come to lay plaint before you of Nabigant of the Rock that challengeth me of the land whereof I am your man, and saith that he will defend it against none but you only. Sir, the day is full nigh, and if you come not to the day, I shall have lost my quarrel, and you held me thereof in covenant what time I became your man.' 'Right fainly will I go,' saith Messire Gawain. He goeth his way thither accordingly by leave of the King and Lancelot, and saith that he will return to them the speediest he may.

XXI

King Arthur and Lancelot go their way as fast as they may toward the land that was King Fisherman's. Messire Gawain rideth until he cometh to the land of Nabigant of the Rock. Meliot doeth Nabigant to wit that Messire Gawain was come, and that he was ready to uphold his right by him that was his champion. Nabigant was whole of the wound he gat at the assembly, and held Messire Gawain of full small account for the cowardize that he saw him do, and bid his knights not meddle betwixt them two, for, and Messire Gawain had been four knights he thought to vanquish them all. He issueth forth of his castle all armed, and is come there where Messire Gawain awaited him. Messire Gawain seeth him coming, and so draweth on one side, and Nabigant, that was stark outrageous, setteth his spear in rest and cometh toward Messire Gawain without another word, and smiteth him on the shield so that he maketh his spear fly all in pieces. And Messire Gawain catcheth him right in the midst of his breast, and pierceth him with his spear through the thick of his heart, and he falleth to the ground dead; and the knights run upon Messire Gawain; but he lightly delivereth himself of them, and Meliot of Logres likewise. Messire Gawain entereth the castle by force, doing battle against all the knights, and holdeth

them in such a pass as that he maketh them do homage to
Meliot of Logres, and deliver up to him the keys of the castle.
He maketh them come to an assembly from the whole of the
land they had reft away from him, and thereafter departeth and
followeth after King Arthur. In the forest, he overtaketh a
damsel that was going on her way a great pace.

XXII

'Damsel,' saith Messire Gawain, 'Lord God guide you,
whither away so fast?' 'Sir,' saith she, 'I am going to
the greatest assembly of knights you saw ever.' 'What
assembly?' saith Messire Gawain. 'Sir,' saith she, 'At the
Palace Meadow, but the knight I am seeking is he that won
the Circlet of Gold at the Meadow of the Tent. Fair Sir, can
you give me any tidings of him?' saith she. 'Damsel,' saith
Messire Gawain, 'What would you do herein?' 'Certes, Sir,
I would right fain find him. My Lady, that kept the Circlet of
Gold for the son of the Widow Lady, that won it aforetime,
hath sent me to seek him.' 'For what intent, damsel?' saith
Messire Gawain. 'Sir, my Lady sendeth for him and beseecheth him by me, for the sake of the Saviour of the World,
that if he had ever pity of dame or damsel, he will take vengeance on Nabigant that hath slain her men and destroyed her
land, for she hath been told how he that won back the Golden
Circlet ought of right to take vengeance upon him.'

XXIII

'Damsel,' saith Messire Gawain, 'Be not any longer troubled
hereof, for I tell you that the knight that won the Golden
Circlet by prize of arms hath killed Nabigant already.' 'Sir,'
saith she, 'How know you this?' 'I know the knight well,'
saith he, 'And I saw him slay him, and behold, here is the
Circlet of Gold that I have as a token hereof, for that he
beareth it to him that hath won the Graal, to the intent that
your Lady may be quit of her charge.' Messire Gawain
showeth her the Golden Circlet in the casket of ivory, that he
kept very nigh himself. Right joyful was the damsel that
the matter had thus fallen out, and goeth her way back again to
tell her Lady of her joy. Messire Gawain goeth on his way
toward the assembly, for well knoweth he that, and King

Arthur and Lancelot have heard the tidings, there will they be. He goeth thitherward as fast as he may, and as straight, and scarce hath he ridden away or ever he met a squire that seemed right weary, and his hackney sore worn of the way.   Messire Gawain asked him whence he came, and the squire said to him, ' From the land of King Arthur, where is great war toward, for that none knoweth not what hath become of him.   Many folk go about saying that he is dead, for never sithence that he departed from Cardoil, and Messire Gawain and Lancelot with him, have no tidings been heard of him ; and he left the Queen at Cardoil to take his place, and also on account of her son's death, and the most part say that he is dead.   Briant of the Isles and my Lord Kay with him are burning his land, and carrying off plunder before all the castles.   Of all the Knights of the Table Round are there now no more than five and thirty, and of these are ten sore wounded, and they are in Cardoil, and there protect the land the best they may.'

XXIV

When Messire Gawain heareth these tidings, they touch his heart right sore, so that he goeth the straightest he may toward the assembly, and the squire with him that was sore fordone. Messire Gawain found King Arthur and Lancelot, and the knights were come from all the kingdom to the piece of ground. For a knight was come thither that had brought a white destrier and borne thither a right rich crown of gold, and it was known throughout all the lands that marched with this, that the knight that should do best at the assembly should have the destrier and the crown, for the Queen that ware it was dead, and it would behove him to guard and defend the land whereof she had been Lady.   On account of these tidings had come thither great plenty of folk and of folk.   King Arthur and Messire Gawain and Lancelot set them of one side.   The story saith that at this assembly King Arthur bare the red shield that the damsel gave him ; Messire Gawain had his own, such as he was wont to bear, and Lancelot a green shield that he bare for the love of the knight that was slain for helping him in the forest.   They struck into the assembly like lions unchained, and cast down three knights at their first onset.   They searched the fellowships on every side, smote down knights and overthrew horses.

XXV

King Arthur overtook no knight but he clave his shield to the boss: all swerved aside and avoided his buffets. And Messire Gawain and Lancelot are not idle on the other hand, but each held well his place. But the more part had wonderment looking at the King, for he holdeth him at bay like a lion when the staghounds would attack him. The assembly lasted throughout on such wise, and when it came to an end, the knights said and adjudged that the Knight of the Red Shield had surpassed all other in doing well. The knight that had brought the crown came to the King, but knew him not a whit: 'Sir,' saith he, 'You have by your good deeds of arms won this crown of gold and this destrier, whereof ought you to make great joy, so only you have so much valour in you as that you may defend the land of the best earthly Queen that is dead, and whether the King be alive or dead none knoweth, wherefore great worship will it be to yourself and you may have prowess to maintain the land, for right broad is it and right rich and of high sovranty.'

XXVI

Saith King Arthur, 'Whose was the land, and what was the name of the Queen whose crown I see?' 'Sir, the King's name was Arthur, and the best king in the world was he; but in his kingdom the more part say that he is dead. And this crown was the crown of Queen Guenievre that is dead and buried, whereof is sore sorrow. The knights that may not leave Cardoil lest Briant of the Isles should seize the city, they sent me to the kingdom of Logres and charged me with the crown and destrier for that I have knowledge of the isles and foreign lands; wherefore they prayed me I should go among the assemblies of knights, that so I might hear tidings of my Lord King Arthur and my Lord Gawain and Lancelot, and, so I might find them, that I should tell them how the land hath fallen into this grievous sorrow.' King Arthur heareth tidings whereof he is full sorrowful. He draweth on one side, and the knights make the most grievous dole in the world. Lancelot knoweth not what he may do, and saith between his teeth that now hath his joy come to an end and his knighthood is of no

avail, for that he hath lost the high Queen, the valiant, that
heart and comfort gave him and encouragement to do well.
The tears ran down from his comely eyes right amidst his face
and through the ventail, and, had he durst make other dole, yet
greater would it have been. Of the mourning the King made
is there nought to speak, for this sorrow resembleth none
other. He holdeth the crown of gold, and looketh full oft at
the destrier for love of her, for he had given it her; and
Messire Gawain may not stint of making dole.

XXVII

'Certes,' saith he, 'Now may I well say that the best Queen
in the world and of most understanding is dead, nor never
hereafter shall be none of equal worth.' 'Sir,' saith Lancelot
to the King, 'So it please you, and Messire Gawain be willing,
I will go back toward Cardoil, and help to defend your land to
the best I may, for sore is it discounselled, until such time as
you shall be come from the Graal.' 'Certes,' saith Messire
Gawain to the King, 'Lancelot hath spoken well, so you grant
him your consent.' 'That do I with right good will,' saith the
King, 'And I pray him right heartily that he go thither and be
guardian of my land and the governance thereof, until such
time as God shall have brought me back.' Lancelot taketh
leave of the King and goeth his way back, all sorrowing and
full of discontent.

BRANCH XXII

INCIPIT

OF Lancelot the story is here silent, and so beginneth another branch of the Graal in the name of the Father, and of the Son, and of the Holy Ghost.

TITLE I

You may well understand that King Arthur is no whit joyful. He maketh the white destrier go after him, and hath the crown of gold full near himself. They ride until they come to the castle that belonged to King Fisherman, and they found it as rich and fair as you have heard told many a time. Perceval, that was there within, made right great joy of their coming, as did all the priests and ancient knights. Perceval leadeth King Arthur, when he was disarmed, into the chapel where the Graal was, and Messire Gawain maketh present to Perceval of the Golden Circlet, and telleth him that the Queen sendeth it to him, and relateth also how Nabigant had seized it, and moreover, how Nabigant was dead. The King offereth the crown that had been Queen Guenievre's. When Perceval knew that she was dead, he was right sorrowful thereof in his heart, and wept and lamented her right sweetly. He showeth them the tomb of King Fisherman, and telleth them that none had set the tabernacle there above the coffin, but only the commandment of Our Lord, and he showeth them a rich pall that is upon the coffin, and telleth them that every day they see a new one there not less rich than is this one. King Arthur looketh at the sepulchre and saith that never tofore hath he seen none so costly. A smell issueth therefrom full delicate and sweet of savour. The King sojourneth in the castle and is highly

266

honoured, and beholdeth the richesse and the lordship and the great abundance that is everywhere in the castle, insomuch that therein is nought wanting that is needful for the bodies of noble folk.   Perceval had made set the bodies of the dead knights in a charnel beside an old chapel in the forest, and the body of his uncle that had slain himself so evilly.   Behind the castle was a river, as the history testifieth, whereby all good things came to the castle, and this river was right fair and plenteous.   Josephus witnesseth us that it came from the Earthly Paradise and compassed the castle around and ran on through the forest as far as the house of a worshipful hermit, and there lost the course and had peace in the earth.   All along the valley thereof was great plenty of everything continually, and nought was ever lacking in the rich castle that Perceval had won.   The castle, so saith the history, had three names.

II

One of the names was Eden, the second, Castle of Joy, and the third, Castle of Souls.   Now Josephus saith that none never passed away therein but his soul went to Paradise.   King Arthur was one day at the castle windows with Messire Gawain. The King seeth coming before him beyond the bridge a great procession of folk one before another; and he that came before was all clad in white, and bare a full great cross, and each of the others a little one, and the more part came singing with sweet voices and bear candles burning, and there was one behind that carried a bell with the clapper and all at his neck. 'Ha, God,' saith King Arthur, 'What folk be these?' 'Sir,' saith Perceval, 'I know them all save the last. They be hermits of this forest, that come to chant within yonder before the Holy Graal, three days in the week.'

III

When the hermits came nigh the castle, the King went to meet them, and the knights adore the crosses and bow their heads before the good men.   As soon as they were come into the holy chapel, they took the bell from the last and smote thereon at the altar, and then set it on the ground, and then began they the service, most holy and most glorious.   The history witnesseth us that in the land of King Arthur at this time was there not a single chalice. The Graal appeared at the sacring of the mass, in five several manners that none ought not to tell, for the secret things of the sacrament ought none to tell openly but he unto whom God hath given it. King Arthur beheld all the changes, the last whereof was the change into a chalice. And the hermit that chanted the mass found a brief under the corporal and declared the letters, to wit, that our Lord God would that in such vessel should His body be sacrificed, and that it should be set upon record. The history saith not that there were no chalices elsewhere, but that in all Great Britain and in the whole kingdom was none. King Arthur was right glad of this that he had seen, and had in remembrance the name and the fashion of the most holy chalice. Then he asked the hermit that bare the bell, whence this thing came? 'Sir,' saith he to Messire Gawain, 'I am the King for whom you slew the giant, whereby you had the sword wherewith St John was beheaded, that I see on this altar. I made baptize me before you and all those of my kingdom, and turn to the New Law, and thereafter I went to a hermitage by the sea, far from folk, where I have been of a long space. I rose one night at matins and looked under my hermitage and saw that a ship had taken haven there. I went thither when the sea was retreated, and found within the ship three priests and their clerks, that told me their names and how they were called in baptism. All three were named Gregory, and they came from the Land of Promise, and told me that Solomon had cast three bells, one for the Saviour of the World, and one for His sweet Mother, and one for the honour of His saints, wherefore they had brought this hither by His commandment into this kingdom for that we had none here. They told me that and I should bear it into this castle, they would take all my sins upon themselves, by Our Lord's pleasure, in such sort as that I should be quit thereof. And I in like manner have brought it hither by the commandment of God, who willeth that this should be the pattern of all those that shall be fashioned in the realm of this island where never aforetime have been none.' 'By my faith,' saith Messire Gawain to the hermit, 'I know you right well for a worshipful man, for you held your covenant truly with me.' King Arthur was right glad of this thing, as were all they that were within. It seemed him that the noise thereof was like the noise that he had heard sound ever since he had moved from Cardoil. The hermits went their way each to his hermitage when they had done the service.

IV

One day, as the King sate at meat in the hall with Perceval and Messire Gawain and the ancient knights, behold you therewithal one of the three Damsels of the Car that cometh, and she was smitten all through her right arm. 'Sir,' saith she to Perceval, 'Have mercy on your mother and your sister and on us. Aristot of Moraine, that is cousin to the Lord of the Moors that you slew, warreth upon your mother, and hath carried off your sister by force into the castle of a vavasour of his, and saith that he will take her to wife, and will have all her land that your mother ought to hold of right, maugre your head. But never had knight custom so cruel as he, for when he shall have espoused the damsel, whomsoever she may be, yet will he never love her so well but that he shall cut off her head with his own hand, and so thereafter go seek for another to slay in like manner. Natheless in one matter hath he good custom, that never will he do shame to none until such time as he hath espoused her. Sir, I was with my Lady your sister when he maimed me in this manner. Wherefore your mother sendeth you word and prayeth you that you succour her, for you held her in covenant that so you would do and she should have need thereof and you should know it; for and you consent to her injury and loss, the shame will be your own.' Perceval heard these tidings, and sore sorrowful was he thereof. 'By my head,' saith the King to Perceval, 'I and my nephew, so please you, will go to help you.' 'Sir,' saith he, 'Gramercy, but go and achieve your own affair also, for sore need have you thereof; wherefore I pray and beseech you that you be guardian of the castle of Camelot, if that my lady mother shall come thither, for thereof make I you lord and champion, and albeit the castle be far away from you, yet garnish it and guard it, for it is builded in a place right fair.'

V

Lords, think not that it is this Camelot whereof these tellers of tales do tell their tales, there, where King Arthur so often held his court. This Camelot that was the Widow Lady's stood upon the uttermost headland of the wildest isle of Wales by the sea to the West. Nought was there save the hold and the forest and the waters that were round about it. The other Camelot, of King Arthur's, was situate at the entrance of the kingdom of Logres, and was peopled of folk and was seated at the head of the King's land, for that he had in his governance all the lands that on that side marched with his own.

BRANCH XXIII

Title I

Of Perceval the story is here silent, and saith that King Arthur and Messire Gawain have taken leave of Perceval and all them of the castle. The King leaveth him the good destrier that he won, with the golden crown. They have ridden, he and Messire Gawain together, until they are come to a waste ancient castle that stood in a forest. The castle would have been right fair and rich had any folk wonned therein, but none there were save one old priest and his clerk that lived within by their own toil. The King and Messire Gawain lodged there the night, and on the morrow went into a right rich chapel that was therein to hear mass, and it was painted all around of right rich colours of gold and azure and other colours. The images were right fair that were there painted, and the figures of them for whom the images were made. The King and Messire Gawain looked at them gladly. When the mass was said, the priest cometh to them and saith: 'Lords,' saith he, 'These imagings are right fair, and he that had them made is full loyal, and dearly loved the lady and her son for whom he had them made. Sir,' saith the priest, 'It is a true history.' 'Of whom is the history, fair Sir?' saith King Arthur. 'Of a worshipful vavasour that owned this hold, and of Messire Gawain, King Arthur's nephew, and his mother. Sir,' saith the priest, 'Messire Gawain was born there within and held up and baptized, as you may see here imaged, and he was named Gawain for the sake of the lord of this castle that had that name. His mother, that had him by King Lot, would not that it should be known. She set him in a right fair coffer, and prayed the good man of this castle that he would carry him away and leave him where he might perish, but and if he would not do so, she would make another do it. This Gawain, that was loyal and would not that the child should be put to death, made seal letters at the pillow-bere of his cradle that he was of lineage royal on the one side and the

271

other, and set therein gold and silver so as that the child might
be nurtured in great plenty, and spread above the child a right
rich coverlid. He carried him away to a far distant country,
and so came one early morning to a little homestead where
dwelt a right worshipful man. He delivered the child to him
and his wife, and bade them they should keep him and nurture
him well, and told them that it might be much good should
come to them thereof. The vavasour turned him back, and
they took charge of the child and nurtured him until that he
were grown, and then took him to Rome to the Holy Father
and showed him the sealed letters. The Holy Father saw them
and understood that he was the son of a King. He had pity
upon him, and gave him to understand that he was of his
kindred. After that, he was elected to be Emperor of Rome.
But he would not be Emperor lest he should be reproached of
his birth that had before been concealed from him. He departed
thence, and lived afterwards within yonder. Now is it said
that he is one of the best knights in the world, insomuch that
none durst take possession of this castle for dread of him, nor
of this great forest that lieth round about it. For, when the
vavasour that dwelt here was dead, he left to Messire Gawain,
his foster-son, this castle, and made me guardian thereof until
such time as Messire Gawain should return.'

II

The King looketh at Messire Gawain, and seeth him stoop
his head toward the ground for shame. 'Fair nephew, be not
ashamed, for as well might you reproach me of the same. Of
your birth hath there been great joy, and dearly ought one to
love the place and honour it, where so good a knight as are
you was born.' When the priest understood that it was Messire
Gawain, he made great cheer to him, and was all ashamed of
that he had recorded as concerning his birth. But he saith to
him : 'Sir, small blame ought you to have herein, for you were
confirmed in the law that God hath established and in loyalty
of marriage of King Lot and your mother. This thing King
Arthur well knoweth, and our Lord God be praised for that
you have come hither !'

BRANCH XXIV

Title I

HERE the story is silent of the kingdom, and of King Arthur and Messire Gawain that remain in the castle to maintain and guard it until they shall have garnished it of folk. Here speaketh it word of the knight's son of the Waste Manor, there whither the brachet led Messire Gawain where he found the knight that Lancelot had slain. He had one son whose name was Meliant, and he had not forgotten his father's death; rather, thereof did wrath rankle in his heart. He heard tell that Briant of the Isles had great force and great puissance, and that he warred upon King Arthur's land, insomuch as that he had already slain many of his knights. Thitherward goeth he, and is come to where Briant was in a castle of his own. He telleth him how Lancelot had slain his father in such sort, and prayeth him right courteously that he would make him knight, for that right fain would he avenge his father, and therefore would he help him in the war the best he might. Briant made much joy thereof, and made him knight in right costly sort, and he was the comeliest knight and the most valiant of his age in Briant's court, and greatly did he desire to meet with Lancelot. They marvelled much in the land and kingdom what had become of him. The more part thought that he was dead, albeit dead he was not, but rather sound and hale and whole, had it not been for the death of Queen Guenievre, whereof the sorrow so lay at his heart that he might not forget it. He rode one day amidst a forest, and overtook a knight and a damsel that made great joy together, singing and making disport. 'By God,' saith the damsel, 'If this knight that cometh here will remain, he shall have right good lodging. It is already nigh eventide, and never will he find hostel so good

K

to-day.' 'Damsel,' saith Lancelot, 'Of good hostel have I sore need, for I am more than enough weary.' 'So be all they,' saith she, 'that come from the land of the rich King Fisherman, for none may suffer the pain and travail and he be not good knight.'

II

' Ah, damsel,' saith Lancelot, ' Which is the way to the castle whereof you speak?' 'Sir,' saith the knight, ' You will go by this cross that you see before you, and we will go by that other way, to a certain hold. Haply we shall find you at the castle or ever you depart thence.' Lancelot goeth his way and leaveth them. 'By my head,' saith the damsel to the knight, ' This that goeth there is Lancelot. He knoweth me not, albeit I know him well, and I hear that he is sore troubled of his sorrow and mis-ease. Natheless, please God, I will have vengeance of him or ever he departeth from the castle whither he goeth to harbour. He made marry perforce a knight that loved me better than aught beside, and to a damsel that he loved not a whit. And so much might he still better perceive when he saw that she ate not at his table, but was seated along with the squires, and that none did aught for her at the castle. But the knight will not abandon her for his own honour, and for that I should be blamed thereof.' The evening draweth on and Lancelot goeth toward the castle, that was right uneath to find and in an unfrequented part. He espieth it at the head of the forest, and seeth that it is large and strong, with strong barbicans embattelled, and at the entrance of the gateway were fifteen heads of knights hanging. He found without a knight that came from the forest, and asked him what castle it was, and he made answer that it was called the Castle of the Griffon. ' And why are these heads hanging at this door?' 'Sir,' saith he, ' The daughter of the lord of the castle is the fairest in the world and that is known in any kingdom, and needs must she be offered to wife to all knights that harbour within. He that can draw a sword that is fixed in a column in the midst of the hall, and fetch it forth, he shall have her of right without forfeit.

III

' All these have made assay whose heads you see hanging at the door, but never might none of them remove the sword, and

on this occasion were they beheaded. Now is it said that none
may draw it forth, unless he that draweth be better knight
than another, and needs must he be one of them that have been
at the Graal. But, and you be minded to believe me, fair Sir,'
saith the knight, 'You will go elsewhither, for ill lodging is it
in a place where one must needs set body and life in adventure
of death, and none ought to be blamed for escaping from his
own harm. Sir, the castle is right fell, for it hath underground, at the issue of a cavern that is there, a lion and a
griffon that have devoured more than half a hundred knights.'
'Sir,' saith Lancelot, 'It is evening, nor know I how I may go
farther this day, for I know not whither I go sith that I know
not the places nor the ways of the forest.' 'Sir,' saith the
knight, 'I speak only for your own good, and God grant you
depart hence, honour safe.' Lancelot findeth the door of the
castle all open, and entereth in, all armed, and alighteth before
the master-hall. The King was leaning at the windows, and
biddeth stall his horse.

IV

Lancelot is entered into the hall, and findeth knights and
damsels at the tables and playing at the chess, but none did he
find to salute him nor make him cheer of his coming save the
lord only, for such was the custom of the castle. The lord
bade him be disarmed. 'Sir,' saith he, 'Right well may you
allow me wear my arms, for they be the fairest garniture and
the richest I have.' 'Sir,' saith the lord of the castle, 'No
knight eateth armed within yonder, but he that cometh armed
in hither disarmeth himself by my leave. He may take his arms
again without gainsay, so neither I nor other desire to do him a
hurt.' With that two squires disarm him. The lord of the
castle maketh bring a right rich robe wherein to apparel him.
The tables were set and the meats served. The damsel issued
forth of her chamber and was accompanied of two knights as far
as the hall. She looketh at Lancelot, and seeth that he is a
right comely knight, and much liketh her of his bearing and
countenance, and she thinketh to herself that sore pity would it
be so comely knight should have his head smitten off.

V

Lancelot saluted the damsel and made great cheer, and when they had eaten in hall, forthwith behold you, the damsel where she cometh that Lancelot overtook in the forest with the knight. 'Sir,' saith she to the lord of the castle, 'You have harboured this night your deadly enemy that slew your brother at the Waste Manor.' 'By my faith,' saith the lord of the manor, 'I think not so, for him would I not have harboured, nor will I not believe it for true until such time as I have proved it. Sir,' saith he to Lancelot, 'Make the demand that the others make!' 'What is it?' saith Lancelot. 'See there my daughter! Ask her of me, and if you be such as you ought to be, I will give her to you.' 'Sir,' saith Lancelot, 'No knight is there in the world so good but ought to plume him upon having her to wife, so always she were willing, and, so I thought that you would be willing to give her to me, I would willingly ask you.' Lancelot spake otherwise than as he thought, for the departing of the Queen and the sorrow thereof lay so at his heart that never again might he lean upon any love in the world, neither of dame nor damsel. He asked his daughter of the knight of the castle, and came before him to save the custom so that he might not have blame thereof. And he showed him the sword that is in the column, all inlaid with gold. 'Go,' saith he, 'and fulfil the custom, as other knights have done.' 'What is it?' saith Lancelot. 'They might not draw forth the sword from this column, and so failed of my daughter and of their lives.' 'Lord God,' saith Lancelot, 'Defend me from this custom!' And he cometh toward the column as fast as he may, and seizeth the sword with both hands. So soon as he touched it, the sword draweth it forth with such a wrench that the column quaked thereof. The damsel was right joyful thereat, albeit she misdoubted the fellness and cruelty of her father, for never yet had she seen knight that pleased her so much to love as he. 'Sir,' saith the other damsel, 'I tell you plainly, this is Lancelot, the outrageous, that slew your brother. Natheless, is it no lie that he is one of the best knights of the world, albeit by the stoutness of his knighthood and his valour many an outrage hath he done, and more shall he yet do and he escape you, and, so you will believe me, you will never allow him to depart thus; sith that and you kill him or slay him you will save the life of many a knight.' The daughter of the lord of the castle is sore displeased of the damsel for this that she saith, and looketh at Lancelot from time to time and sigheth, but more durst she not do. Much marvelleth she, sith that Lancelot hath drawn the sword forth of the column, that he asketh her not of her father as his own liege woman, but he was thinking of another thing, and never was he so sorrowful of any lady as he was for the Queen. But whatsoever thought or desire he may have therein, he telleth the lord of the castle that he holdeth him to his covenant made at such time as the sword was still fixed in the column. 'I have a right not to hold thereto,' saith the lord of the castle, 'Nor shall I break not my vow and I fail you herein; for no man is bound to give his daughter to his mortal enemy. Sith that you have slain my brother, you are my mortal enemy, and were I to give her to you, she ought not to wish it, and were she to grant you her love she would be a fool and a madwoman.' Right sorrowful is the damsel of this that she heareth her father say. She would fain that Lancelot and she were in the forest, right in the depth thereof. But Lancelot had no mind to be as she was thinking. The lord of the castle made guard the gateway of the castle well, in such sort that Lancelot might issue therefrom on no side. Afterward he bade his knights privily that they take heed on their lives that they be all ready on the morrow and all garnished of their arms, for that it was his purpose to smite off Lancelot's head and hang it above all the others.

VI

The daughter of the lord knew these tidings and was right sorrowful thereof, for she thinketh never more to have joy at heart and he shall be slain in such manner. She sendeth him greeting by her own privy messenger, as she that loveth him better than aught else living in the world, and so biddeth and prayeth him be garnished of his arms, and ready to protect his life, for that her father is fain to smite off his head. 'Sir,' saith the messenger, 'Your force would avail you nought as against my lord, for to-morrow there will be a dozen knights all armed at the issue of the gate whereby you entered to-night, and he saith that he purposeth to cut off your head there where he cut the heads off the other knights. Without the gate there will likewise be another dozen knights all armed. No

knight is there in the world so good as that he might issue
forth of this castle through the midst of these four and twenty
knights, but my lady sendeth you word that there is a cavern
under this castle that goeth therefrom underground as far as
the forest, so that a knight may well pass thereby all armed,
but there is therein a lion, the fiercest and most horrible in the
world, and two serpents that are called griffons, that have the
face of a man and the beaks of birds and eyes of an owl and
teeth of a dog and ears of an ass and feet of a lion and tail of
a serpent, and they have couched them therewithin, but never
saw no man beasts so fell and felonous.   Wherefore the damsel
biddeth you go by that way, by everything that you have ever
loved, and that you fail her not, for she would fain speak with
you at the issue of the cavern in an orchard that is nigh a right
broad river not far from this castle, and will make your destrier
be brought after you underground.' 'By my head,' saith
Lancelot, ' And she had not conjured me in such sort, and were
it not for love of herself, I would have rather set myself in
hazard with the knights than with the wild beasts, for far
fainer would I have delivered myself from them, and so I might,
than go forth in such-wise.' 'She sendeth you word,' saith
the messenger, 'that so you do not thus, no further trouble
will she take concerning you.   She doth it of dread lest she
lose your love; and here behold a brachet that she sendeth
you by me that you will carry with you into the cavern.   So
soon as you shall see the serpent griffons that have couched
them therein, you shall show them this and cast her down before
them.   The griffons love her as much as one beast may love
another, and shall have such joy and such desire to play with
the brachet that they will leave you alone, and have such good
will toward you that they will not look at you after to do you
any hurt.   But no man is there in the world, no matter how
well soever he were armed, nor how puissant soever he were
in himself, might never pass them otherwise, but he should be
devoured of them.   But no safeguard may you have as against
the lion but of God only and your own hardiment.' 'Tell my
damsel,' saith Lancelot, ' that all her commandment will I do,
but this cowardize resembleth none other, that I shall go fight
with beasts and leave to do battle with knights.' This was
then repeated to the damsel, that marvelled her much thereat,
and said that he was the hardiest knight in the world.

VII

Lancelot armed him toward daybreak, and had his sword girt, his shield at his neck, and his spear in his hand. So he entered into the cavern, all shamefast, and the brachet followeth after, that he deigned not to carry, and so cometh he to the place where the griffons were. So soon as they heard him coming they dress them on their feet, and then writhe along as serpents, then cast forth such fire, and so bright a flame amidst the rock, as that all the cavern is lighted up thereof, and they see by the brightness of light of their jaws the brachet coming. So soon as they have espied her, they carry her in their claws and make her the greatest cheer in the world. Lancelot passeth beyond without gainsay, and espieth, toward the issue of the cavern, the lion that was come from the forest all famished. He cometh thither right hardily, sword drawn. The lion cometh toward him, jaws yawning, and claws bared, thinking to fix them in his habergeon, but Lancelot preventeth him and smiteth him so stoutly that he cutteth off thigh and leg together. When the lion feeleth himself thus maimed, he seizeth him by the teeth and the claws of his fore feet and rendeth away half the skirt of his habergeon. Thereupon Lancelot waxeth wroth. He casteth his shield to the ground and approacheth the lion closer. He seeth that he openeth his jaws wide to avenge himself, and thrusteth his sword the straightest he may into his gullet, and the lion giveth out a roar and falleth dead. The damsel, that had come into the cavern, heareth that the lion is dead.

VIII

Lancelot issued forth and so cometh into the orchard beside the forest, and wiped his sword on the freshness of the green grass. Thereupon behold you the damsel that cometh. 'Sir,' saith she to Lancelot, 'Are you wounded in any place?' 'Damsel, nowhere, thank God!' Another damsel leadeth a horse into the orchard. The damsel of the castle looketh at Lancelot. 'Sir,' saith the damsel, 'Meseemeth that you are not over joyous.' 'Damsel,' saith he, 'If I be not, I have good right, for I have lost the thing in the world that most I loved.' 'And you have won me,' saith she, 'so you remain not here,

that am the fairest damsel in this kingdom, and I have saved
you your life for this, that you grant me your love, for mine
own would I fain give unto you.' 'Gramercy, damsel,' saith
Lancelot, 'Your love and your good will fain would I have;
but neither you nor none other damsel ought not to have
affiance in me, and I might so soon set carelessly aside the
love to whom my heart owed its obedience, for the worthiness
and the courtesy that were lodged in her. Nor never hereafter, so long as I live, shall I love none other in like manner;
wherefore all others commend I to God, and to yourself, as for
leave-taking to one at whose service I fain would be; I say
that if you shall have need of me, and so I be in place and free,
I will do all I may to protect your honour.'

IX

'Ha, God!' saith the damsel, 'How am I betrayed, sith
that I am parted from the best knight in the world! Lancelot,
you have done that which never yet no knight might do! Now
am I grieved that you should escape on such wise, and that
your life hath been saved in this manner by me. Better should
I love you mine own dead, than another's living. Now would
I fain that you had had your head smitten off, and that it were
hanging with the others! So would I solace myself by behold-
ing it!' Lancelot took no account of that he heard, for the
grief that lay at his heart of the Queen. He mounteth on his
horse and issueth forth of the orchard by a postern gate, and
entereth into the forest, and commendeth him to God. The
lord of the Castle of the Griffons marvelleth much that Lancelot delayeth so long. He thinketh that he durst not come
down, and saith to his knights, 'Let us go up and cut off his
head, sith that he durst not come down.' He maketh search for
him all through the hall and the chambers, but findeth him not.
'He hath gone,' saith he, 'through the cavern, so have the
griffons devoured him.' So he sendeth the twain most hardy of
his knights to see. But the brachet had returned after the
damsel, whereof the griffons were wroth, and they forthwith
seized on the two knights that entered into their cavern and
slew them and devoured.

X

When the lord of the castle knew it, he went into the chamber where his daughter was, and found her weeping, and thinketh that it is for the two knights that are dead. News is brought him that the lion is dead at the issue of the cavern, and thereby well knoweth he that Lancelot is gone. He biddeth his knights follow after him, but none was there so hardy as that he durst follow. The damsel was right fain they should go after him, if only they might bring him back to the castle, for so mortally was she taken of his love that she thought of none other thing. But Lancelot had her not in remembrance, but only another, and rode on sadly right amidst the forest, and looked from time to time at the rent the lion had made in his habergeon. He rideth until he is come toward evening to a great valley where was forest on the one side and the other, and the valley stretched onward half a score great leagues Welsh. He looketh to the right, and on the top of the mountain beside the valley he seeth a chapel newly builded that was right fair and rich, and it was covered of lead, and had at the back two quoins that seemed to be of gold. By the side of this chapel were three houses dight right richly, each standing by itself facing the chapel. There was a right fair grave-yard round about the chapel, that was enclosed at the compass of the forest, and a spring came down, full clear, from the heights of the forest before the chapel and ran into the valley with a great rushing ; and each of the houses had its own orchard, and the orchard an enclosure. Lancelot heareth vespers being chanted in the chapel, and seeth the path that turned thitherward, but the mountain is so rugged that he could not go along it on horseback. So he alighteth, and leadeth his horse after him by the reins until he cometh nigh the chapel.

XI

There were three hermits therewithin that had sung their vespers, and came over against Lancelot. They bowed their heads to him and he saluted them, and then asked of them what place was this? And they told him that the place there was Avalon. They make stable his horse. He left his arms without the chapel and entereth therein, and saith that never hath he seen none so fair nor so rich. There were within three other places, right fair and seemly dight of rich cloths of silk and rich corners and fringes of gold. He seeth the images and the crucifixes all newly fashioned, and the chapel illumined of rich colours; and moreover in the midst thereof were two coffins, one against the other, and at the four corners four tall wax tapers burning, that were right rich, in four right rich candle-sticks. The coffins were covered with two palls, and there were clerks that chanted psalms in turn on the one side and the other. 'Sir,' saith Lancelot to one of the hermits, 'For whom were these coffins made?' 'For King Arthur and Queen Guenievre.' 'King Arthur is not yet dead,' saith Lancelot. 'No, in truth, please God! but the body of the Queen lieth in the coffin before us, and in the other is the head of her son, until such time as the King shall be ended, unto whom God grant long life! But the Queen bade at her death that his body should be set beside her own when he shall end. Hereof have we the letters and her seal in this chapel, and this place made she be builded new on this wise or ever she died.'

XII

When Lancelot heareth that it is the Queen that lieth in the coffin, he is so straitened in his heart and in his speech that never a word may he say. But no semblant of grief durst he make other than such as might not be perceived, and right great comfort to him was it that there was an image of Our Lady at the head of the coffin. He knelt down the nighest he might to the coffin, as it had been to worship the image, and set his face and his mouth to the stone of the coffin, and sorroweth for her right sweetly. 'Ha, Lady,' saith he, 'But that I dread the blame of the people, never again would I seek to depart from this place, but here would I save my soul and pray for yours; so would it be much recomforting to me that I should be so nigh, and should see the sepulchre wherein your body lieth that had so great sweetness and bounty. God grant me of your pleasure, that at my death I may still be a-nigh, and that I may die in such manner and in such place as that I may be shrouded and buried in this holy chapel where this body lieth.' The night cometh on. A clerk cometh to the hermits and saith, 'Never yet did no knight cry mercy of God so sweetly, nor of

His sweet Mother, as did this knight that is in the chapel.'
And the hermits make answer that knights for the most part do
well believe in God. They come to the chapel for him and bid
him come thence, for that meat is ready and he should come to
eat, and after that go to sleep and rest, for it is full time so to
do. He telleth them that as for his eating this day it is stark
nought, for a desire and a will hath taken him to keep vigil in
the chapel before one of the images of Our Lady. No wish had
he once to depart thence before the day, and he would fain that
the night should last far longer than it did. The good men
durst not force him against his will; they say, rather, that the
worshipful man is of good life who will keep watch in such
manner throughout the night without drink or meat, for all that
he seemeth to be right weary.

XIII

Lancelot was in the chapel until the morrow before the
tomb. The hermits apparelled them to do the service that they
chanted each day, mass for the soul of the Queen and her son.
Lancelot heareth them with right good will. When the masses
were sung, he taketh leave of the hermits and looketh at the
coffin right tenderly. He commendeth the body that lieth
therein to God and His sweet Mother; then findeth he without
the chapel his horse accoutred ready, and mounteth forthwith,
and departeth, and looketh at the place and the chapel so long
as he may see them. He hath ridden so far that he is come nigh
Cardoil, and findeth the land wasted and desolate, and the towns
burnt, whereof is he sore grieved. He meeteth a knight that
came from that part, and he was wounded full sore. Lancelot
asketh him whence he cometh, and he saith, ' Sir, from towards
Cardoil. Kay the Seneschal, with two other knights, is leading
away Messire Ywain li Aoutres toward the castle of the Hard
Rock. I thought to help to rescue him, but they have wounded
me in such sort as you see.' ' Are they ever so far away?'
saith Lancelot. ' Sir, they will pass just now at the head of
this forest; and so you are fain to go thither, I will return with
you right willingly and help you to the best I may.' Lancelot
smiteth his horse with the spurs forthwith, and the knight after
him, and espieth Kay the Seneschal, that was bringing Messire
Ywain along at a great pace, and had set him upon a trotting

hackney, for so he thought that none would know him.   Lancelot overtaketh him and crieth, ' By my head, Kay the Seneschal,
shame had you enough of that you did to King Arthur when
you slew his son, and as much more ought you now to have of
thus warring upon him again ! '   He smiteth his horse of his
spurs, lance in rest, and Kay the Seneschal turneth toward
him, and they mell together with their spears on their shields,
and pierce them in such sort that an ells-length of each shaft
passeth through beyond.

XIV

The lances were strong so as that they brast not.   They
draw them back to themselves so stoutly and come together so
fiercely that their horses stagger and they lose the stirrups
Lancelot catcheth Kay the Seneschal at the passing beyond, in
the midst of the breast, and thrusteth his spear into him so far
that the point remained in the flesh, and Kay to-brast his own ;
and sore grieved was he when he felt himself wounded.   The
knight that was wounded overthrew one of the two knights.
Kay is on the ground, and Lancelot taketh his horse and setteth
Messire Ywain li Aoutres thereupon, that was right sore
wounded so as that he scarce might bear it.   Kay the Seneschal
maketh his knight remount, and holdeth his sword grasped in
his fist as though he had been stark wood.   Lancelot seeth
the two knights sore badly wounded, and thinketh that and he
stay longer they may remain on the field.   He maketh them go
before him, and Kay the Seneschal followeth them behind, himself the third knight, that is right wroth of the wound he
feeleth and the blood that he seeth.   Lancelot bringeth off his
knights like as the wild-boar goeth among the dogs, and Kay
dealeth him great buffets of his sword when he may catch him,
and Lancelot him again, and so they depart, fencing in such
sort.

XV

When Kay the Seneschal seeth that he may not harm him,
he turneth him back, full of great wrath, and his heart pricketh
to avenge him thereof and he may get at him, for he is the
knight of the court that most he hateth.   He is come back to
the Castle of the Hard Rock.   Briant of the Isles asketh him

who hath wounded him in such sort, and he telleth him that he was bringing thither Ywain li Aoutres when Lancelot rescued him. 'And the King,' saith Briant, 'Is he repaired thither?' 'I have heard no tidings of him at all,' saith Kay, 'For no leisure had I to ask of any.' Briant and his knights take much thought as concerning Lancelot's coming, for they are well persuaded that Lancelot hath come for that the King is dead and Messire Gawain, whereof they make right great joy. Kay the Seneschal maketh him be disarmed and his wound searched. They tell him he need not fear it shall be his death, but that he is right sore wounded.

XVI

Lancelot is entered into the castle of Cardoil, and his wounded knights withal, and findeth the folk in sore dismay. Great dole make they in many places and much lamentation for King Arthur, and say that now nevermore may they look for succour to none, and he be dead and Messire Gawain. But they give Lancelot joy of that he hath rescued Messire Ywain li Aoutres, and were so somewhat comforted and made great cheer. The tidings thereof came to the knights that were in the castle, and they all come forward to meet him save they that were wounded, and so led him up to the castle, and Messire Ywain with him and the other knight that was wounded. All the knights of the castle were right glad, and ask him tidings of King Arthur, and whether he were dead or no. And Lancelot telleth them that he was departed from him at the Palace Meadow, where he won the white destrier and the crown of gold there where the tidings were brought to him that Queen Guinievre was dead.

XVII

'Then you tell us of a truth that the King is on live, and Messire Gawain?' 'Both, you may be certain!' saith Lancelot. Thereupon were they gladder than before. They told him of their own mischance, how Briant of the Isles had put them to the worse, and how Kay the Seneschal was with him to do them hurt. For he it is that taketh most pains to do them evil. 'By my head,' saith Lancelot, 'Kay the Seneschal

ought of right to take heed and with-hold him from doing you
ill, but he departed from the field with the point of my spear
in him when I rescued Messire Ywain.'

XVIII

The knights are much comforted of the coming of Lancelot,
but he is much grieved that he findeth so many of them
wounded. Meliant of the Waste Manor is at the castle of the
Hard Rock, and good fellow is it betwixt him and Kay the
Seneschal. He is right glad of the tidings he hath heard, that
Lancelot is come, and saith that he is the knight of the world
that most he hateth, and that he will avenge him of his father
and he may meet him. There come before the castle of Cardoil
one day threescore knights armed, and they seize upon their
booty betwixt the castle and the forest. Lancelot issueth forth,
all armed, and seven of the best of the castle with him. He
cometh upon them after that they have led away their plunder.
He overtaketh one knight and smiteth him with his spear right
through the body, and the other knights make an onset upon
the others and many to-brake their spears, and much clashing
was there of steel on armour; and there fell at the assembly on
one side and the other full a score knights, whereof some were
wounded right sore. Meliant of the Waste Manor espied
Lancelot, and right great joy made he of seeing him, and
smiteth him so stout a buffet on the shield that he to-breaketh
his spear.

XIX

Lancelot smiteth him amidst the breast so grimly that he
maketh him bend backwards over the saddle behind, and so
beareth him to the ground, legs uppermost, over his horse's
croup, and trampleth him under his horse's feet. Lancelot was
minded to alight to the ground to take him, but Briant of the
Isles cometh and maketh him mount again perforce. The
numbers grew on the one side and the other of knights that
came from Cardoil and from the Hard Rock. Right great was
the frushing of lances and the clashing of swords and the
overthrow of horses and knights. Briant of the Isles and
Lancelot come against each other so stoutly that they pierce
their shields and cleave their habergeons, and they thrust with

their spears so that the flesh is broken under the ribs and the shafts are all-to-splintered. They hurtle against each other so grimly at the by-passing that their eyes sparkle as it were of stars in their heads, and the horses stagger under them. They hold their swords drawn, and so return the one toward the other like lions. Such buffets deal they upon their helms that they beat them in and make the fire leap out by the force of the smiting of iron by steel. And Meliant cometh all armed toward Lancelot to aid Briant of the Isles, but Lucan the Butler cometh to meet him, and smiteth him with his spear so stoutly that he thrusteth it right through his shield and twisteth his arm against his side. He breaketh his spear at the by-passing, and Meliant also breaketh his, but he was wounded passing sore.

XX

Thereupon he seizeth him by the bridle and thinketh to lead him away, but the knights and the force of Briant rescue him. The clashing of arms lasted great space betwixt Briant of the Isles and Lancelot, and each was mightily wrath for that each was wounded. Either seized other many times by the bridle, and each was right fain to lead the other to his own hold, but the force of knights on the one side and the other disparted them asunder. Thus the stour lasted until evening, until that the night sundered them. But Briant had nought to boast of at departing, for Lancelot and his men carried off four of his by force right sore wounded, besides them that remained dead on the field. Briant of the Isles and Meliant betook them back all sorrowful for their knights that are taken and dead. Lancelot cometh back to Cardoil, and they of the castle make him right great joy of the knights that they bring taken, and say that the coming of the good knight Lancelot should be great comfort to them until such time as King Arthur should repair back and Messire Gawain. The wounded knights that were in the castle turned to healing of their wounds, whereof was Lancelot right glad. They were as many as five and thirty within the castle. Of all the King's knights were there no more save Lancelot and the wounded knight that he brought along with him.

BRANCH XXV

TITLE I

HERE the story is silent of Lancelot and the knights that are at Cardoil, and saith that King Arthur and Messire Gawain are in the castle where the priest told Messire Gawain how he was born. But they cannot depart thence at their will, for Ahuret the Bastard that was brother of Nabigant of the Rock, that Messire Gawain slew on account of Meliot of Logres, knoweth well that they are therewithin, and hath assembled his knights and holdeth them within so strait that they may not depart without sore damage. For he hath on the outer side a full great plenty of knights, and the King and Messire Gawain have with them but only five of the forest and the country that are upon their side, and they hold them so strait within that they may not issue out from thence; yea, the brother of Nabigant sweareth that they shall not depart thence until such time as he shall have taken Messire Gawain, and taken vengeance on his fellow of his brother whom he slew. The King saith to Messire Gawain that he hath much shame of this that they are so long shut up therewithin, and that he better loveth to die with honour than to live with shame within the castle. So they issued forth, spears in rest, and Ahuret and his knights, whereof was there great plenty, made much joy thereat.

II

The King and Messire Gawain strike among them, and each overthroweth his man; but Ahuret hath great shame of this that he seeth his knights put to the worse by so few folk. He setteth his spear in rest and smiteth one of King Arthur's knights through the body and beareth him down dead. Then returneth he to Messire Gawain, and buffeteth him so strongly that he pierceth his shield, but he maketh drop his own spear and loseth his stirrups, and Messire Gawain waxeth wroth and smiteth him so grimly and with such force that he maketh him bend back over the hinder bow of his saddle. But Ahuret was strong and of great might, and leapeth back between the bows and cometh toward King Arthur that he saw before him, but he knew him not. He left Messire Gawain, and the King smiteth him with such a sweep that he cutteth off his arm, spear and all. There was great force of knights, so that they ran upon them on all sides; and never would they have departed thence sound and whole, but that thereupon Meliot of Logres cometh thither with fifteen knights, for that he had heard tidings of Messire Gawain, how he was besieged in a castle there, where he and King Arthur between them were in such plight that they had lost their five knights, so that they were not but only two that defended themselves as best they might, as they that had no thought but to remain there, for the odds of two knights against thirty was too great.

III

Thereupon, behold you, Meliot of Logres with fifteen knights, and they come thither where the King and Messire Gawain are in such jeopardy, and they strike so stoutly among them that they rescue King Arthur and Messire Gawain from them that had taken them by the bridle, and so slay full as many as ten of them, and put the others to flight, and lead away their lord sore maimed. And Messire Gawain giveth Meliot much thanks of the bounty he hath done, whereby he hath saved them their lives; and he giveth him the castle, and is fain that he hold it of him, for in no place might he have better employment, and that well hath he deserved it of his service in such need. Meliot thanketh him much, and prayeth Messire Gawain instantly that and he shall have need of succour he will come to aid him, in like manner as he would do by him everywhere. And Messire Gawain telleth him that as of this needeth him not to make prayer, for that he is one of the knights of the world that most he ought of right to love. The King and Messire Gawain take leave of Meliot, and so depart, and Meliot garnisheth the castle that was right fair and rich and well-seated.

BRANCH XXVI

Title I

OF Meliot the story is here silent, and saith that King Arthur and Messire Gawain have ridden so far that they are come into the Isle of Avalon, there where the Queen lieth. They lodge the night with the hermits, that made them right great cheer. But you may well say that the King is no whit joyful when he seeth the coffin where the Queen lieth and that wherein the head of his son lieth. Thereof is his dole renewed, and he saith that this holy place of this holy chapel ought he of right to love better than all other places on earth. They depart on the morrow when they have heard mass. The King goeth the quickest he may toward Cardoil, and findeth the land wasted and desolate in many places, whereof is he right sorrowful, and understandeth that Kay the Seneschal warreth upon him with the others. He marvelleth much how he durst do it He is come to Cardoil. When they of the castle know it they come to meet him with right great cheer. The tidings went throughout all the land, and they of the country were right joyous thereof, for the more part believed that he was dead. They of the castle of the Hard Rock knew it, but little rejoiced they thereat. But Kay the Seneschal was whole of his wound and bethought him that great folly would he do to remain longer there to war upon the King, for well knew he that and the King held him and did that which he had proclaimed, his end were come. He departeth from the castle, where he had sojourned of a long while, and crossed again stealthily over-sea, and came into Little Britain, and made fast a castle for fear of the King, that is called Chinon, and was there long time, without the King warring upon him, for enough adventures had he in other parts.

II

To Cardoil was the King repaired and Messire Gawain.

You may well understand that the land was much rejoiced thereof, and that all the knights were greatly comforted, and knights came back to the court from all parts. They that had been wounded were whole again. Briant of the Isles stinted not of his pride nor of his outrage, but rather stirred up the war the most he might, he and Meliant still more, and said that never would he cease therefrom until death, nor never would he have rest until such time as he should have vengeance of Lancelot. The King was one day at Cardoil at meat, and there was in the hall great throng of knights, and Messire Gawain sate beside the King. Lancelot sate at the table, and Messire Ywain the son of King Urien, and Sagramors li Desirous, and Ywain li Aoutres, and many more other knights round about the table, but there were not so many as there wont to be. Messire Lucan the Butler served before the King of the golden cup. The King looked round about the table and remembered him of the Queen. He was bent upon thinking rather than on eating, and saw that his court was much wasted and worsened of her death. And what time the King was musing in such sort, behold you a knight come into the hall all armed before the King; and he leaneth on the staff of his spear. 'Sir,' saith the knight, 'Listen, so please you, to me, and all these others, listen! Madeglant of Oriande sendeth me here to you, and commandeth that you yield up the Table Round to him, for sith that the Queen is dead, you have no right thereof, for he is her next of kin and he that hath the best right to have and to hold it; and, so you do not this, you he defieth as the man that disinheriteth him, for he is your enemy in two manner of ways, for the Table Round that you hold by wrong, and for the New Law that you hold. But he sendeth you word by me, that so you will renounce your belief and take Queen Jandree his sister, that he will cry you quit as of the Table Round and will be of your aid everywhere. But and if you do not this, have never affiance in him. And so sendeth he word to you by me!'

III

Therewith the knight departeth, and the King remaineth all heavy in thought, and when they had eaten, he rose from the tables and all the knights. He speaketh to Messire Gawain and Lancelot, and taketh counsel with all the others. 'Sir,' saith Messire Gawain, ' You will defend yourself the best you may, and we will help you to smite your enemies. Great Britain is all at your will. You have not as yet lost any castle. Nought hath been broken down nor burnt but open ground and cottages and houses, whereof is no great harm done to yourself, and the shame thereof may lightly be amended. King Madeglant is of great hardiment as of words, but in arms will he not vanquish you so soon. If that he warreth upon you toward the West, send thither one of the best knights of your court that may maintain the war and defend the land against him.'

IV

The King sojourned at Cardoil of a long space. He believed in God and His sweet Mother right well. He brought thither from the castle where the Graal was the pattern whereby chalices should be made, and commanded make them throughout all the land so as that the Saviour of the world should be served more worshipfully. He commanded also that bells be cast throughout his land after the fashion of the one he had brought, and that each church should have one according to the means thereof. This much pleased the people of his kingdom, for thereby was the land somewhat amended. The tidings came to him one day that Briant and Meliant were riding through his land with great routs of folk, and were minded to assiege Pannenoisance ; and the King issued forth of Cardoil with great throng of knights all armed, and rode until he espied Briant and his people, and Briant him again. They ranged their battles on both sides, and came together with such might and so great a shock as that it seemed the earth shook ; and they melled together at the assembly with their spears so passing grimly as that the frushing thereof might be heard right far away. Some fourteen fell in the assembly that rose up again never more. Meliant of the Waste Manor searcheth for Lancelot in the midst of the stour until he findeth him, and runneth upon him right sturdily and pierceth his shield with his spear. Lancelot smiteth him such a sweep amidst the breast, that he thrusteth his spear right through his shoulder, and pinneth him so strongly that the shaft is all to-brast, and the end thereof remaineth in his body. And Meliant, all stricken through as he is, runneth upon him and passeth his spear right through the shield and through the arm, in such sort that he pinneth it to his side. He passeth beyond and breaketh his spear, and afterward returneth to Lancelot, sword in fist, and dealeth him a buffet on the helm so grimly that he all to-battered it in. Lancelot waxeth right wroth thereof, and he grieveth the more for that he feeleth him wounded. He cometh toward Meliant, sword drawn, and holding him well under cover of his shield and cover of his helm, and smiteth Meliant so fiercely that he cleaveth his shoulder down to the rib in such sort that the end of the spear wherewith he had pierced him fell out therefrom. Meliant felt himself wounded to the death, and draweth him back all sorrowful, and other knights run upon Lancelot and deliver assault. Messire Ywain and Sagramors li Desirous and Messire Gawain were on the other side in great jeopardy, for the people of Briant of the Isles came from all parts, and waxed more and more, and on all sides the greater number of knights had the upper hand therein. King Arthur and Briant of the Isles were in the midst of the battle, and dealt each other right great buffets. Briant's people come thither and take King Arthur by the bridle, and the King defendeth himself as a good knight, and maketh a ring about him amongst them that attack him, the same as doth a wild boar amongst the dogs. Messire Ywain is come thither and Lucan the Butler, and break through the press by force. Thereupon, behold you Sagramors li Desirous, that cometh as fast as his horse may gallop under him, and smiteth Briant of the Isles right before his people with such a rush that he beareth him to the ground in a heap, both him and his horse. Briant to-brast his thigh bone in the fall that he made. Sagramors holdeth sword drawn and would fain have thrust it into his body, when the King crieth to him that he slay him not.

V

Briant's people were not able to succour their lord. Nay, rather, they drew back on all sides, for the stour had lasted of a long space. So they tended the dead and the wounded, of whom were enough on one side and the other. King Arthur made carry Briant of the Isles to Cardoil, and bring along the other knights that his own knights had taken. Right joyous were the folks at Cardoil when the King came back. They bore Méliant of the Waste Manor on his shield to the Hard Rock, but he scarce lived after. The King made Briant of the Isles be healed, and held him in prison of a long while, until Briant gave him surety of all his lands and became his man. The King made him Seneschal of all his lands, and Briant served him right well.

VI

Lancelot was whole of his wound, and all the knights of theirs. King Arthur was safely stablished, and redoubted and dreaded of all lands and of his own land like as he wont to be. Briant hath forgotten all that is past, and is obedient to the King's commands, and more privy is he of his counsel than ever another of the knights, insomuch that he put the others somewhat back, whereof had they much misliking. The felony of Kay the Seneschal lay very nigh the King's heart, and he said that and any would take vengeance upon him for the same, greatly would he love him thereof, for so disloyally hath he wrought against him that he durst not let the matter be slurred over; and a sore misfortune is it for the world when a man of so poor estate hath slain so high a man as his son for no misdeed, and that strangers ought by as good right as they that knew him or himself take vengeance upon him thereof, so that others might be adread of doing such disloyalty.

VII

Briant was feared and redoubted throughout all Great Britain. King Arthur had told them that they were all to be at his commandment. And one day while the King was at Cardoil, behold you! a damsel that cometh into the hall and saith unto him: 'Sir, Queen Jandree hath sent me over to you, and biddeth you do that whereof her brother sent you word by his knight. She is minded to be Lady and Queen of your land, and that you take her to wife, for of high lineage is she and of great power, wherefore she biddeth you by me that you renounce the New Law and that you believe in the God in whom she believeth, and, so you do not this, you may not have affiance in your land, for King Madeglant hath as now made ready his host to enter into the chief of your land, and hath sworn his oath that he will not end until he shall have passed all the borders of the isles that march upon your land, and shall come upon Great Britain with all his strength, and so seize the Table Round that ought to be his own of right. And my Lady herself would come hither but for one thing, to wit, that she hath in her such disdain of them that believe in the New Law, that she deigneth not behold none of them, for, so soon as she was stablished Queen, made she her eyes be covered for that she would not look upon none that were of that believe. But the Gods wherein she believeth did so much for her, for that she loveth and worshippeth them, that she may discover her eyes and her face, and yet see not at all, whereof is she right glad, for that the eyes in her head are beautiful and gentle. But great affiance hath she in her brother, that is mighty and puissant, for he hath her in covenant that he will destroy all them that believe in the New Law, in all places where he may get at them, and, when he shall have destroyed them in Great Britain and the other islands, so that my Lady might not see none therein, so well is she with the Gods wherein she believeth. that she will have her sight again all whole, nor until that hour is she fain to see nought.'

VIII

'Damsel,' saith the King, 'I have heard well that which you tell me of this that you have in charge to say; but tell your Lady on my behalf, that the Law which the Saviour of the world hath established by His death and by His crucifixion never will I renounce, for the love that I have in Him. But tell her that she believe in God and in His sweet Mother, and that she believe in the New Law, for by the false believe wherein she abideth is she blinded in such sort, nor never will she see clear until she believe in God. Tell her moreover, I send her word that never more shall there be Queen in my land save she be of like worth as was Queen Guenievre.' 'Then I tell you plainly,' saith she, 'that you will have betimes such tidings as that good for you they will not be.' The damsel departeth from Cardoil, and cometh back to where the Queen was, and telleth her the message King Arthur sendeth her. 'True,' saith she, 'I love him better than all in the world, and yet refuseth he my will and my commandment. Now may he no longer endure!' She sendeth to her brother King Madeglant, and telleth him that she herself doth defy him and he take not vengeance on King Arthur and bring him not into prison.

BRANCH XXVII

TITLE I

THIS history saith that the land of this King was full far away from the land of King Arthur, and that needs must he pass two seas or ever he should approach the first head of King Arthur's land. He arrived in Albanie with great force of men with a great navy. When they of the land knew it, they garnished them against him and defended their lands the best they might; then they sent word to King Arthur that King Madeglant was come in such manner into the land, with great plenty of folk, and that he should come presently to succour them or send them a knight so good as that he might protect them, and that in case he doth not so, the land will be lost. When King Arthur understood these tidings, it was not well with him. He asked his knights whom he might send thither. And they say, let him send Lancelot thither, for that he is a worthy knight and a kingly, and much understandeth of war, and hath in him as much loyalty as hath ever another that they know. The King maketh him come before him.

II

'Lancelot,' saith the King, 'Such affiance have I in you and in your knighthood, that it is my will to send you to the furthest corner of my land, to protect it, with the approval of my knights, wherefore I pray and require you that you do your power herein as many a time have you done already in my service. And I will give you in command forty knights.' 'Sir,' saith Lancelot, 'Against your will am I not minded to be, but in your court are there other knights full as good, or better than I, whom you might well send thither. But I would not that you should hold this of cowardize in me, and right willingly will I do your pleasure, for none ought I to serve more willingly than you.' The King giveth him much thanks of this that he saith. Lancelot departeth from the court, and taketh forty knights with him, and so cometh into the land of Albanie where King Madeglant hath arrived. When they of the land knew that Lancelot was come, great joy had they thereof in their hearts, for ofttimes had they heard tell of him and of his good knighthood. They were all at his commandment, and received him as their champion and protector.

III

King Madeglant one day issued forth of his ships to do battle against Lancelot and them of the land. Lancelot received him right stoutly, and slew many of his folk, and the more part fled and would fain have drawn them to their ships, but Lancelot and his people went after and cut a part of them to pieces. King Madeglant, with as many of his men as he might, betaketh himself to his own ship privily, and maketh put to sea the soonest he may. They that might not come to the ships remained on dry land, and were so cut up and slain. Madeglant went his way discomfited. Of ten ships full of men that he had brought he took back with him but two. The land was in peace and assured in safety. Lancelot remained there of a long space. They of the country loved him much and gave themselves great joy of his valour and his great bounty, insomuch that most of them say ofttimes that they would fain have such a knight as was he for king, by the goodwill of King Arthur, for that the land is too far away; but and if he would set there a knight or other man that might protect the land, they would take it in right good part, and he should hold the land of him, for they might not safeguard it at their will without a champion, for that land without a lord may but little avail. They of the land loved Lancelot well, as I tell you. King Arthur was at Cardoil, and so were his knights together with him. He thought to be assured in his kingdom and to live peaceably; but what time he sate at meat one day in Cardoil, behold you thereupon a knight that cometh before the Table Round without saluting him. 'Sir,' saith he, 'Where is Lancelot?' 'Sir,' saith the King to the knight, 'He is not in this country.' 'By

my head,' saith the knight, 'that misliketh me. Wheresoever
he be, he is your knight and of your household; wherefore
King Claudas sendeth you word that he is his mortal enemy,
and you also, if so be that for love of him you receive him from
this day forward, for he hath slain his sister's son, Meliant of
the Waste Manor, and he slew the father of Meliant likewise,
but the father belongeth not to King Claudas.

IV

'Meliant was the son of his sister-german, wherefore much
grieveth he of his death.' 'Sir knight,' saith the King, 'I
know not how the covenant may be between them as of this
that you tell me, but well know I that King Claudas holdeth
many a castle that King Claudas ought not of right to have,
whereof he disherited his father, but meet is it that each should
conquer his own right. But so much I tell you plainly, that
never will I fail mine own knight and he be such as durst defend
himself of murder, but and if he hath no will to do this, then
well may I allow that right be done upon him. But, sith that
he will not love his own death, neither I nor other ought greatly
to love him and he refuse to redress his wrong. When Lancelot shall know these tidings, I know well that such is his valour
and his loyalty that he will readily answer in reason, and will do
all that he ought to do to clear himself of such a charge.' 'Sir,'
saith the knight, 'You have heard well that I have told you.
Once more, I tell you plainly, King Claudas sendeth you word
that so you harbour his enemy henceforward and in such
manner as you have done heretofore, he will be less than pleased
with you.'

V

With that the knight departeth, and the King remaineth at
Cardoil. He sendeth for Briant of the Isles, his seneschal, and
a great part of his knights, and demandeth counsel of them
what he may do. Messire Ywain saith that he killed Meliant
in the King's service, as one that warred upon his land, albeit
the King had done him no wrong, and had so made common
cause with the King's enemies without demanding right in his
court. Nor never had Meliant appealed Lancelot of murder nor
of treason, nor required him of the death of his father. Rather,

Lancelot slew him in open war, as one that warred upon his lord
by wrong.   Sir,' saith Messire Ywain to the King, ' Howsoever
Lancelot might have wrought in respect of Meliant, your land
ought not to be called to account, for you were not in the kingdom, nor knew not that either had done other any wrong, and
therefore say I that King Claudas will do great wrong and he
bring plaint or levy war against you on this account.'   ' Messire
Ywain,' saith Briant of the Isles, ' matter of common knowledge
is it that Lancelot slew the lord of the Waste Manor and
Meliant his son after the contention that was betwixt King
Arthur and me.   But, after that he had slain the father, he
ought of right to have taken good heed that he did no wrong to
the son, but rather ought he to have sought peace and accord.'

VI

' Briant,' saith Messire Gawain, ' Lancelot is not here ; and,
moreover, he is now on the King's business.   Well know you
that Meliant came to you and that you made him knight, and
that thereafter he warred upon the King's land without reasonable occasion.   The King was far away from the land as he
that made pilgrimage to the Graal.   He was told tidings that
his land was being put to the worse, and he sent Lancelot to
protect it.   He accordingly maintained the war as best he might
until such time as the King was returned.   Meliant knew well
that the King was come back, and that never had he done
wrong to none in his court that wished to demand right therein.
He neither came thither nor sent, either to do right or to
demand right, whether he did so for despite or whether it was
for that he knew not how to do it.   In the meanwhile he
warred upon the King, that had never done him a wrong nor
refused to do him a right.   Lancelot slew him in the King's
war and upon his land in defence thereof.   There was peace of
the war, as was agreed on between you and the King, but and
if any should therefore hold Lancelot to blame of the death of
Meliant, meseemeth that therein is he wrong.   For the others
are not held to answer for them that they slew ; but and if
you wish to say that Lancelot hath not slain him with reason,
howsoever he may have wrought aforetime in respect of his
father, I am ready to maintain his right by my body on behalf
of his.'

VII

'Messire Gawain,' saith Briant of the Isles, 'You will not as at this time find none that will take up your gage on account of this affair, nor ought any to make enemies of his friends, nor ought you to counsel me so to do. King Madeglant warreth upon him and King Claudas maketh war upon him also. They will deliver attacks enough. But I should well allow, for the sake of saving his land and keeping his friends, that the King should suffer Lancelot to remain at a distance from his court for one year, until tidings should have come to King Claudas that he had been bidden leave thereof, so as that King Arthur might have his good will and his love.' Sagramors li Desirous leapeth forward. 'Briant of the Isles,' saith Sagramors, 'Ill befall him that shall give such counsel to a lord of his knight, and the knight have well served his lord, albeit he may have slain in his wars a knight without murder and without treason, that he should give him his leave! Right ill will Lancelot hitherto have bestowed his services, and the King on this account give him his leave! After that, let King Claudas come! Let him lay waste and slay, and right great worship shall King Arthur have thereof! I say not this for that Lancelot hath need be afeared of King Claudas body to body, nor of the best knight in his land, but many things befall whereof one taketh no heed; and so King Arthur give leave to Lancelot from his court, it will be counted unto him for cowardize, and neither I nor you nor other knight ought never more to have affiance in him.' 'Lord,' saith Briant of the Isles, 'Better would it avail the King to give Lancelot leave for one year, than it would to fight for him ten years and have his land wasted and put to the worse.'

VIII

Thereupon, behold you! Orguelleux of the Launde come, that had not been at the court of a long time, and it had been told him whereof these words were. 'Briant,' saith Orguelleux of the Launde, 'Evil fare the knight that would fain grieve and harm with their lord them that have served him well! Sith that Lancelot is not here, say nought of him that ought not to be said. The court of King Arthur hath been as much renowned and made honoured by Lancelot as by ever another knight that is in it, and, but for him, never would his court have been so redoubted as it is. For no knight is there so cruel to his foes nor so redoubted throughout all Great Britain as is Lancelot, and, for that King Arthur loveth you, make him not that he hate his knights, for such four or such six be there in his castle as may depart therefrom without returning, the loss whereof should scarce be made good by us. Lancelot hath well served the King aforetime, and the King well knoweth how much he is worth; and if so be that King Claudas purposeth to war on King Arthur for Lancelot's sake, according as I have heard, without any reason, and King Arthur be not more craven than he wont to be, he may well abide his warfare and his strife so treason harm him not. For so many good knights hath King Arthur yet, that none knoweth such knights nor such King in the world beside.'

BRANCH XXVIII

Title I

THIS story saith that Briant would have been wroth with a will against Orguelleux of the Launde, had it not been for the King, and Orguelleux against him, for Orguelleux heeded no danger when anger and ill-will carried him away. Therewithal the talk came to an end. When the King learnt the tidings that Madeglant was discomfited and that the land of Albanie was in peace, he sent word to Lancelot to return back. They of the land were very sorrowful when he departed, for great affiance had they in his chivalry. So he came back thither where King Arthur was. All they of the land made great joy, for well loved was he of many, nor were there none that hated him save of envy alone. They told him the tidings of King Claudas, and also in what manner Briant had spoken. Lancelot took no notice outwardly, as he that well knew how to redress all his grievances. He was at the court of a long while, for that King Claudas was about to send over thither some one of his knights. Briant of the Isles would fain that the King should have given him his leave, for more he hated him than ever another knight in the court, sith he it was that many a time had harmed him more than any other. By Briant's counsel, King Claudas sent his knight to King Arthur's court, wherein did he not wisely, for that he thereby renewed a matter whereof afterward came right great mischief, as this title witnesseth.

II

Madeglant of Oriande heard say that Lancelot was repaired back, and that the land of Albanie was all void save for the folk of the country. He maketh ready his navy at once and cometh back to the land in great force. He burneth the land and layeth it waste on every side, and doth far worse therein than he did aforetime.   They of the land sent over to King Arthur and told him of their evil plight, warning him that, and he send them not succour betimes, they will leave the land and yield up the castles, for that they might not hold them longer.   He took counsel, the King with his knights, whom he might send thither, and they said that Lancelot had already been there and that now another knight should be sent thither.   The King sent thither Briant of the Isles, and lent him forty knights. Briant, that loved not the King in his heart, came into the land, but only made pretence of helping him to defend it.   One day fell out a battle betwixt Madeglant and Briant and all their men.   Briant was discomfited, and had many of his knights killed.   Madeglant and his people spread themselves over the land and laid the towns in ruins and destroyed the castles, that were disgarnished, and put to death all them that would not believe in their gods, and cut off their heads.

III

All they of the land and country longed with sorrow for Lancelot, and said that had he remained there, the land would not have been thus destroyed, nor might they never have protection of no knight but of him alone.   Briant of the Isles returned back, as he that would the war against King Arthur should increase on every side, for, what good soever the King may do him, he loveth him not, nor never will so long as he is on live.   But no semblant thereof durst he show, for, sith that the best of his knights had been slain in the battle, so had he no power on his side, as against Lancelot and the good knights of his fellowship, whereof he would fain that there had been not one.

IV

King Arthur was at Cardoil on one day of Whitsuntide. Many were the knights that were come to this court whereof I tell you.   The King was seated at meat, and the day was fair and clear, and the air clean and fresh.   Sagramors li Desirous and Lucan the Butler served before the King.   And what time they had served of the first meats, therewithal behold you, a

quarrel, like as it had been shot from a cross-bow, and striketh
in the column of the hall before the King so passing strong that
there was not a knight in the hall but heard it when it struck
therein. They all looked thereat in great wonderment. The
quarrel was like as it were of gold, and it had about it a many
costly precious stones. The King saith that quarrel so costly
cometh not from a poor place. Lancelot and Messire Gawain
say that never have they seen one so rich. It struck so deep in
the column that the iron point thereof might not be seen, and a
good part of the shaft was also hidden. Thereupon, behold
you, a damsel of surpassing great beauty that cometh, sitting on
a right costly mule, full well caparisoned. She had a gilded
bridle and gilded saddle, and was clad in a right rich cloth of
silk. A squire followed after her that drove her mule from
behind. She came before King Arthur as straight as she
might, and saluted him right worshipfully, and he made answer
the best he might. 'Sir,' saith she, 'I am come to speak and
demand a boon, nor will I never alight until such time as you
shall have granted it to me. For such is my custom, and for
this am I come to your court, whereof I have heard such tidings
and such witness in many places where I have been, that I know
you will not deny me herein.'

V

'Damsel, tell me what boon you would have of me?' 'Sir,'
saith she, 'I would fain pray and beseech you that you bid the
knight that may draw forth this quarrel from this column go
thither where there is sore need of him.' 'Damsel,' saith the
King, 'Tell me the need.' 'Sir,' saith she, 'I will tell it you
plainly when I shall see the knight that shall have drawn it
forth.' 'Damsel,' saith the King, 'Alight! Never, please
God, shall you go forth of my court denied of that you ask.'
Lucan the Butler taketh her between his arms and setteth her
to the ground, and her mule is led away to be stabled. When
the damsel had washen, she was set in a seat beside Messire
Ywain, that showed her much honour and served her with a
good will. He looked at her from time to time, for she was
fair and gentle and of good countenance. When they had
eaten at the tables, the damsel prayeth the King that he will
hasten them to do her business. 'Sir,' saith she, 'Many a

L

good knight is there within yonder, and right glad may he be that shall draw it forth, for I tell you a right good knight is he, sith that none may achieve this business save he alone.' 'Fair nephew,' saith the King, 'Now set your hand to this quarrel and give it back to the damsel.' 'Ha, sir,' saith he, 'Do me not shame! By the faith that I owe you, I will not set my hand forward herein this day, nor ought you to be wroth hereof. Behold, here have you Lancelot with you, and so many other good knights, that little worship should I have herein were I to set myself forward before them.' 'Messire Ywain,' saith the King, 'Set your hand hereto! It may be that you think too humbly of yourself herein.' 'Sir,' saith Messire Ywain, 'Nought is there in the world that I would not do for you, but as for this matter I pray you hold me excused.' 'Sagramors, and you, Orguelleux of the Launde, what will you do?' saith the King. 'Sir,' say they, 'When Lancelot hath made assay, we will do your pleasure, but before him, so please you, we will not go.'

VI

'Damsel,' saith the King, 'Pray Lancelot that he be fain to set his hand, and then the rest shall go after him if needs be.' 'Lancelot,' saith the damsel, 'By the thing that most you love, make not mine errand bootless, but set your hand to the quarrel and then will the others do that they ought of right to do. For no leisure have I to tarry here long time.' 'Damsel,' saith Lancelot, 'Ill do you, and a sin, to conjure me for nought, for so many good knights be here within, that I should be held for a fool and a braggart and I put myself forward before all other.' 'By my head,' saith the King, 'Not so! Rather will you be held as a knight courteous and wise and good, as now you ought to be, and great worship will it be to yourself and you may draw forth the quarrel, and great courtesy will it be to aid the damsel. Wherefore I require you, of the faith you owe me, that you set your hand thereto, sith that the damsel prayeth you so to do, before the others.'

VII

Lancelot hath no mind to disobey the King's commandment; and he remembered that the damsel had conjured him by the

thing that most he loved; nor was there nought in the world
that he loved so much as the Queen, albeit she were dead, nor
never thought he of none other thing save her alone. Then
standeth he straight upright, doth off his robe, and cometh
straight to the quarrel that is fixed in the column. He setteth
his hand thereunto and draweth it forth with a right passing
strong wrench, so sturdily that he maketh the column tremble.
Then he giveth it to the damsel. 'Sir,' saith she to King
Arthur, 'Now is it my devoir to tell you plainly of my errand;
nor might none of the knights here within have drawn forth
the quarrel save only he; and you held me in covenant how he
that should draw it forth should do that which I shall require
of him, and that he might do it, nor will I pray nor require of
him nought that is not reason. Needs must he go to the Chapel
Perilous the swiftest he may, and there will he find a knight
that lieth shrouded in the midst of the chapel: He will take of
the cloth wherein he is shrouded and a sword that lieth at his
side in the coffin, and will take them to the Castle Perilous;
and when he shall there have been, he shall return to the castle
where he slew the lion in the cavern wherein are the two
griffons, and the head of one of them shall he take and bring to
me at Castle Perilous, for a knight there lieth sick that may not
otherwise be healed.'

VIII

'Damsel,' saith Lancelot, 'I see that you reckon but little of
my life, so only that your wish be accomplished.' 'Sir,' saith
she, 'I know as well as you what the enterprise is, nor do I no
whit desire your death, for, and were you dead, never would
the knight be whole for whose sake you undertake it. And
you will see the fairest damsel that is in any kingdom, and the
one that most desireth to see you. And, so you tarry not,
through her shall you lightly get done that you have to do.
See now that you delay it not, but do that is needful swiftly
sith that it hath been laid upon you, for the longer you tarry,
the greater will be the hazard of mischance befalling you.' The
damsel departeth from the court and taketh her leave and goeth
her way back as fast as she may, and saith to herself: 'Lancelot, albeit you have these pains and this travail for me, yet
would I not your death herein, but of right ought I to rejoice
in your tribulation, for into two of the most perilous places in

the world are you going.   Greatly ought I to hate you, for you reft me of my friend and gave him to another, and while I live may I never forget it.'   The damsel goeth her way, and Lancelot departeth from the court and taketh leave of the King and of all the others.   He issueth forth of Cardoil, all armed, and entereth into the forest that is deep, and so goeth forth a great pace, and prayeth God guide him into safety.

BRANCH XXIX

TITLE I

THEREWITHAL the story is silent of Lancelot, and saith that Briant of the Isles is repaired to Cardoil. Of the forty knights that he took with him, but fifteen doth he bring back again. Thereof is King Arthur right sorrowful, and saith that he hath the fewer friends. They of the land of Albanie have sent to King Arthur and told him that and he would not lose the land for evermore he must send them Lancelot, for never saw they knight that better knew how to avenge him on his enemies and to do them hurt than was he. The King asketh Briant of the Isles how it is that his knights are dead in such sort? 'Sir,' saith Briant, 'Madeglant hath great force of people, and what force of men soever may run upon them, they make a castle of their navy in such sort that none may endure against them, and never did no folk know so much of war as do they. The land lieth far away from you, and more will it cost you to hold it than it is worth; and, if you will believe my counsel, you will trouble yourself no more about it, and they of the country would be well counselled and they did the same.' 'Briant,' saith the King, 'This would be great blame to myself. No worshipful man ought to be idle in guarding and holding that which is his own. The worshipful man ought not to hold of things so much for their value as for their honour, and if I should leave the land disgarnished of my aid and my counsel, they will take mine, and will say that I have not heart to protect my land; and even now is it great shame to myself that they have settled themselves there and would fain draw away them of the land to their evil law. And I would fain that Lancelot had achieved that he hath undertaken, and I would have sent him there, for none would protect the land better than he, and, were he now there along with forty knights and with them of the country, Madeglant would make but short stay there.' 'Sir,' saith Briant, 'They of the country reckon nought of you nor any other but Lancelot only, and they say that and you send him there they will make him King.' 'It may well be that they say so,' saith the King, 'But never would Lancelot do aught that should be against my will.' 'Sir,' saith Briant, 'Sith that you are not minded to believe me, I will say no more in this matter, but in the end his knighthood will harm you rather than help you and you take no better heed thereof than up to this time you have done.'

BRANCH XXX

Title I

OF Briant of the Isles the story is here silent, whom King the believeth too much in many things, and saith that Lancelot goeth his way right through the forest, full heavy in thought. He had not ridden far when he met a knight that was right sore wounded. He asked him whence he came and who had wounded him in such manner. 'Sir,' saith he, 'I come from the Chapel Perilous, where I was not able to defend me against an evil folk that appeared there; and they have wounded me in such sort as you see, and but for a damsel that came thereinto from the forest I should not have escaped on live. But she aided me on such condition that and I should see a knight they call Lancelot, or Perceval, or Messire Gawain, I should tell which of them soever I should first meet withal that he should go to her without delay, for much she marvelleth her that none of them cometh into the chapel, for none ought to enter there but good knights only. But much do I marvel, Sir, how the damsel durst enter there, for it is the most marvellous place that is, and the damsel is of right great beauty; natheless she cometh thither oftentimes alone into the chapel. A knight lieth in the chapel that hath been slain of late, that was a fell and cruel knight and a hardy.' 'What was his name?' saith Lancelot. 'He was named Ahuret the Bastard,' saith the knight; 'And he had but one arm and one hand, and the other was smitten off at a castle that Messire Gawain gave Meliot of Logres when he succoured him against this knight that lieth in the coffin. And Meliot of Logres hath slain the knight that had assieged the castle, but the knight wounded him sore, so that he may not be whole save he have the sword wherewith he wounded him, that lieth in the coffin at his side, and some of

311

the cloth wherein he is enshrouded ; and, so God grant me to meet one of the knights, gladly will I convey unto him the damsel's message.' 'Sir Knight,' saith Lancelot, 'One of them have you found. My name is Lancelot, and for that I see you are wounded and in evil plight, I tell it you thus freely.' 'Sir,' saith the knight, 'Now may God protect your body, for you go in great peril of death. But the damsel much desireth to see you, I know not for what, and well may she aid you if she will.'

II

'Sir Knight, God hath brought us forth of many a peril, and so will He also from this and it be His pleasure and His will.' With that, Lancelot departeth from the knight, and hath ridden so far that he is come at evensong to the Chapel Perilous, that standeth in a great valley of the forest, and hath a little church-yard about it that is well enclosed on all sides, and hath an ancient cross without the entrance. The chapel and the grave-yard are overshadowed of the forest, that is right tall. Lancelot entereth therein all armed. He signeth him of the cross and blesseth him and commendeth him to God. He seeth in the grave-yard coffins in many places, and it seemeth him that he seeth folk round about that talk together, the one with another. But he might not hear that they said. He might not see them openly, but very tall they seemed him to be. He is come toward the chapel and alighteth of his horse, and seeth a shed outside the chapel, wherein was provender for horses. He goeth thither to set his own there, then leaneth his shield against his spear at the entrance of the chapel, and entereth in, where it was very dark, for no light was there save only of a single lamp that shone full darkly. He seeth the coffin that was in the midst of the chapel wherein the knight lay.

III

When he had made his orison before an image of Our Lady, he cometh to the coffin and openeth it as fast as he may, and seeth the knight, tall and foul of favour, that therein lay dead. The cloth wherein he was enshrouded was displayed all bloody. He taketh the sword that lay at his side and lifteth the winding-sheet to rend it at the seam, then taketh the knight by the head to lift him upward, and findeth him so heavy and so ungain that scarce may he remove him. He cutteth off the half of the cloth wherein he is enshrouded, and the coffin beginneth to make a crashing so passing loud that it seemed the chapel were falling. When he hath the piece of the cloth and the sword he closeth the coffin again, and forthwith cometh to the door of the chapel and seeth mount, in the midst of the grave-yard as it seemed him, great knights and horrible, and they are apparelled as it were to combat, and him thinketh that they are watching for him and espy him.

IV

Thereupon, behold you, a damsel running, her kirtle girt high about her, right through the grave-yard a great pace. 'Take heed you move not until such time as it is known who the knight is!' She is come to the chapel. 'Sir Knight, lay down the sword and this that you have taken of the winding-sheet of the dead knight!' 'Damsel,' saith Lancelot, 'What hurt doth it you of this that I have?' 'This,' saith she, 'That you have taken it without my leave; for I have him in charge, both him and the chapel. And I would fain,' saith she, 'know what is your name?' 'Damsel,' saith he, 'What would you gain of knowing my name?' 'I know not,' saith she, 'whether I shall have either loss or gain thereof, but high time already is it that I should ask you it to my sorrow, for many a time have I been deceived therein.' 'Damsel,' saith he, 'I am called Lancelot of the Lake.' 'You ought of right,' saith she, 'to have the sword and the cloth; but come you with me to my castle, for oftentimes have I desired that you and Perceval and Messire Gawain should see the three tombs that I have made for your three selves.'

V

'Damsel,' saith he, 'No wish have I to see my sepulchre so early betimes.' 'By my head,' saith she, 'And you come not thither, you may not issue from hence without tribulation; and they that you see there are earthly fiends that guard this grave-yard and are at my commandment.' 'Never, damsel, please God,' saith Lancelot, 'may your devils have power to harm a Christian.' 'Ha, Lancelot,' saith she, 'I beseech and pray you that you come with me into my castle, and I will save your life as at this time from this folk that are just now ready to fall upon you; and, so you are not willing to do this, yield me back the sword that you have taken from the coffin, and go your way at once.' 'Damsel,' saith Lancelot, 'Into your castle may I not go, nor desire I to go, wherefore pray me no more thereof, for other business have I to do; nor will I yield you back the sword, whatsoever may befall me, for a certain knight may not otherwise be healed, and great pity it were that he should die.' 'Ha, Lancelot,' saith she, 'How hard and cruel do I find you towards me! And as good cause have I to be sorry that you have the sword as have you to be glad. For, and you had not had it upon you, never should you have carried it off from hence at your will; rather should I have had all my pleasure of you, and I would have made you be borne into my castle, from whence never should you have moved again for nought you might do; and thus should I have been quit of the wardenship of this chapel and of coming thereinto in such manner as now oftentimes I needs must come.

VI

'But now am I taken in a trap, for, so long as you have the sword, not one of them that are there yonder can do you evil nor hinder you of going.' Of this was Lancelot not sorry. He taketh leave of the damsel, that departeth grudgingly, garnisheth him again of his arms, then mounteth again on his horse and goeth his way right through the grave-yard. He beholdeth this evil folk, that were so foul and huge and hideous, it seemed as if they would devour everything. They made way for Lancelot, and had no power to hurt him. He is issued forth of the grave-yard and goeth his way through the forest until daylight appeared about him, fair and clear. He found the hermit there where he had heard mass, then ate a little, then departed and rode the day long until setting of the sun, but could find no hold on the one side nor the other wherein he might lodge, and so was benighted in the forest.

VII

Lancelot knew not which way to turn, for he had not often
been in the forest, and knew not how the land lay nor the paths
therein. He rode until he found a little causeway, and there
was a path at the side that led to an orchard that was at a
corner of the forest, where there was a postern gate whereby
one entered, and it was not made fast for the night. And the
orchard was well enclosed with walls. Lancelot entered in and
made fast the entrance, then took off his horse's bridle and let
him feed on the grass. He might not espy the castle that was
hard by for the abundance of trees and the darkness of the
night, and so knew not whither he was arrived. He laid his
shield for a pillow and his arms at his side and fell on sleep.
But, had he known where it was he had come, little sleep
would he have had, for he was close to the cavern where he
slew the lion and where the griffons were, that had come in
from the forest all gorged of victual, and were fallen on sleep,
and it was for them that the postern gate had been left
unbolted. A damsel went down from a chamber by a trap-
door with a brachet on her arm for fear of the griffons, and as
she went toward the postern-gate to lock it, she espied Lancelot,
that lay asleep in the midst of the orchard. She ran back to
her Lady the speediest she might, and said unto her: 'Up,
Lady!' saith she, 'Lancelot is sleeping in the orchard!' She
leapt up incontinent and came to the orchard there where
Lancelot was sleeping, then sate her down beside him and
began to look at him, sighing the while, and draweth as near
him as she may. 'Fair Lord God,' saith she, 'what shall I do?
and I wake him first he will have no care to kiss me, and if I
kiss him sleeping he will awake forthwith; and better hap is it
for me to take the most I may even in such-wise than to fail of
all, and, moreover, if so be I shall have kissed him, I may hope
that he will not hate me thereof, sith that I may then boast that
I have had at least so much of that which is his own.' She set
her mouth close to him and so kissed him the best and fairest
she might, three times, and Lancelot awakened forthwith. He
leapt up and made the cross upon him, then looked at the
damsel, and said: 'Ha, God! where, then, am I?' 'Fair
sweet friend,' saith she, 'You are nigh her that hath all set
her heart upon you and will remove it never.' 'I cry you

mercy, damsel,' saith Lancelot, ' and I tell you, for nought that may befall, one that loveth me, please God, never will I hate! but that which one hath loved long time ought not so soon to fall away from the remembrance of a love that is rooted in the heart, when she hath been proven good and loyal, nor ought one so soon to depart therefrom.'

VIII

' Sir,' saith she, ' This castle is at your commandment, and you will remain therein, and well may you know my thought towards you.   Would that your thought were the same towards me.'   ' Damsel,' saith he, ' I seek the healing of a knight that may not be healed save I bring him the head of one of your serpents.'   ' Certes, Sir, so hath it been said.   But I bade the damsel say so only for that I was fain you should come back hither to me.'   ' Damsel,' saith he, ' I have come back hither, and so may I turn back again sith that of the serpent's head is there no need.'   ' Ha, Lancelot,' saith she, ' How good a knight are you, and how ill default do you make in another way!   No knight, methinketh, is there in the world that would have refused me save only you.   This cometh of your folly, and your outrage, and your baseness of heart!   The griffons have not done my will in that they have not slain you or strangled you as you slept, and, so I thought that they would have power to slay you, I would make them come to slay you now.   But the devil hath put so much knighthood into you that scarce any man may have protection against you.   Better ought I to love you dead than alive.   By my head, I would fain that your head were hanged with the others that hang at the entrance of the gateway, and, had I thought you would have failed me in such wise I would have brought my father hither to where you were sleeping, and right gladly would he have slain you.

IX

' None that knoweth the covenant between me and you ought to hold you for a good knight; for you have cozened me of my right according to the tenor and custom of the castle if that through perversity or slothfulness you durst not take me when you have won me.'   ' Damsel,' saith Lancelot, ' You may say your will. You have done so much for me sithence that I came hither that I ought not to be afeard of you, for traitor is the man or woman that kisseth another to procure his hurt.' 'Lancelot, I took but that I might have, for well I see that none more thereof may I have never again.' He goeth to put the bridle on his destrier, and then taketh leave of the damsel, that parteth from him right sorrowfully; but Lancelot would no longer tarry, for great throng of knights was there in the castle, and he was not minded to put him in jeopardy for nought. He issueth forth of the orchard, and the damsel looketh after him as long as she may see him. After that, cometh she to her chamber, sad and vexed at heart, nor knoweth she how she may bear herself, for the thing in the world that most she loveth is far away, and no joy may she have thereof.

X

Lancelot rideth right amidst the forest until it is day, and cometh at the right hour of noon to the Castle Perilous, where Meliot of Logres lay. He entered into the castle. The damsel that was at King Arthur's court cometh to meet him. 'Lancelot,' saith she, 'Welcome may you be!' 'Damsel,' saith he, 'Good adventure may you have!' He was alighted at the mounting-stage of the hall. She maketh him mount up the steps and afterward be disarmed. 'Damsel,' saith he, 'Behold, here is some of the winding-sheet wherein the knight was shrouded, and here is his sword; but you befooled me as concerning the serpent's head.' 'By my head,' saith the damsel, 'that did I for the sake of the damsel of the Castle of Griffons that hateth you not a whit, for so prayed she me to do. Now hath she seen you, and so will she be more at ease, and will have no cause to ask me thereof.'

XI

The damsel leadeth Lancelot to where Meliot of Logres lay. Lancelot sitteth him down before him and asketh how it is with him? 'Meliot,' saith the damsel, 'This is Lancelot, that bringeth you your healing.' 'Ha, Sir, welcome may you be!' 'God grant you health speedily,' said Lancelot. 'Ha, for God's sake,' saith Meliot, 'What doth Messire Gawain? Is he hearty?' 'I

left him quite hearty when I parted from him,' saith Lancelot,
' And so he knew that you had been wounded in such sort, full
sorry would he be thereof and King Arthur likewise.'   ' Sir,'
saith he, ' The knight that assieged them maimed me in this
fashion, but was himself maimed in such sort that he is dead
thereof.   But the wounds that he dealt me are so cruel and so
raging, that they may not be healed save his sword toucheth
them and if they be not bound with some of the winding-sheet
wherein he was shrouded, that he had displayed about him, all
bloody.'   ' By my faith,' saith the damsel, ' Behold them here !'
' Ha, Sir,' saith he, ' Gramercy of this great goodness !   In
every way appeareth it that you are good knight, for, but for
the goodness of your knighthood, the coffin wherein the knight
lieth had never opened so lightly, nor would you never have
had the sword nor the cloth, nor never till now hath knight
entered therein but either he were slain there, or departed
thence wounded right grievously.'   They uncover his wounds,
and Lancelot unbindeth them, and the damsel toucheth him of
the sword and the winding-sheet, and they are assuaged for
him.   And he saith that now at last he knoweth well he need
not fear to die thereof.   Lancelot is right joyful thereof in his
heart, for that he seeth he will be whole betimes ; and sore
pity had it been of his death, for a good knight was he, and
wise and loyal.

XI

' Lancelot,' saith the lady, ' Long time have I hated you on
account of the knight that I loved, whom you reft away from me
and married to another and not to me, and ofttimes have I put
myself to pains to grieve you of some ill deed for that you did
to me, for never was I so sorrowful for aught that befell me.
He loved me of right great love, and I him again, and never
shall that love fail.   But now is it far further away from me
than it was before, and for this bounty that you have done,
never hereafter need you fear aught of my grievance.'   ' Damsel,'
saith Lancelot, ' Gramercy heartily.'   He was lodged in the
castle the night richly and worshipfully, and departed thence
on the morrow when he had taken leave of the damsel and
Meliot, and goeth back a great pace toward the court of King
Arthur, that was sore dismayed, for Madeglant was conquering
his islands and great part of his land.   The more part of the

lands that he conquered had renounced the New Law for fear of death and held the false believe. And Messire Gawain and many other knights were departed from King Arthur's court for that the King trusted more in Briant of the Isles than he did in them.

XIII

For many times had King Arthur sent knights against Madeglant since Lancelot was departed from the court, to the intent that they should put to rebuke the enemies of his land, but never saw he one come back from thence nought discomfited. The King of Oriande made much boast that he would fulfil for his sister all that she had bidden him, for he thought that King Arthur would yield himself up betimes unto him and yield all his land likewise. The King greatly desired the return of Lancelot, and said ofttimes that and he had been against his enemies as nigh as the others he had sent they would not have durst so to fly against him. In the midst of the dismay wherein was King Arthur, Lancelot returned to the court, whereof was the King right joyous. Lancelot knew that Messire Gawain and Messire Ywain were not there, and that they held them aloof from the court more willingly than they allowed on account of Briant of the Isles, that King Arthur believed in more than ever a one of the others. He was minded to depart in like sort, but the King would not let him, but said to him rather, 'Lancelot, I pray and beseech you, as him that I love much, that you set your pains and your counsel on defending my land, for great affiance have I in you.' 'Sir,' saith Lancelot, 'My aid and my force shall fail you never; take heed that yours fail not me.' 'Of right ought I not to fail you,' saith the King, 'Nor will I never, for I should fail myself thereby.'

XIV

The history saith that he gave Lancelot forty knights in charge, and that he is come into an island where King Madeglant was. Or ever he knew of his coming, Lancelot had cut off his retreat, for he cut his cables and beat his anchors to pieces and broke up his ships. After that, he struck among the people of Madeglant, and slew as many of them as he would, he and his knights. The King thought to withdraw him back, both him and his fellowship, into safety as he wont, but he found himself right ill bested. Lancelot drove him toward the sea, whither he fled, but only to find himself no less discomfit there, and slew him in the midst of his folk, and all his other knights were slain and cast into the sea. This island was freed of him by Lancelot, and from thence he went to the other islands that Madeglant had conquered and set again under the false Law, and there did away the false Law from them that had been set thereunder by fear of death, and stablished the land in such sort as it had been tofore. He roved so long from one island to another that presently he came to Albanie where he had succoured them at first.

XV

When they of the land saw him come, they well knew that the King of Oriande was dead and the islands made free, whereof made they great joy. The land was some deal emptied of the most puissant and the strongest, for they were dead along with their lord. Lancelot had brought with him some of the best knights and most puissant. He was come with a great navy into the land and began to destroy it. They of the land were misbelievers, for they believed in false idols and in false images. They saw that they might not defend the land, sith that their lord was dead. The more part let themselves be slain for that they would not renounce the evil Law, and they that were minded to turn to God were saved. The kingdom was right rich and right great that Lancelot conquered and attorned to the Law of Our Lord in such wise. He made break all the false images of copper and latten wherein they had believed tofore, and whereof false answers came to them of the voices of devils. Thereafter he caused be made crucifixes and images in the likeness of Our Lord, and in the likeness of His sweet Mother, the better to confirm them of the kingdoms in the Law.

XVI

The strongest and most valiant of the land assembled one day and said that it was high time a land so rich should no longer be without a King. They all agreed and came to Lancelot and told him how they would fain that he should be

King of the realm he had conquered, for in no land might he be better employed, and they would help him conquer other realms enow.   Lancelot thanked them much, but told them that of this land nor of none other would he be King save by the good will of King Arthur only; for that all the conquest he had made was his, and by his commandment had he come thither, and had given him his own knights in charge that had helped him to reconquer the lands.

XVII

King Claudas had heard tell how Lancelot had slain the King of Oriande and that none of the islands might scarce be defended against him.   He had no liking of him, neither of his good knighthood nor of his conquest, for well remembered he of the land that he had conquered from King Ban of Benoic that was Lancelot's father, and therefore was he sorry of the good knighthood whereof Lancelot was everywhere held of worth and renown, for that he was tenant of his father's land.   King Claudas sent a privy message to Briant and bore him on hand that, and he might do so much as that King Arthur should forbid Lancelot his court, and that it were ill with him with the King, he would have much liking thereof and would help him betimes to take vengeance on his enemies, for, so Lancelot were forth of his court, and Messire Gawain, the rest would scarce abide long time, and thus should they have all their will of King Arthur's land.   Briant sent word back to King Claudas that Messire Gawain and Messire Ywain began to hold them aloof from the court, and that as for most part of the other he need not trouble him a whit, for he might so deal as that in short time Lancelot should be well trounced, would they or nould they.

XVIII

Tidings are come to King Arthur's court that the King of Oriande is dead and his people destroyed, and that Lancelot hath conquered his kingdom and slain the King, and reconquered all the lands wherein he had set the false Law and the false believe by his force and by dread of him.   And the more part say in the court that they of the realm of Oriande nor those of the other islands will not let Lancelot repair to court, and are doing their endeavour to make him King; and nought is there in the world, and he command them, they will not do, and that never was no folk so obedient to any as are they of all these lands to him.   Briant of the Isles cometh one day privily to King Arthur, and saith: ' Sir,' saith he, ' Much ought I to love you, for that you have made me Seneschal of your land; whereby meseemeth you have great affiance in me, and my bounden duty is it to turn aside that which is evil from you and to set forward your good everywhere, and, did I not so, no whit loyal should I be towards you.

XIX

' Tidings are come to me of late that they of the kingdom of Oriande and Albanie and of the other islands that are your appanages have all leagued together, and have sworn and given surety that they will aid one another against you, and they are going presently to make Lancelot their King, and will come down upon your land as speedily as they may wheresoever he may dare lead them, and they have sworn their oath that they will conquer your kingdom just as you now hold it, and, so you be not garnished against them betimes, you may have thereof sore trouble to your own body as well as the loss whereof I tell you.'   ' By my head,' saith the King, ' I believe not that Lancelot durst think this, nor that he would have the heart to do me evil.'   ' By my head,' saith Briant, ' Long time have I had misgivings both of this and of him, but one ought not to tell one's lord all that one knows, for that one cannot be sure either that it be not leasing or that folk wish to meddle in his affairs out of envy.   But nought is there in the world that I will conceal from you henceforward for the love that you bear me and for that you have affiance in me, and so may you well have, for I have abandoned my land for you that marched with your own, whereby you may sorely straiten your enemies, for well you know that in your court is there no knight of greater puissance than am I.'

XX

' By my head,' saith the King, ' I am fain to love you and hold you dear, nor shall you never be removed from my love nor from my service for nought that may be said of any, so manifestly have I seen your goodness and your loyalty.   I will bid Lancelot by my letters and under my seal that he come to speak with me, for sore need have I thereof, and when he shall be here we will take account of this that you have told me, for this will I not, that he nor none other that may be my knight shall dare rise in arms against me, for such power ought lord of right to have over his knight, and to be feared and dreaded of him, for elsewise is he feeble, and lordship without power availeth nought.'

XXI

The King sent his letters by his messenger to Lancelot. The messenger sought him until he found him in the kingdom of Oriande, and delivered him the letters and the seal of the King. So soon as he knew that which the letters say, he took leave of them of the land, that were right sorrowful. He departed thence and came back to Cardoil, bringing with him all the knights that he had in charge, and told the King that he had reconquered for him all the islands, and that the King of Oriande was dead and that his land was attorned to the Law of Our Lord. The King bade Briant of the Isles that he should make forty knights come armed under their cloaks ready to take Lancelot prisoner as soon as he should command them. The tidings come to Lancelot, there where he was in his hostel, that the King had made knights come all armed to the palace. Lancelot bethought him that some need had arisen and that he would arm himself likewise, so he made him be armed and came to the hall where the King was. 'Sir,' saith Briant, 'Lancelot thinketh him of something, for he hath armed himself at his hostel, and is come hither in such manner and at such time without your leave, and he may do something more yet. You ought well to ask him wherefore he wisheth to do you evil, and in what manner you have deserved it.' He biddeth him be called before him. 'Lancelot,' saith the King, 'Wherefore are you armed?' 'Sir, I was told that knights had come in hither armed, and I was feared lest some mishap had befallen you, for I would not that any evil should betide you.' 'You come hither for another thing,' saith the King, 'according to that I have been given to wit, and, had the hall been void of folk, you hoped to have slain me.' The King commandeth him be taken forthwith without gainsay of any. The knights that were armed did off their cloaks and leapt toward him on all sides, for they durst not disobey the King's commandment, and the more part were men of Briant of the Isles.

XXII

Lancelot seeth them coming towards him with their keen swords and saith, 'By my head, an evil guerdon do you return me of the services I have done for you.' The knights come to him all together swords drawn, and run upon him all at once. He goeth defending himself, as far as the wall of the hall, whereof he maketh a castle to his back, but before he cometh thither he hath slain or wounded seven. He began to defend himself right stoutly on all sides, but they gave him great buffets of their swords, and no fair play is it of thirty or forty blows to one. Nor ought none believe that one single knight might deliver himself from so many men, seeing that they were eager to take him and do him a hurt. Lancelot defended him the best he might, but the numbers were against him, and, anyway, or ever he let himself be taken he sold himself right dear, for of the forty knights he harmed at least a score, and of them was none that was not sore wounded and the most part killed; and he caught Briant of the Isles, that was helping to take him, so sore that he made his sword drink the blood of his body, in such sort that the wound was right wide. The knights laid hold on Lancelot on all sides, and the King commanded that none should harm him, but that they should bring him to his dungeon in the prison. Lancelot marvelled him much wherefore the King should do this, nor might he understand wherefore this hatred was come so lately. He is put in the prison so as the King hath commanded. All they of the court are sorry thereof, save Briant and his knights, but well may he yet aby it dear, so God bring Lancelot out of prison. Some say, 'Now is the King's court lost, sith that Messire Gawain and the other knights have thus forsaken it, and Lancelot is put in prison for doing well, ill trust may the others have therein.' They pray God yet grant Briant of the Isles an evil guerdon, for well know they that all this is of his procurement. And of an evil guerdon shall he not fail so God protect Lancelot and bring him forth of prison.

BRANCH XXXI

TITLE I

THEREUPON the story is silent of Lancelot, and cometh back to Perceval that had not heard these tidings, and if he had known them, right sorrowful would he have been thereof. He is departed from his uncle's castle that he hath reconquered, and was sore grieved of the tidings that the damsel that was wounded brought him of his sister that Aristot had carried away by force to the house of a vavasour. He was about to take her to wife and cut off her head on the day of the New Year, for such was his custom with all them that he took. Perceval rideth one day, all heavy in thought, and taketh his way as fast as he may toward the hermitage of his uncle King Hermit. He is come thither on an eventide, and seeth three hermits issued forth of the hermitage. He alighteth and goeth to meet them so soon as he seeth them. 'Sir,' say the hermits, 'Enter not in, for they are laying out a body there.' 'Who is it?' saith Perceval. 'Sir,' say the hermits, 'It is the good King Pelles that Aristot slew suddenly after mass on account of one of his nephews, Perceval, whom he loveth not, and a damsel is laying out the body there within.' When Perceval heard the news of his uncle that is dead, thereof was he right grieved at heart, and on the morrow was he at his uncle's burial. When mass was sung, Perceval would have departed, as he that had great desire to take vengeance on him that had done him such shame.

II

Thereupon behold you the damsel that is his. 'Sir,' saith she, 'Full long time have I been seeking you. Behold here the head of a knight that I carry hanging at the bow of my saddle, in this rich casket of ivory that you may see, and by none ought

325

he to be avenged but by you alone.   Discharge me thereof, fair Sir, of your courtesy, for I have carried it too long a time, and this King Arthur knoweth well and Messire Gawain, for each hath seen me at court along with the head, but they could give me no tidings of you, and my castle may I not have again until such time as he be avenged.'   'Who, then, was the knight, damsel?' saith Perceval.   'Sir, he was son of your uncle Bruns Brandalis, and were he on live, would have been one of the best knights in the world.'   'And who slew him, damsel?' saith Perceval.   'Sir, the Knight of the Deep Forest that leadeth the lion, foully in treason there where he thought him safe.   For had he been armed in like manner as was the other, he would not have slain him.'   'Damsel,' said Perceval, 'This grieveth me that he hath slain him, and it grieveth me likewise of mine uncle King Hermit, whom I would avenge more willingly than all the men in the world, for he was slain on my account.

III

'Most disloyal was this knight, and foully was he fain to avenge him when he slew a holy man, a hermit that never wished him ill on account of me and of none other.   Right glad shall I be and I may find the knight, and so, methinketh, will he be of me, for me he hateth as much as I do him, as I have been told, and Lord God grant, howsoever he may take it, that I may find him betimes.   'Sir,' saith the damsel, 'So outrageous a knight is he that no knight is there in the world so good but he thinketh himself of more worth than he, and sith that he hateth you with a will, and he knew that you were here, you and another, or you the third, he would come now at once, were he in place and free.'   'Damsel,' saith Perceval, 'God give him mischief of his coming, come whensoever he may!'   'Sir,' saith she, 'The Deep Forest there, where the Red Knight leadeth the lion, is towards the castle of Aristot, and, or ever you come by adventure into the forest, you may well hear some tidings of him!'

BRANCH XXXII

INCIPIT

HERE beginneth the last branch of the Graal in the name of the Father, and of the Son, and of the Holy Ghost.

TITLE I

The story saith that Perceval went his way through the forest. He saw pass before him two squires, and each carried a wild deer trussed behind him that had been taken by hounds. Perceval cometh to them a great pace and maketh them abide. 'Lords,' saith he, 'Whither will you carry this venison?' 'Sir,' say the squires, 'To the castle of Ariste, whereof Aristot is lord.' 'Is there great throng of knights at the castle?' saith Perceval. 'Sir,' say the squires, 'Not a single one is there, but within four days will be a thousand there, for Messire is about to marry, whereof is great preparation toward. He is going to take the daughter of the Widow Lady, whom he carried off by force before her castle of Camelot, and hath set her in the house of one of his vavasours until such time as he shall espouse her. But we are right sorrowful, for she is of most noble lineage and of great beauty and of the most worth in the world. So is it great dole that he shall have her, for he will cut her head off on the day of the New Year, sith that such is his custom.' 'And one might carry her off,' saith Perceval, 'would he not do well therein?' 'Yea, Sir!' say the squires, 'Our Lord God would be well pleased thereof, for such cruelty is the greatest that ever any knight may have. Moreover, he is much blamed of a good hermit that he hath slain, and every day desireth he to meet the brother of the damsel he is about to take, that is one of the best knights in the world. And he saith that he would slay him more gladly than ever another knight on live.' 'And where is your lord?' saith Perceval, 'Can you give

me witting?' 'Yea, Sir,' say the squires, 'We parted from
him but now in this forest, where he held melly with a knight
that seemeth us to be right worshipful and valiant, and saith
that he hath for name the Knight Hardy.   And for that he told
Aristot that he was a knight of Perceval's and of his fellowship,
he ran upon him, and then commanded us to come on, and said
that he should vanquish him incontinent.   We could still hear
just now the blows of the swords yonder where we were in the
forest, and Aristot is of so cruel conditions that no knight may
pass through this forest, but he is minded to slay him.'

II

When Perceval heard these tidings, he departed from the
squires, and so soon as they were out of sight he goeth as great
pace thither as they had come thence.   He had ridden half a
league Welsh when he heard the buffets they were dealing one
another on the helm with their swords, and right well pleased
was he for that the Knight Hardy held so long time melly with
Aristot in whom is there so much cruelty and felony.   But
Perceval knew not to what mischief the Knight Hardy had been
wounded through the body of a spear, so that the blood rayed
out on all sides; and Aristot had not remained whole, for he was
wounded in two places.   So soon as Perceval espied them, he
smiteth his horse of his spurs, lance in rest, and smiteth Aristot
right through the breast with such force that he maketh him lose
his stirrups and lie down backwards over the hinder bow of the
saddle.   After that saith he : 'I am come to my sister's wedding,
of right ought it not to be made without me.'

III

Aristot, that was full hardy, set himself again betwixt the
bows of the saddle in great wrath when he seeth Perceval, and
cometh towards him like as if he were wood mad, sword in
hand, and dealeth him such a buffet on the helm as that it is
all dinted in thereby.   The Knight Hardy draweth back when
he seeth Perceval, for he is wounded to the death through the
body.   He had held the stour so long time that he could abide
no more.   But or ever he departed, he had wounded Aristot

in two places right grievously. Perceval felt the blow that was heavy, and that his helmet was dinted in. He cometh back to Aristot and smiteth him so passing strongly that he thrusteth the spear right through his body and overthroweth him and his horse all of a heap. Then he alighteth over him and taketh off the coif of his habergeon and unlaceth his ventail. ' What have you in mind to do?' said Aristot. 'I will cut off your head,' said Perceval, 'and present it to my sister whom you have failed.' 'Do not so!' saith Aristot, 'But let me live, and I will forgo my hatred.' 'Your hatred might I well abide henceforward, meseemeth,' saith Perceval, 'But one may not abide you any longer, for well have you deserved this, and God willeth not to bear with you.' He smiteth off his head incontinent and hangeth it at his saddle-bow, and cometh to the Knight Hardy, and asketh him how it is with him. 'Sir,' saith he, 'I am very nigh my death, but I comfort me much of this that I see you tofore I die.' Perceval is remounted on his horse, then taketh his spear and leaveth the body of the knight in the midst of the launde, and so departeth forthwith and leadeth the Knight Hardy to a hermitage that was hard by there, and lifteth him down of his horse as speedily as he may. After that, he disarmed him and made him confess to the hermit, and when he was shriven of his sins and repentant, and his soul had departed, he made him be enshrouded of the damsel that followed him, and bestowed his arms and his horse on the hermit for his soul, and the horse of Aristot likewise.

IV

When mass had been sung for the knight that was dead, and the body buried, Perceval departed. 'Sir,' saith the damsel that followed him, 'Even now have you much to do. Of this cruel knight and felonous you have avenged this country. Now, God grant you find betimes the Red Knight that slew your uncle's son. I doubt not but that you will conquer him, but great misgiving have I of the lion, for it is the cruellest beast that saw I ever, and he so loveth his lord and his horse as never no beast loved another so much, and he helpeth his lord right hardily to defend him.'

V

Perceval goeth toward the great Deep Forest without
tarrying, and the damsel after. But, or ever he came thither,
he met a knight that was wounded right sore, both he and his
horse. 'Ha, Sir,' saith he to Perceval, 'Enter not into this
forest, whence I have scarce escaped with much pains. For
therein is a knight that had much trouble of rescuing me from
his lion; and no less am I in dread to pass on forward, for
there is a knight that is called Aristot, that without occasion
runneth upon the knights that pass through the forest.' 'Of
him,' saith the damsel, 'need you have no fear, for you may see
his head hanging at the knight's saddle-bow.'

VI

'Certes,' saith the knight, 'Never yet was I so glad of any
tidings I have heard, and well know I that he that slew him is
not lacking of great hardiment.' The knight departeth from
Perceval, but the lion had wounded his horse so passing sore in
the quarters that scarce could he go. 'Sir Knight,' saith
Perceval, 'Go to the hermit in the Deep Forest, and say I bade
him give you the destrier I left with him, for well I see that
you have sore need thereof, and you may repay him in some
other manner, for rather would he have something else than the
horse.' The knight giveth him much thanks of this that he
saith. He cometh to the hermit the best he may, and telleth
him according as he had been charged, and the hermit biddeth
him take which destrier he will for the love of the knight that
had slain the evil-doer, that did so many evil deeds in this
forest. 'And I will lend you them both twain if you will.'
'Sir,' saith the knight, 'I ask but for one of them.' He taketh
Aristot's horse, that seemed him the better, and straightway
mounteth thereon, and abandoneth his own, that might go no
further. He taketh leave of the hermit, and telleth him he will
right well repay him, but better had it befallen him and he had
not taken the horse, for thereof was he slain without reason
thereafter. A knight that was of the household of Aristot
overtook him at the corner of the forest, and knew his lord's
horse and had heard tell that Aristot was dead, wherefore he
went into the forest to bury him. He smote the knight

through the body with his spear and so slew him, then took the horse and went away forthwith. But, had Perceval known thereof, he would have been little glad, for that he asked the knight to go for the horse, but he did it only for the best, and for that he rode in great misease.

VII

Perceval goeth toward the Deep Forest, that is full broad and long and evil seeming, and when he was entered in, he had scarce ridden a space when he espied the lion that lay in the midst of a launde under a tree and was waiting for his master, that was gone afar into the forest, and the lion well knew that just there was the way whereby knights had to pass, and therefore had abided there. The damsel draweth her back for fear, and Perceval goeth toward the lion that had espied him already, and came toward him, eyes on fire and jaws yawning wide. Perceval aimeth his spear and thinketh to smite him in his open mouth, but the lion swerved aside and he caught him in the fore-leg and so dealt him a great wound, but the lion seizeth the horse with his claws on the croup, and rendeth the skin and the flesh above the tail. The horse, that feeleth himself wounded, catcheth him with his two hinder feet or ever he could get away, so passing strongly that he breaketh the master-teeth in his jaw. The lion gave out a roar so loud that all the forest resounded thereof. The Red Knight heareth his lion roar, and so cometh thither a great gallop, but, or ever he was come thither, Perceval had slain the lion. When the knight saw his lion dead, right sorry was he thereof. 'By my head,' saith he to Perceval, 'When you slew my lion you did it as a traitor!' 'And you,' saith Perceval, 'adjudged your own death when you slew my uncle's son, whose head this damsel beareth.' Perceval cometh against him without more words, and the knight in like manner with a great rushing, and breaketh his spear upon his shield. Perceval smiteth him with such force that he thrusteth his spear right through his body and beareth him to the ground dead beside his horse. Perceval alighteth of his own when he hath slain the knight, and then mounteth him on the Red Knight's horse for that his own might carry him no longer.

VIII

'Sir,' saith the damsel, 'My castle is in the midst of this forest, that the Red Knight reft away from me long ago. I pray you now come with me thither that I may be assured thereof in such sort as that I may have it again wholly.' 'Damsel,' saith Perceval, 'This have I no right to deny you.' They ride amidst the forest so long as that they come to the castle where the damsel ought to be. It stood in the fairest place of all the forest, and was enclosed of high walls battlemented, and within were fair-windowed halls. The tidings were come to the castle that their lord was dead. Perceval and the damsel entered in. He made the damsel be assured of them that were therein, and made them yield up her castle that they well knew was hers of right inheritance. The damsel made the head be buried that she had carried so long, and bade that every day should mass be done within for the soul of him. When Perceval had sojourned therein as long as pleased him, he departed thence. The damsel thanked him much of the bounty he had done her as concerning the castle that she had again by him, for never again should it be reconquered of another, as well she knew.

IX

Josephus telleth us in the scripture he recordeth for us, whereof this history was drawn out of Latin into Romance, that none need be in doubt that these adventures befell at that time in Great Britain and in all the other kingdoms, and plenty enow more befell than I record, but these were the most certain. The history saith that Perceval is come into a hold, there where his sister was in the house of a vavasour that was a right worshipful man. Each day the damsel made great dole of the knight that was to take her, for the day was already drawing somewhat nigh, and she knew not that he was dead. Full often lamented she the Widow Lady her mother, that in like sort made great dole for her daughter. The vavasour comforted the damsel right sweetly and longed for her brother Perceval, but little thought he that he was so near him. And Perceval is come to the hold all armed, and alighteth at the mounting-stage before the hall. The vavasour cometh

to meet him, and marvelleth much who he is, for the more part
believed that he was one of Aristot's knights. 'Sir,' saith the
vavasour, 'Welcome may you be!' 'Good adventure may
you have, Sir!' saith Perceval. He holdeth Aristot's head in
his hand by the hair, whereof the vavasour marvelled much
that he should carry a knight's head in such-wise. Perceval
cometh to the master-chamber of the hall, where his sister was,
that bewailed her right sore.

X

'Damsel,' saith he to his sister, 'Weep not, for your wedding
hath failed. You may know it well by this token!' He
throweth the head of Aristot before her on the ground, then
saith unto her: 'Behold here the head of him that was to take
you!' The damsel heareth Perceval her brother that was
armed, and thereby she knoweth him again. She leapeth up
and maketh him the greatest joy that ever damsel made to
knight. She knoweth not what to do. So joyful is she, that
all have pity on her that see her of her weeping for the joy
that she maketh of her brother. The story saith that they
sojourned therewithin and that the vavasour showed them
much honour. The damsel made cast the knight's head into
a river that ran round about the hold. The vavasour was
right glad of his death for the great felony that he had in him,
and for that needs must the damsel die in less than a year and
she had espoused him.

XI

When Perceval had been therein as long as it pleased him,
he thanked the vavasour much of the honour he had done him
and his sister, and departed, he and his sister along with him
on the mule whereon she had been brought thither. Perceval
rode so long on his journeys that he is come to Camelot
and findeth his mother in great dole for her daughter that
should be Queen, for she thought surely that never should she
see her more. Full sorrowful was she moreover of her brother,
the King Hermit that had been killed in such-wise. Perceval
cometh to the chamber where his mother was lying and might
not stint of making dole. He taketh his sister by the hand and
cometh before her. So soon as she knoweth him she beginneth

to weep for joy, and kisseth them one after the other. 'Fair son,' saith she, 'Blessed be the hour that you were born, for by you all my great joy cometh back to me! Now well may I depart, for I have lived long enow.' 'Lady,' saith he, 'Your life ought to be an offence to none, for to none hath it ever done ill, but, please God, you shall not end in this place, but rather you shall end in the castle that was your cousin's german, King Fisherman, there where is the most Holy Graal and the sacred hallows are.' 'Fair son,' saith she, 'You say well, and there would I fain be.' 'Lady,' saith he, 'God will provide counsel and means whereby you shall be there; and my sister, and she be minded to marry, will we set in good place, where she may live worshipfully.' 'Certes, fair brother,' saith she, 'None shall I never marry, save God alone.' 'Fair son,' saith the Widow Lady, 'The Damsel of the Car goeth to seek you, and I shall end not until such time as she hath found you.' 'Lady,' saith he, 'In some place will she have tidings of me and I of her.' 'Fair son,' saith the Lady, 'The damsel is here within that the felonous knight wounded through the arm, that carried off your sister, but she is healed.' 'Lady,' saith he, 'I am well avenged.' He telleth her all the adventures until the time when he reconquered the castle that was his uncle's. He sojourned long time with his mother in the castle, and saw that the land was all assured and peaceable. He departed thence and took his leave, for he had not yet achieved all that he had to do. His mother remained long time, and his sister, at Camelot, and led a good life and a holy. The lady made make a chapel right rich about the sepulchre that lay between the forest and Camelot, and had it adorned of rich vestments, and stablished a chaplain that should sing mass there every day. Sithence then hath the place been so builded up as that there is an abbey there and folk of religion, and many bear witness that there it is still, right fair. Perceval was departed from Camelot and entered into the great forest, and so rode of a long while until he had left his mother's castle far behind, and came toward evening to the hold of a knight that was at the head of the forest. He harboured him therein, and the knight showed him much honour and made him be unarmed, and brought him a robe to do on. Perceval seeth that the knight is a right simple man, and that he sigheth from time to time.

XII

'Sir,' saith he, 'Meseemeth you are not over joyous.'
'Certes, Sir,' saith the knight, 'I have no right to be, for a
certain man slew mine own brother towards the Deep Forest
not long since, and no right have I to be glad, for a worshipful
man was he and a loyal.' 'Fair Sir,' saith Perceval, 'Know you
who slew him?' 'Fair Sir, it was one of Aristot's knights, for
that he was sitting upon a horse that had been Aristot's, and
whereon another knight had slain him, and a hermit had lent
him to my brother for that the Red Knight's lion had maimed
his own.' Perceval was little glad of these tidings, for that he
had sent him that had been slain on account of the horse.
'Sir,' saith Perceval, 'Your brother had not deserved his
death, methinketh, for it was not he that slew the knight.'
'No, Sir, I know it all of a truth, but another, that slew the
Red Knight of the Deep Forest.' Perceval was silent thereupon. He lay the night at the hostel and was harboured right
well, and on the morrow departed when he had taken leave.
He wandered until he came to a hermitage there where he heard
mass. After the service, the hermit came unto him and said:
'Sir,' saith he, 'In this forest are knights all armed that are
keeping watch for the knight that slew Aristot and the Red
Knight and his lion as well. Wherefore they meet no knight
in this forest but they are minded to slay him for the knight
that slew these twain.' 'Sir,' saith Perceval, 'God keep me
from meeting such folk as would do me evil.'

XIII

With that he departed from the hermitage and took leave of
the hermit, and rideth until that he is come into the forest and
espieth the knight that sitteth on Aristot's horse for that he hath
slain the other knight. A second knight was with him. They
abide when they see Perceval. 'By my head,' saith one of
them, 'This same shield bare he that slew Aristot, as it was
told us, and, like enough, it may be he.' They come toward
him, full career. Perceval seeth them coming, and forgetteth
not his spurs, but rather cometh against them the speediest he
may. The two knights smote him upon the shield and brake

their spears.   Perceval overtaketh him that sitteth on Aristot's horse and thrusteth an ell's length of his spear through his body and so overthroweth him dead.

XIV

After that, he cometh to the other knight, that fain would have fled, and smiteth off the shoulder close to his side, and he fell dead by the side of the other.   He taketh both twain of their destriers, and knotteth the reins together and driveth them before him as far as the house of the hermit, that had issued forth of his hermitage.   He delivered unto him the horse of Aristot, and the other of the knight that he had sent thither. 'Sir,' saith Perceval, 'Well I know that and you shall see any knight that hath need of it and shall ask you, you will lend him one of these horses, for great courtesy is it to aid a worshipful man when one seeth him in misfortune.'   'Sir,' saith the hermit, 'But now since, were here three knights.   So soon as they knew that the two were dead whose horses you had delivered unto me, they departed, fleeing the speediest they might.   I praised them much of their going, and told them they did well not to die on such occasion, for that the souls of knights that die under arms are nigher to Hell than to Paradise.'

XV

Perceval, that never was without sore toil and travail so long as he lived, departed from the hermitage and went with great diligence right through the midst of the forest, and met a knight that came a great gallop over against him.   He knew Perceval by the shield that he bare.   'Sir,' saith he, 'I come from the Castle of the Black Hermit, there where you will find the Damsel of the Car as soon as you arrive, wherefore she sendeth you word by me that you speed your way and go to her to ask for the chess-board that was taken away from before Messire Gawain, or otherwise never again will you enter into the castle you have won.   Sir,' saith he, 'Haste, moreover, on account of a thing most pitiful that I heard in this forest.   I heard how a knight was leading a damsel against her will, beating her with a great scourge.   I passed by the launde on the one side and he on the other, so that I espied him through the underwood that was between us; but it seemed me that the damsel was bemoaning her for the son of the Widow Lady that had given her back her castle, and the knight said that for love of him he would put her into the Serpent's pit. An old knight and a priest went after the knight to pray him have mercy on the damsel, but so cruel is he, that so far from doing so, he rather waxed sore wroth for that they prayed it of him, and made cheer and semblant as though he would have slain them.' The knight departed from Perceval and taketh leave, and Perceval goeth along the way that the knight had come, thinking that he would go after the damsel, for he supposeth certainly that it is she to whom he gave back her castle, and would fain know what knight it is that entreateth her in such fashion. He hath ridden until he is come into the deepest of the forest and the thickest. He bideth awhile and listeneth and heareth the voice of the damsel, that was in a great valley where the Serpent's pit was, wherein the knight was minded to set her. She cried right loud for mercy, and wept, and the knight gave her great strokes of the scourge to make her be still. Perceval had no will to tarry longer, but rather cometh thither as fast as he may.

XVI

So soon as the damsel seeth Perceval, she knoweth him again. She claspeth her two hands together and saith, 'Ha, Sir, for God's sake have mercy! Already have you given me back the castle whereof this knight would reave me.' The horse whereon Perceval sat, the knight knew him. 'Sir,' saith he, 'This horse was the horse of Messire the Red Knight of the Deep Forest! Now at last know I that it was you that slew him!' 'It may well be,' saith Perceval, 'And if that I slew him, good right had I to do so, for he had cut off the head of a son of mine uncle, the which head this damsel carried of a long time.' 'By my head,' saith the knight, 'Sith that you slew him, you are my mortal enemy!' So he draweth off in the midst of the launde and Perceval likewise, and then they come together as fast as their horses may carry them, and either giveth other great buffets in the midst of their breast with their spears the most they may. Perceval smiteth the knight so passing hard that he overthroweth him to the ground right over the croup of his horse, and in the fall that he made, he to-brake him the

M

master-bone of his leg so that he might not move. And Perceval alighteth to the ground and cometh where the knight lay. And he crieth him mercy that he slay him not. And Perceval telleth him he need not fear death, nor that he is minded to slay him in such plight as he is, but that like as he was fain to make the damsel do he will make him do. He maketh alight the other old knight and the priest, then maketh the knight be carried to the Pit of the Serpent and the worms, whereof was great store. The pit was dark and deep. When that the knight was therein he might not live long for the worms that were there. The damsel thanked Perceval much of this goodness and of the other that he had done her. She departeth and returneth again to her castle, and was assured therein on all sides, nor never thereafter had she dread of no knight, for the cruel justice that Perceval had done on this one.

XVII

The son of the Widow Lady of his good knighthood knoweth not how to live without travail. He well knoweth that when he hath been at the Black Hermit's castle, he will in some measure have achieved his task. But many another thing behoveth him to do tofore, and little toil he thinketh it, whereof shall God be well pleased. He hath ridden so far one day and another, that he came into a land where he met knights stout and strong there where God was neither believed in nor loved, but where rather they adored false images and false Lord-Gods and devils that made themselves manifest. He met a knight at the entrance of a forest. 'Ha, Sir!' saith he to Perceval, 'Return you back! No need is there for you to go further, for the folk of this island are not well-believers in God. I may not pass through the land but by truce only. The Queen of this land was sister of the King of Oriande, that Lancelot killed in the battle and all his folk, and seized his land, wherein all the folk were misbelievers. Now throughout all the land they believe in the Saviour of the World. Thereof is she passing sorrowful, and hateth all them that believe in the New Law, insomuch as that she would not look upon any that believed, and prayed to her gods that never might she see none until such time as the New Law should be overthrown; and God, that hath power to do this, blinded her forthwith. Now

she supposeth that the false gods wherein she believeth have
done this, and saith that when the New Law shall fall, she will
have her sight again by the renewal of these gods, and by their
virtue, nor, until this hour, hath she no desire to see. And I
tell you this,' saith the knight, ' because I would not that you
should go thither as yet, for that I misdoubt of your being
troubled thereby.' ' Sir, gramercy,' saith Perceval, ' But no
knighthood is there so fair as that which is undertaken to set
forward the Law of God, and for Him ought one to make
better endeavour than for all other. In like manner as He
put His body in pain and travail for us, so ought each to put
his own for Him.' He departeth from the knight, and was
right joyous of this that he heard him say that Lancelot had
won a kingdom wherein he had done away the false Law.
But and he knew the tidings that the King had put him in
prison, he would not have been glad at all, for Lancelot was of
his lineage and was therefore good knight, and for this he
loved him right well.

XVIII

Perceval rideth until nightfall, and findeth a great castle
fortified with a great drawbridge, and there were tall ancient
towers within. He espied at the door a squire that had the
weight of a chain on his neck, and at the other end the chain
was fixed to a great bulk of iron. The chain was as long as
the length of the bridge. Then cometh he over against
Perceval when he seeth him coming. ' Sir,' saith he, ' Meseemeth you believe in God ? ' ' Fair friend, so do I, the best
I may.' ' Sir, for God's sake, enter not this castle ! ' ' Wherefore, fair friend ? ' saith Perceval. ' Sir,' saith he, ' I will tell
you. I am Christian, even as are you, and I am thrall within
there and guard this gate, as you see. But it is the most cruel
castle that I know, and it is called the Raving Castle. There
be three knights within there, full young and comely, but so
soon as they see a knight of the New Law, forthwith are they
out of their senses, and all raving mad, so that nought may
endure between them. Moreover, there is within one of the
fairest damsels that saw I ever. She guardeth the knights so
soon as they begin to rave, and so much they dread her that
they durst not disobey her commandment in aught that she
willeth, for many folk would they evilly entreat were it not for

her. And for that I am their thrall they put up with me, and
I have no fear of them, but many is the Christian knight that
hath come in hither that never hath issued hence.' 'Fair sweet
friend,' saith Perceval, 'I will enter in thither and I may, for I
should not know this day how to go elsewhither, and true it is
that greater power hath God than the devil.' He entereth into
the castle and alighteth in the midst of the courtyard.

XIX

The damsel was at the windows of the hall, that was of
passing great beauty. She cometh down as soon as she may,
and seeth Perceval come in and the cross on his shield, and
knoweth well thereby that he is Christian. 'Ha, Sir, for God's
sake,' saith she, 'Come not up above, for there be three of the
comeliest knights that ever were seen that are playing at tables
and at dice in a chamber, and they are brothers-german. They
will all go out of their senses so soon as they shall see you!'

XX

'Damsel,' saith Perceval, 'Please God, so shall they not, and
such a miracle is good to see, for it is only right that all they
who will not believe in God should be raving mad when they
see the things that come of Him.' Perceval goeth up into the
hall, all armed, for all that the damsel saith. She followeth
him as fast as she may. The three knights espied Perceval all
armed and the cross on his shield, and forthwith leapt up and
were beside themselves. They rolled their eyes and tore
themselves and roared like devils. There were axes and
swords in the hall that they go to lay hold on, and they are
fain to leap upon Perceval, but no power have they to do so,
for such was the will of God. When they saw that they might
not come a-nigh him, they ran either on other and so slew themselves between them, nor would they stint their fighting together
for the damsel. Perceval beheld the miracle of these folks that
were thus killed, and the damsel that made right great dole
thereof. 'Ha, damsel,' saith he, 'Weep not, but repent you
of this false belief, for they that are unwilling to believe in
God shall die like mad folks and devils!' Perceval made the
squires that were there within bear the bodies out of the hall,
and made them be cast into a running water, and straightway

slew all the other, for that they were not minded to believe.
The castle was all emptied of the misbelieving folk save only
the damsel and those that waited upon her, and the Christian
thrall that guarded the gate. Perceval set him forth of the
chain, then led him up into the hall and made him disarm him.
He found sundry right rich robes. The damsel, that was of
right great beauty, looked at him and saw that he was a full
comely knight, and well pleased she was with him. She
honoured him in right great sort, but she might not forget the
three knights that were her brothers, and made sore dole for
them.

XXI

'Damsel,' saith Perceval, 'Nought availeth it to make this
dole, but take comfort on some other manner.' Perceval looked
at the hall from one end to the other and saw that it was right
rich, and the damsel, in whom was full great beauty, stinted of
making dole to look at Perceval. She seeth that he is comely
knight and gentle and tall and well furnished of good conditions,
wherefore he pleaseth her much, and forthwith beginneth she
to love him, and saith to herself that, so he would leave his
God for the god in whom she believed, right glad would she
be thereof, and would make him lord of her castle, for it
seemed her that better might she not bestow it, and, sith that
her brothers are dead, there may be no bringing of them back,
and therefore better would it be to forget her dole. But little
knew she Perceval's thought, for had she known that which
he thinketh, she would have imagined not this; for, and had
she been Christian he might not have been drawn to love her in
such sort as she thinketh, sith that Josephus telleth us that
never did he lose his virginity for woman, but rather died
virgin and chaste and clean of his body. In this mind was she
still, nor never might she refrain her heart from him. Thinketh
she rather that, and he knew she was minded to love him, right
joyous would he be thereof, for that she is of so passing beauty.
Perceval asketh the damsel what she hath in her thought?
'Sir,' saith she, 'Nought think I but only good and you will.'
'Damsel,' saith Perceval, 'Never, please God, shall there be
hindrance of me but that you renounce this evil Law and
believe in the good.' 'Sir,' saith she, 'Do you renounce yours
for love of me, and I will do your commandment and your will.'

XXII

'Damsel,' saith Perceval, 'Nought availeth to tell me this. Were you man like as you are woman, your end would have come with the others. But, please God, your tribulation shall lend itself to good.' 'Sir,' saith she, 'So you are willing to promise me that you will love me like as knight ought to love damsel, I am well inclined to believe in your God.' 'Damsel, I promise you as I am a Christian that so you are willing to receive baptism, I will love you as he that firmly believeth in God ought to love damsel.' 'Sir,' saith she, 'I ask no more of you.' She biddeth send for a holy man, a hermit that was in the forest appurtenant, and right gladly came he when he heard the tidings. They held her up and baptized her, both her and her damsels with her. Perceval held her at the font. Josephus witnesseth us in this history that she had for name Celestre. And great joy made she of her baptism, and her affections turned she unto good. The hermit remained there with her, and taught her to understand the firm believe, and did the service of Our Lord. The damsel was of right good life and right holy, and ended thereafter in many good works.

XXIII

Perceval departed from the castle, and gave thanks to Our Lord and praise, that He hath allowed him to conquer a castle so cruel and to attorn it to the Law. He went his way a great pace, all armed, until he came into a country wherein was great grief being made, and the more part said that he was come that should destroy their Law, for that already had he won their strongest castle. He is come towards an ancient castle that was at the head of a forest. He looketh and seeth at the entrance of the gateway a full great throng of folk. He seeth a squire come forth thence, and asketh him unto whom belongeth the castle. 'Sir,' saith he, 'It is Queen Jandree's, that hath made her be brought before her gate with the folk you see yonder, for she hath heard tell how the knights of the Raving Castle are dead, and another knight that hath conquered the castle hath made the damsel be baptized, wherefore much she marvelleth how this may be. She is in much dread of losing her land, for her brother Madeglant of Oriande is dead, so that she may no longer look to none for succour, and she hath been told how the knight that conquered the Raving Castle is the Best Knight of the World, and that none may endure against him. For this doubtance and fear of him she is minded to go to one of her own castles that is somewhat stronger.' Perceval departeth from the squire and rideth until they that were at the entrance of the gateway espied him. They saw the Red Cross that he bare on his shield, and said to the Queen, 'Lady, a Christian knight is coming into this castle.' 'Take heed,' saith she, 'that it be not he that is about to overthrow our Law!' Perceval cometh thither and alighteth, and cometh before the Queen all armed. The Queen asketh what he seeketh.

XXIV

'Lady,' saith he, 'Nought seek I save good only to yourself so you hinder it not.' 'You come,' saith she, 'from the Raving Castle, there where three brothers are slain, whereof is great loss.' 'Lady,' saith he, 'At that castle was I, and now fain would I that your own were at the will of Jesus Christ, in like manner as is that.' 'By my head,' saith she, 'And your Lord hath so great power as is said, so will it be.' 'Lady, His virtue and His puissance are far greater than they say.' 'That would I fain know,' saith she, 'presently, and I am fain to pray you that you depart not from me until that it hath been proven.' Perceval granteth it gladly. She returned into her castle and Perceval with her. When he was alighted he went up into the hall. They that were within marvelled them much that she should thus give consent, for never, sithence that she had been blind, might she allow no knight of the New Law to be so nigh her, and made slay all them that came into her power, nor might she never see clear so long as she had one of them before her. Now is her disposition altered in such sort as that she would fain she might see clear him that hath come in, for she hath been told that he is the comeliest knight of the world and well seemeth to be as good as they witness of him.

XXV

Perceval remained there gladly for that he saw the lady's cruelty was somewhat slackened, and it seemed him that it

would be great joy and she were willing to turn to God, and
they that are within there, for well he knoweth that so she
should hold to the New Law, all they of the land would be of
the same mind. When Perceval had lain the night at the
castle, the Lady on the morrow sent for all the more powerful
of her land, and came forth of her chamber into the hall where
Perceval was, seeing as clear as ever she had seen aforetime.
' Lords,' saith she, ' Hearken ye all, for now will I tell you the
truth like as it hath befallen me. I was lying in my bed last
night, and well know ye that I saw not a whit, and made my
orisons to our gods that they would restore me my sight. It
seemed me they made answer that they had no power so to do,
but that I should make be slain the knight that was arrived
here, and that and I did not, sore wroth would they be with
me. And when I had heard their voices say that nought might
they avail me as for that I had prayed of them, I remembered
me of the Lord in whom they that hold the New Law believe.
I prayed Him right sweetly that, and so it were that He had
such virtue and such puissance as many said, He would make
me see clear, so as that I might believe in Him. At that hour
I fell on sleep, and meseemed that I saw one of the fairest
Ladies in the world, and she was delivered of a Child therewithin, and He had about Him a great brightness of light like
it were the sun shone at right noonday.

XXVI

' When the Child was born, so passing fair was He and so
passing gentle and of so sweet semblant that the looks of Him
pleased me well ; and meseemed that at His deliverance there
was a company of folk the fairest that were seen ever, and they
were like as it had been birds and made full great joy. And
methought that an ancient man that was with Her, told me that
My Lady had lost no whit of her maidenhood for the Child.
Well pleased was I the while this thing lasted me. It seemed
me that I saw it like as I do you. Thereafter, methought I saw
a Man bound to a stake, in whom was great sweetness and
humility, and an evil folk beat Him with scourges and rods
right cruelly, so that the blood ran down thereof. They
would have no mercy on Him. Of this might I not hold myself but that I wept for pity of Him. Therewithal I awoke

and marvelled much whence it should come and what it might
be.   But in anyway it pleased me much that I had seen it.   It
seemed me after this, that I saw the same Man that had been
bound to the stake set upon a cross, and nailed thereon right
grievously and smitten in the side with a spear, whereof had I
such great pity that needs must I weep of the sore pain that I
saw Him suffer.   I saw the Lady at the feet of the cross, and
knew her again that I had seen delivered of the Child, but none
might set in writing the great dole that she made.   On the
other side of the cross was a man that seemed not joyful, but he
recomforted the Lady the fairest he might.   And another folk
were there that collected His blood in a most holy Vessel that
one of them held for it.

XXVII

'Afterward, methought I saw Him taken down of hanging
on the cross, and set in a sepulchre of stone.   Thereof had I
great pity, for, so long as meseemed I saw Him thus, never
might I withhold me from weeping.   And so soon as the pity
came into my heart, and the tears into my eyes, I had my sight
even as you see.   In such a Lord as this ought one to believe,
for He suffered death when He might lightly have avoided it
had He so willed, but He did it to save His people.   In this
Lord I will that ye all believe, and so renounce our false gods,
for they be devils and therefore may not aid us nor avail us.
And he that will not believe, him will I make be slain or die a
shameful death.'   The Lady made her be held up and baptized,
and all them that would not do the same she made be destroyed
and banished.   This history telleth us that her name was
Salubre.   She was good lady and well believed in God, and so
holy life led she thereafter that in a hermitage she died.
Perceval departed from the castle right joyous in his heart of the
Lady and her people that believed in the New Law.

BRANCH XXXIII

Title I

AFTERWARD, this title telleth us that Meliot of Logres was departed from Castle Perilous sound and whole, by virtue of the sword that Lancelot had brought him, and of the cloth that he took in the Chapel Perilous. But sore sorrowful was he of the tidings he had heard that Messire Gawain was in prison and he knew not where, but he had been borne on hand that two knights that were kinsmen of them of the Raving Castle that had slain one another, had shut him in prison on account of Perceval that had won the castle. Now, saith Meliot of Logres, never shall he have ease again until he knoweth where Messire Gawain is. He rideth amidst a forest, and prayeth God grant him betimes to hear witting of Messire Gawain. The forest was strange and gloomy. He rode until nightfall but might not find neither hold nor hermitage. He looketh right amidst the forest before him and seeth a damsel sitting that bemoaneth herself full sore. The moon was dark and the place right foul of seeming and the forest gloomy of shadow. 'Ha, damsel, and what do you here at this hour?' 'Sir,' saith she, 'I may not amend it, the more is my sorrow. For the place is more perilous than you think. Look,' saith she, 'up above, and you will see the occasion wherefore I am here.' Meliot looketh and seeth two knights all armed hanging up above the damsel's head. Thereof much marvelleth he. 'Ha, damsel,' saith he, 'Who slew these knights so foully?' 'Sir,' saith she, 'The Knight of the Galley that singeth in the sea.' 'And wherefore hath he hanged them in such wise?' 'For this,' saith she, 'that they believed in God and His sweet Mother. And so behoveth me to watch them here for forty days, that none take them down of hanging, for and they were taken hence he would lose his castle, he saith, and would cut off

346

my head.' 'By my head,' saith Meliot, 'Such watch is foul shame to damsel, and no longer shall you remain here.' 'Ha, Sir,' saith the damsel, 'Then shall I be a dead woman, for he is of so great cruelty that none scarce might protect me against him.'

II

'Damsel,' saith Meliot, 'Foul shame would it be and I left here these knights in such wise for the reproach of other knights.' Meliot made them graves with his sword, and so buried them the best he might. 'Sir,' saith the damsel, 'And you take not thought to protect me, the knight will slay me. To-morrow, when he findeth not the knights, he will search all the forest to look for me.' Meliot and the damsel together go their way through the forest until they come to a chapel where was wont to be a hermit that the Knight of the Galley had destroyed. He helpeth down the damsel of his horse, and afterward they entered into the chapel, where was a great brightness of light, and a damsel was there that kept watch over a dead knight. Meliot marvelleth him much. 'Damsel,' said Meliot, 'When was this knight killed?' 'Sir, yesterday the Knight of the Galley slew him on the sea-shore, wherefore behoveth me thus keep watch, and in the morning will he come hither or ever he go to the castle where Messire Gawain hath to-morrow to fight with a lion, all unarmed, and my Lady, that is mistress both of me and of this damsel you have brought hither, will likewise be brought to-morrow to the place where the lion is to slay Messire Gawain, and she in like sort will be afterward delivered to the lion and she renounce not the New Law wherein the knight that came from Raving Castle, whereof she is lady, hath made her believe; and we ourselves shall be in like manner devoured along with her. But this damsel would still have taken respite of my death and she had still kept guard over the knights that were so foully hanged above her. Natheless, sith that you have taken them down from where they were hanging, you have done a right good deed, whatsoever betide, for the Lord of the Red Tower will give his castle to the knight for this.' Meliot is right joyous of the tidings that he hath heard of Messire Gawain that he is still on live, for well knoweth he, sith that the Knight of the Galley will come

by the chapel there, that he will come thither or ever Messire
Gawain doth battle with the lion. 'Sir,' saith the damsel of the
chapel, 'For God's sake, take this damsel to a place of safety,
for the knight will be so wood mad of wrath and despite so
soon as he cometh hither, that he will be fain to smite off her
head forthwith, and of yourself also have I great fear.'

III

'Damsel,' saith Meliot, 'The knight is but a man like as am
I.' 'Yea, Sir, but stronger is he and more cruel than seem you
to be.' Meliot was in the chapel the night until the morrow,
and heard the knight coming like a tempest, and he brought
with him the lady of the castle and reviled her from time to
time, and Meliot seeth him come, and a dwarf that followeth
after him a great pace. He crieth out to him: 'Sir, behold
there the disloyal knight through whom you have lost your
castle. Now haste! Avenge yourself of him! After that
will we go to the death of Messire Gawain?' Meliot, so soon
as he espieth him, mounteth and maketh his arms ready. 'Is
it you,' saith the Knight of the Galley, 'that hath trespassed on
my demesne and taken down my knights?' 'By my head,
yours were they not! Rather were they the knights of God,
and foul outrage have you done herein when you slew them so
shamefully.' He goeth toward the knight without more words,
and smiteth him so passing strong amidst the breast that he
pierceth the habergeon and thrusteth all the iron of his spear
into his body and afterward draweth it back to him with a
great wrench. And the knight smiteth him so hard on his
shield that he maketh an ell's length pass beyond, for right
wroth was he that he was wounded. The dwarf crieth to
him, 'Away, then! The knight endureth against you that
have slain so many of them!' The Knight of the Galley
waxeth wood wrath. He taketh his career, and cometh as
fast as his horse may carry him, and smiteth Meliot so strongly
that he breaketh his spear in such sort that he maketh both
him and his horse stagger. But Meliot catcheth him better,
for he thrusteth the spear right through his body and hurleth
against him at the by-passing with such stoutness and force
that he maketh him fall dead to the ground from his horse.
The dwarf thought to escape, but Meliot smote off his head,

whereof the damsels gave him great thanks, for many a mischief had he wrought them.

IV

Meliot buried the knight that he found in the chapel dead, then told the damsels that he might abide no longer, but would go succour Messire Gawain and he might. The damsels were horsed to their will, for one had the horse of the knight that was slain and the other the horse of the dwarf. The other damsel was come upon a mule, and they said that they would go back, for the country was made all safe by the death of the knight. They thanked Meliot much, for they say truly that he hath rescued them from death. Meliot departeth from the damsels and goeth right amidst the forest as he that would most fain hear tidings of Messire Gawain. When he had ridden of a long space, he met a knight that was coming all armed at a great pace. 'Sir Knight,' saith he to Meliot, 'Can you tell me tidings of the Knight of the Galley?' 'What have you to do therein?' saith Meliot. 'Sir, the Lord of the Red Tower hath made bring Messire Gawain into a launde of this forest, and there, all unarmed, must he do battle with a lion. So my lord is waiting for the Knight of the Galley, that is to bring two damsels thither that the lion will devour when he shall have slain Messire Gawain.' 'Will the battle be presently?' saith Meliot. 'Yea, Sir,' saith the knight, 'Soon enough betimes, for Messire Gawain hath already been led thither and there bound to a stake until such time as the lion shall be come. Then will he be unbound, but even then two knights all armed will keep watch on him. But tell me tidings of the Knight of the Galley, and you have seen him?' 'Go forward,' saith he, 'and you will hear tidings of him.' Meliot departeth thereupon, a great gallop, and cometh nigh the launde whereunto Messire Gawain had been brought. He espied the two knights that kept guard over him, and if that Messire Gawain were in fear, little marvel was it, for he thought that his end had come. Meliot espied him bound to an iron staple with cords about the body on all sides so that he might not move. Meliot hath great pity thereof in his heart, and saith to himself that he will die there sooner than Messire Gawain shall die. He clappeth spurs to his horse when he cometh nigh the knights, and overtaketh one of them with such a rush that he thrusteth his spear right through his body, and beareth him down dead. The other was fain to go to the castle for succour when he saw his fellow dead. Meliot slew him forthwith. He cometh to Messire Gawain, and so unbindeth him and cutteth the cords wherewith he is bound. 'Sir,' saith he, 'I am Meliot of Logres, your knight.'

V

When Messire Gawain felt himself unbound, no need to ask whether he had joy thereof. The tidings were come to the Red Court that Queen Jandree was christened and baptized, and that the Knight was come that had such force and puissance in him that none might endure against him for the God in whom he believed, and they knew likewise that the Knight of the Galley was dead, and Messire Gawain unbound and the knights that guarded him slain. They say that there may they not abide, so they depart from the castle and say that they will cross the sea to protect their bodies, for that there they may have no safety.

VI

When Meliot had delivered Messire Gawain he made him be armed with the arms, such as they were, of one of the knights he had slain. Messire Gawain mounted on a horse such as pleased him, and right great joy had he at heart. They marvel much how it is that they of the castle have not come after them, but they know not their thought nor how they are scared. 'Meliot,' saith Messire Gawain, 'You have delivered me from death this time and one other, nor never had I acquaintance with any knight that hath done so much for me in so short a time as have you.' They departed the speediest they might and rode nigh enow to the castle, but they heard none moving within nor any noise, nor saw they none issue forth, and much marvelled they that none should come after them. They rode until they came to the head of the forest and caught sight of the sea that was nigh enough before them, and saw that there was a great clashing of arms at the brink of the sea. A single knight was doing battle with all them that would fain have entered into a ship, and held stour so stiffly against them that he toppled the more part into the sea. They went thither as fast as they might, and when they drew nigh to the ship they knew that it was Perceval by his arms and his shield. Or ever they reached it, the ship was put off into the midst of the sea, wherein he was launched of his own great hardiment, and they went on fighting against him within the ship. 'Meliot,' saith Messire Gawain, 'See you, there is Perceval the Good Knight, and now may we say of a truth that he is in sore peril of death; for that ship, save God bethink Him thereof, shall arrive in such manner and in such a place as that never more shall we have no witting of him, and, so he perish for ever, no knight on live may have power to set forward the Law of our Lord.'

VII

Messire Gawain seeth the ship going further away, and Perceval that defendeth himself therein against them that set upon him. Right heavy is he that he came not sooner, or ever the ship had put off from the land. He turneth back, he and Meliot together, and right sorrowful was Messire Gawain of Perceval, for they knew not in what land he might arrive, and, might he have followed, right gladly would he have gone after him to aid him. They have ridden until they meet a knight. Messire Gawain asketh him whence he cometh, and he saith from King Arthur's court. 'What tidings can you tell us thereof?' saith Messire Gawain. 'Sir, bad enough!' saith he. 'King Arthur hath neglected all his knights for Briant of the Isles, and hath put one of his best knights in prison.' 'What is his name?' saith Messire Gawain. 'Sir, he is called Lancelot of the Lake. He had reconquered all the islands that had been reft of King Arthur, and slain King Madeglant, and conquered the land of Oriande that he turned to the belief of the Saviour of the World, and, so soon as he had conquered his enemies, King Arthur sent for him forthwith and straightway put him in his prison by the counsel of Briant of the Isles. But King Arthur will have a surfeit of friends betimes; for King Claudas hath assembled his folk in great plenty to reconquer the kingdom of Oriande and come back upon King Arthur by the counsel of Briant of the Isles that betrayeth the King, for he hath made him his Seneschal and commander of all his land.' 'Sir Knight,' saith Messire Gawain, 'Needs must the King miscarry that setteth aside the counsel of his good knights for the leasings of a traitor.' Thereupon the knight departed from Messire Gawain. Right heavy is he of this that he hath said, that the King hath put Lancelot in prison. Never tofore did he aught whereby he wrought so much to blame.

BRANCH XXXIV

Title I

HEREUPON the story is silent of Messire Gawain and Meliot and speaketh of King Claudas that hath assembled a great folk by the counsel of Briant of the Isles to come into the land of King Arthur, for he knoweth that it is disgarnished of the good knights that wont there to be, and he knoweth all the secret plottings of the court and what power King Arthur hath withal. He draweth toward his land the nighest he may, and hath won back the kingdom of Oriande all at his will. But they of Albanie still hold against him and challenge the land the best they may. Tidings thereof come to the court of King Arthur, and they of the country sent him word that so he send them not succour betimes they will yield up the land to King Claudas, and oftentimes they long after Lancelot, and say that so they had a defender like him, the islands would be all at peace. The King sent Briant of the Isles thither many times, that ever incontinent returned thence discomfit, but never sent he thither him that should have power to protect the land against King Claudas. King Arthur was sore troubled, for no witting had he of Messire Gawain nor Messire Ywain nor of others whereby his court had use of right to be feared and dreaded and of high renown throughout all other kingdoms. The King was one day in the hall at Cardoil, right heavy; and he was at one of the windows, and remembered him of the Queen and of his good knights that he wont to see oftener at court, whereof the more part were dead, and of the adventures that wont to befall therein whereof they saw none no longer. Lucan the Butler seeth him right heavy and draweth nigh unto him quietly.

353

II

'Sir,' saith he, 'Meseemeth you are without joy.' 'Lucan,' said the King, 'Joy hath been somewhat far from me sithence that the Queen hath been dead, and Gawain and the other knights have held aloof from my court so that they deign come hither no longer. Moreover, King Claudas warreth upon me and conquereth my lands so that no power have I to rescue me for default of my knights.' 'Sir,' saith Lucan, 'Herein is there nought whereof you have right to accuse any save yourself alone. For you have done evil unto him that hath served you, and good unto them that are traitors to you. You have one of the best knights in the world and the most loyal in your prison, wherefore all the other hold them aloof from your court. Lancelot had served you well by his good will and by his good knighthood, nor never had he done you any disservice whereof you might in justice have done him such shame ; nor never will your enemies withhold them from you nor have dread of you save only through him and other your good knights. And know of a truth that Lancelot and Messire Gawain are the best of your court.' 'Lucan,' saith King Arthur, 'So thought I ever again to have affiance in him, I would make him be set forth of my prison, for well I know that I have wrought dis- courteously toward him ; and Lancelot is of a great heart, wherefore would he not slacken of his despite for that which hath been done unto him until such time as he should be avenged thereof, for no king is there in the world, how puissant soever he be, against whom he durst not well maintain his right.'

III

'Sir,' saith Lucan, 'Lancelot well knoweth that and you had taken no counsel but your own, he would not have been thus entreated, and I dare well say that never so long as he liveth will he misdo in aught towards you, for he hath in him much valour and loyalty, as many a time have you had good cause to know. Wherefore, and you would fain have aid and succour and hold your realm again, behoveth you set him forth of the prison, or otherwise never will you succeed herein, and, if you do not so, you will lose your land by treason.' The King held by the counsel of Lucan the Butler. He made bring Lancelot before

him into the midst of the hall, that was somewhat made ean of
his being in prison, but he bore him as he wont, nor might none
look at him to whom he seemed not to be good knight.
' Lancelot,' saith the King, ' How is it with you ? ' ' Sir,' saith
he, ' It hath been ill with me long time, but, please God, it
shall be better hereafter.' ' Lancelot,' saith the King, ' I
repent me of this that I have done to you, and I have bethought
me much of the good services I have found in you, wherefore I
will do you amends thereof at your will, in such sort as that the
love between us shall be whole as it was tofore.'

IV

' Sir,' saith Lancelot, ' Your amends love I much, and your
love more than of any other; but never, please God, will I
misdo you for aught that you may have done to me, for it is well
known that I have not been in prison for no treason I have done,
nor for no folly, but only for that it was your will.   Never will
it be reproached me as of shame, and, sith that you have done
me nought whereof I may have blame nor reproach, my devoir
it is to withhold me from hating you ; for you are my lord, and
if that you do me ill, without flattery of myself the ill you do me
is your own ; but, please God, whatsoever you have done me,
never shall my aid fail you, rather, everywhere will I set my
body in adventure for your love, in like sort as I have done
many a time.'

V

In the court of King Arthur was right great joy of the most
part when they heard that Lancelot was set forth of prison, but
not a whit rejoiced were Briant and his folk. The King
commanded that Lancelot should be well cared for and made
whole again, and that all should be at his commandment. The
court was all overjoyed thereof, and they said : now at last
might the King make war in good assurance. Lancelot was
foremost in the King's court and more redoubted than was ever
another of the knights. Briant of the Isles came one day before
the King. ' Sir,' saith he, ' Behold, here is Lancelot that
wounded me in your service, wherefore I will that he know I
am his enemy.' ' Briant,' saith Lancelot, ' And if that you
deserved it tofore, well may you be sorry thereof, and sith that

you wish to be mine enemy, your friend will I not be. For well may I deem of your love according as I have found it in you.' 'Sir,' saith Briant to the King, 'You are my lord, and I am one you are bound to protect. You know well that so rich am I in lands and so puissant in friends that I may well despise mine enemy, nor will I not remain at your court so long as Lancelot is therein. Say not that I depart thence with any shame as toward myself. Rather thus go I hence as one that will gladly avenge me, so I have place and freedom, and I see plainly and know that you and your court love him far better than you love me, wherefore behoveth me take thought thereof.' 'Briant,' saith the King, 'Remain as yet, and I will make amends for you to Lancelot, and I myself will make amends for him to you.'

VI

'Sir,' saith Briant, 'By the faith that I owe to you, none amends will I have of him nor other until such time as I have drawn as much blood of his body as did he of mine, and I will well that he know it.' With that Briant departeth from the court all wrathful, but if that Lancelot had not feared to anger the King, Briant would not have ridden a league English or ever he had followed and forced him to fight. Briant goeth toward the Castle of the Hard Rock, and saith that better would it have been for the King that Lancelot were still in prison, for that such a plea will he move against him and he may bring it to bear, as that he shall lose thereof the best parcel of his land. He is gone into the land of King Claudas, and saith that now at last hath he need of his aid, for Lancelot is issued forth of the King's prison and is better loved at court than all other, so that the King believeth in no counsel save his only. King Claudas sweareth unto him and maketh pledge that never will he fail him, and Briant to him again.

BRANCH XXXV

Title I

HEREWITHAL is the story silent of Briant and talketh of Perceval, that the ship beareth away right swiftly; but so long hath he held battle therein that every one hath he slain of them that were in the ship save only the pilot that steereth her, for him hath he in covenant that he will believe in God and renounce his evil Law. Perceval is far from land so that he seeth nought but sea only, and the ship speedeth onward, and God guideth him, as one that believeth in Him and loveth Him and serveth Him of a good heart. The ship ran on by night and by day as it pleased God, until that they saw a castle and an island of the sea. He asked his pilot if he knew what castle it was. 'Certes,' saith he, 'Not I, for so far have we run that I know not neither the sea nor the stars.' They come nigh the castle, and saw four that sounded bells at the four corners of the town, right sweetly, and they that sounded them were clad in white garments. They are come thither.

II

So soon as the ship had taken haven under the castle, the sea withdraweth itself back, so that the ship is left on dry land. None were therein save Perceval, his horse, and the pilot. They issued forth of the ship and went by the side of the sea toward the castle, and therein were the fairest halls and the fairest mansions that any might see ever. He looketh underneath a tree that was tall and broad and seeth the fairest fountain and the clearest that any may devise, and it was all surrounded of rich pillars, and the gravel thereof seemed to be gold and precious stones. Above this fountain were two men sitting, their beards and hair whiter than driven snow, albeit they seemed young of visage. So soon as they saw Perceval they dressed them to meet him, and bowed down and worshipped the shield that he bare at his neck, and kissed the cross and then the boss wherein were the hallows. 'Sir,' say they, 'Marvel not of this that we do, for well knew we the knight that bare this shield tofore you. Many a time we saw him or ever God were crucified.' Perceval marvelleth much of this that they say, for they talk of a time that is long agone.

III

'Lords, know ye then how he was named?' Say they, 'Joseph of Abarimacie, but no cross was there on the shield before the death of Jesus Christ. But he had it set thereon after the crucifixion of Jesus Christ for the sake of the Saviour that he loved so well.' Perceval took off the shield from his neck, and one of the worshipful men setteth upon it as it were a posy of herbs that was blooming with the fairest flowers in the world. Perceval looketh beyond the fountain and seeth in a right fair place a round vessel like as it were ivory, and it was so large that there was a knight within, all armed. He looketh thereinto and seeth the knight, and speaketh unto him many times, but never the more willeth the knight to answer him. Perceval looketh at him in wonderment, and cometh back to the good men and asketh them who is this knight, and they tell him that he may know not as yet. They lead him to a great hall and bear his shield before him, whereof they make right great joy, and show thereunto great worship. He seeth the hall right rich, for hall so rich and so fair had he seen never. It was hung about with right rich cloths of silk, and in the midst of the hall was imaged the Saviour of the World so as He is in His majesty, with the apostles about Him, and within were great galleries that were full of folk and seemed to be of great holiness, and so were they, for had they not been good men they might not there have remained.

IV

'Sir,' say the two Masters to Perceval, 'This house that you see here so rich, is the hall royal.' 'By my faith,' saith Perceval, 'So ought it well to be, for never saw I none so much of worth.'

He looketh all around, and seeth the richest tables of gold and ivory that he saw ever. One of the Masters clappeth his hands thrice, and three and thirty men come into the hall all in a company. They were clad in white garments, and not one of them but had a red cross in the midst of his breast, and they seemed to be all of an age. As soon as they enter into the hall they do worship to God Our Lord and set out their cups. Then went they to wash at a great laver of gold, and then went to sit at the tables. The Masters made Perceval sit at the most master-table with themselves. They were served thereat right gloriously, and Perceval looked about him more gladlier than he ate.

V

And while he was thus looking, he seeth a chain of gold come down above him loaded with precious stones, and in the midst thereof was a crown of gold. The chain descended a great length and held on to nought save to the will of Our Lord only. As soon as the Masters saw it descending they opened a great wide pit that was in the midst of the hall, so that one could see the hole all openly. As soon as the entrance of this pit was discovered, there issued thence the greatest cry and most dolorous that any heard ever, and when the worshipful men hear it, they stretched out their hands towards Our Lord and all began to weep. Perceval heareth this dolour, and marvelleth much what it may be. He seeth that the chain of gold descendeth thither and is there stayed until they have well-nigh eaten, and then draweth itself again into the air and so goeth again aloft. But Perceval knoweth not what became thereof, and the Master covereth the pit again, that was right grisly to see, and pitiful to hear were the voices that issued therefrom.

VI

The Good Men rose from the tables when they had eaten, and gave thanks right sweetly to Our Lord; and then returned thither whence they had come. 'Sir,' saith the Master to Perceval, 'The chain of gold that you have seen is right precious and the crown of gold likewise. But never may you issue

forth from hence save you promise to return so soon as you shall
see the ship and the sail crossed of a red cross ; otherwise may
you not depart hence.' 'Tell me,' saith he, 'of the chain of gold
and the crown, what it may be ?' 'We will tell you not,' saith
one of the Masters, 'save you promise that which I tell you.'
'Certes, Sir,' saith Perceval, 'I promise you faithfully, that so
soon as I shall have done that I have to do for my lady my
mother and one other, that I will return hither, so I be on live
and I see your ship so marked as you say.' 'Yea, be you faith-
ful to the end herein, and you shall have the crown of gold upon
your head so soon as you return, and so shall you be seated in
the throne, and shall be king of an island that is near to this,
right plenteous of all things good, for nought is there in the
world that is there lacking that is needful for man's body.
King Hermit was the king thereof that thus hath garnished it,
and for that he approved himself so well in this kingdom, and
that they who are in the island consented thereto, is he chosen
to be king of a greater realm.   Now they desire that another
worshipful man be sent them for king, that shall do for them as
much good as did he, but take you good heed, sith that you will
be king therein, that the island be well garnished ; for, and you
garnish it not well, you will be put into the Poverty-stricken
Island, the crying whereof you have but now since heard, and
the crown thereof will again be reft from you.   For they that
have been kings of the Plenteous Island and have not well
approved them, are among the folk that you saw in the Poverty-
stricken Island, lacking in all things good.   And so I tell you
that King Hermit, whom you will succeed, hath sent thither a
great part of his folk.   There are the heads sealed in silver,
and the heads sealed in lead, and the bodies whereunto these
heads belonged ; I tell you that you must make come thither
the head both of the King and of the Queen.   But of the other
I tell you that they are in the Poverty-stricken Island.   But we
know not whether they shall ever issue forth thence.'

VII

'Sir,' saith Perceval, 'Tell me of the knight that is all armed
in the ivory vessel, who he is, and what is the name of this
castle ?'   'You may not know,' saith the Master, 'until your
return.   But tell me tidings of the most Holy Graal, that you

reconquered, is it still in the holy chapel that was King Fisherman's?' 'Yea, Sir,' saith Perceval, 'And the sword wherewith
S. John was beheaded, and other hallows in great plenty.' 'I
saw the Graal,' saith the Master, 'or ever Joseph, that was
uncle to King Fisherman, collected therein the blood of Jesus
Christ. Know that well am I acquainted with all your lineage,
and of what folk you were born. For your good knighthood
and for your good cleanness and for your good valour came you
in hither, for such was Our Lord's will, and take heed that you
be ready when place shall be, and time shall come, and you shall
see the ship apparelled.' 'Sir,' saith Perceval, 'Most willingly
shall I return, nor never would I have sought to depart but for
my lady my mother, and for my sister, for never have I seen
no place that so much hath pleased me.' He was right well
harboured the night within, and in the morning, or ever he
departed, heard a holy mass in a holy chapel the fairest that he
had seen ever. The Master cometh to him after the mass and
bringeth him a shield as white as snow. Afterwards, he saith,
'You will leave me your shield within for token of your coming
and will bear this.' 'Sir,' saith Perceval, 'I will do your pleasure.' He hath taken leave, and so departeth from the rich
mansion, and findeth the ship all apparelled, and heareth sound
the bells at his forth-going the same as at his coming. He
entereth into the ship and the sail is set. He leaveth the land
far behind, and the pilot steereth the ship and Our Lord God
guideth and leadeth him. The ship runneth a great speed, for
far enough had she to run, but God made her speed as He
would, for He knew the passing great goodness and worth of
the knight that was within.

VIII

God hath guided and led the ship by day and by night until
that she arrived at an island where was a castle right ancient,
but it seemed not to be over-rich, rather it showed as had it
been of great lordship in days of yore. They cast anchor, and
Perceval is come toward the castle and entereth in all armed.
He seeth the castle large, and the dwelling-chambers fallen
down and the house-place roofless, and he seeth a lady sitting
before the steps of an old hall. She rose up as soon as she saw
him, but she was right poorly clad. It seemed well by her

body and her cheer and her bearing that she was a gentle-woman, and he seeth that two damsels come with her that are young of age and are as poorly clad as is the lady. 'Sir,' saith she to Perceval, 'Welcome may you be. No knight have I seen enter this castle of a long time.' 'Lady,' saith Perceval, 'God grant you joy and honour!' 'Sir,' saith she, 'Need have we thereof, for none scarce have I had this long while past.' She leadeth him into a great ancient hall that was right poorly garnished. 'Sir,' saith she, 'Here will you harbour you the night, and you would take in good part that we may do and you knew the plight of this castle.' She maketh him be unarmed of a servant that was there within, and the damsels come before him and serve him right sweetly. The lady bringeth him a mantle to do on. 'Sir,' saith she, 'Within are no better garments wherewith to show you honour than this.' Perceval looketh on the damsels and hath great pity of them, for so well shapen were they of limb and body as that nature might not have better fashioned them, and all the beauty that may be in woman's body was in them, and all the sweetness and simpleness.

IX

'Lady,' saith Perceval, 'Is this castle, then, not yours?' 'Sir,' saith she, 'So much is all that remaineth unto me of all my land, and you see there my daughters of whom is it right sore pity, for nought have they but what you see, albeit gentle-women are they and of high lineage, but their kinsfolk are too far away, and a knight that is right cruel hath reft us of our land sithence that my lord was dead, and holdeth a son of mine in his prison, whereof I am right sorrowful, for he is one of the comeliest knights in the world. He had not been knight more than four years when he took him, and now may I aid neither myself nor other, but I have heard tell that there is a knight in the land of Wales that was the son of Alain li Gros of the Valleys of Camelot, and he is the Best Knight in the World, and this Alain was brother of Calobrutus, whose wife was I, and of whom I had my son and these two daughters. This know I well, that and the Good Knight that is so near akin to them were by any adventure to come into this island, I should have my son again, and my daughters that are disherited would have their lands again freely, and so should I be brought out of

sore pain and poverty. I am of another lineage that is full far
away, for King Ban of Benoic that is dead was mine uncle, but
he hath a son that is a right good knight as I have been told, so
that and one of these two should come nigh me in any of these
islands right joyous should I be thereof.'

X

Perceval heareth that the two damsels are his uncle's
daughters, and hath great pity thereof. 'Lady,' saith he,
'How is he named that is in prison?' 'Sir,' saith she,
'Galobruns, and he that holdeth him in prison is named Gohaz
of the Castle of the Whale.' 'Is his castle near this, Lady?'
saith he. 'Sir, there is but an arm of the sea to cross, and in
all these islands of the sea is there none that hath any puissance
but he only, and so assured is he that no dread hath he of any.
For none that is in this land durst offend against him. Sir, one
thing hath he bid me do, whereof I am sore grieved, that and I
send him not one of my daughters, he hath sworn his oath that
he will reave me of my castle.' 'Lady,' saith Perceval, 'An
oath is not always kept. To the two damsels, please God,
shall he do no shame, and right heavy am I of that he hath done
already, for they were daughters of mine uncle. Alain li Gros
was my father and Galobrutus my uncle, and many another
good man that now is dead.'

XI

When the damsels heard this, they kneeled down before him,
and began to weep for joy and kiss his hands, and pray him for
God's sake have mercy on them and on their brother. And he
saith that he will not depart from their land until he hath done
all he may. He remaineth the night in the castle and his
mariner likewise. The lady made great joy of Perceval, and
did him all the honour she might. When the morrow came
they showed him the land of the King that had reft them of
their land, but the lady could not tell him where her son was
in prison. He departeth and cometh back to his ship when he
hath taken leave of the lady and the damsels, and right glad
was he to know that the damsels were so nigh to him of kin.
So he prayeth God grant him that he may be able to give them

back their land and bring them out of the poverty wherein they
are. He roweth until that he is come under a rock, wherein
was a cave at top round and narrow and secure like as it were
a little house. Perceval looketh on that side, and seeth a man
sitting within. He maketh the ship draw nigh the rock, then
looketh and seeth the cutting of a way that went upwards
through the rock. He is come forth of the ship and goeth up
the little path until he cometh into the little house. He findeth
within one of the comeliest knights in the world. He had a
ring at his feet and a collar on his neck with a chain whereof
the other end was fixed by a staple into a great ledge of the
rock. He rose up over against Perceval as soon as he saw him.
'Sir Knight,' saith Perceval, 'You are well made fast.' 'Sir,
that irketh me,' saith the knight, 'Better should I like myself
elsewhere than here.' 'You would be right,' saith Perceval,
'For you are in right evil plight in the midst of this sea. Have
you aught within to eat or to drink?' 'Sir,' saith he, 'The
daughter of the Sick Knight that dwelleth in the island hard
by, sendeth me every day in a boat as much meat as I may eat,
for she hath great pity of me. The King that hath imprisoned
me here hath reft her castles like as he hath those of my lady
my mother.' 'May none remove you hence?' 'Sir, in no wise,
save he that set me here, for he keepeth with him the key of
the lock, and he told me when he departed hence that never
more should I issue forth.' 'By my head,' saith Perceval, 'but
you shall! And you were the son of Galobrutus, you were the
son of mine uncle,' saith Perceval, 'and I of yours, so that it
would be a reproach to me for evermore and I left you in this
prison.'

XII

When Galobruns heareth that he is his uncle's son, great joy
hath he thereof. He would have fallen at his feet, but Perceval
would not, and said to him, 'Now be well assured, for I will
seek your deliverance.' He cometh down from the rock, and
so entereth the ship and roweth of a long space. He looketh
before him and seeth a right rich island and a right plenteous,
and on the other side he seeth in a little islet a knight that is
mounted up in a tall tree that was right broad with many
boughs. There was a damsel with him, that had climbed up
also for dread of a serpent, great and evil-favoured, that had

issued from a hole in a mountain. The damsel seeth Perceval's
ship coming, and crieth out to him. 'Ha, Sir,' saith she,
'Come to help this King that is up above, and me that am a
damsel!' 'Whereof are you afeard, damsel?' saith Perceval.
'Of a great serpent, Sir,' saith she, 'that hath made us climb
up, whereof ought I not to be sorry, for this King hath carried
me off from my father's house, and would have done me shame
of my body and this serpent had not run upon him.' 'And
what is the King's name, damsel?' saith Perceval. 'Sir, he is
called Gohaz of the Castle of the Whale. This great land is
his own that is so plenteous, and other lands enow that he hath
reft of my father and of other.' The King had great shame of
this that the damsel told him, and made answer never a word.
Perceval understandeth that it was he that held his cousin in
prison, and is issued from the ship forthwith, sword drawn.
The serpent seeth him, and cometh toward him, jaws yawning,
and casteth forth fire and flame in great plenty. Perceval
thrusteth his sword right through the gullet. 'Now may you
come down,' saith he to the King. 'Sir,' saith he, 'The key
of a chain wherewith a certain knight is bound hath fallen, and
the serpent seized it.' Perceval rendeth open the throat and
findeth the key forthwith, all red-hot with the fire of the
serpent. The King cometh down, that hath no dread of aught,
but cometh, rather, as he ought, to thank Perceval of the
goodness he had done him, and Perceval seizeth him between
his arms and beareth him away to the ship.

XIII

'Sir Knight,' saith Gohaz, 'Take heed what you do, for I am
King of this land.' 'Therefore,' saith Perceval, 'I do it. For,
had it been another I should do it not.' 'Ha, Sir,' saith the
damsel, 'Leave me not here to get forth as I may, but help me
until that I shall be in the house of my father, the Sick Knight,
that is sore grieved on my account.' Perceval understandeth
that it is the damsel of whom Galobruns spake such praise.
He goeth to bring her down from the tree, then bringeth her
into the ship, and so goeth back toward the rock where his
cousin was. 'Sir Knight,' saith Gohaz, 'Where will you put
me?' 'I will put you,' saith he, 'as an enemy, there, where
you have put the son of mine uncle in prison; so shall I avenge

me of you, and he also at his will.' When the King heard this, he was glad thereof not a whit, and the damsel was loath not a whit, whom he had thus disherited. They row until they come to the rock. Perceval issueth forth of the ship, and bringeth Gohaz up maugre his head. Galobruns seeth him coming and maketh great joy thereof, and Perceval saith to him : ' Behold here your mortal enemy ! Now do your will of him ! ' He taketh the key and so looseth him of the irons wherein he was imprisoned.

XIV

' Galobruns,' saith Perceval, ' Now may you do your pleasure of your enemy ? ' ' Sir,' saith he, ' Right gladly ! ' He maketh fast the irons on his feet that he had upon his own, and afterward setteth the collar on his neck. ' Now let him be here,' saith he, ' in such sort and in such prison as he put me ; for well I know that he will be succoured of none.' After that, he flingeth the key into the sea as far as he might, and so seemed it to Galobruns that he well avenged himself in such wise, and better than if he had killed him. Perceval alloweth him everything therein at his will. They enter into the ship and leave Gohaz all sorrowing on the rock, that never thereafter ate nor drank. And Perceval bringeth his cousin and the damsel, and they row until that they come into their land, and Perceval maketh send for all the folk of King Gohaz and maketh all the more powerful do sure homage to Galobruns and his sisters in such sort that the land was all at their will. He sojourned there so long as it pleased him, and then departed and took leave of the damsel and Galobruns, that thanked him much for the lands that he had again through him.

XV

Perceval hath rowed until that he is come nigh a castle that was burning fiercely with a great flame, and seeth a hermitage upon the sea hard by. He seeth the hermit at the door of the chapel, and asketh him what the castle is that hath caught fire thus. ' Sir,' saith the hermit, ' I will tell you. Joseus, the son of King Pelles, slew his mother there. Never sithence hath the castle stinted of burning, and I tell you that of this castle and one other will be kindled the fire that shall burn up the world

and put it to an end.' Perceval marvelleth much, and knew
well that it was the castle of King Hermit his uncle. He
departeth thence in great haste, and passeth three kingdoms
and saileth by the wastes and deserts on one side and the other
of the sea, for the ship ran somewhat a-nigh the land. He
looketh and seeth on an island twelve hermits sitting on the sea-
shore. The sea was calm and untroubled, and he made cast the
anchor so as to keep the ship steady. Then he saluteth the
hermits, and they all bow down to him in answer. He asketh
them where have they their repair, and they tell him that they
have not far away twelve chapels and twelve houses that
surround a grave-yard wherein lie twelve dead knights that we
keep watch over. They were all brothers-german, and right
worshipful men, and none thereof lived more than twelve years
knight save one only, and none of them was there but won
much land and broad kingdoms from the misbelievers, and they
all died in arms; and the name of the eldest was Alain li Gros,
and he came into this country from the Valleys of Camelot to
avenge his brother Alibans of the Waste City that the Giant
King had slain, and he took vengeance on him thereof, but he
died thereafter of a wound that the Giant had given him.
'Sir,' saith one of the hermits, 'I was at his death, but nought
was there he so longed after as a son of his, and he said that his
name was Perceval. He was the last of the brothers that died.'

XVI

When Perceval heard this he had pity thereof, and issued
forth of the ship and came to land, and his mariner with him.
He prayed the hermits that they would lead him to the grave-
yard where the knights lay, and gladly did they so. Perceval
is come thither and seeth the coffins right rich and fair, and the
chapels full fairly dight, and every coffin lay over against the
altar in each chapel. 'Lords, which coffin is that of the Lord
of Camelot?' 'This, the highest,' say the hermits, 'and the
most rich, for that he was eldest of all the brethren.' Perceval
kneeleth down before it, then embraceth the coffin and prayeth
right sweetly for the soul of his father, and in like manner he
went to all the other coffins. He harboured the night with the
hermits, and told them that Alain li Gros was his father and all
the other his uncles. Right joyous were the hermits for that

he was come thither, and the morrow, or ever he departed, he heard mass in the chapel of his father and in the others where he might. He entered into the ship and sped full swift, and so far hath the ship run that he draweth nigh the islands of Great Britain. He arriveth at the head of a forest under the Red Tower whereof he had slain the lord, there where Meliot delivered Messire Gawain. He is issued forth of the ship and leadeth forth his horse and is armed, and commendeth the pilot to God. He mounteth on his destrier, all armed, and goeth amidst the land that was well-nigh void of people, for he himself had slain the greater part thereof, albeit he knew it not. He rideth so long, right amidst the country, that he cometh toward evensong to a hold that was in a great forest, and he bethought him that he would go into the hermitage, and he cometh straight into the hold, and seeth a knight lying in the entrance of the gate on a straw mattress, and a damsel sate at the bed's head, of passing great beauty, and held his head on her lap.

XVII

The knight reviled her from time to time, and said that he would make cut off her head and he had not that he desired to have, for that he was sick. Perceval looked at the lady that held him and served him full sweetly, and deemed her to be a good lady and a loyal. The Sick Knight called to Perceval. 'Sir,' saith he, 'Are you come in hither to harbour?' 'Sir,' saith Perceval, 'So please you, I will harbour here.' 'Then blame me not,' saith the knight, 'of that you shall see me do unto my wife.' 'Sir,' saith Perceval, 'Sith that she is yours, you have a right to do your pleasure, but in all things ought one to be heedful on one's way.' The knight made him be carried back into the dwelling, for that he had been in the air as long as pleased him, and commanded his wife that she do much honour to the knight that is come to lodge within. 'But take heed,' saith he, 'that you be not seen at the table, but eat, as you are wont, at the squire's table, for, until such time as I have the golden cup I desire, I will not forego my despite against you.'

XVIII

Perceval unarmed him. The lady had brought him a surcoat of scarlet for him to do on, and he asked her wherefore her

lord reviled her and rebuked her in such sort, and she told him
all the story how Lancelot had married her to him, and how her
lord ever sithence had dishonoured her. 'Sir,' saith she, 'Now
hath he fallen into misease, sithence then, and he hath a brother
as sick as he is, and therefore hath Gohaz of the Castle of the
Whale reft him of his land, whereof is he right sorry, and my
lord hath never been heal since that he heard thereof. And
well you know that such folk wax wroth of a little, and are
overjoyed when they have a little thing that pleaseth them,
for they live always in desire of somewhat. My lord hath
heard tell of a cup of gold that a damsel beareth, that is
right rich and of greater worth than aught he hath seen this
long time, and a knight goeth with the damsel that beareth the
cup, and saith that none may have it save he be the Best Knight
in the World. My lord hath told me many times, sithence he
heard tidings thereof, that never shall the despite he hath
toward me be forgone, until that he shall have the cup.
But he is so angry withal with his brother that hath lost his
land, that I aby it right dear, for I do all his will and yet may
I have no fair treatment of him. Howbeit, for no ill that he
may do, nor no churlishness that he may say, will I be against
him in nought that he hath set his mind on. For I would have
him, and I had him, blessed be Lancelot through whom it was
so. As much as I loved him in health, so much love I him in
his sickness, and more yet, for I desire to deserve that God
shall bring him to a better mind.'

XIX

'Lady,' saith Perceval, 'Great praise ought you to have of
this that you say; but you may well tell him of a truth that
the sick King his brother hath all his land freely and his
daughter, for I was at the reconquering thereof, and know
the knight well that gave it back unto him. But of the golden
cup can I give you no witting.' 'Sir,' saith she, 'The damsel
is to bear it to an assembly of knights that is to be held hard
by this, under the White Tower. There hath she to give it
to the best knight, and him that shall do best at the assembly,
and the knight that followeth the damsel is bound to carry it
whither he that shall win it may command, and if he would
fain it should be given to another rather than to himself.'

'Lady,' saith Perceval, 'Well meseemeth that he who shall win the cup by prize of arms will be right courteous and he send it to you, and God grant that he that hath it may do you such bounty as you desire.' 'Sir,' saith she, 'Methinketh well, so Lancelot were there, either he or Messire Gawain, that, and they won it, so they remembered them of me, and knew how needful it were to me, they would promise me the cup.' 'Lady,' saith Perceval, 'By one of these twain ought you well to have it, for greater prize now long since have they won.' She goeth to her lord and saith to him: 'Sir,' saith she, 'Now may you be more joyous than is your wont, for that your brother hath his land again all quit. For the knight that is within was at the reconquering.' The Sick Knight heard her and had great joy thereof. 'Go!' saith he to his wife, 'and do great honour to the knight, but take heed you sit not otherwise than you are wont.' 'Sir,' saith she, 'I will not.'

XX

The damsel maketh Perceval sit at meat. When he had washen, he thought that the lady should have come to sit beside him, but she would not disobey her lord's commandment. When Perceval was set at the table and he had been served of the first meats, thereupon the lady went to sit with the squires. Perceval was much shamed that she should sit below, but he was not minded to speak, for she had told him somewhat of her lord's manner. Howbeit, he lay the night in the hold, and, on the morrow when he had taken leave, he departed, and bethought him in his courage that the knight would do good chivalry and great alms that should do this sick knight his desire as concerning the cup, in such sort as that his wife should be freed of the annoy that she is in, for that all knights that knew thereof ought to have pity of her. Perceval goeth his way as he that hath great desire to accomplish that he hath to do, and to see the token of his going again to the castle where the chain of gold appeared to him, for never yet saw he dwelling that pleased him so much. He hath ridden so far that he is come into the joyless forest of the Black Hermit, that is so loathly and horrible that no leaves nor greenery are there by winter nor by summer, nor was song of bird never heard therein, but all the land is gruesome and burnt, and wide are the cracks therein. He hath scarce gone thereinto or ever he hath overtaken the Damsel of the Car, that made full great joy of him. 'Sir,' saith she, 'Bald was I the first time I saw you; now may you see that I have my hair.' 'Certes, yea!' saith Perceval, 'And, as methinketh, hair passing beautiful.' 'Sir,' saith she, 'I was wont to carry my arm at my neck in a scarf of gold and silk, for that I thought the service I did you in the hostel of King Fisherman your uncle had been ill bestowed; but now well I see that it was not; wherefore now carry I the one arm in the same manner as the other; and the damsel that wont to go a-foot now goeth a-horseback; and blessed be you that have so approved you in goodness by the good manner of your heart, and by your likeness to the first of your lineage, whom you resemble in all good conditions. Sir,' saith she, 'I durst not come nigh the castle, for there be archers there that shoot so sore that none may endure their strokes, and hereof will they stint not, they say, until such time as you be come thither. But well know I wherefore they will cease then, for they will come to shut you up within to slay and to destroy. Natheless all they that are within will have no power, nor will they do you evil, save only the lord of the castle; but he will do battle against you right gladly.'

XXI

Perceval goeth toward the castle of the Black Hermit, and the Damsel of the Car after. The archers draw and shoot stoutly. Perceval goeth forward a great gallop, but they know him not on account of the white shield. They think rather that it is one of the other knights, and they lodge many arrows in his shield. He came nigh a drawbridge over a moat right broad and foul and horrible, and the bridge was lowered so soon as he came, and all the archers left of shooting. Then knew they well that it was Perceval who came. The door was opened to receive him, for they of the gate and they of the castle within thought to have power to slay him. But so soon as they saw him, they lost their will thereof and were all amated and without strength, and said that they would set this business on their lord that was strong enough and puissant enough to slay one man. Perceval entered all armed into a great hall, and found it filled all around with a great throng of

folk that was right foul to look on. He that was called the
Black Hermit was full tall and seemed to be of noble lordship,
and he was in the midst of the hall, all armed. 'Sir,' say his
men, 'And you have not defence of yourself, never no counsel
nor aid may you have of us!'

XXII

We are yours to guard, to protect, and oftentimes have we
defended you; now defend us in this sore need.' The Black
Hermit sate upon a tall black horse, and was right richly armed.
So soon as Perceval espieth him, he cometh with such a rush
against him that he maketh all the hall resound, and the Black
Hermit cometh in like sort. They mell together with such
force that the Black Hermit breaketh his spear upon Perceval,
but Perceval smiteth him so passing stoutly on the left side
upon the shield, that he beareth him to the ground beside his
horse, so that in the fall he made he to-frushed two of the great
ribs in the overturn. And when they that were therein saw
him fall, they opened the trap-door of a great pit that was in
the midst of the hall. So soon as they had opened it, the
foulest stench that any smelt ever issued thereout. They take
their lord and cast him into this abysm and this filth. After
that, they come to Perceval, and so yield the castle and put
them at his mercy in everything. Thereupon, behold you, the
Damsel of the Car that cometh. They deliver up to her
the heads sealed in gold, both the head of the King and of the
Queen, and she departeth forthwith, for well knoweth she that
Perceval will achieve that he hath to do without her. She
departeth from the castle and goeth the speediest she may
toward the Valleys of Camelot. And all they of the castle that
had been the Black Hermit's are obedient to Perceval to do his
will, and they have him in covenant that never more shall
knights be harassed there in such sort as they had been there-
tofore, but rather that they should receive gladly any knights
that should pass that way, like as in other places. Perceval
departed from the castle rejoicing for that he had drawn them
to the believe of Our Lord, and every day was His service done
therein in holy wise, like as it is done in other places.

XXIII

Hereof ought the good knight to be loved that by the goodness of his heart and the loyalty of his knighthood hath achieved all the emprises he undertook, without reproach and without blame. Perceval hath ridden until he hath overtaken the damsel that carried the rich cup of gold and the knight that was along with her. Perceval saluteth him, and the knight maketh answer, may he be blessed of God and of His sweet Mother. ' Fair Sir,' saith Perceval, ' Is this damsel of your company ?' Saith the knight, ' Rather am I of hers. But we are going to an assembly of knights that is to be under the White Tower to the intent to prove which knight is most worth, and to him that shall have the prize of the assembly shall be delivered this golden cup.' ' By my head,' saith Perceval, 'That will be fair to see !' He departeth from the knight and the damsel, and goeth his way a great pace amidst the meadows under the White Tower, whither the knights were coming from all parts, and many of them were already armed to issue forth. So soon as it was known that the damsel with the cup was come thither, the fellowships assembled on all sides, and great was the clashing of arms. Perceval hurleth into the assembly in such sort that many a knight he smiteth down and overthroweth at his coming, and he giveth so many blows and so many receiveth that all they that behold marvel much how he may abide. The assembly lasted until evensong, and when it came to an end the damsel came to the knights and prayed and required that they would declare to her by right judgment of arms which had done the best. The more part said that he of the white shield had surpassed them all in arms, and all agreed thereto. The damsel was right glad, for well she knew that they spake truth. She cometh to Perceval ; ' Sir,' saith she, ' I present you this cup of gold for your good chivalry, and therefore is it meet and right you should know whence the cup cometh. The elder Damsel of the Tent where the evil custom was wont to be, sent it to Messire Gawain, and Messire Gawain made much joy thereof. And it came to pass on such-wise that Brundans, the son of the sister of Briant of the Isles, slew Meliot of Logres, the most courteous knight and the most valiant that was in the realm of Logres, and thereof was Messire Gawain so sorrowful that he knew not how to contain himself. For Meliot had twice rescued him from death, and King Arthur once.   He was liegeman of Messire Gawain.   Wherefore he prayeth and beseecheth you on his behalf that you receive not the cup save you undertake to avenge him.   For he was loved of all the court, albeit he had haunted it but little.   Brundans slew him in treason when Meliot was unawares of him.'   'Damsel,' saith Perceval, 'Were there no cup at all, yet natheless should I be fain to do the will of Messire Gawain, for never might I love the man that had deserved his hatred.'   He taketh the cup in his hand.   'Damsel,' saith he, ' I thank you much hereof, and God grant I may reward you for the same.'   'Sir,' saith she, ' Brundans is a right proud knight, and beareth a shield party of vert and argent.   He is minded never to change his cognisance, for that his father bore the same.'   Perceval called the knight that was of the damsel's company.   ' I beseech you,' saith he, 'of guerdon and of service, that you bear this cup for me to the hold of the Sick Knight, and tell his wife that the Knight of the White Shield that was harboured there within hath sent it her by you.'   'Sir,' saith the knight, ' This will I do gladly to fulfil your will.'   He taketh the cup to furnish out the conditions of the message, and so departeth forthwith.

XXIV

Perceval lay the night in the castle of the White Tower, and departed thence on the morrow as he that would fain do somewhat whereof he might deserve well of Messire Gawain.   Many a time had he heard tell of Meliot of Logres and of his chivalry and of his great valour.   He was entered into a forest, and had heard mass of a hermit, from whom he had departed.   He came to the Castle Perilous that was hard by there where Meliot lay sick, lay wounded, when Lancelot brought him the sword and the cloth wherewith he touched his wounds.   He entered into the castle and alighted.   The damsel of the castle, that made great dole, came to meet Perceval.   'Damsel,' saith he, ' Wherefore are you so sorrowful ? '   'Sir,' saith she, ' For a knight that I tended and healed herewithin, whom Brundans hath killed in treason, and God thereof grant us vengeance yet, for so courteous knight saw I never.'   While she was speaking in this manner, forthwith behold you a damsel that cometh.   'Ha, Sir,' saith she to Perceval, 'Mount you again and come to aid us, for none other knight find I in this land nor in this forest

but only you all alone!' 'What need have you of my aid?'
saith Perceval. 'A knight is carrying off my lady by force, that
was going to the court of King Arthur.' 'Who is your lady?'
saith Perceval. 'Sir, she is the younger Damsel of the Tent
where Messire Gawain overthrew the evil customs. For God's
sake, hasten you, for he revileth her sore for her love of the
King and of Messire Gawain.' Perceval remounteth forthwith
and issueth forth of the castle on the spur. The damsel bringeth
him on as fast as the knight can go. They had not ridden far
before they came a-nigh, and Perceval heard the damsel crying
aloud for mercy, and the knight said that mercy upon her he
would not have, and so smote her on the head and neck with
the flat of his sword.

XXV

Perceval espied the knight and saw that the cognisance of his
shield was such as that which had been set forth to him. 'Sir,'
saith he, 'Too churlishly are you entreating this damsel!
What wrong hath she done you?' 'What is it to you of me
and of her?' 'I say it,' saith Perceval, 'for that no knight
ought to do churlishly to damsel.' 'He will not stint for you
yet!' saith Brundans. He raiseth his sword and dealeth the
damsel a buffet with the flat so passing heavy that it maketh her
stoop withal so that the blood rayeth out at mouth and nose.
'By my head,' saith Perceval, 'On this buffet I defy thee, for
the death of Meliot and for the shame you have done this
damsel.' 'Neither you nor none other may brag that you have
heart to attack me, but you shall aby it right dear!' 'That
shall you see presently,' saith Perceval, and so draweth back the
better to let drive at him, and moveth towards him as fast as his
horse may run, and smiteth him so passing sore that he pierceth
his shield and bursteth his habergeon and then thrusteth his
spear into his body with such force that he overthroweth him all
in a heap, him and his horse, in such sort that he breaketh both
legs in the fall. Then he alighteth over him, lowereth his coif,
unlaceth the ventail, and smiteth off his head. 'Damsel,' saith
he, 'Take it, I present it to you. And, sith that you are going
to King Arthur's court, I pray and beseech you that you carry it
thither and so salute him first for me, and tell Messire Gawain
and Lancelot that this is the last present I look ever to make
them, for I think never to see them more. Howbeit, whereso-

ever I may be, I shall be their well-wisher, nor may I never withdraw me of my love, and I would fain I might make them the same present of the heads of all their enemies, but that I may do nought against God's will.' The damsel giveth him thanks for that he hath delivered her from the hands of the knight, and saith that she shall praise him much thereof to the King and Messire Gawain. She goeth her way and carrieth off the head, and Perceval biddeth her to God. He returned back to Castle Perilous, and the damsel made great joy thereof when she understood that he had slain Brundans. Perceval lay there that night, and departed on the morrow after that he had heard mass. When he came forth of the castle he met the knight by whom he had sent the cup to the Sick Knight's wife. Perceval asketh how it is with him. 'Sir,' saith he, 'I have carried out your message right well, for never was a thing received with such good will. The Sick Knight hath forgone his grudge against his wife. She eateth at his table, and the household do her commandment.' 'This liketh me right well,' saith Perceval, 'and I thank you of doing this errand.' 'Sir,' saith the knight, 'No thing is there I would not do for you, for that you made my brother Knight Hardy there where you first saw him Knight Coward.' 'Sir,' saith Perceval, 'Good knight was your brother and a right good end he made, but a little it forthinketh me that he might have still been living had he abided in his cowardize.' 'Sir,' saith he, 'Better is he dead, sith that he died with honour, than that he should live with shame. Yet glad was I not of his death, for a hardy knight he was, and yet more would have been, had he lived longer.'

XXVI

Perceval departeth from the knight and commendeth him to God. He hath wandered so far one day and another that he is returned to his own most holy castle, and findeth therein his mother and his sister that the Damsel of the Car had brought thither. The Widow Lady had made bear thither the body that lay in the coffin before the castle of Camelot in the rich chapel that she had builded there. His sister brought the cere-cloth that she took in the Waste Chapel, and presented there where the Graal was. Perceval made bring the coffin of the other knight that was at the entrance of his castle within the chapel likewise, and place it beside the coffin of his uncle, nor never thereafter might it be removed. Josephus telleth us that Perceval was in this castle long time, nor never once moved therefrom in quest of no adventure; rather was his courage so attorned to the Saviour of the World and His sweet Mother, that he and his sister and the damsel that was therein led a holy life and a religious. Therein abode they even as it pleased God, until that his mother passed away and his sister and all they that were therein save he alone. The hermits that were nigh the castle buried them and sang their masses, and came every day and took counsel of him for the holiness they saw him do and the good life that he led there. So one day whilst he was in the holy chapel where the hallows were, forthwith, behold you, a Vcice that cometh down therein : 'Perceval,' saith the Voice, 'Not long shall you abide herein; wherefore it is God's will that you dispart the hallows amongst the hermits of the forest, there where these bodies shall be served and worshipped, and the most Holy Graal shall appear herein no more, but within a brief space shall you know well the place where it shall be.' When the Voice departed, all the coffins that were therein crashed so passing loud that it seemed the master-hall had fallen. He crosseth and blesseth him and commendeth him to God. On a day the hermits came to him. He disparted the holy relics among them, and they builded above them holy churches and houses of religion that are seen in the lands and in the islands. Joseus the son of King Hermit, remained therein with Perceval, for he well knew that he would be departing thence betimes.

XXVII

Perceval heard one day a bell sound loud and high without the manor toward the sea. He came to the windows of the hall and saw the ship come with the white sail and the Red Cross thereon, and within were the fairest folk that ever he might behold, and they were all robed in such manner as though they should sing mass. When the ship was anchored under the hall they went to pray in the most holy chapel. They brought the richest vessels of gold and silver that any might ever see, like as it were coffins, and set therein one of the three bodies of knights that had been brought into the chapel, and the body of King Fisherman, and of the mother of Perceval. But no savour in the world smelleth so sweet.   Perceval took leave of Joseus and commended him to the Saviour of the World, and took leave of the household, from whom he departed in like manner.   The worshipful men that were in the ship signed them of the cross and blessed them likewise.   The ship wherein Perceval was drew far away, and a Voice that issued from the manor as she departed commended them to God and to His sweet Mother. Josephus recordeth us that Perceval departed in such wise, nor never thereafter did no earthly man know what became of him, nor doth the history speak of him more.   But the history telleth us that Joseus abode in the castle that had been King Fisherman's, and shut himself up therein so that none might enter, and lived upon that the Lord God might send him.   He dwelt there long time after that Perceval had departed, and ended therein. After his end, the dwelling began to fall.   Natheless never was the chapel wasted nor decayed, but was as whole thereafter as tofore and is so still.   The place was far from folk, and the place seemed withal to be somewhat different.   When it was fallen into decay, many folk of the lands and islands that were nighest thereunto marvel them what may be in this manor. They dare a many that they should go see what was therein, and sundry folk went thither from all the lands, but none durst never enter there again save two Welsh knights that had heard tell of it.   Full comely knights they were, young and joyous-hearted.   So either pledged him to other that they would go thither by way of gay adventure; but therein remained they of a long space after, and when again they came forth they led the life of hermits, and clad them in hair shirts, and went by the forest and so ate nought save roots only, and led a right hard life; yet ever they made as though they were glad, and if that any should ask whereof they rejoiced in such wise, ' Go,' said they to them that asked, ' thither where we have been, and you shall know the wherefore.'   In such sort made they answer to the folk.   These two knights died in this holy life, nor were none other tidings never brought thence by them.   They of that land called them saints.

XXVIII

Here endeth the story of the most Holy Graal.   Josephus, by whom it is placed on record, giveth the benison of Our Lord to all that hear and honour it. The Latin from whence this history was drawn into Romance was taken in the Isle of Avalon, in a holy house of religion that standeth at the head of the Moors Adventurous, there where King Arthur and Queen Guenievre lie, according to the witness of the good men religious that are therein, that have the whole history thereof, true from the beginning even to the end. After this same history beginneth the story how Briant of the Isles renounced King Arthur on account of Lancelot whom he loved not, and how he assured King Claudas that reft King Ban of Benoic of his land. This story telleth how he conquered him and by what means, and how Galobrus of the Red Launde came to King Arthur's court to help Lancelot, for that he was of his lineage. This story is right long and right adventurous and weighty, but the book will now forthwith be silent thereof until another time.

The Author's Conclusion

For the Lord of Neele made the Lord of Cambrein this book be written, that never tofore was treated in Romance but one single time besides this; and the book that was made tofore this is so ancient that only with great pains may one make out the letter. And let Messire Johan de Neele well understand that he ought to hold this story dear, nor ought he tell nought thereof to ill-understanding folk, for a good thing that is squandered upon bad folk is never remembered by them for good.

Explicit

the Romance of Perceval the nephew of
King Fisherman.